Food, Politics, and
Agricultural Development

Westview Special Studies in Social, Political, and Economic Development

Food, Politics, and Agricultural Development:
Case Studies in the Public Policy of
Rural Modernization
edited by Raymond F. Hopkins, Donald J. Puchala,
and Ross B. Talbot

This collection of studies on the politics of agricultural development in key countries and regions of Asia and Africa focuses on the political forces that have shaped the development of new agricultural patterns and have modernized rural areas. The studies substantiate the assertion that political rather than technical factors hold the key to improved agriculture and economic development, and emphasize the need for steady and significant increases in food production in the developing countries themselves.

Raymond F. Hopkins is associate professor of political science and director of public policy programs at Swarthmore College. Donald J. Puchala is professor of political science at Columbia University and associate dean of the Columbia University School of International Affairs. Ross B. Talbot is professor of political science at Iowa State University.

Food, Politics, and Agricultural Development:
Case Studies in the Public Policy of Rural Modernization

edited by Raymond F. Hopkins,
Donald J. Puchala, and Ross B. Talbot

Westview Press / Boulder, Colorado

Westview Special Studies in
Social, Political, and Economic Development

Copyright © 1979 by Westview Press, Inc.

Published in 1979 in the United States of America by
  Westview Press, Inc.
  5500 Central Avenue
  Boulder, Colorado 80301
  Frederick A. Praeger, Publisher

Library of Congress Cataloging in Publication Data
Main entry under title:
Food, politics, and agricultural development.
  (Westview special studies in social, political, and economic development)
  1. Agriculture and state—Addresses, essays, lectures. 2. Food supply—Addresses, essays, lectures. 3. Rural development—Addresses, essays.
I. Hopkins, Raymond F. II. Puchala, Donald James, 1939- III. Talbot, Ross B.
HD1415.F64   338.1'8   79-10209
ISBN: 0-89158-389-0

Printed and bound in the United States of America

Contents

Tables and Figures

Figure

About the Contributors

Pamela R. Aall, a graduate of Radcliffe College and the School of International Affairs at Columbia University, is a consultant to the Rockefeller Foundation's International Relations program.

Robert H. Bates is an associate professor of political science at the California Institute of Technology. He is author of *Unions, Parties, and Political Development* and *Rural Responses to Industrialization: A Study of Village Zambia.* His current research is on the impact of public policy on rural farm families in contemporary Africa.

Thomas P. Bernstein is an associate professor of political science at Columbia University and a research associate in the East Asian Institute. He is the author of *Up to the Mountains and Down to the Villages: The Transfer of Youth from Urban to Rural China,* a study of the management of educated unemployment in the PRC. He has also written on the collectivization of agriculture in China and the Soviet Union, and is now working on a full-scale study of rural transformation in those two countries.

J. D. Esseks is an associate professor of political science at Northern Illinois University. A graduate of Harvard University, Esseks has written on political economy issues facing sub-Saharan Africa and on farmland preservation in the United States.

Don F. Hadwiger, professor of political science at Iowa State University, has written books and articles on the agricultural policy process, agricultural research policy, commodity policy, rural development, the Department of Agriculture, and the history and structure of agricultural politics. He previously served in staff positions in Congress, the USDA, and the Washington Research Project.

Ronald J. Herring teaches political economy, public policy, and politics of South Asia, specializing in developmental issues, at Northwestern University. His research in Sri Lanka, India, and Pakistan has centered on land reform and rural credit, stressing consequences for economic rationality and social justice. His published work has appeared in a variety of journals and the forthcoming book, *Land to the Tiller: Agrarian Reform in South Asia*. Herring is currently editor of the journal *Comparative Political Studies*.

Raymond F. Hopkins is professor of political science at Swarthmore College. He has recently published articles on the politics of international food affairs in *Foreign Policy* and *International Organization* and has coauthored a book on *Global Food Interdependence* with Donald Puchala. He is now completing a study of the political economy of international food assistance.

Charles R. Kennedy, Jr. is an instructor of political science at the University of Texas at Austin. His dissertation concerning the politics of land reform in Pakistan, India, Iran, and Japan was presented at the 6th Annual South Asian Conference at Madison, Wisconsin, in November 1977. Other research interests include methodological issues in class analysis and United States–Third World relationships.

Ali Akhtar Khan is a Ph.D. candidate in political science at Northern Illinois University with special interest in political economy and organizational development. He has worked for the Food Institute, East-West Center, Honolulu, Hawaii as a Fellow, for FAO/UNDP as an advisor (Rural Institutions) to Sri Lanka, and for the Comilla Academy for Rural Development, Bangladesh, as research associate.

Young Whan Kihl, professor of political science at Iowa State University, has published numerous works on contemporary Korea including *Elections and Party Politics in Korea* (coedited with C. I. Eugene Kim). He is also the author of *Conflict Issues and International Civil Aviation Decisions: Three Cases*. His scholarly works appear in various professional journals including *Asian Survey*, the *Journal of Politics*, and *American Political Science Review*.

Norman K. Nicholson is an associate professor of political science at Northern Illinois University, DeKalb, and is currently on leave with the Office of Rural Development, Agency for International Development, Washington.

Donald J. Puchala is professor of political science at Columbia University and associate dean of the Columbia School of International Affairs. He is the author of *International Politics Today* (1971), and most recently coeditor with Raymond Hopkins of *The Global Political Economy of Food*. His forthcoming publications will include *Global Food Interdependence: Challenge to American Policy* (also with Hopkins).

Ann T. Schulz is a research associate professor at Clark University. She has written on Iranian politics, international politics in the Middle

East, and comparative local politics. Dr. Schulz is the coeditor of *Nuclear Proliferation and the Near-Nuclear Countries* (Ballinger, 1975), the editor of *International and Regional Politics in the Middle East and North Africa; An Annotated Bibliography* (Gale, 1977), and the author of *Local Politics and Nation-States: Cases Studies in Politics and Policy* (ABC-Clio, forthcoming). She has also served as a consultant on regional development administration.

Jane Staveley studied at Columbia University, receiving a master's degree in international affairs and a certificate from the Institute on Western Europe. She has been involved in research on the politics of food, focusing on agricultural development in Taiwan and cooperation between Canada and the United States on food aid. She is at present economics editor at Praeger Publishers.

Ross B. Talbot is professor of political science at Iowa State University. His research and publications have been in the areas of world and U.S. agricultural and food politics and policies. Recent publications include *The Chicken War* and *The World Food Problem and U.S. Food Politics and Policies, 1977—A Readings Book* (both published by the Iowa State University Press in 1978).

Preface

Agricultural development is a crucial element in any society's transformation to a modern industrial state. In this process, the provision of food to a growing nonagricultural labor force is a necessity and the securement of investable resources is a further and often vital contribution by agriculture. Political science has paid relatively little attention to this process compared to the attention given it by economics and sociology. Yet the politics of agricultural development interact in important ways with the social and economic aspects of modernization. Indeed, agricultural policy issues and their resolution probably lie at the heart of forces shaping the future political and economic landscape in most developing countries. The papers for this volume were planned with this concern in mind.

Many of the chapters were first drafted as contributions to panels on the politics of agricultural development at International Studies Association meetings in St. Louis in February 1977 and Washington in February 1978. These include the contributions by Hadwiger and Talbot, Puchala and Staveley, Kihl, Herring and Kennedy, and Esseks and Nicholson. The other contributions were invited to add important dimensions to the initial collection. The major burden of editing and revising chapters occurred in the summer and fall of 1978. While Puchala and Hopkins took major responsibility for preparing the introduction, Talbot bore the heaviest burden of editing and preparing the manuscript for publication.

The editors are particularly grateful to our authors who cheerfully responded to suggestions and who peacefully tolerated delays. At Westview Press we sincerely appreciate the encouragement and assistance of Lynne Rienner, Miriam Gilbert, and Vicki Groninger. For assistance in preparing final copy for the press, and in the editorial process, we acknowledge with much gratitude the work of Kay Maas and Claudette McMahon.

Raymond F. Hopkins

1
The Politics
of Agricultural Modernization

Donald J. Puchala
Raymond F. Hopkins

The history of every modern country includes an account of how agricultural change occurred. The forces that stimulated rural populations to adopt new farming techniques or to abandon the land for urban society have also stirred major political struggles. In each country the struggle for advantage in the countryside presents unique factors; but in each this struggle—over control of land or the income from its product—has had important consequences for the values, stability, and form of politics of the country. Today, the politics of agriculture in the less-developed countries turn on issues of access to land and control of credit, markets, or other economic relationships.

This volume brings together a group of essays that review salient aspects of agricultural change in particular countries. Even though the essays vary in tone, emphasis, and historical or geographical scope, all address similar questions: What role has government generally, and particular government politics specifically, played in the success or failure of agricultural modernization? What political forces has the agricultural sector unleashed, and under what circumstances? Overall, how has the chosen path of agricultural modernization in each case reflected colonial or national politics; and how, in turn, has this affected national politics?

Our fundamental purpose here is to provide case studies of agricultural modernization that emphasize the political aspects and ingredients of development. In doing this we seek to complement the literature of agricultural economics as applied to rural development. Theoretical and technical writings on agricultural modernization are voluminous; the better known recent works are sound, sophisticated, enlightening, and basic to our understanding of development.[1] Nonetheless, many of those who approach problems of rural development from agronomic and economic perspectives pay scant attention to politics and government and their roles in agriculture. Such underemphasis frequently renders analysis incomplete, since public policies toward agriculture influence prices, investment, planting decisions, marketing strategies, land tenure patterns, crop mixes, imports and exports, and rural incomes in every country of the world. Understanding the origins, contents, and impacts of such policies, then, must be fundamental to understanding agricultural development. Even more important, analyses of development that omit the influence of political factors can become theoretical exercises offering little guidance in practical problem solving. For example, development proposals that call for utilizing market forces and matching supply to demand via prices utilize impeccable economic logic. But such prescriptions border on fantasy where government policies regulate commodity and food prices to serve ends other than agricultural development, where they encourage uneconomic factor mixes for political reasons, or where they ration capital for industrialization and thereby inhibit rural investment. Similarly, agronomic prescriptions that anticipate higher yields from better seeds, more fertilizer, and adequately proportioned water are obviously sound. Yet they become practicable only under conditions where information inputs and capital are accessible to rural populations who have been appropriately educated and motivated to innovate. Whether such conditions exist is largely a function of government policy and administrative capacity, and these, in turn, result from political considerations that often have little to do with agriculture as such.

The Meaning of Rural Modernization

Rural modernization is a complex phenomenon. Although its modes have varied considerably throughout history, and presently vary from region to region, certain general outcomes signal its occurrence. First, agricultural *production and productivity* increase substantially as modernization proceeds. Enhanced productivity tends to be especially marked with regard to labor and land, and these increases are most frequently the results of *changing technology*, the second general feature of agricultural modernization. Even though the extent and impacts of technological change differ from country to country, sustained development eventually requires technological change in all cases.

More broadly conceived, rural modernization is an aspect of the structural transformation of economies, a step in the progression that has led countries and peoples from traditional feudal agrarianism to modern urban industrialism.[2] During modernization, labor moves from agriculture to industry as heightened productivity and improved marketing and distribution systems make it possible for those few working in the countryside to feed the many working in the cities. Concurrently, the farmers' greater participation in the cash economy combines with escalating demand for their products to produce a heightened rural well-being, an increase in disposable income, and an enhanced demand for both agricultural inputs and consumer goods. Rural demand stimulates urban industry, and reinvested profits promote further industrial growth, thus creating new urban employment, new demands for food, and further incentives to agriculture. Of course it is a simplification to believe that national economic development and industrialization result solely or even primarily from the rising interdependence of rural and urban demand. But this is not the point. Rather, what is important here is that structural transformation, as reflected in shifting linkages between sectors, is both a result and an index of rural modernization.

Many features of rural modernization are readily observable in the statistical series and quantitative records of countries. Table 1.1, for example, highlights the rural modernization of several countries in terms of production, productivity, input technology, and structural transformation. Equally relevant and revealing would be figures showing that, typically, during or after agricultural modernization rural wage rates move in tandem with urban ones, rural unemployment and underemployment diminish (partly through migration), rural literacy and education levels rise notably, rural savings and capital increase, and living standards markedly improve, at least for the "successful" farmers. Also, while some of the rural populace are gaining these advantages, others are losing out—squeezed off the bud or impoverished as new technologies and government policies disadvantage them.

There are other aspects of rural modernization that are less quantifiable, but certainly important. For one thing, "successful" peasants typically become farmers during modernization—much more an attitudinal or psychological transformation than a physical one. With this comes a new attentiveness to markets and a new receptivity to innovation, new expectations concerning economic and social mobility within and between generations, new openness to information, a penchant for organization, and, usually, a heightened and more effective political participation. In addition, traditional fatalism in the countryside tends to give way to awareness and confidence in science applied to agriculture. Parochialism diminishes as modern transport

TABLE 1.1

AGRICULTURAL MODERNIZATION AND STRUCTURAL TRANSFORMATION

United States, Japan, Denmark and France, 1880-1960

1960=100

Country	1880	1900	1910	1930	1950	1960
A. Total Production						
United States	29	46	48	60	84	100
Japan	28	42	53	69	71	100
Denmark	24	31	41	66	76	100
France	43	47	53	62	60	100
B. Output Per Male Worker						
United States	15	18	19	25	52	100
Japan	22	34	43	57	57	100
Denmark	22	30	36	51	67	100
France	22	24	28	40	47	100
C. Output Per Hectare						
United States	63	62	63	69	81	100
Japan	36	49	57	71	73	100
Denmark	26	33	44	64	67	100
France	43	47	50	60	62	100
D. Percent Male Workers in Non-Agriculture						
United States	45	57	64	74	85	91
Japan	21	35	43	57	60	74
Denmark	46	53	55	62	77	77
France	51	56	60	67	NA	80

Source: Yujiro Hayami and Vernon Ruttan, Agricultural Development: An International Perspective (Baltimore: Johns Hopkins Press, 1971),pp. 327-331.

and communications obviate rural isolation: Lifestyles in the countryside become more secular, urbane, and comfortable as material and
intellectual poverty recede.[3] In many aspects the American farmer
approximates this ideal, as described by Hadwiger and Talbot in
Chapter 2.

What parts do politics and public policy play in the course of such
"typical" rural modernization? What roles do public policy and the policy process play in initiating and nurturing the economic, social, and
attitudinal transformations involved in evolution from primitive to
modern agriculture? Conversely, when, how, and why does public policy, either by commission or omission, hinder, divert, or stifle such
transformations? These are the central substantive concerns of our book
and the main themes of the collected essays that compose it. Readers will
discover, however, that few pat and simple answers emerge to questions
about government's role in agricultural modernization, mainly because
experiences are so varied and complex. There is no ready formula for
agricultural development, no universally reliable policy guideline, no
widely prescribable doctrine of innovation and reform, no superior
ideology of development. Agriculture has been modernized with a low
degree of governmental intervention, as in the United States, and with a
high degree, as in Japan.[4] It has also floundered under a low degree of
intervention, as in India during the First and Second Five Year Plans,
and under a high degree, as in the Soviet Union in the 1930s.[5] Similarly,
agriculture has been admirably developed under capitalist systems, as in
North America and Western Europe, and under socialist ones, as in the
People's Republic of China and Cuba.[6] But modernization has also
lagged under both systems, as evidenced by Brazil and Poland.[7] Land
redistribution has furthered development in countries like Taiwan; it
was relatively inconsequential in Chile, and it probably set back development in nineteenth century Ireland and in present-day Bolivia.[8]

Analyzing Rural Modernization Policies

Methodologically, this book is a set of exercises in the comparative
analysis of agricultural modernization policies. Those engaged in these
exercises begin by assuming that policy outcomes range along a
continuum from "success" to "failure," although the criteria for such
judgments vary widely. Even the seeming "success" of American
agricultural modernization has been challenged recently for its excessive
resource depletion, capital-intensiveness, and environmental pollution,
as Hadwiger and Talbot note in Chapter 2. Young Kihl finds a success in
the declining food self-sufficiency of Korea (see Chapter 6), while a
similar decline in Iran seems a failure to Schulz (Chapter 7). Even the

critique of tractor policy in Pakistan offered by Herring and Kennedy (Chapter 8) indicates debate and ambiguity over the employment and production effects of tractor subsidization, although the effects on income distribution clearly enhance inequalities.

Aside from divergency in evaluating outcomes, we will see from our analyses that outcomes are shaped at different times and places by a combination of factors that we shall term "policy components." In other words, they are shaped by the contents of policies. Analyzing a particular government's policy consists in identifying and accounting for the components of its attitude and actions toward its rural sector either consciously or inadvertently. Evaluating that policy means assessing the appropriateness of the various components (singly or in combination) under prevailing geographic, social, economic, political, and cultural conditions, and studying their effects on agricultural production, rural life, and the political role of agricultural groups.

Policy components assume specific forms and are of great variety and uncertain duration in the modernization process of different countries, yet standard classification is possible. All development policies, for example, are directed toward explicit and/or implicit goals; all prescribe a degree of official intervention into agricultural markets; all embody means or modes of execution; all concern the allocation of resources; all establish or suppress institutions of various kinds. Each of these classifications warrants some elaboration.

The Goals and Priorities of Agricultural Policy

Generally speaking, agricultural modernization is most readily furthered by agricultural policy when modernization is the goal of such policy. Ironically, this has not always been (nor is it presently) the case. In some countries governmental attitudes toward the countryside and its inhabitants reflect indifference to rural modernization; in other countries policies toward agriculture reflect governmental preoccupations with development in other sectors. For both the Soviet Union and the People's Republic of China priorities in agricultural policy have revolved around ideological aims at creating "new socialist men"; ideological socialization ranked as more important than productivity or production, as Bernstein notes in Chapter 4. India's agricultural policy under the First Five Year Plan set goals of nation-building and integrating above rural development. Iran subordinates development to regime maintenance. Japan's aspirations for Taiwanese agriculture during the colonial period had a good deal more to do with imperial integrity than with rural modernization (see Chapter 5). The point is that governmental goals in agricultural policy vary: some pursuits aid modernization, and others clearly hamper it.

Acceptability of Market Structures and Processes

In some countries agricultural development has been encouraged by official reliance on market forces as the means and motors of development—that is, the logic of supply and demand, the efficiency of giving production cues with prices, and the simplicity of adjustment and transformation via open competition. In such cases public policies have mandated government intervention in economic intercourse only to protect property, legalize contracts, standardize weights and measures, or occasionally control abuses and negative effects of the market (see Bates, Chapter 9, on negative externalities). In great contrast, agricultural development in some other countries has been conditioned so widely by public intervention that the effect has been complete suppression of market forces. Under such regimes, market structures are replaced by administrative ones, and market dynamics are superseded by plans, production directives, and rationing schemes. Obviously, the great majority of development regimes fall somewhere between high reliance on market forces, as in early America, and comprehensive regulation, as in the Soviet Union.[9] The Japanese development experience, for example, has rather elegantly interwoven market forces and administrative controls.[10] The important analytical point is that the degree and utility of reliance on free markets embodied in rural development policies do not vary by accident among national cases, and the analyst should therefore be attentive to the reasons for and appropriateness of market versus nonmarket emphases under varying conditions.

policies for market protection

policies for market intervention

Means Adopted to Pursue Policy Goals

Again, the array of ways that governments have gone about pursuing their ends in agriculture, including modernization, is extensive. Some have emphasized fiscal manipulation, as in Brazilian attempts to force heightened productivity by raising land taxes.[11] Financial means, too, have been used in a variety of ways to channel public funds into forming an infrastructure, subsidizing inputs, prices, and incomes, compensating expropriated landowners, providing credit, furthering research and extension services, and educating farm families. In countries such as Cuba and China where agricultural modernization has been only an aspect of broader programs of rural improvement, public funds have also been directed into health, recreational, cultural, and educational facilities intended ultimately to enhance the human resources invested in agriculture.[12]

The primary legislative means to furthering agricultural modernization in a great many countries has been the land reform law, in which there is great variety. A number of land reforms have been punitively directed and draconically enforced against larger landholders, sometimes under the banner of heightened efficiency, sometimes out of intentions to eliminate aliens and absentees, and sometimes as unabashed campaigns of class warfare in the countryside. In this latter regard, Stalin's drive against the kulaks is notorious.[13] As noted earlier, there are few general lessons to be drawn from experience with land reform and its relation to agricultural modernization. As an agricultural policy, many governments, especially in Latin America, still continue to look at adjusting land tenure, however, as the final step toward rural improvement. The policy analyst's task is to determine what kinds of land reform best contribute to rural modernization and what kinds are least productive.

Border controls and foreign relations are also means that serve rural development ends. In some cases where conditions are propitious, governments find that integrating their agricultural sector or parts of it with the world economy supports internal development; in other instances, isolating agriculture has been a preferred strategy. Where cash crops for export are important sources of development capital, as with many coffee, cocoa, sugar, and cotton producing countries, export taxes and foreign policies aimed at stable markets and enhanced earnings are bound to development programs that rely on exchange earnings for financing, as in Ghana (see Bates, Chapter 9). On the other hand, where unreasonable foreign competition, in grains or processed food, for example, threatens bankruptcy even to efficient local farmers, tariff protection and consequent insulation from the world economy become ingredients of planning for rural development. Interestingly, almost every country that has experienced rural modernization passed through a high tariff period during initial and middle phases of development. Other ways in which foreign policy means serve rural modernization ends typically include relying on external markets for agricultural inputs, looking to more advanced countries, multinational firms, and international organizations for information and technology, and seeking development capital from abroad (as does Iran, see Chapter 6). Remarkable strides toward rural modernization in Taiwan and South Korea, and in Israel as well, can be attributed in considerable measure to American public and private development assistance.[14] But then too a measure of early American agricultural growth also followed from overseas investment.[15] Finally, while there is controversy about the efficacy of foreign food aid as a stimulant to rural development, some governments have managed to integrate aid into modernization programs in an imaginative way—in the form of "food-for-work" on rural infrastructure projects, or as "crop insurance" to encourage experiments with new technologies.[16]

Development in the countryside does not usually occur spontaneously. People generally do not change their modes of living and livelihood, even when desperate, until they are convinced that change will either bring rewards or avoid punishments. The task of executing policies aimed at change therefore involves governments in the search for appropriate administrative instruments. Styles of official promotion and enforcement during rural modernization range from gentle urging to brutal coercion, although, typically, incentives and enticements are preferred over sanctions. The Chinese government continues to rely rather heavily, though hardly exclusively, on symbols and propaganda—slogans, campaigns, wall posters, verbal exhortation, exemplary behavior, and the like—and the Indian government has also used such methods with some effect.[17]

Many governments direct their market interventions at providing incentives for innovation, for instance in cases where genetically superior seeds are publicly subsidized and fertilizers are distributed below cost to encourage their adoption. Some governments, such as the Japanese, have effectively mobilized rural elites and farmers' organizations to lead modernization drives. Still others, like the Chinese nationalist government, have linked their agricultural extension services with their gendarmerie to monitor compliance with official policies (see Chapter 5 on Taiwan), and elsewhere, in a few cases, development goals have been enforced by imprisoning or executing recalcitrant peasants.

Origins and Allocation of Resources for Development

No policy can help attain goals without resources, and experience in many countries reveals that rural modernization requires substantial investments of time, energy, intellect, and money. The origins of resources for agricultural development, however, differ considerably over time and space. In North America and in some European countries and their colonies, investing in rural development was, by and large, a private-sector undertaking. Opportunities were signalled by expectations of high return; initiative followed from individual entrepreneurship; capital came from private institutions and was granted to the state from a stock of uninhabited or expropriated property. Early public investment in these cases was limited to supporting research and sometimes funding the development of infrastructure (although in

North America even infrastructure was privately financed and engineered until well into the twentieth century). The official policy, if it can be called that, was to promote the uninhibited operations of private capital markets by interfering as minimally as possible.

Elsewhere, of course, the origins of resources for development were to be found in the public sector—planning and administration became surrogates for entrepreneurship; ministries of development or rural reform and marketing boards replaced private financial institutions and commodity exchange; and fiscal receipts served the function of private savings. Policy under these conditions embodies an orchestration of fiscal means, revenue needs, and anticipated costs of development strategies. In instances where public revenues turn out either inadequate or unreliable, governments may choose to finance development through domestic inflation, as Brazil did during the 1960s, or through foreign borrowing, as Peru, Sudan, and other countries in Asia and Africa have done in recent years.[18] Ultimately, there is no "better" or "poorer" way to finance rural modernization, since much depends on the location of resources, the relative allurement of alternative investment opportunities, the strength and integrity of bureaucratic institutions, and the level of entrepreneurship in different countries at different times. Needless to say, much also depends on the magnitude of the development task and the rapidity with which it must be accomplished.

There are, however, "better" and "poorer" investment strategies for rural modernization, or at least there are some lessons to be learned from experience. There is, of course, the standard economic rule of thumb that advises investment *to compensate for scarce factors*—by rendering them more plentiful or more productive. Investing in mechanization, for example, compensates for scarce labor, investing in fertilizer raises the productivity of scarce land, investing in irrigation makes more efficient use of scarce water, sinking new wells makes water more abundant, and so on. Repeating this scarcity dictum would be a trivial exercise were it not for the fact that it is so often, and disappointingly, overlooked in many countries' agricultural development programs, especially in those, like Pakistan's, where mechanization in agriculture becomes a goal in itself, pursued without regard to land, labor, and capital ratios (see Chapter 8). The connection between factor scarcities and investment strategies therefore bears monitoring. If capital-intensive technology is subsidized at the same time that rural unemployment is growing, for instance, one may immediately suspect that advantaged groups, such as large landholders or urban elites, have substantial influence over the policy.

The sequence of investment targets is also important. Early investments to improve the quality of human resources tend, for example, to correlate rather closely with later accomplishments in agricultural production and productivity. Government drives to promote literacy in the countryside before promoting more elaborate programs of technological change unquestionably contributed to progress in rural modernization in the United States, Europe, Japan, Taiwan, and China.[19] The productive impact was particularly noteworthy in China, where, since the revolution of 1949, rural education has been combined with measures to improve the health and nutrition of the rural population. Similarly, early investment in transport and communications also appears to be directly linked to making rapid strides toward modernization. Overcoming bottlenecks in marketing and distribution by providing roads, railroads, and waterways, and integrating farmers into information networks via media and extension services, contribute significantly to the shift from subsistence agriculture to the specialization in production and new rural-urban divisions of labor which necessarily accompany modernization. Furthermore, early investments in agronomic research have tended to speed rural modernization and to bring benefits which far outweigh the cost of research establishments. European accomplishments are a testament to this, the Dutch, Danish, and British especially. But this has also been the case for Japan, Canada, and the United States, as Hadwiger, Talbot, and Aall point out in Chapters 2 and 3. The point that fundamental investments to improve the environment for agriculture should come before specific drives to change technology, though obvious, is frequently overlooked in practice, as several of this volume's essays demonstrate (e.g., the chapters by Schulz and Bates).

Institutions for Rural Modernization

As the countryside changes, farms and other producing units are altered in structure and function, markets are established or superseded, schools are founded, financial and credit facilities such as banks and cooperatives emerge, research and extension services are introduced, and farmers organize for economic and political action. A good deal has already been said about created and transformed infrastructure during rural modernization. What needs to be underlined is that promoting or suppressing various rural institutions and political movements is inevitably a component of official development policies. Moreover, building institutions that are appropriate to conditions in the countryside and complementary both to farmers' needs and govern-

mental objectives is a challenging problem for policymakers. Contrariwise, encouraging inappropriate or ill-designed institutions, such as
many cooperatives in Africa in the 1960s proved to be, can be a formula
for failure.

Agricultural production units assume considerable variety, and,
although different kinds usually coexist in any country, governments
tend to emphasize particular ones as vehicles for development.
Compare, for example, American official encouragement of the "family
farm" with Danish emphasis on the cooperative, Soviet promotion of
the kolkholz or collective farm, Tanzanian ujamaa villages, and the
elaborately tiered Chinese system of teams, brigades, and communes.
Which institutions are deemed ideologically superior depends ultimately on one's leanings; which ones are appropriate vehicles for
rapidly raising production and productivity depends on prevailing
socio-cultural milieus and peculiar problems of resources and
agronomy in given countries. Therefore, connections between kinds of
producing units and kinds of development outcomes under varying
contexts warrant monitoring. Much the same can be said for marketing
institutions and credit facilities. Which contribute best to rural
modernization? Traditional money lenders who charge usurious rates of
interest but lend to even the poorest applicant? Modern banks that
charge reasonable interest but lend to only some applicants? Or
government ministries that charge nominal interest but lend for
certain projects or to certain people only?

Farmers' organizations and rural political associations deserve special
attention in the analysis of rural modernization. Experience in Japan
and Taiwan has shown that farmers' associations can be exploited by
governments as vehicles of modernization and carriers of technological
change—in effect, as extensions of extension services. Conversely, as in
the United States, an elite "subsystem" can capture the benefits of
government largely for itself. With appropriately recruited and
rewarded leadership, organizations can serve as instruments of
surveillance and even agents to enforce compliance with official policies
whether they favor current rural elites (as in Pakistan) or seek to displace
them (as has occurred in Taiwan). More generally, farmers' organizations have been channels through which information about the impacts
of policies has flowed back to governments. As such they have proven
essential to monitoring the effects of policy and crucial to the
governmental capacity for timely adjustment. What is important for
policy analysis, and what some of the following essays discuss is the
extent to which governments have used or abused various farm
organizations during rural development. Another question that is

examined is what has resulted from their various attitudes and actions toward these organizations?

Finally, there are the institutions of technological innovations *per se*—research and extension services. It is fair to say that in every successful case of rural modernization that we are aware of government has been instrumental in fusing science and technology with agriculture. Even in the United States, where much of the technological development was in the private sector, federal and state investment in university research in agronomy and forestry was notable in the nineteenth century, when the land grant college network was established. The European tradition of public subsidization of agricultural research is, of course, much older, especially in plant and animal genetics in Russia, Prussia, and England. On the other hand, underemphasis on technology and low funding for agricultural research proved costly to both Indian and Chinese rural modernization during the 1950s, and insufficient research and technological innovation currently poses a major obstacle to rural development in Africa.

Extension services are equally important. If a government does not have the capacity to reach farmers directly, broad-gauged policies of rural development cannot be executed effectively or monitored adequately. Creating, maintaining, and effectively using an agricultural extension service appears to be an ingredient of every successful case of rural modernization. The absence or ineffectiveness of such structures contributed to the failure of the land reform efforts in Bolivia in the 1950s (where newly "landed" peasants could not be shown how to use their resources) and to lagging production growth in some Indian states where agricultural extension agents preferred not to go into the countryside to meet farmers.

Encompassing all these institutional developments and a phenomenon inextricably linked to agricultural and rural modernization is the expansion of government. All the kinds of changes in agriculture that we have reviewed have reflected or spurred the expansion of state power in the countryside. There are two reasons for this. First, for traditional agricultural patterns to be supplanted by new rural institutions and practices—such as changed land-tenure systems or ownership distribution, increased credit, and new planting and marketing techniques—new (usually national) bases for authority and the settlement of conflicts are required and facilitated. That is, rural change can be the forerunner as well as the product of new government, as has happened in China. Second, new practices require expanded services—new types of production inputs, regulation of diseases, rules to insure that wider markets operate securely, and an expansion of physical infrastructure, education, and extension work. The concern of comparative policy analysis is to determine which of these have worked successfully within varying contexts.

Policy Analysis and Comparative Case Studies

If we could know which combinations of official goals, degrees of intervention, political and administrative means, sources and uses of resources, and institutional emphases would yield successful rural modernization under various conditions, our capacity to prescribe would be a good deal more advanced than it is at present. Unfortunately, we have not yet accumulated the systematic knowledge required to guide governments toward courses of action that are simultaneously economically efficient, politically practicable, socioculturally appropriate, and agriculturally productive. That we lack this knowledge is a major justification for this volume and a recurrent theme of its chapters.

Implicitly or explicitly there are at least six issues on the policy agendas of countries undergoing rural modernization—land ownership, degree of foreign control, scale biases of technology, rural versus urban biases, food versus nonfood production, and the instrumental versus the consummatory role of the rural populace in modernization. Some or all of the policy components identified earlier affect the practical resolution of each of these issues. Moreover, these issues are not independent of each other. Their resolution leads to the particular policy configuration of a given country. Of course, this "configuration" may or may not be stable over time and may or may not be conducive to growth in agricultural productivity. The case studies of six countries that follow, along with the three region-oriented analyses (Chapters 3, 9, and 10), do not systematically review the manner in which each of these issues was resolved nor the apparent effects of each. Each chapter's analysis does, however, examine some or most of these issues.[20]

Land Ownership

Keith Griffin, among others, has argued that redistribution of land ownership would be the most effective means of reducing rural inequality and poverty and would increase production and total income in most contexts.[21] He notes that small farmers tend to use land more completely and with higher yields and value added per hectare, as evidenced by studies in Bangladesh, Malaysia, Sri Lanka, Indonesia, Thailand, Pakistan, India, and the Philippines.[22] Yet land reforms have frequently been inconsequential or outright failures, since much more than simply redistribution is required, including considerable political "costs." Two questions really come up with respect to land: What form shall "ownership" take (i.e., shall individual communities or the government be given title), and how equitable should distribution be? Land ownership, as we see in the Iranian, Russian, and Chinese cases (Chapters 4 and 7) can be used most importantly for political ends, either to reinforce traditional rule or to revolutionize a society. When development goals (e.g., production growth with or without equity) are uppermost, economic rather than political calculations are presumably determinative. In any event, policy elements such as goals, resources, and institutions will all be affected by the way a regime settles the question of land ownership.

External Control

As we noted in several cases, notably Pakistan, Iran, Korea, and Taiwan, there has been a heavy reliance on external inputs and a tolerance of foreign control in agricultural development. Interestingly, both China and Taiwan have achieved considerable equity among their rural populace while following or being subject to quite opposite degrees of foreign control, especially since 1949. Furthermore, Cuba, which sought to reduce foreign control after 1960, has met with some difficulties as sugar production has declined and general dependence on the Soviet Union has replaced that previously enjoyed by the United States. The effects of foreign involvement and influence, therefore, generally depend on the context; for example, they can be said to have been favorable in Taiwan, mixed in Iran and Africa, and detrimental in Pakistan and China.

Technology

Different technologies carry with them different "biases"; in particular, most capital-intensive technologies, such as tractors, are not scale-neutral but rather give advantage to the larger, wealthier farmers (as the Pakistan case makes clear; see Chapter 8). The most obvious "non-transferable" element in the American experience, according to Hadwiger and Talbot (Chaper 2), is our specific technology. Technology "choice" has a major effect on the policy options available to developing countries. Different choices produced different options for the earlier developers of Europe, according to Aall (Chapter 3). More important than the technological inputs that capital investment can buy may be the forms of the technology: Which kinds of farms and farmers does it advantage? Is it scale-neutral or does it favor extensive or intensive cultivation? Even though the effects of the "green revolution" have been more scale-neutral than many expected, continuing technological innovation of the same kind in less agronomically favorable areas may well lead to wide-spread impoverishment and a more volatile political role for rural areas.[23] If policy decisions resolve the issue of kind of technology in favor of one with a large farm bias (usually through subsidies and provision of services for farm commodities), then the "choice" of equitable land distribution would work at cross-purposes to the goal of increased production. Hence, the effect of technology may be as important for equity as for production if it favors large landowners for certain regions to the absolute disadvantage of others.

Rural Versus Urban

A fourth issue for policy resolution is the question of whether to favor rural or urban populaces.[24] As we noted earlier, all development involves intersectoral stimulation—industry in towns and agriculture in the countryside advance together, as Aall notes pointedly for England. However, production in one sector may be supported by the other through direct intersectoral transfers as well, usually through government taxes. Classically, the city has advanced at the expense of the rural population, whether through cheap-food policies, confiscation of export earnings, or other causes. This pattern, whether found in the United States, the Soviet Union, or Ghana, is no longer likely to yield the same growth effects. And in the wake of such intersectoral transfers, the basis for rural tensions, given the diffusion of expectations, is now much greater. Bates's discussion of the discontent among Ghanaian cocoa growers (Chapter 9) illustrates this point.

Food Versus Nonfood

A fifth issue is whether food self-sufficiency should be encouraged through extra-market incentives. Iran and Korea, with their declining food production compared to demand, have chosen to subsidize consumer prices, though not totally at producers' expense. The government has instead paid a subsidy to maintain a differential between higher farm and lower urban retail prices. Other related policies do harm farmers. For instance, when higher earning export crops or cheaper food imports (e.g., food aid) create incentives to move away from food production, this shift will also affect the urban-rural terms of trade because cheaper food prices generally favor the urban population. Policies in Iran, Pakistan, and elsewhere favoring export crops and/or imported extensive-type technologies for food production are surprising in the wake of the global food shortages of 1973-74 and the projections of substantial and growing food deficits in less developed countries as a whole—expected to be 185 million tons by 1990, up from

21 million tons in 1975.[25] Nicholson and Esseks (Chapter 10) discuss a number of the problems food shortages pose for policy makers in developing countries.

Role of the Rural Populace

A final issue is the political role played by the rural populace in policy making. Modernization through revolution has been advanced as rural "classes" aided revolutionary efforts in China, Russia, Cuba, and elsewhere (see Bernstein, Chapter 4).[26] At the opposite extreme, the countryside may be viewed as politically impotent, serving principally as a supplier of capital through "profits" captured by the government to support urban industrialization. In the Soviet Union, the Russians may have played both these roles from 1917 through 1937. The goals of policies, of course, are important in reflecting or establishing these alternative roles in modernization. At one extreme the well-being of the rural populace may be regarded as an end in itself and, hence, growth in their consumption becomes a critical yardstick for evaluating policy. At the other extreme, rural people are seen as an instrument of production whose immiscibility is irrelevant to policy evolution, except as it may have a negative effect on production or political stability.

Although some consultants believe that they can knowledgeably and confidently offer advice on these issues, we recommend caution. There is at present a respected body of theoretical knowledge concerned with the economics of development and an equally impressive body in the fields of theoretical and applied agronomy and the cognate sciences. Drawing on these helps achieve a better and more systematic understanding of rural modernization but can hardly complete the intellectual task, since, as noted earlier, they fail to take into account the economic, social, and cultural factors that shape politics and affect policy implementation. In contrast to theoretical scientific analyses, there is also a wealth of practical experience with agricultural modernization—scores of cases, historical and contemporary, libraries of description, documentation, anecdotal insights, and case-study materials that can be mined by scholars in the search for a more complete and systematic understanding of relationships between public policies and rural transformation. What these case analyses can show is that under particular conditions certain combinations of policy components produced particular results—some good, some bad. Multiplying cases and reconfirming relationships increases the generality of the findings, and, ultimately, such comparative research and inductive logic can yield systematic knowledge. This book's collection of case studies of rural modernization is a preliminary and very small step in the direction of such knowledge. We

certainly do not recommend that Third World governments delay efforts
at agricultural development while scholars accumulate more complete
knowledge about the process. There is no time for this. We do suggest
that governmental efforts will become more successful as our
understanding becomes more complete and contextually relevant.
There is an urgency, then, in the task that we have proposed to our
colleagues and begun work on in the chapters of this volume.

Notes

1. Bruce F. Johnston and Peter Kilby, *Agriculture and Structural
Transformation* (New York: Oxford University Press, 1975); Yujiro Hayami
and Vernon W. Ruttan, *Agricultural Development: An International Perspective* (Baltimore and London: The Johns Hopkins Press, 1971); Theodore
W. Schultz, *Transforming Traditional Agriculture* (New Haven: Yale University Press, 1964); Laurence Hewes, *Rural Development: World Frontiers* (Ames,
Iowa: The Iowa State University Press, 1974); Melvin G. Blasee, ed., *Institutions
in Agricultural Development* (Ames, Iowa: The Iowa State University Press,
1971); Keith Griffin, *The Political Economy of Agrarian Change* (Cambridge,
Mass.: Harvard University Press, 1974).

2. Johnston and Kilby, *Agriculture and Structural Transformation*, pp. 34-
75.

3. Daniel Lerner, *The Passing of Traditional Society* (New York: The Free
Press, 1958), pp. 19-75.

4. Cf. John T. Schlebecker, *Whereby We Thrive: A History of American
Farming, 1607-1972* (Ames, Iowa: The Iowa State University Press, 1975);
Murray R. Benedict, *Farm Policies of the United States: A Study of Their
Origins and Development* (New York: Twentieth Century Fund, 1956); Gilbert
C. Fite, *American Agriculture and Farm Policy Since 1900* (Washington,
D.C.: The American Historical Association, Waverly Press, 1964); Yujiro
Hayami, *A Century of Agricultural Growth in Japan* (Minneapolis and
Tokyo: University of Minnesota Press and University of Tokyo Press, 1975).

5. John W. Mellor, *The Economics of Agricultural Development* (Ithaca,
N.Y.: Cornell University Press, 1966), pp. 223-244; John W. Mellor et al.,
Developing Rural India (Ithaca, N.Y.: Cornell University Press, 1968), pp. 31-
93; Lazar Volin, *A Century of Russian Agriculture* (Cambridge, Mass.: Harvard
University Press, 1970), pp. 203-274.

6. Schlebecker, *Whereby We Thrive*; Benedict Stavis, *People's Communes
and Rural Development in China* (Ithaca: Cornell University Rural Development Committee, RLG no. 3, 1975); Benedict Stavis, *Making Green Revolution:
The Politics of Agricultural Development in China* (Ithaca: Cornell University
Rural Development Committee, 1974); Elizabeth and Graham Johnson,
Walking on Two Legs: Rural Development in South China (Ottawa: International Development Research Center, 1976); Sterling Wortman, "Agriculture
in China," *Scientific American* 232, no. 6 (June 1975):13-21; Edward Boorstein,

The Economic Transformation of Cuba (New York and London: Monthly Review Press, 1968); Teresa Castro, *Cuba and Castro* (New York: Random House, 1961).

7. G. Edward Schuh, *The Agricultural Development of Brazil* (New York: Praeger, 1970); William H. Nicholls, "The Transformation of Agriculture in a Semi-Industrialized Country: The Case of Brazil," in Erik Thorbecke, ed., *The Role of Agriculture in Development* (New York; Columbia University Press, 1968), pp. 311-378; Gordon W. Smith, "Brazilian Agricultural Policy, 1950-1967," in Howard S. Ellis, ed., *The Economy of Brazil* (Berkeley, Calif.: University of California Press, 1969), pp. 213-265; Tomaz Wybraniec, "Peasant Farming in Poland: Performance and Prospects," Paper presented at Conference on Soviet and Peasant Affairs, August 1967. On socialist and communist experiences more generally, see W. A. Douglas Jackson, ed., *Agrarian Policies and Problems in Communist and Non-Communist Countries* (Seattle and London: University of Washington Press, 1971).

8. Cf. Chapter 1, Stuart Thomas, "Authoritarian Politics: The Case of the Chilean Agrarian Reform" (Ph.D. diss., Columbia University, Department of Political Science, 1978); Pamela Aall McPherson, "Politics and Agriculture in Nineteenth Century Ireland" (New York: Columbia University, Institute on Western Europe, 1977); Frances M. Foland, "Agrarian Reform in Latin America," *Foreign Affairs* 48, no. 1 (October 1969):97-112.

9. Schlebecker, *Whereby We Thrive*, pp. 71-86; Volin, *Century of Russian Agriculture*, pp. 235-274.

10. Hayami and Ruttan, *Agricultural Development*, pp. 111-168; Johnston and Kilby, *Agriculture and Structural Transformation*, pp. 182-240; Hayami, *Century of Agricultural Growth in Japan*, pp. 44-86.

11. Gordon W. Smith, "Brazilian Agricultural Policy," p. 215.

12. Stavis, *People's Communes*, pp. 136-165; Boorstein, *Economic Transformation of Cuba, passim;* Carmelo Mesa-Lago, *Cuba in the 1970's* (Albuquerque, N.M.: University of New Mexico Press, 1978), pp. 30-61.

13. Volin, *Century of Russian Agriculture*, pp. 203-235.

14. Cf. Chapters 5 and 6 in this volume.

15. Gilbert C. Fite and Jim E. Reese, *An Economic History of the United States* (Boston: Houghton Mifflin, 1965), pp. 135, 163-185, 380-405.

16. U. K. Srivastava et al., *Food Aid and International Economic Growth* (Ames, Iowa: The Iowa State University Press, 1975), pp. 37-64, 113-123.

17. Stavis, *Making Green Revolution*, pp. 22-54; Mellor et al., *Developing Rural India*, pp. 33-55.

18. G. Edward Schuh, *Agricultural Development of Brazil*, pp. 4-17. See also G. Edward Schuh, "Effects of Some General Economic Development Policies on Agricultural Development," *American Journal of Agricultural Economics* 50, no. 5 (December 1968):1283-1293.

19. Note especially the Japanese case as described by Hayami, *Century of Agricultural Growth in Japan*, pp. 107ff.

20. If our introduction had been prepared before the chapters were completed, more systematic treatment by the authors of these issues would have occurred.

21. Keith Griffin, *The Political Economy of Agrarian Change* (Cambridge: Harvard University Press, 1974); and Keith Griffin, *Land Concentration and Rural Poverty* (New York: Holmes and Meier, 1976).

22. Azizur Rehman Khan, *The Economy of Bangladesh* (London: Macmillan, 1972), pp. 131-136; Keith Griffin, *Political Economy of Agrarian Change*, pp. 39-45; and R. Albert Berry and William R. Cline, "Farm Size, Factor Productivity, and Technical Change in Developing Countries," manuscript draft, 1976.

23. Vernon Ruttan, for instance, argues that the initial effects of the green revolution were to increase productivity rather generally in the areas where it was adopted early, at least after four to five years, but that new productivity gains may come more slowly and with far less equity, thus spurring revolutionary impulses in the countryside. In Vernon W. Ruttan, "Induced Institutional Innovation and the Green Revolution," *Philippine Economic Journal* (1977).

24. For a discussion of "urban biases" endemic in many countries' policies, see Michael Lipton, *Why the Poor Stay Poor* (Cambridge: Harvard University Press, 1976).

25. See *Food Needs of Developing Countries: Projections of Production and Consumption to 1990* (Washington: International Food Policy Research Institute, 1977), pp. 44-53.

26. This point is well made by Scott, who notes that peasants rather than proletariat have been more important in twentieth century revolutions, a rather un-Marxist argument. See James Scott, "Hegemony and the Peasantry," *Politics and Society* 7, no. 3 (1977):267-295.

2
The United States:
A Unique Development Model

Don F. Hadwiger
Ross B. Talbot

It is really too much to try to state the relevance of U.S. agriculture for developing countries, given that we could not have been more surprised at the outcome of our own agricultural experience. Indeed, we do not fully understand what is happening to ourselves, and some students of American agriculture are far from being reconciled to what they do perceive. Many feel a sense of anxiety and concern about the world impact of U.S. agribusiness. There are those who believe that economic and political necessity may ultimately cause the United States to restructure and redirect its own food production/distribution institutions and procesess.

We will establish a kind of dual interpretation in our study of the relevancy of U.S. agricultural development to the conditions and problems of agriculture in the developing nations. In the first section, we present a brief history of U.S. agriculture, with particular reference to nineteenth century developments, exploring for comparability and possible transferability, especially in matters of policy development and impact. In the second half of the paper, we examine a second interpretation of U.S. agriculture—i.e., the exceptionalist interpretation. This school of thought contends that U.S. agriculture is distinctive in its many-faceted reality. Attempting what may seem to be paradoxical, we conclude that there are "lessons" to be learned from American agriculture which could be of value to the developing nations, notwithstanding the "exceptionalist" quality of the American experience.

History of U.S. Agriculture

U.S. agriculture is probably looked upon with some envy, because its high productivity is obvious and because it is said to have fostered the egalitarian values that are the basis for a democratic society. The high productivity achieved in the United States, however, has had some barely tolerable side effects. And egalitarian values have never been secure, championed in our early history by farmer aristocrats such as Thomas Jefferson whose own enterprise did not embody these values. In this century, the symbolism of equality manifested in the family farm has been undermined by the elimination of the small farm as the major production unit.

Our purpose in this section is to discuss, in historical perspective, the relevance of U.S. farm policies for developing nations. Any such discussion must recognize at least two major complexities. First, public policy has been only one causative factor in agricultural development. Therefore, it is necessary to try to sort out the distinctive influence of policy as it has interacted with social structure, technology, the natural environment, and events such as the Civil War. Second, we have always had not one but several structures of agriculture in this country, each similar to structures found in some other countries. Our agricultural policy has accommodated each of these structures, although not without showing bias toward some. It is this policy bias—the reasons for it and the consequences of it—that may be of concern to developing countries, and therefore it is the principal subject of this section.

In the United States, as in some other countries, farming developed under conditions of "land abundance." Rapid geographic expansion of the American nation happened mainly at the initiative of frontier farmers and ranchers, although they were supported by federal policies.

The pace of development was moderated somewhat by the need to wait for new technology to accommodate natural environments. Expansion in the South awaited the cotton gin; settlement beyond the rivers awaited the development of alternative forms of freight transport; farm settlement west of the Mississippi awaited the development of barbed wire, windmills, binders, and gangplows; permanent farm settlement on the High Plains awaited the creation of irrigation systems and—in this century—the development of dry-land farming. Yet the choice of farming structure and the kinds of commodities to be produced was much more the result of cultural values and market demand.

Farming structures were originally of two major types—small, freeholding farms and plantations using slave labor, with a few locations featuring corporate landholding and landed estates. The plantation economy that dominated Southern politics was always embarrassed by the national values of individualism and equality, and, indeed, the "peculiar institution" of slavery was a major cause of this nation's Civil War. The Northern victory in that war resulted in a continuation and reaffirmation of a symbolic policy favoring small freeholders, but the Southern plantations were ultimately replaced by concentrated landholding. In recent years—as technology ended the need for unskilled labor—Southern agriculture developed large-scale industrial farms.[1]

The South has continued to be a major agricultural region (with a predominantly agricultural economy until recently), often with a specialized agriculture highly dependent on federal assistance. The great concentrations of landholding in the South supported a structure of elites that provided national leaders who helped secure federal policies amenable to large-farm agriculture, notwithstanding the national-legal symbolisms favoring small-farm freeholding.

Indeed, during the recent half century, Southerners who held strategic positions in Congress were sometimes artful and sometimes crude, but usually successful in manipulating the national fondness for small farmers into support for policies encouraging the national development of large-farm agriculture. In the notable case of the USDA's Bureau of Agricultural Economics, social scientists employed by the federal government to analyze U.S. agriculture were effectively prevented from addressing the total range of rural interests.[2] Recognition of the interests of large landholders was a condition for Southern—and later, Far Western—participation in the coalitions that passed federal farm legislation.

Thus, in the process of developing a full range of federal farm programs, Southern large-farm agriculture often exerted influence out of proportion to its economic significance in the nation or even within the South. Yet farmer aristocrats, mostly from Southern states, were powerful political resonators during the nineteenth century on issues where large-farm and small-farm interests were perceived to coincide. These included monetary, credit, and tariff policies and regulation of railroads and other "middlemen." Subsequently, other major agricultural regions played leading roles in the establishment of agricultural policy—particularly the Midwest, which was always the center of support for land policies favoring small-farm freeholding, and the Plains region, whose late-blooming, very unstable, commercial agriculture was most inclined to seek direct governmental assistance and which spawned the Populists and some other radical movements in American agriculture.

In a political system responsive to popular elections, U.S. farmers had great potential for influence. They comprised a majority of all Americans, at least until 1870, when they were 53 percent of all persons gainfully employed.[3] Their numbers continued to increase up to World War I, at which time farming was still the largest single occupation of

Americans. But numbers often proved a poor measure of power. In the Constitutional period, for example, most rural freeholders could not or did not vote, although they comprised "the great mass of White America."[4]

There was another sense in which most U.S. farmers were less potent than their numbers suggested. As Lester Milbrath has commented, a major determinant of political participation is a person's distance from the center of affairs.[5] The political centers (geographic, social, and/or psychological) are loaded with political stimuli, and those who reside there are likely to be relatively well informed, highly involved, confident, and committed to the system. In contrast, those on the periphery do not have a strong sense of belonging or capacity to work within it, as indicated by the rise of farmer protest groups and ultimately the Populist Party of the 1890s. The Populists, who tried to speak for the majority of small farmers and workers, perceived themselves to be outside the centers of power—the major party coalitions, the financial centers, corporations, government agencies, and the press. And when their program was coopted by the Democratic Party, the conflict between farmers and the industrial establishment became one of those infrequent causes of a party realignment. Yet the Democrats, running on the Populists' redistributive program, failed to win enough support from common people in the presidential election of 1896, partly because farmers lacked social status. Clanton has pointed out this additional handicap of those on the periphery of the system: "In the context of their period of origin, it was not [the] Populists' principles that were retrogressive—merely the fact that they were championed by and in the name of farmers and laborers. The path to reform could be made much smoother almost overnight if these same principles were embraced by urban, middle-class spokesmen and championed in the name of the middle class."[6]

The Populists were a movement founded for all common people, but their membership and leadership were found within the ranks of middle or large commercial farmers. An economic division between well-off commercial farmers on the one hand and marginal farmers and farm workers on the other was shaping up even during the years of Populism. Fred Shannon, referring to the presumed equality of opportunity in farming, said that although "there has been a spate of twaddle about the agricultural ladder up which hired laborers climbed to tenancy and then to ownership, by the end of the nineteenth century the compilers of the Industrial Commission Report had to concede that regardless of whatever advantage the agricultural ladder may once have accorded the day laborer or tenant, that device after 1880 was mainly filled by freeholders skidding down into tenancy or work for hire."[7] Shannon found that by 1900, in the North Central United States, 37.8 percent of all persons working farms were laborers making an average of $117 per year; another 19 percent were tenants, part tenants, and managers; only 43.2 percent owned or held equity in their farms.

Federal policy toward farmers proceeded through a number of stages. During the nineteenth century, according to Murray Benedict, agriculture was affected most directly by federal laws setting the mode for distributing public lands, by the federal monetary system, and by protective tariffs.[8] At first, land distribution policy had the goal of obtaining revenues, and land was sold in large segments. Pressure from "Western" spokesmen resulted in a succession of land laws beginning in 1800 (the Homestead Act of 1862 is the most famous) which permitted small-farm purchases and ultimately provided small farms free of charge to settlers.[9]

Tariffs designed to spur industry and monetary systems designed to provide a stable currency were usually resisted by farmer spokesmen, with some success.

There seemed to be no governmental remedy for the farm depressions that added to the miseries of nineteenth century farmers, one of which extended from the 1870s to 1896. The underlying economic problem was overproduction because of rapid expansion of cropland[10]—a problem that many countries might welcome today. The widespread farmer protest at the grass-roots level which culminated in the organization of the Populist Party did produce a radical policy agenda, but this great farmer movement failed to capture the presidency or Congress for its leaders (and thus failed to achieve many of its major objectives).

Federal legislation during the latter part of the nineteenth century did include regulation of rail rates and practices, a chief objective of the farmers' movements. New agricultural research and education agencies were established in the 1860s; that is, the Department of Agriculture was chartered as an information-gathering agency, and state agriculture colleges were supported by federal land grants and subsidies. In 1887 the agricultural experiment stations were given federal support, and extension education for farmers was begun at the turn of the century.[11] These new public institutions supported by scientists, agricultural societies, and other elites were of little moment to nineteenth century farmers, although their impact since that time has, of course, been enormous.

The geographical expansion of agriculture slowed after 1900, and with rising demand for products, farmers enjoyed two decades of relative prosperity, during which the more progressive purchased new mechanical technology.[12]

Federal agricultural credit institutions had their beginnings during this period. During World War I, the national government fixed farm prices, but this did not prevent farmers from reaping profits from war-related demand. Those farmers who used their profits and their credit to capitalize the new technology found themselves endangered by very low prices during the 1920s. Consequently, these "successful" farmers, supported by the agricultural education/research establishment and agribusiness suppliers, developed a new political structure for agriculture. During the 1920s that new structure enacted laws supporting cooperatives and regulating middlemen; under the New Deal administration it achieved agricultural price supports and other types of federal subsidies. Over time, the new commercial farmers became part of a subsystem with the following identifiable components:

1. It was based on a subculture with a well-developed socialization process whose norms sanctioned subsystem interaction and support. The political actors generally shared commercial-farm backgrounds and often had attended land grant colleges of agriculture. Subsequently, they experienced continual interaction with other groups and leaders at the universities, in the marketplace, through the farm media, in the general farm organizations, and in the activities of government agencies.

2. A rough hierarchy of goals was more or less agreed to, with the preeminent goals being productivity and efficiency. Farm income as an important political objective was given emphasis, but it was to be achieved by a combination of production efficiency and adequate market prices.

3. There were material and status supports for many individuals who contributed to the subsystem goals. For its participants, this subsystem displaced the national value system, which had placed a low status value on farming and on agricultural service functions. Within the subsystem, however, there were increasingly sharp status distinctions between the commercial farmers and those in technical service functions on the one hand and the subsistence farmers and farm workers on the other hand. Their interests were largely ignored by the subsystem.

4. The subsystem featured a discrete and integrated economic subsystem with its own monitoring agencies and market information mechanisms and even its own academic discipline—agricultural economics.

5. The subsystem also developed a set of remarkable political mechanisms and processes including the following:

   a. A coalition of groups representing major commodities, programs for which were coordinated within the congressional agricultural committees.[13]

  b. A cooperating bureaucracy that included the bureaus of the U.S. Department of Agriculture[14] as well as the land grant institutions.

  c. A rural electorate whose large swing votes (outside the South) were noticeably responsive to prices for principal commodities.[15]

  d. Client organizations that exercised grass roots control over the relevant federal bureaucracies while using these bureaucracies as a vehicle for developing their membership.[16] Lowi called the agricultural subsystem "the new feudalism" because each of at least ten bureaucracies was run by its own clientele.[17]

This has by no means been a stable subsystem throughout the past forty years, nor has it exercised unchallenged control over agricultural policies. Within the subsystem there has been much organizational, commodity, and partisan conflict, particularly in choosing mechanisms to stabilize and maintain adequate farm prices. Because of this conflict, and also because of the declining number of farmers, coalitions enacting these programs have included outside groups such as labor unions. Outside groups imposed several major agricultural policies and transformed others from their original purpose. The food stamp program, for example, originated as a way to dispose of farm surplus, but was recast by a national "hunger lobby" into a major welfare program, over vigorous subsystem opposition. Environmental interests achieved controls on the use of pesticides—a mainstay of commercial agricultural production. And in this era of world food scarcity, even foreign policy elites have influenced agricultural trade and surplus disposal policies. But outside groups have yet to restrain the trend toward large production units within American agriculture.

The agricultural subsystem itself has undergone transformation as the more substantial roles are being assumed by processors and farm suppliers, including credit institutions.

In reviewing the influence of public policies on the structure of U.S. agriculture, we may say that these policies—especially those supported by the subsystem, such as price stabilization and agricultural research— did aid in improving productivity. Up to a point, they also encouraged development of viable family farms, as contrasted with the oligopolistic structure that characterized other segments of our economy (including non-farm segments of the agricultural economy).[18] Even within farming, however, policies developed by this subsystem were permissive toward large farms, large landowners, and corporate agriculture. Major agricultural programs ultimately contributed to the enlargement of farms and the virtual elimination of small farms as significant producers. One can say, in a broader way, that federal policy for agriculture was quite influential in the displacement of labor from farming.

Relevance of the U.S. Experience

Of what relevance is the U.S. experience in helping developing countries choose a framework for agricultural policy? Our abundant food output is surely desirous to them. They may want to achieve it using a different mix of resources—less capital and energy, and more labor, for instance. For many agricultural sectors in developing countries, the "ideal" economic solution appears to be a labor-intensive yet technologically advanced system. This solution is feasible, according to economist Keith Griffin.[19] And it minimizes the displacement of rural people to the cities.

Predictions vary as to the social consequences of massive rural-to-urban migration. In one rather optimistic assessment, based on current performance, four scholars suggested that rural-urban migrants typically improve their situation by moving to cities. They observed, "Not everyone is employed immediately, but a large fraction of migrants find jobs in a reasonably short period."[20] Less optimistically, Hayami and Ruttan state as a general proposition that "in most less developed countries, labor will increasingly be more abundant relative to land"[21]— that is, the cities will hardly absorb even the rural population increase, much less those actually displaced through labor-saving technology.

Assuming that countries do want policies that maintain much of their population in agriculture, is the American political experience relevant, even if not to be emulated? Or is it unique and uninstructive? On the side that it is entirely unique, one could argue that the mix of agricultural structures in developing countries is different from what ours was at an earlier state of development—ours in the nineteenth century having been characterized mainly by small holdings, theirs today mainly by large holdings. But, on the other hand, small-holders may become more typical in developing countries because they are more efficient. Geoffrey Paige, who examined political instability in 135 "export sectors" within seventy developing countries, stated that "in most export crops, the small holding is the most efficient form of agricultural organization." He also says, "As market pressures increase, most agricultural systems tend toward the efficient organization of the small holding."[22] Based on the American political experience, Paige maintains that these economically viable small-holders are likely to be politically weak and dependent on outside political parties and interest groups.[23]

As we have seen, this was true of U.S. farmers in the nineteenth century, despite their potential electoral strength. But as we also observed, the U.S. agricultural subsystem, supported by elites from Southern large landholders and the larger family enterprises elsewhere, was responsible in large measure for an economic and political environment that facilitated the wholesale displacement of labor from farming.

What the American experience suggests, therefore, is that an efficient, labor-intensive agriculture will not be the product of a policy developed by an agricultural subsystem such as ours. To put it another way, nations that let farmers make farm policy should be prepared to see a majority of them move into town.

Having noted possible historical parallels between the earlier U.S. agricultural structure and that of other countries, we should also take note that American agriculture is, of course, a product of a particular culture. And this American culture has been heavily influenced, in turn, by both agricultural experience and agrarian myths, especially those that portray the United States as an exceptionalist culture because of its agrarian experience and aspirations. It is important to observe, too, that modern-day U.S. agriculture is distanced from its own mythology and distinct in many basic ways from the agriculture of developing nations.

The "Exceptionalism" of U.S. Agriculture: Myths and Realities

There is a school of American "exceptionalism" whose general thesis is that the history of nation building, as exemplified by the United States, is unique in terms of time, resources, migrations, and institutions. Stated with the utmost succinctness, a huge and unexploited continent, with an abundance of productive soils and a conducive climate, became inhabited by independent (not peasant) farmers. This happened in a gradual way, although the mass migrations from Europe in the latter decades of the nineteenth century and the early decades of the twentieth century stepped up the tempo of settlement and development in rural America. During these periods of migration and development, a dual revolution was unfolding—one in farm technology and the other in local self-government.

This school contends that we need to understand this uniqueness, this exceptionalism, in the American experience so we will not continue to act (from whatever motives in both the formulation and the im-plementation of domestic and international policies) as if American agrarian ideas and institutions were as exportable as corn and soybeans. Indeed, even the appropriateness of the American model for the United States is debatable. Some would hold that the modern American agribusiness model is the best of all possible worlds; at the other extreme, there are those who believe that this model is really leading directly to a national disaster because of its dependence on cheap energy, expensive technology, and dangerous chemicals.

A special variant of the modern American "exceptionalist" school can be found in a widely read and influential series of studies by David Potter, especially in his *People of Plenty*.[24] He has advanced the thesis that the development of the American democracy has come about because the nature of American "abundance" has enabled us to build a unique and exceptional political system. More significantly, in terms of his analysis, Americans have developed a national character that centers around the admiration and accumulation of an "unusual plenty of available goods or other useable wealth," which he calls an "economic abundance." According to Potter's interpretation, we have misunderstood our own "exceptionalism": "Democracy paced the growth of our abundance, and abundance broadened the base of our democracy. . . . Our message to the world has become involved in a dilemma: to other peoples, our democracy has seemed attainable but not especially desirable; our abundance has seemed infinitely desirable but quite unattainable."[25]

Myths of American Agriculture

In this section we will outline what we hold to be the central myths of American agriculture and relate them to the exceptionalist thesis. Indeed, our argument is that these agrarian myths constitute a considerable segment of the core of the exceptionalist theory.

We believe that these myths continue to be valuable in terms of explaining some significant aspects of the American set of operative ideals. They have been powerful inspirational and motivational tools in the development of the American political system, and they retain a remarkable potency even today. It is our contention that these agrarian myths, in their historic forms, are seriously outdated, misleading, and even dangerous, and especially so if we view them as items of export. More positively, we are advocating that the American's and the foreigner's understanding of these myths must be modernized. The potency of the historic imageries must be understood in order to be appreciated, but the history of American agriculture in, say, 1877 must be viewed as a phenomenon radically different from the agribusiness agriculture of 1977. Once these agrarian myths have become modernized (that is, new "forms of consciousness" are created), then both this nation and the developing nations will come to the realization that the realities of modern American agriculture are vastly different from those of nineteenth century agrarianism, which we have viewed as a kind of limited and exportable utility. In the rural America of today, agrarianism is being transformed into an agribusiness reality. One could hold that this marvellously productive, incredibly resource-consumptive, capital-intensive model might be the envy of the new nations, but surely it is not a viable candidate for their emulation.

Let us examine just a few of the more outstanding examples of the American rural myth/ideology in order to lay the groundwork for our proposition that a modernization of American agrarian ideologies is necessary and that the current U.S. agribusiness model is not exportable.

The first and still the most potent rural myth is the Jeffersonian concept of the family farm, which is, philosophically, a kind of immanent version of the Protestant ethic. That is, the virtues of goodness are to be found in those who clear the forests, cultivate the soil, and work with fervor and faith to produce an abundance of food and fiber.[26] In truth, the family farm has become mythologized in the American mind by literature and the arts, not least by television and certainly by contemporary music. This family farm myth has been a powerful influence on American political life, supporting an ideology of individualism that still has political efficacy. It could perhaps be argued that the family farm was the backbone of the American republic, at least for the first hundred years of this nation's independence. More to the point of this essay is the danger of believing that Jefferson's freeholder, family farmer is an accurate portrayal of the commercial farmer of today. A farmer in a business suit, with an appreciation of applied biology, a flair for understanding and tinkering with farm machinery, and a willingness to experiment with the relevant innovations of modern science, is more characteristic of the modern American farmer. And that model is not exportable to the poor nations. For whatever motives and with whatever intentions, the family farm myth has been transformed into an ideology that is misleading and probably dangerous, both to Americans and to the developing nations. The middle-class, highly capitalized, science/technology-oriented American farm business bears a poor relationship to the Jeffersonian concept of the family farm.

Second, we should take note of Daniel Boorstin's argument that "the frontier" thesis has been the single most dynamic and persuasive theme relative to understanding American political life and institutions. We should recollect Frederick Jackson Turner's basic premise: "The Western wilds, from the Alleghanies to the Pacific, constituted the richest free gift that was ever spread out before civilized man. . . . Never again can such an opportunity come to the sons of men."[27] The Turner thesis—i.e., the significance of the frontier in shaping American national character and institutions—has probably been subjected to more furious debate than any other interpretation of American history. For our purposes, however, the principal emphasis must be on the uniqueness of the American frontier. Turner mourned its passing because that meant the decline of agrarian democracy; Potter has claimed that the operative ideal imbedded within the frontier thesis was really "economic abundance"; Grant McConnell gloried in Turner's thesis and then bitterly decried its passing.[28]

To the modern farmer-businessman, however, the new frontier is technology—hybrids, self-propelled combines, huge tractors, pesticides, chemical fertilizers, all of which have been utilized to transform the potential of this land of plenty into an actual abundance, and usually a surplus of food. Perhaps logically today's environmentalists may argue that this is the road to self-destruction and national ruination. But thus far at least, the subliminally conveyed theme of modern advertising to the effect that "bigger is better" seems to exemplify most clearly the modern American version of the frontier—that is, "technology is good, and bigger technology is even better." We must note, however, that some of the most perceptive "establishment" scholars are having second thoughts and raising serious doubts.[29]

Third, William Graham Sumner's social Darwinism—neatly depicted in agrarian terminology in his principal theme, "root, hog, or die"—is a kind of American version of Adam Smith's "hidden hand of God." We believe that this ideology of a fiercely competitive capitalism has been of notable importance in the development of American agriculture. Two points need to be made, however. One is that the ideology of capitalism has encountered a stalwart competitor among modern farmers in the ideology of "parity" (i.e., the idea that the government should guarantee that farm income be stable and roughly equal to that of the middle-class generally). The second point is that social Darwinism is not exportable. The technology-parity dichotomy has created an ideology that, when made operational, has demanded the movement of millions of American rural people to the cities and suburbs. In at least the short- and medium-run, an obverse ideal is most needed in the developing nations: to keep peasant-farmers and farm laborers in a rural environment and still improve their opportunities for a better economic, social, and political life.

Fourth, the New Deal farm programs have, in a real sense, constituted the modern ideology for the American farmer. Some of those programs have been outlined in the first section of this essay. Our point here, however, is that the ostensible and original purpose of these programs was to aid economic redistribution; the principal winners were to be the tenant, small-scale farmer. Nevertheless, we now realize that most of these programs have actually favored those who are already advantaged; that is, the winners have been and still are the middle-income and especially the large-scale farmer-businessmen. One might justifiably argue that if some of the New Deal farm programs, such as those administered by the Farm Security Administration and the Resettlement Administration, had been given sufficient political protection and economic sustenance, this scenario could have been radically altered. But this kind of a "rural revolution" would have demanded a very considerable alteration of the scheme of things, characterized by what might properly be referred to as "Madisonian politics" functioning in a technological society. To summarize: the New Deal–type farm programs have been enormously expensive both in terms of U.S. Treasury and consumer costs, and the economic advantages have heavily accrued to the haves rather than the have-nots in American agriculture. Like the earlier ideological myths, this complex ideological framework is not exportable, in terms of economic feasibility, social equity, or political stability.

Finally, the twin and generally contradictory myths of free trade (i.e., the long-run comparative advantages principle) and "infant industry" protectionism (i.e., industries in the early, takeoff stages should be given governmental protection until they can become competitive internationally) have often been in evidence in American politics. Indeed, they are currently the basis for a double-barreled ideology which claims that "the right to export U.S. farm products and the right to restrict the imports of farm products are inalienable prerogatives of the American farmer." In our judgment, this ideological contradiction is not a helpful export, assuming that we are primarily concerned with economic development in the Fourth World because protectionism is not appropriate for agriculture there. We realize that this is certainly a highly debatable proposition. Nevertheless, there seems to be a persuasive amount of evidence that a policy of national self-sufficiency is not in the long-run economic interests of a nation, developed or developing. One could argue, admittedly, that the developing nations must engage in protectionist practices simply as a countervailing strategy to the protectionist practices (e.g., trade barriers that protect U.S. dairy products) of the developed nations. We agree; however, our

contention is that a wiser course of action—one which would be in the
long-run interests of all—would be to accept and adhere to the
principles of comparative advantage and competitive trade.

Agribusiness Industry of the United States:
Modernizing the Myths

The American farm/food economy of today is unique, exceptional,
and nonexportable, at least to the Fourth World nations (those in
extreme poverty). Again, there are two faces to the exceptionalist
argument. One is that the U.S. public needs to comprehend (both
cognitively and affectively) the changing realities that are taking place
within American agriculture so we may know what it is we are actually
offering for export. Second, the Fourth World nations should at least
understand the American food economy so their decisions concerning its
applicability to their conditions can be based on reality rather than on
mythology.

In order to help clarify our overview, we have included a crude but
useful flow chart to depict the food agribusiness industry of the United
States.[30] This food and fiber industry is as remote from the traditional,
commercial rural economies of Fourth World countries as the space age
is from the bullock and the hoe. Hired farm labor (i.e. nonfamily labor)
cost $4.8 billion in 1973, as contrasted to $10.4 billion for machinery and
other equipment and $14.7 billion for feed and seeds. Moreover, farm
assets (physical and financial) more than doubled in value from 1968 to
1976—from $281 billion to $586 billion; total farm production expenses
increased from $31.8 billion in 1964 to $73.4 billion in 1974. From 1959
to 1976, the number of farms decreased by over one-third (from over 4.1
to almost 2.8 million farms), and farm size advanced from 288 to 389
acres per farm. In essence, the U.S. agribusiness industry is highly and
increasingly capital-intensive; it is one of the major segments in a very
complex industrial economy.

U.S. agriculture has now experienced two "revolutions," and, "if
there is a third agricultural revolution it will likely be in the tradition of
the first two—a major change in sources of power."[31] According to
Wayne Rasmussen and Jane Porter, the "first American agricultural
revolution" occurred during the middle 1800s, when "the noble horse
was harnessed to machines."[32] The second "revolution" took place after
World War II and is still continuing. From 1950 to 1973, total farm
output increased by 52 percent, and output per unit of input increased by
45 percent; farm production per hour of farm labor grew by 27 percent,
while land used for crops declined by 6 percent and labor used in
farming by 60 percent.[33] "Five- and seven-bottom plows became

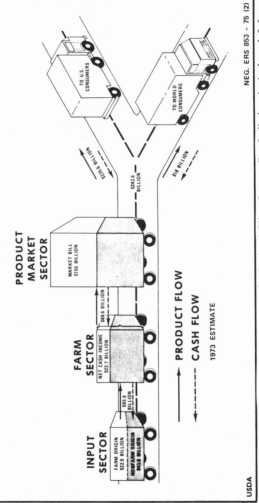

HOW PRODUCTS AND CASH FLOW THROUGH OUR FOOD AND FIBER SYSTEM

FIGURE 2.1

Source: USDA—Economic Research Service, The Food and Fiber System—How It Works, Agricultural Information Bulletin 383, March 1975, p. 2.

commonplace, and the tractors could pull these monsters through almost any terrain. . . . The single-row planter gave way to six- and eight-row drills of greater size and efficiency. . . . The self-propelled combine came into use . . . [as did the] spindle cotton picker and the tractor-mounted cotton stripper."[34]

This second revolution was not restricted to technological advances in farm machinery. Schlebecker also describes the revolutionary changes in seeds, fertilizers, insecticides and herbicides, vaccines, and animal nutrition. As he observes, all this was not done without economic and social costs, although "very few seemed seriously interested in undoing what had been done."[35]

There is another myth that portrays farming as a "way of life" that one can ostensibly enter rather inexpensively and thereupon enjoy the blissful fruits of a rustic experience. As a matter of fact, entry into U.S. commercial farming has become extremely difficult: Class IA farmers (those who gross $100,000 a year or more from sale of farm commodities) were capitalized (on the average, per farm) at almost $950,000 by January 1974. In terms of decision making, the farmer-businessman should be of a fairly high order of intelligence; as Schlebecker notes, "The [necessary] technological knowledge demanded a comparatively high level of education as well as of practical skill. If the farmer could not understand the owner's manual he was lost."[36] On the other hand, "farming as a business" undermined the self-sufficiency of the farm family and the farming operation. The farmer has become essentially a risk-taking, highly competitive entrepreneur; he is less and less independent of and more and more dependent on the vagaries and caprices of a world-wide food economy.

The American farming industry is highly pluralistic in terms of regions and subregions, states, crops, climate, soils, animals, and especially economic classes. There is no "average" American farmer, although we often try to view him as average. For example, realized net income per farm for all farms averaged $9,826 in 1974. However, Class IA farmers had an average net income per farm of $84,300 that year, as contrasted to $1,026 for Class VI (sales of less than $2,500). Nevertheless, Class VI farm units averaged $13,930 per farm in off-farm income in 1973, thereby accruing a total income (including nonmoney income from farm food and housing) of $15,012 per unit.

Also worthy of note—and this has been rather consistently true since 1963, with the exception of 1973—is that "total net income from farming" and "income from off-farm sources" for all farmers and farm people have run fairly even (e.g., in 1974 it was $29.6 billion for the former as compared to $25.5 billion for the latter). By early 1977, both urban and rural food-purchasing habits had become so alike that the

Bureau of Labor Statistics decided to aggregate all of us into one general category—food consumers. In terms of political sociology, the modern U.S. farmer has become distinctly middle class.

Next, the burgeoning U.S. agribusiness industry should be viewed in terms of social costs, although we need to remember that certain conditions were "inherited," so to speak, while others were created. On the inherited side, there is the issue of race—especially in terms of minority Americans in rural areas. Median farm-family income for Whites was $10,750 in 1974, as contrasted to $8,265 for Blacks "and other races." However, there are at least two features of this median income data that need to be emphasized here. One is that median-income figures paper over a considerable amount of poverty within Black farm families. According to a joint Census-USDA report, based on 1975 data, "the proportion of Black farm families below the low-income level—45 percent—is about five times as high as the national average for all families and about four times as that for White farm families [12.7 percent]."[37]

The second feature is of considerable importance in understanding the impact of the agribusiness industry on farm-racial patterns. That is, Blacks (including other minorities) are migrating to the city in dramatic numbers, and this has been occurring since the end of World War II. In 1970, 90.4 percent of the U.S. farm population was White, 7.7 percent Black "and other races." By 1975, the respective figures were 93.1 percent as contrasted to 6.9 percent. To be more interpretive this data would need to be broken down into at least South versus non-South, but for our purposes, this description is sufficient. In summary, the dynamics of U.S. agribusiness are causing "excess" Black labor to be exported to the American cities. The point at issue is: developing nations should not emulate U.S. labor-migration practices either. One of their most basic problems is how to use vast numbers of underemployed or unemployed farm laborers productively in rural areas.

Finally, the American farmer-businessman seems to be gradually transforming himself into a different type of political animal. J. K. Galbraith's analysis continues to be perceptive: success in American politics is based on the organization and effective use of countervailing power.[38] American farmers have long understood this concept in theory; they simply have been unable to put this theory into disciplined political and economic practice (for reasons we cannot elaborate here).

A century ago, with the founding of the Granger movement, farmers thought the ballot box would provide the necessary countervailing power. A century later we can observe the vastly more sophisticated, but still only marginally successful, efforts of the American Farm Bureau Federation, with its various and usually profitable farm input and family-protection programs (gasoline, insurance, fertilizers, etc.) and its less-than-effective output program—the American Agricultural Marketing Association. With somewhat varied ideologies and practices, the National Farmers Union, the National Farm Organization, the National Council of Farmer Cooperatives, and a multiplicity of commodity and cooperative organizations are in pursuit of quite identical goals, although their strategies and programs are not necessarily in agreement. Our point is that this situation is unique to a highly capitalized, agribusiness-type industry. Furthermore, this pursuit of countervailing power by the American farmer must be understood within the uniqueness—the exceptionalism—of the American experience.

The gist of our argument is as follows: The peasant farmer of the developing world desperately needs to develop types of political power that he can and will utilize to improve his social and economic condition. Indeed, he now seems to be in the process of doing so, at least in a few of the developing nations. In the developing world, however, the power of the national government will have to be far more direct and controlling than is true in the American farm economy. Farmer discipline of a much higher order of magnitude will need to be legitimated. The common good will have to be specified much more precisely and pursued much more authoritatively than is true in rural America. (Brazil may be the exception that only proves the rule.) The rural infrastructure must be modernized, but these developments will have to occur within the framework and dictates of a nationally planned economy, not through the subtle but persuasive influences of a private, agribusiness-type complex.

Transferring the American Agribusiness Model to the Fourth World

We have presented two quite generalized and seemingly paradoxical responses to the question we posed at the beginning of this essay, namely, is the U.S. agribusiness model of any value to the Fourth World nations in terms of the development problems they confront? Both interpretations have led us to the conclusion, "yes, in part; if done eclectically and pragmatically." This eclectic-pragmatic interpretation seems to contain the seeds of hope and promise. After all, there is a certain operational common sense in the classical economic theory of demand and supply, in understanding that every political-economic system must employ in some form the essential factors of production— land, labor, capital, and entrepreneurial skills—in appreciating and utilizing at least the basic elements of input-output analysis. Importantly, development specialists from Eastern and Western nations have learned a good deal about what not to do and presumably what should be done for Fourth World nations to appreciably increase their production of food, and to improve, in terms of equity, its distribution.[39] We point to two comprehensive studies among the many which could be cited: Uma Lele, *The Design of Rural Development*, and John Mellor, *The New Economics of Growth*.[40]

We make no claim to have studied all of the development literature. However, our overall impression is that the easy optimism of the 1950s, and the often healthy pessimism of the 1960s, have come to at least some fruition in the cautiously constructed, empirically based, interdisciplinary-oriented (at least avowedly so) studies of the genre referred to above.

Studying the literature does not necessarily lead to the conclusion that the U.S. agribusiness model is of no particular utility to a Fourth World nation. A recent and excellent study by the OECD's Development Center[41] contains a brief section on "the United States as a model of appropriate technology." But the "lessons" learned seem to have been derived, and perhaps quite perceptively so, more from nineteenth century American agriculture than from the agribusiness model we have been describing and analyzing. Examples of these "lessons" come from Jequier:

> A society which for some reason or other is suddenly forced to rely on its own resources can often do so; . . . the crucial importance of demand, or rather of need for the products and the technologies which were formerly imported; . . . the development of new industries is not necessarily incompatible with the absence of craftsmen and a structural shortage of skilled labour; . . . the ability to innovate, and to innovate successfully, on a continuous basis; . . . a high proportion of the inventors and entrepreneurs can come from the rural communities.[42]

Precisely so, and even these observations seriously understate the uniqueness of the American experience—at least that would be the argument of the exceptionalist.

According to this more skeptical view, we have apotheosized the Lockean creed (i.e., natural rights, labor theory of value, and private property) without even an understanding of its essential features; then, to compound this intellectual felony, we have proceeded to act as if "all the world is still America" (to update and vulgarize Locke's "state of nature" assumption). Epigrammatically, Robert Packenham contends that this misunderstanding of our unique "liberal roots" has caused us to adopt four erroneous "doctrines": (1) "change and development are easy"; (2) "all good things go together"; (3) "radicalism and revolution are bad"; and (4) "distributing power is more important than accumulating power."[43]

We must assume that the reader will be able to appreciate the historical meaning of these uniquely American propositions. We ask only that the U.S. agribusiness model be placed alongside two quotations—one culture-based, the other ideology-based. According to H. A. Oluwassanmi,

> More than two-thirds of the economically active African population live in rural communities and earn their living from farming. Although there are pockets of highly developed and highly specialized agriculture all over the continent, African farming has retained its essentially traditional character: small-scale operating units scattered over wide geographic areas, hoe and cutlass as the main means of cultivation; natural regeneration through shifting cultivation as the major method of maintaining soil fertility; and communal systems of land holding.[44]

The second quotation is from a recent study by Mahbub ul Haq, a Pakistani economist who is presently Director of the Policy Planning and Program Review Department of the World Bank. "Land reforms and public ownership of major industries in the developing nations have become the key elements in any institutional reforms."[45]

Assuming the perceptiveness of both of these insights (which we do), it seems to be a fair observation that the American agribusiness model is unique and exceptional, but that it still offers both positive and negative lessons which should not be ignored. More pointedly, we must ask, can (and will) political and economic elites, in both the developing and developed nations, be perceptively eclectic in their selections from the American experience and pragmatic in their applications (either recommended or implemented) of those choices to Fourth World cultures, with results that will be humane, effective, and durable?

Notes

1. Richard Rodefeld coined the term "large-scale industrial farms" to describe those on which more than half of the work is performed by hired workers. See testimony of Richard D. Rodefeld, in *Hearings on the Role of Giant Corporations in the American and World Economies, Part 3, before the Subcommittee on Monopoly of the U.S. Senate Select Committee on Small Business, 1972.*

2. Richard S. Kirkendall, *Social Scientists and Farm Politics in the Age of Roosevelt* (Columbia, Mo.: University of Missouri Press, 1966), pp. 227-228.

3. Wayne D. Rasmussen, "American Agriculture: A Short History," mimeographed, based on Wayne D. Rasmussen, *A Documentary History of American Agriculture*, 4 vols. (New York; Random House, 1975).

4. Thomas R. Dye and L. Harmon Zeigler, *The Irony of Democracy: An Uncommon Introduction to American Politics* (Belmont, Calif.: Duxbury Press, 1972), p. 28.

5. Lester W. Milbrath, *Political Participation: How and Why Do People Get Involved in Politics?* (Chicago: Rand McNally, 1965), pp. 113-14.

6. O. Gene Clanton, *Kansas Populism: Ideas and Men* (Lawrence, Kansas: The University Press of Kansas, 1969), p. 243.

7. Fred A. Shannon, *American Farmers' Movements* (Princeton, N.J.: Van Nostrand, 1957), p. 9.

8. Murray R. Benedict, *Farm Policies of the United States 1790-1950* (New York: Octagon Books, 1966), pp. 3-60.

9. Thomas LeDuc, "History and Appraisal of U.S. Land Policy to 1862," and Paul W. Gates, "The Homestead Act: Free Land Policy in Operation, 1862-1935," both in *Land Use Policy and Problems in the United States*, ed. Howard W. Ottoson (Lincoln, Neb.: University of Nebraska Press, 1963), pp. 1-46.

10. Gilbert C. Fite, *American Agriculture and Farm Policy Since 1900* (New York: MacMillan, 1964), pp. 4-9.

11. Gladys L. Baker, Wayne D. Rasmussen, Vivian Wise, and Jane M. Porter, *Century of Service: The First 100 Years of the U.S. Department of Agriculture* (U.S. Department of Agriculture, 1963), pp. 1-25, 43-45.

12. Gilbert C. Fite, *American Agriculture.*

13. Charles Jones, "Representation in Congress: The Case of the House Agriculture Committee," *American Political Science Review* 55 (June 1961):358-67.

14. Described by Wayne Rasmussen and Gladys Baker, *The U.S. Department of Agriculture* (New York: Praeger Publishers, 1972).

15. Agnes Campbell et al., *The American Voter* (New York: John Wiley and Sons, 1960), p. 417.

16. Charles M. Hardin, *The Politics of Agriculture: Soil Conservation and the Struggle for Power in Rural America* (Glencoe, Illinois: The Free Press, 1952).

17. Theodore Lowi, *The End of Liberalism* (New York; W. W. Norton, 1969).

18. Harold Breimyer, *Individual Freedom and the Economic Organization of Agriculture* (Urbana: University of Illinois Press, 1965).

19. Keith Griffin, *The Political Economy of Agrarian Change* (London: Macmillan, 1974).

20. George Beier, Anthony Churchill, Michael Cohen, and Bertrand Renaud, "The Task Ahead for the Cities of the Developing Countries," *World Development* 4 (May 1976):377-78.

21. Yujiro Hayami and Vernon W. Ruttan, *Agricultural Development: An International Perspective* (Baltimore: Johns Hopkins Press, 1971), p. 293.

22. Jeffery M. Paige, *Agrarian Revolution: Social Movements and Export*

Agriculture in the Underdeveloped World (New York: The Free Press, 1975), pp. 15-16.

23. Ibid., p. 46.

24. Subtitled *Economic Abundance and the American Character* (Chicago: The University of Chicago Press, 1954).

25. Ibid., p. 10.

26. A. Whitney Griswold's *Farming And Democracy* (New Haven: Yale University Press, 1952) is the classic analysis, although he seriously questions the validity of the basic myth.

27. *The Frontier in American History* (1920; reprint ed., New York: Henry Holt and Co., 1940), p. 261. Also see Daniel Boorstin, *The Genius of American Politics* (Chicago: University of Chicago Press, 1953).

28. *The Decline of Agrarian Democracy* (Berkeley: University of California Press, 1952).

29. An excellent sample of what might be viewed as the "revisionist" school in agricultural economics is a recent article by Earl O. Heady, "Externalities of American Agricultural Policy," *The University of Toledo Law Review* 7, no. 3 (Spring 1976):795-835.

30. The data used in this section, unless a specific source is cited, has been extracted from the following USDA publications, nearly all of which are written by persons in the Economic Research Service:

   a) *The Food and Fiber System: How It Works*, Agriculture Information Bulletin no. 383 (March 1975).

   b) *Social And Economic Characteristics of the Population in Metro and Nonmetro Countries, 1970*, Agricultural Economic Report no. 272 (March 1975).

   c) *Balance Sheet of the Farming Sector: By Value of Sales Class, 1960-73*, Supplement no. 1, Agriculture Information Bulletin no. 376 (April 1975).

   d) *State Farm Income Statistics*, Supplement to Statistical Bulletin no. 547 (September 1975).

   e) *Fact Book of U.S. Agriculture*, Miscellaneous Publication no. 1063 (revised March 1976), published by the USDA's Office of Communication.

   f) *Balance Sheet of the Farming Sector, 1976*, Agriculture Information Bulletin no. 403 (September 1976).

   g) *Changes in Farm Production and Efficiency*, Statistical Bulletin no. 561 (September 1976).

   h) *The American Farmer*, a collection of articles from *The Farm Index* (January 1975–January 1976), published in 1976.

31. Wayne D. Rasmussen, "The American Farmer: The First 200 Years," *The Farm Index*, January 1975, p. 12.

32. "Land of Turmoil," *The Farm Index*, April 1976, p. 4.

33. Rasmussen, "The American Farmer."

34. John T. Schlebecker, *Whereby We Thrive: A History of American Farming, 1607-1972* (Ames, Iowa: Iowa State University Press, 1975), pp. 295-97.

35. Ibid., p. 314.

36. Ibid., p. 304.

37. *Farm Population,* Series Census-ERS, P-27, no. 47, September 1976, p. 8.

38. *American Capitalism: The Concept of Countervailing Power* (rev. ed., Boston: Houghton Mifflin, 1956).

39. For example, see D. Gale Johnson, *World Food Problems and Prospects* (Washington, D.C.: American Enterprise Institute for Public Policy Research, June 1975), especially Chapter 7.

40. (Baltimore: Johns Hopkins Press, 1975); and (Ithaca, New York: Cornell University Press, 1976), respectively. Lele's study is subtitled *Lessons from Africa;* Mellor's, *A Study for India and the Developing World.*

41. Nicolas Jequier, *Appropriate Technology: Problems and Promises* (Paris: OECD, 1976). "Appropriate" is used synonymously with "intermediate" in this study. The current fashion in development literature is to emphasize the ways and means whereby relatively simple, low-priced, small-scale technological tools and methods can be devised and utilized by peasant farmers to improve the quantity and quality of the food and fiber produced.

42. Ibid., pp. 28-30.

43. Robert A. Packenham, *Liberal America and the Third World: Political Development Ideas in Foreign Aid and Social Science* (Princeton, N.J.: Princeton University Press, 1973).

44. "African Institutions and Rural Development," *Land Tenure Center Newsletter,* July-September 1976, p. 15.

45. *The Poverty Curtain: Choices of the Third World* (New York: Columbia University Press, 1976), p. 67.

3
Agricultural Modernization in England, France, and Denmark

Pamela R. Aall

This chapter will examine various degrees of governmental involvement in European agricultural history, with the hope of learning some
lessons that might be applicable to the economic and social decisions
facing developing countries in the twentieth century.[1]

The three countries examined represent various routes to agricultural
modernization. England developed an efficient, productive agriculture
concentrated in the hands of a few wealthy landowners. France tied
agricultural reforms to political reform and promoted equality to the
detriment of productivity. Denmark managed to achieve both equality
and productivity as a result of a combination of governmental policy
and private initiative. Other countries in Europe, such as the
Netherlands and Ireland, could have served equally well as examples of
modernization successes and failures, but it seems to me that the lessons
drawn from England, France, and Denmark are least complicated by
national idiosyncracies and, therefore, most accessible to decision
makers in modern developing countries.

To introduce a note of caution, let us examine a few of the similarities
and differences between premodernization Europe and twentieth
century developing countries. The similarities include low income and
wealth per capita, with vast inequalities in the distribution of wealth;
poorly developed infrastructures and mechanisms for economic
integration within the societies; subsistence agriculture organized such
that the landlord's gain is the tenant's loss; low-technology agriculture
and low output per unit of input; little capital formation anywhere in
the economy; and little literacy and schooling.

Among the most important differences is the fact that no technology
gap divided the wealthy and poor countries in medieval Europe: the
technology in use at the time was the only technology available. Hence,
modernization through technological innovations could occur only
over centuries. Although the Industrial Revolution introduced immense

possibilities for improved agricultural productivity, the difference between scattering seed by hand and using the seed drill is not as vast as the difference between using an ox-drawn wooden plow and a tractor.

Another distinction lies in the attitude toward government: in medieval Europe the concept of the strong central government was not well developed. In fact, in most cases, the central government was too weak or too busy consolidating power to intervene directly in agricultural affairs. Modern concepts—the welfare state, long-term planning, national taxation, government subsidies—were not factors in Europe's agricultural modernization process. In European history, agriculture developed concurrently with other social, economic, and political structures, including modern government.

Feudalism: The Common Heritage

The base for the development of modern European agriculture is the feudal system, which existed in some variation in nearly every corner of Europe.[2] The feudal system was an organization of society along strict lines of well-defined relationships, but it also provided the framework for the political and economic spheres as well. The central focus of the medieval feudal system, and the unit around which the three spheres were defined, was the manor.

The manor contained a cross-section of life in microcosm and was often a self-sufficient unit. In the center of the manor were the lord's manse, the serfs' dwellings, the artisan shops, and the barns and shelters for the animals; in the periphery were the vast fields and forests owned by the lord and farmed or maintained by the serfs. In theory, the king was the overlord of the land, and all lesser lords were his vassals; in practice, some of the vassals were stronger than the king and at times could control or overthrow him. The lines of responsibility, however, were clear and often upheld. The vassal had the right to the income from the land, in return for which he owed goods, services, and loyalty to his overlord. Thus, while feudalism dictated the social relationships on a grand scale, the manor governed the social relationships on the more humble scale of everyday life.

The political organization imposed by the manor system sprang from the lord's position as main forger and enforcer of manorial law. The lord had the right to create and collect taxes, to raise an army, and to decide juridical questions that arose within the manor. These rights gave him control over most of the important functions performed by modern government and made him, in essence, king over his fiefdom. The sources of his political power flowed from two fronts: the prestige of his overlord and the wealth and security of his own holdings.

The manor coordinated the two important factors of production of the medieval economy: land and labor.[3] The land was, by and large, the property of the lord, as was the labor produced by the serfs. In return, the serfs received a place to live, a small plot of land, and protection from the forages of passing armies or competing lords. This arrangement lent itself to economic stability bordering on stasis. The produce of the land served to feed the manor or to pay for essential goods and services; the excess profit was taxed away by the lord or used directly to finance the lord's warring ambitions. It was the lack of this third traditional factor— capital—that caused agriculture to remain virtually unchanged for several centuries, and it was the development of a money economy, in which capital accumulation was possible, that sparked the transition from medieval to modern agricultural times.[4]

The legacy of farming in the Middle Ages has affected agriculture up to the establishment of modern agribusiness. Under the manorial system, the vast majority of people lived not on the land they farmed, but in villages clustering around the protecting manse of the lord. The land spread out from the village in all directions until it became forest, marsh, river, sea, or another lord's property. This land was divided into blocks, or "cultures," of eight to ten acres. Often, the size of the culture was determined by the area's topography and the soil it boasted. These cultures were broken down further into strips of different sizes, strips that formed the basic unit of a peasant's allotted land. Usually a peasant farmed several strips, not in the same block, but scattered among numerous blocks. Consequently, the distance from strip to strip could be great, and the farmers wasted time travelling from one to the other. A probable reason for this inefficient method of land allocation is that the land was divided as it was reclaimed; thus, each reclamation resulted in an extra strip for every peasant. The customary inheritance patterns dictated that a peasant's strips be subdivided among his male progeny, and the result after generations was a prevalence of tiny, tired plots.

The location of the strips meant that farming had to be a communal occupation, with the times for ploughing, sowing, and harvesting closely coordinated. Pushing back the limits of the farmland was also a joint enterprise. All the livestock fed on common pastureland. Although this community effort was necessary for survival, it did not encourage the develoment of individual methods or radical innovation in agricultural techniques.[5]

Most farming was done by field rotation, either in a two- or three-field system. Productivity was very low by today's standards, since returns on seeding were only four- to five-fold and the chronic shortage of hay for livestock meant that many animals had to be slaughtered in the fall. This seasonal slaughtering reduced the amount of manure that could be applied to the cultivated fields each year.[6]

Besides land, the other important factor of production was labor provided by the serfs. Serfs differed from slaves in that they could work part-time on plots that they did not own technically, but which fed their families and livestock. In addition, there were legal conditions regarding a serf's freedom: in England, a peasant could become a freeman if he escaped capture for one year and one day. In other respects, however, the serf's lot was as unfortunate as the slave's; burdened with obligations to the lords, serfs were often overwhelmed by seigneurial taxes, rents, and demands for services. As the external threats diminished in the late Middle Ages, the benefits of the feudal relationship to the serf decreased proportionately.

Feudalism and the manor system declined at different rates and in different ways in each European country: in France and Germany, strong traces still remained in the nineteenth century[7]; the system had declined, however, from its thirteenth century apogee. The general causes behind its wane seem common to several European states. One slow agent of change was the development of small industries in the towns. Industry spurred the creation of a money economy and provided demand for food and markets, where peasants could sell excess produce in exchange for money or other goods. Another reason was a modification in the labor force: the plagues that swept Europe in the fourteenth century decimated the population; in addition, increased employment opportunities in the town lured serfs away from manors by providing an alternative and more attractive mode of livelihood.[8] In order to hold their dwindling number of serfs, landlords had to improve the working and living conditions, consequently easing some of the restrictive obligations of manor life. As serf labor declined in the late thirteenth century, the lords were forced to let out excess land in return for money or produce, and, thus, a new class of less dependent landholders arose. Finally, the position of the feudal lord was undermined from the other side of the social spectrum. As central authority under the king emerged as a strong and viable force, it reduced by every means possible the independent authority of the strongest vassals.[9]

Over centuries, national justice, national taxation, and national policy making replaced and destroyed the autocratic position of the feudal lord vis-à-vis his subjects. The traditional feudal system gave way in the end to the nation-state.

England: Development of a
Capitalist Agriculture

England provides an excellent illustration of the processes described in the last section. More so than in any other country, feudalism in England was defeated by the growth of capitalism. Before the modernizing effects of capitalism could make an impact on agriculture, however, it was necessary that favorable conditions exist for the growth of a money economy based on several industries. Those conditions developed partly because of the growth of urban industry and the consequent urban-rural trade and partly because of a peculiar governmental structure that hastened the creation of a strong central government in Great Britain.

The tradition of a strong monarchy goes back farther in England than in France or Denmark. The Viking invasions, which produced chaos and fueled the rise of the feudal lord in France, encouraged the kings of Wessex to counter the deleterious effects of the invasions. Their exertions led to two results: the creation of a strong military force capable of defeating the Danes, and the establishment of local government organized, not around manors, but around fortresses. By 950 an administrative system existed that was composed of a network of "hundredshires." They were responsible ultimately to the king and formed the basis of modern English local government.

The monarchy successfully maintained its central position through military prowess and the absence of orderly opposition. The approval of the king's council was not necessary for the enactment of laws; although only a foolish monarch would ignore the advice of his council, the decision in the end was autocratic, not plutocratic.[10] With the development of the concept of the divine right of kings, the king secured the explicit and highly influential support of the church, a powerful ally against the ambitions of feudal lords. Thus, the structural framework for a strong central government existed in the ninth and tenth centuries, and the kings used it with varying success. Its effectiveness was so apparent, however, that when the Anglo-Saxon kings surrendered to the Normans in 1066, the Norman kings chose to adopt the established administration without alteration. The medieval kings used this administrative base to consolidate and unify the realm of England, and by 1033, the monarchy had succeeded in hobbling the greatest of the feudal lords.

The military and administrative costs incurred in Edward I's reign necessitated the frequent convocation of Parliament, which by this time consisted of several orders of society and had real legislative power.[11] If this body had assumed powers independent of the king, it is possible that the monarchy in England would have been undermined by powerful lords at an early stage. But the Parliament, and the country, were devoted to the idea of monarchy. The last feudal battle, the War of the Roses, would occur over the issue of succession, not legitimacy.[12]

The significance of the War of the Roses for agricultural modernization lies in its destruction of the feudal lords' power and of the manorial system, thereby opening the way for the development of a state-supported capitalism. This development was also encouraged by the slow evolution of a money economy which rolled on independent of politics. Agriculture, as the mainstay of economic life, expanded with population growth from the eleventh century onward. Lands were cleared, marshes drained, and moors claimed for grazing ground. Slowly, too, an infrastructure emerged as roads, canals, and bridges were built to connect village with village and country with town.

The relaxation of social castes, the growth of trade, and the development of the small cottage industries and crafts spurred urban expansion. Expansion of trade provided novelties, which soon became essentials or desired luxuries, and this new supply provoked rising expectation and new demand. The development of trade, infrastructure, transportation, money economy, and industry ate away at the traditional, self-sufficient, isolated social units based on agriculture and did its part to rust the old bonds of the Middle Ages. By feeding a steady rise in prices, these developments also laid the groundwork for the next step in England's agricultural modernization.

It was the result of an act taken for reasons unrelated to economic development.[13] Henry VIII could not have foreseen that the men he favored would be the founders of a new class of agricultural entrepreneurs. His interest in securing his own position, however, provided the base and the means for innovation. As a result of his quarrel with the Pope over ecclesiastical matters, he confiscated monastic and chantry land, distributing the bounty to his own supporters. These supporters were not always of the nobility and consequently did not anticipate a return to feudal power; often they were adventurous, unconventional men whose urban background gave them an appreciation for trade, markets, and making a profit.[14] Furthermore, unlike the feudal lords of the past, they frequently retained ties with their urban lives, managing their farms only part-time or through baliffs and overseers. Farms shed their feudal coats for modern ones; instead of self-sufficient units organized around the manor house and its resident, they were capitalist ventures under absentee landlords.

One sign of the new times was a breakdown in the traditional tenant-landlord relationship. The protective, paternalistic attitude on the part of the landlord, a vestige of the feudal past, gave way to a businesslike arrangement in which profits were the objective. From the landowner's perspective, there were two ways to secure larger profits: the first was to increase productivity; the second, to increase the rent and the turnover of leases so the amount accruing to the landlord would increase faster than prices. Both of these conditions altered the landlord's relationship to the tenants. The first often entailed enclosing land, a practice that had existed since the eleventh century, but was not commonly adopted until the sixteenth century. A landlord could obtain more land for his own use through several means: clearing forests, draining swamps, usurping the common grazing lands, refusing to renew leases, and evicting tenants. Sixteenth century landlords followed all these practices despite the burden that the last three placed on their tenants. In doing so, they started an enclosure movement that was designed to shore up the legitimacy and profits of the new agriculturists and was consequently severely opposed by both the old aristocracy and the peasantry.

The second method of securing profits—through leases—changed tenant-landlord relationships as drastically as the first. Landlords were interested in tenants who would be successful enough to afford a high rent. If a tenant fell on hard times or a likelier prospect appeared, the new landlords felt little qualms about refusing lease renewal or evicting the tenants. In the absence of written contracts, there was little recourse available to the tenantry. As a result, a capitalist class arose comprising landlords and tenants adaptable to the market's requirements and conditions: thrift, savings, reinvestment of profits, monitoring of markets, and earthly rewards for labors.[15] It was the traditional peasants and the inflexible landlords who suffered and were forced to turn to the crown for welfare and subsidies.

In the sixteenth century land provided one outlet for excess capital in England and, with rising food prices, was a sufficiently profitable outlet to attract a great deal of investment funds. If the initial investment in land was due to success in the military and in trading, or to the munificence of the crown, the secondary investment for agricultural improvements—drainage, reclamation, and hedging and ditching enclosed lands—came from profits, rising rents, entry fines, and reduced costs produced by the shift from cultivation to tending livestock. But land served another function in the sixteenth century society in that ownership of land brought social prestige and encouraged social mobility. The classical distinction between landed aristocracy, urban entrepreneurs, knights, yeomen, and peasants was blurred by the ruin of some aristocrats and the good fortune of some members from the lower classes. The purchase of land necessitated wealth, but it also produced wealth, and the growth of a nonnoble landed class with influence at court and abroad antagonized the conservative landowners and stimulated the breakdown of class barriers.[16]

The government was in an ambivalent position during this period. Responsible for the rise of the new gentleman class, it also feared the consequences of its actions. As the enclosure movement spread, the rolls of the poor and unemployed increased, until beggary became a national problem and a governmental concern. Another consequence of the enclosure movement, and of the concurrent switch from grain to cattle or sheep, was the threat of a sudden grain shortage. Although enclosures made farming more efficient, they also made farmers favor livestock over a mixed crop. The possibility of famine increased the possibility of riots and threatened the regime's stability. In addition, the enclosure movement depopulated the countryside, decreasing the aggregate taxable income. Hence, the attitude of the government toward enclosures was negative, and it repeatedly initiated investigations into the enclosure practice through the Privy Council or the Parliament. It attempted to halt the practice through legislation, but the acts were poorly enforced and strongly opposed, so they served more as symbolic dissensions than as laws.[17]

The government's fears became a reality in the early seventeenth century, when large riots occurred in Western England. Sir Thomas More's observation that sheep in England were eating men was more than a vivid metaphorical description; if they were not eating the former tenants literally, they were consuming their major sources of livelihood in the produce from the land.[18] But as Christopher Hill points out, these sporadic riots never led to a full-scaled agrarian revolution (as in Russia and France) because of the heterogeneity of the peasant classes.[19] As some were dispossessed, others profited and identified with the interests of the genteel classes rather than with their former neighbors. The rise of a husbandman from small farmer to merchant inextricably widened the gap between himself and the unsuccessful farmer demoted to agricultural laborer. The cohesion of interests necessary to revolution was lacking.

The surprising aspect of the seventeenth century is the switch in governmental policy toward enclosures.[20] To halt the enclosure movement, Charles I established the land's enclosure commissions which investigated landowners' activities and fined enclosures when proof of their existence could be established. After 1641, however, no governmental action was launched against enclosures, and by the eighteenth century the practice was supported by an Act of Parliament. The impetus behind the shift was the growth in power of the House of Commons, a process that, again, was not directly related to agriculture, but had a lasting effect on it.[21]

The dual nature of Parliament had traditionally favored the House of Lords as the most wealthy, powerful, and influential body. Radical changes in the seventeenth century, however, promoted the position of the House of Commons until it played a major role in governing public policy. As concentrations of wealth slipped from the noble to the bourgeois sectors, the constituency of the House of Commons grew in financial strength. As the radical, reforming zeal of Cromwell undermined the monarchy and the nobility, the constituency of the House of Commons grew in political strength. In its new role, this body was active in promoting the interests of the nonnoble landed class, for it drew most of its members and support from this sector. Enclosures were important to the economic welfare of this class, and the increase in successful attempts to legislate proenclosure acts, from a mild measure of support in the early 1600s to a full endorsement in the mid-eighteenth century, indicates the increase in successful attempts on the part of the House of Commons to legislate public policy in general. Another example of parliamentary strength was the passage in 1640 of the Corn Laws, which levied taxes on imported grain to keep domestic prices artificially high. Despite the opposition of crown, aristocracy, and peasantry, middle class interests were on the ascendancy in the seventeenth century and, by the mid-1700s, had emerged as triumphant.

The Act of Parliament on Enclosures took the process of creating enclosures out of the landlords' hands by establishing legal regulations for the redistribution of farmland. The new lands obtained from clearing forests and draining marshland or common land were divided by an official commission on the basis of prior holdings: those that had more received more. Conditions for the small cottager and landowner became more arduous and forced former farmers into working for wages. This process provoked a moral outcry against enclosures, but the majority of the middle and upper classes felt that the market forces at work in the transformation were also moral forces. A common mode of thought in Protestant England was that poverty resulted from the sin of sloth. The poor, subsistence farmers were lazy and recalcitrant and brought upon themselves the miserable conditions of their lives. In his description of the character of the Puritan, R. H. Tawney captures the essential elements of this attitude:

Convinced that character is all and circumstances nothing, he sees in the

poverty of those who fall by the way, not a misfortune to be pitied and
relieved, but a moral failing to be condemned, and in riches, not an object
of suspicion . . . but the blessing which rewards the triumph of energy and
will.[22]

Since they thought that the switch to industrial labor would do poor
farmers good, the socially concerned of the eighteenth century saw
nothing detrimental about enclosures.

Elsewhere in Europe, agricultural experimentation had been
flourishing throughout the seventeenth century. The Netherlands,
especially, excelled in innovative improvements, in part a result of
Dutch topography. Land reclamation was a natural component of life
in a country shaped by polders, and the proportion of fertile soil to
population fostered techniques aimed at intense use of the land. Added
to this was the Dutch spirit of trade and profits, which lent a capitalist
spark to their efforts. The result was development of new species of
plants designed to enrich the soil as well as to feed livestock. The
revolution caused by clover, which adds nutrients to the earth and can be
sown in normally fallow fields, and turnips, whose versatility and
adaptability make them a cheap fodder for livestock, was perhaps not as
spectacular as the Industrial Revolution but affected as many lives as the
latter period of economic change.

The new crops and the new methods of caring for the soil through
fertilizers, innovations developed by the Dutch, were not introduced in
England until the late seventeenth century and did not catch on until the
mid-eighteenth century. But when they became widespread, they joined
other techniques to create what has been called the "Agricultural
Revolution," a period when the three factors of land, labor, and capital
were available and organized to take advantage of fairly simple
improvements.[23] Land was collected into large estates on which
experiments could take place on a large scale without threatening the
farmer with starvation if they proved unsuccessful. Labor was plentiful,
since supply far exceeded demand. Capital was provided by the
landowners, who had emerged richly endowed from the enclosure
period. The incentive to reform and improve agricultural technology
was provided by a steady rise in agricultural prices beginning in the
eighteenth century; visions of increasing profits spurred the adoption of
more efficient techniques.

A last important factor in general economic growth is information
and its dissemination. The absence of this factor impeded adoption of
the Dutch innovations, but a new breed of eighteenth century
landowners corrected for this defect. Through experimenting in plant

propagation, developing new techniques and machinery, disseminating results, proselytizing about favored innovations, printing pamphlets, and giving lectures, some members of the wealthy, landed English gentry effected changes that otherwise might have taken decades to adopt. Jethro Tull's invention of the seed drill revolutionized cultivation patterns by facilitating planting in rows rather than by scattered handfulls. Charles Viscount Townshend earned the nickname of "Turnip Townshend" for his work in encouraging cultivation of this new crop. Another wealthy innovator was Robert Blackwell, whose experiments in animal husbandry improved the English strain of livestock. Finally, the number of innovative machines and techniques for their use, and the quantity of instructive information available, proliferated in the wake of the profound changes precipitated by the Industrial Revolution.

As technical improvements contributed to agricultural productivity, the workings of the market solved the capital problem of the upper middle-income farmers who were without access to investment sources that the high-income groups enjoyed. In a fashion reminiscent of the earlier Renaissance cycle, the emphasis on capitalism in agriculture caught the eye of urban investors on the lookout for "growth stocks." Creating a flow beneficial to both groups, urban investment in agriculture enhanced productivity—which, in turn, brought greater returns both to the farmer and to the investor. With the growing urban population, demand for food was such that increased supply did not entail lowered prices.

Many of the forces that created the Agricultural Revolution in England were forces of the private sector. In fact, the mythology of the era emphasizes the absence of public intervention in England's great surge forward in industrial and agricultural productivity. The government, however, did play a role—at times quite significant—in the process. When its attempts to halt enclosures had clearly failed, the government did not attempt to legislate stricter controls. Instead, it let the matter drop, clearing the way for a much stronger Parliament (largely representative of landlord interests) to endorse the procedure by official Act of Parliament.

In another vital area, government intervention paved the way for private initiatives through adoption of the Corn Laws in 1640. These laws, in effect until 1846, ensured high grain prices in England by taxing all imports of grain to the level of the domestic market price. The security of a guaranteed satisfactory price and the freedom from foreign competition provided a constant boost to agricultural investment. Governmental export subsidies also ensured that English grain was competitive abroad. The Corn Laws and export subsidies were consistent with the larger economic philosophy of the times: by mercantile prescription, the key to state security was the accumulation of huge amounts of gold through maximal exports and minimal imports.

The shift in governmental policy from mercantilism to espousal of the *laissez-faire* philosophy resulted in a conscious absence of governmental intervention in agriculture. The export subsidies were stopped and the Corn Laws repealed. By the mid-nineteenth century, however, England had a strong and wealthy agricultural class that was equipped to deal with the shock of competition in the open and volatile agricultural commodities markets. Those middle-income farmers who could not adjust were forced out of business, and, thus, the concentration of land and capital accrued naturally to the larger landowners. A consistent trend since the Reformation thus continued.

By the time government actually stepped out of active participation in the agricultural sector, it had already provided a fertile culture for the growth of the elite private sector by encouraging enclosures and through price supports and subsidies. Its role, however, was limited in comparison with the parts played by the French and Danish governments and must be seen in proper perspective. Equally important to this growth of the private sector was the growth in demand for food and an improvement of the techniques of food production. Both of these phenomena can be traced to the development of urban industry, which provoked urban migration and thus increased the demand for food, kept prices high, and provided capital for agricultural improvements. The Industrial Revolution, with its rapid development of useful machines, provided the means to meet the increased demand and, at the same time, provided the means to reduce the amount of labor necessary to farm each acre. To large estate owners, the production of scale made investment in new machinery well worth its initial cost. This process also released labor for the new demands of urban industry. And finally, the work of private gentlemen farmers who took it upon themselves to experiment, innovate, and educate provided a spark to modernization otherwise lacking in England.

The result was that by 1870 England had an efficient system of farming, which might have survived well into this century had not the American and Russian competition been so severe.[24] In a joint effort, the public and private sectors managed to achieve agricultural modernization through consolidation of great amounts of land and capital in a few hands. That modernization can be reached through more equitable means will become clear in the discussion of Danish agriculture. First, however, it might be useful to examine the experience in France, where the government attempted to use agriculture to ensure economic and social equality to the detriment of productivity.

France: Development of an Economy
Based on Peasant Agriculture

Early medieval France and England shared the same economic and social system of feudalism organized around the manor with a strictly defined lord-peasant relationship, a weak monarchy, and a strong church. In France, during the period between 987 and 1491, the efforts of the powerful lords were focused on resisting the growing power of the Capetian and Valois kings, who managed by the end of the fifteenth century to incorporate most of the land within current French borders into the royal realm. Although some of this amalgamation occurred through marriages and allegiances, much was the result of bloody and costly battles between power-hungry rulers.

While the logic of the feudal relationship in England was breaking down, repeated marauding by French and English soldiers confirmed the necessity of seigneurial protection in France. Thus, the grip in which the lord held the peasants was tightened, despite the fact that feudalism as a formal institution had come to an end by 1400, nearly a century earlier than in England.[25] Most peasants in the fifteenth century were freeholders who paid their rent in kind, in labor, or in cash. The labor supply for the lord was augmented by the agricultural workers who had not enough land to farm, but rented themselves out in return for money and, at times, a small plot of soil. The chief landlords were the nobility, the royal family, and the church.

The legal setup of Renaissance France hides the realities of the landlord-peasant relationship. Due to the turbulence of the times and the conditions under which peasants leased lands from the lords, the landlords, in fact, imposed heavier seigneurial duties on their tenants than had many feudal lords. The danger to the countryside of the passing troops convinced many landlords to flee to the cities—or, in this increasingly centralized state, to Paris—leaving their lands in the hands of others to manage. Besides cutting the emotional ties between land and landowners, this movement also served to cut the economic ties. Rents went to Paris and were devoted to the lord's personal expenses, instead of reinvested in the land. Consequently, until the eighteenth century, there was a balance-of-payments deficit in the country. Revenues went to the town, and, except for the area immediately around Paris, little returned to the countryside.[26]

The following description of the conditions that prevailed in France immediately before the Revolution is fairly typical of the conditions for the preceding three centuries.[27] Unlike the case in England, a third of the French land was in the hands of French peasants by 1780, but the plots were often too small to support the farmer's family, much less to yield a profit. Thus, even landholders were forced to augment their income through other means: by cottage industries or, more commonly, by renting additional land to ensure a profitable yield, or by serving as agricultural laborers on another estate. So landholders joined the ranks of tenant farmers, sharecroppers, and agricultural workers in their dependency on the absent landlord. The growing population and resulting competition for leases allowed the landlords to draw up arbitrary and often harshly termed leases and encouraged them to evict tenants or to refuse lease renewal if a more interesting prospect came along. These conditions produced murmurings among the peasantry, which repeatedly demanded sale or lease of some parts of the royal domain to ease the competitive crush.[28]

The arrangements would have been intolerable, provoking perhaps an earlier move to revolt, but for one factor. As a holdover from feudal days, French peasants claimed certain community privileges as part of their natural rights.[29] These privileges, which increased the farmer's access to land and to produce, allowed subsistence farmers to survive where economic laws would have predicted starvation. Among these expected privileges were the right to glean and raise cattle on harvested fields and the right to allow livestock to wander and graze through unenclosed fields. These privileges were important to the peasantry, for they were the only guarantee of its livelihood.

To say that the peasants were naturally suspicious of change is to miss the point. The peasants' continued existence was incompatible with a change that would destroy the old "rights" without establishing new ones. Only a total structural change could hope to improve the peasants' lot and therefore to win their approval.

It is possible that the impetus to do away with this sytem would have come from the noble landlords whose livelihood depended on rents from the lands had they felt that their income was diminished as a result of the inefficient system. The same rising prices that spurred the English "Agricultural Revolution," however, caused the French landlords to tighten their grip.[30] England witnessed the rise of the capitalist farmer after the Reformation. France had no such sanctioned land redistribution. Neither did it have increasing industrial development to feed.

Lack of opportunity would seem to have prohibited the development of a capitalist agriculture in France. Nevertheless, an entrepreneurial class did spring up, not as independent landowners, but as tenants of the lords.[31] The seigneurs, ensconced in towns, leased out everything involved with managing estates—the right to collect taxes and income, the right to half of the sharecroppers' produce, the right to oversee the behavior of the other tenants. In some cases, the seigneurs leased out the leases themselves, allowing tenants to become landlords, in effect. These powerful tenants had every incentive to increase the income obtainable from the farms, as had their English counterparts. They differed from the English, however, in that their position in society was ruled by feudal laws: they were vassals of a great lord rather than independent entrepreneurs. As Lefebvre points out:

> The intrusion of capitalism into agriculture was made in part under the cover of feudal rights, and (this) made them very much more unbearable. It also perverted their very nature because they had been created to support a seigneur who lived in the midst of his peasants, and now they passed into the hands of capitalists who thought only of deriving a profit from them.[32]

The success of these middlemen directly fed their lord's anxiety to keep the system exactly as it was.

Resistance to conditions for efficient agriculture also came from the king, whose primary objective was to bolster his power and throne against any contenders, foreign or domestic. As had the English Tudors, the French kings feared anything that smacked of an enclosure movement—which would have brought more lands, wealth, and influence to the nobility. Consequently, whenever possible, the French kings encouraged their nobles to disdain "la vie de province"—their landholdings and agriculture.[33] Even though this policy made good political sense, as witnessed in Louis XIV's phenomenal success in diverting the attention of his nobility from serious concerns, economically it hindered the development of an efficient agricultural sector. Consequently, before the Revolution, the four major groups involved in agriculture—peasants, middlemen, landlords, and government—shared an interest in maintaining the traditional character of agricultural production in France.

The fiscal mechanism that explains the chronic inability of the peasant farmers to accumulate capital, despite gross profits, was the system of taxation.[34] The Church and nobility were exempt from taxes, so the burden of financing the government fell on the peasantry. The peasants had to pay three kinds of taxes: direct taxes to the government, direct taxes to the seigneur, and indirect taxes on consumer goods. The weight of these taxes was difficult to bear in good times; in times of depression it became intolerable, since taxes remained constant even as prices fell. This was the situation in the decade before the Revolution as the country limped along on the brink of financial crisis. Harvests were inconsistent, direct taxes were high, and, to meet the debts it incurred in the Seven Years' War and in the American Revolution, the government slapped taxes onto consumer goods.[35] The attempt to rectify the financial crisis by squeezing the peasants ignited the peasantry's antimonarchical and antiseigneurial sentiments and made them receptive to the logic of the revolutionaries: that France's economic woes were the result of politics and could be traced to the irresponsible action of the government. The solution must also be political: a complete transformation of state and government to a society based on liberty, equality, and brotherhood.

As is often the case in France, the answer came not as a gradual change but as an explosion inexorably altering the basic assumptions of political life.[36] The effect of the Revolution was to rock every sector of French society, making complacent return to the past impossible. In agriculture, the abrupt break from the past consisted of a complete land reform legislated by the government.[37] Land was confiscated from landlords and clergy and redistributed to the peasants. The new owners got title to the land they farmed before the Revolution, but the competition for land prevented peasants from receiving a larger plot unless they could pay for it.[38] At the level of rural capital holdings, few could afford the additional costs, and the result was that thousands of peasants owned plots sufficiently large to nurture the family, but not to yield a profit.

The French experience is historical proof that good governmental intentions and egalitarian land reform do not necessarily make a fair or productive system of agriculture. As it turned out, the French peasantry continued to live as before, selling what surplus produce existed in good years to the local towns and hoarding the crops in bad years. Land reform was unaccompanied by other essential—although politically less visible—reforms, such as education, credit facilities, availability of new technology, and development of local industry. Without the other inputs, land reform was a sad answer to a stagnating economy.

What the legacy of the Napoleonic era was for France is argued still, but nearly all sides agree that one great achievement of the period was the Napoleonic Code, in which laws of the *ancien régime* and of the Revolution were compiled and enforced in equal measure throughout France. In this way, the Revolution's concern for equality in the agricultural world became a further legal hindrance to enlarging the size of the farms, since the law stipulated that all sons of a farmer must receive an equal portion of the farm upon his death. The subdivisions continued throughout the nineteenth century. At the end of the 1800s, there were over four thousand farms of under five hectares, while little over a hundred farms exceeded forty hectares. And as the Restoration period illustrates, rights written into law do not translate necessarily into rights enjoyed: equality in the franchise depended on the ablity to pay a three-hundred-franc direct tax, and liberty to hold office depended on the ability to pay a fee of one thousand francs.[39] The link between politics and food, forged by the Revolution, continued during the Restoration; thus, when the post-Napoleonic depression induced a relative decrease in income and bad harvests drove the price of food up, the blame fell on the monarchy and contributed to the 1830 Revolution.

By this time, France had experienced nearly fifty years of turbulence: the Revolution, the Napoleonic era, and the Restoration. Civil war, blockades, empire building, and depressions had occupied most of her attention and wealth and had served to reduce the inflow of new information and techniques to a trickle. As a result, while England was refining and experimenting with new methods of industry and agriculture, France clung to its old modes. Without the tradition of the individual entrepreneur, imbedded in English society, the likelihood of an economic transformation occurring spontaneously by the work of enlightened private persons was slim in France. The only source of physical capital, human resources, wealth, and information capable of inspiring a transformation was the government, and until the Second Empire, there was little interest on the government's part in this area. The groundwork for modernization had been laid in part by Napoleon, whose demand for war supplies had encouraged the mechanization of certain industries. The Restoration government had also promoted the development of a system of railway lines, but depressions and politics ate away at that program until it slowed to an imperceptible crawl by the end of the July Monarchy. France needed a push to get rolling again, and it came with the gold rushes from abroad.

In 1848, gold was discovered in California, and in 1851 in Australia. Much of this gold flooded into Europe, especially to England and France. In France, gold replaced silver as the official currency, and the Bank of France started a spectacular buildup of reserves, which increased tenfold from 1847 to 1869. The influx of gold provided the capital for general economic transformation; the government provided the policy. Napoleon III had a natural predilection for economics, which he had studied in exile. During his stay in England, he read influential *laissez-*

faire theorists like Smith and Ricardo and had ample time to absorb the results of England's Industrial Revolution. Upon his return to France, he set forth a policy of transformation that was to strengthen France's economy while turning the citizenry's thoughts from politics to economics. Hence, the policy had two goals: to make France rich and to make the government secure.

With this in mind, the government set about developing the structure for a new economy. Eight days after the coup in which Napoleon III rose from president to emperor, the government issued a decree to construct a line of railroads within Paris. In 1852, it permitted the Paris-Lyons line to begin, starting the north-south line that was to speed delivery of produce far beyond the maximum velocity of the canal boats. Within the reign of the Second Empire, the length of France's railroad lines increased from 2,200 miles to 14,570 miles. The government did not establish national companies to run the railroads, but managed to retain substantial control by appointing a few large private companies to take over from the numerous small companies responsible for the railroads in the past. The effect of the development of railroads on agriculture was enormous, changing the market for agricultural goods from the local town squares to the capitals all over Europe. The demand for agricultural goods increased, demand spurred production, sales produced profits, and, for the first time, farmers had extra capital to reinvest in their farms.[40]

The government recognized the lack of capital formation as a hindrance to agricultural efficiency; in response, it encouraged the establishment of the Credit Foncier in 1852 for the benefit of the agricultural community. The Credit Foncier provided long-term mortgages repayable in annual installments; its capital was secured by the issue of government bonds. At last, an apparatus was created to guide capital to the rural districts.

Napoleon III instituted a third innovation that was to spur transformation. Using his imperial perogative, he negotiated treaties with most of the European nations to reduce or eliminate tariffs, to end quotas, and to grant most-favored-nation clauses to treaty partners. In so doing, he violated the hard-fought rights of the French middle class, who had controlled France since 1815. This commercial middle class had agitated for firm protectionist measures to shelter France's industry and agriculture from the innovating shocks of foreign competition. Since Parliament was increasingly composed of its members, the middle class was granted its desires without opposition. As Napoleon negotiated, he removed the buffers, exposed industry and agriculture, and thus spurred them on to efficiency.

Napoleon's reign was liberal in economics only; in politics he was authoritarian. His actions antagonized the powerful industrialists and the middle class as well as the peasant farmers, and his abdication represented, in part, the triumph of these three groups. After his exile, the French elite and citizenry again opted for democracy in the form of the Third Republic. And with democracy came the same protectionist influences that had been prevalent prior to Napoleon III. The result was that as American and Russian grain started to pour into Europe, the French government again slapped on high tariffs and strict quotas. The speed of the Second Empire's industrial revolution was checked, and France again sacrificed agricultural transformation for politics.

Denmark: A Flexible Agricultural Economy

Denmark differs from England and France in size, wealth, and importance, as well as in its course to agricultural modernization. Its status as a small, peripheral state, however, did not deter its government from instituting social programs as radical as those of the French Revolution. It was not deterred either from encouraging an agricultural growth as profitable as that of the English. The result of these actions was Denmark's emergence from underdevelopment to prosperity in less than a century.[41]

The agricultural history of Denmark since the thirteenth century is one of alternating cycles of freedom and repression. The Danes share with the other Scandinavians an unusual respect for justice and equality.[42] The early Vikings evolved the system of trial by peers and organized the earliest modern parliament, established in Iceland in the tenth century. This dedication to equality manifested itself in Denmark in the system of community farming that flourished by the thirteenth century. At this time, the Danish agricultural sector was as strong as the trading and marauding sectors, and the country was settled, cultivated, and dotted with villages forming the social center of agricultural life. The land surrounding the villages was divided into strips which the villagers owned. Often, a system of cooperative farming developed in which the farmer-owners would pool land and resources and run the farm as a commune. Each farmer had one vote in determining village policy and received his share of the produce in compensation.

This system did not endure. As some farmers did better than others, they bought up their neighbors' lands, leasing them out again to the former owner or the highest bidder. Thus, both the apex and the decline of a medieval expression of political and social equality occurred in Denmark in the thirteenth century.

The commitment to equality broke down in other areas as well. A notion predating the introduction of Christianity was that the king derived his power from the people in the form of a representative parliament. Although the crown often passed from father to son, kingship was not hereditary; its conferral faced a parliamentary vote. The momentum of this system depended on a strong parliament and a weak king. In the early Middle Ages rising wealthy landowners paid their taxes to the king in the form of military service. They thereby developed into a service class dependent on the king for special dispensations. The kings encouraged the relationship, because it provided them with eager and loyal followers. In time, the nobles realized the security of their position allowed them to increase their rights and privileges at the cost of the king's power, transforming the previously satisfactory relationship into one of tension, anger, and bitterness. The ensuing split between noble and king governed much of Denmark's history until the late eighteenth century.

In lieu of the nobles' support, the Danish kings found a new ally in the Church—which had been firmly established by the mid-twelfth century. Eventually, the Church and not the people bestowed blessings on kingship and enabled the rulers to grow in strength and influence and to establish a dynastic monarchy. The kings' power was not absolute, since each ruler signed an agreement restricting his rights, but nearly all the monarchs until the mid-nineteenth century could assume complete authority if they so wished.

The purpose of this overview of medieval political life is to mark the road Denmark took from freedom and equality to feudalism. The effect of this progression on farmers was severe. As landowners, all farmers paid taxes to the king. In total expenditure, the share of these taxes grew as the king centralized his power. Over time, it became crippling for the small farmers. They sold their land to nobles or to the Church, leasing the farms back from the new owners. Thus, they became bound to the land in a manner that differed from the feudal relationship, for here, as in France, there was no concept of mutual obligation between landlord and tenant. If the tenant could not meet the cash payments, he had to provide physical labor. In the years between 1250 and 1400, the number of landowning farmers fell from 50 percent to under 15 percent of all farmers.

Analogies to the situation in nineteenth century Ireland are not inappropriate, especially since the practice of creating big estates by coalescing lands gained more currency in the late fifteenth and sixteenth centuries.[43] In a movement started by the king, nobles began to exchange their far-flung plots for land adjacent to the main estate, thereby enlarging the size of their contiguous holdings. Peasants who leased their farms were thrown into instability, for no guarantee existed that their lease would be renewed. As the nobles' estates swelled in size, they demanded more labor from their tenant farmers. This condition worsened as new profit-oriented men brought up the estates of nobles who were impoverished by war with Sweden. Any remnants of the feudal lord's obligations were wiped out on these new estates; the landlords' demands forced tenants to neglect their own plots. This period—the late seventeenth and early eighteenth century—saw the deterioration of the peasant's position in society. It was confirmed by a law passed in the early 1700s decreeing that no man could leave his estate-by-birth between the ages of fourteen and thirty-six. At least feudal England provided an escape clause, however harsh, for serfs.

Outside of agriculture, the economy was growing as a result of economic decisions made by the kings Erik of Pomerania and Christian II (his successor). To bolster their importance in the northern trade routes, these rulers claimed rights to trade that was formerly controlled by Hanseatic merchants and gave to market towns along the trade routes wider economic rights. By the seventeenth century, then, a strong urban bourgeoisie, dependent on trade and the king, had developed. Although the growth of towns spurred demand for food, the industries that grew up in England did not flourish in Denmark, where most nonagricultural life centered on trade. The growth of the middle class did have a long-term effect on agriculture, however, in providing access to powerful positions on the king's council. A natural alliance sprang up between the middle class and the ruler against the nobles; as a consequence, more input from commoners in policy making became apparent. This access to power would have a significant effect in the latter part of the eighteenth century.

The ideas of the Enlightenment spread throughout Europe in the eighteenth century, reaching Prussia, Poland, and even the cold shores of Sweden. In Scandinavia, Denmark had far closer ties to the continent and was therefore more susceptible to the radical and often humane ideas of the *philosophes*. The effects of this worldly dose of philosophy were intensified by the teachings of the Lutheran church, which by this time had a firm grip on Danish society. Because one of the main tenets of Lutheranism is universal education, the church agitated for its institution despite aristocratic opposition throughout the century. In 1789, while the Jacobites were toppling the *ancien régime*, a school commission was set up in Denmark to study the possibilities of establishing public schools to bring education to the masses. Its report led eventually to the School Law of 1814, which provided free education for all. In fact it called for a heavy fine on parents who refused to educate their children either in school or at home. The potential objections of the aristocracy were skirted by funding the school system through public taxation. At the same time, the government established teachers' training colleges, supplemented in 1840 by folk high schools, the curricula of which focused on agriculture.[44] In a quiet way, this reform had as much impact on Danish life and society as the bold and radical actions of the French Revolution had on France.

School reform was not the only change instituted for the benefit of the peasants. Under the leadership of Count Christian Reventlow, a whole program of reforms was initiated, with the aim of creating an independent peasant class.[45] Laws were passed to ensure peasant compensation for improvements to leased property, to prevent the landlord from inflicting corporal punishment on the farmers, to end the obligatory bond of peasants with the land they farmed. Common fields were abolished and separate strips were consolidated. In an unusually early move, the government provided loans to the peasants for the purchase of plots of land and encouraged farmers to move from the villages to farmhouses on their own property. In 1819, it issued regulations on the minimum dimensions of farms supporting families, decreeing that farms must conform to or exceed these measurements. The result was the growth of small- to medium-sized farms; this almost assuredly produced a surplus for selling in the marketplace.

Traditional resistance to land reform was circumvented by a law which stipulated that redistribution of land was compulsory if even one landowner in a village called for it. This measure broke the back of the age-old practice of communal farming and provided farmers with the opportunity of following their own judgment instead of the communal policy of the village. The individual plots not only led to greater efficiency as peasants bought their plots outright but also allowed lands previously used for livestock to be cultivated.

By 1814, 60 percent of Danish farmers owned the plots they farmed. The growing self-sufficiency and resulting pride of these new farmers, coupled with the remarkable educational advances, eventually led to political expression in a country just awakening to the possibilities of a constitutional monarchy.

Due to separatist mutterings in Schleswig and Holstein, the monarchy was forced to introduce assemblies in four provinces in 1831. The limited representative bodies nurtured the growth of political sophistication and the development of political parties. Yet the rural community was reluctant to join urban liberals and radicals in their demand for greater democracy, for the farmers recognized that their well-being was the result of government intervention. They did use the opportunity, however, to press directly for further reforms. One particular thorn in the side of the rural class was the limitation of the conscription to rural communities. When the king declined to grant an extension of the draft to all sectors, the farmers put aside their reluctance and joined with the liberals to form a farmers' party, the Bondesvennernes Selskap, in 1846.[46]

The granting of political rights proceeded rapidly in Denmark, and by 1848, the National Liberals, a party more conservative than the farmers' party, persuaded the king to accept a national constitution. It guaranteed religious and personal freedoms, freedom of speech, and a representative parliament. Farmers benefited immensely from this acquisition of political power. In the same year they achieved the extension of the conscription and the establishment of the *Kreditforeninger* (credit societies), savings and loans associations for the farming community.

Better education, better living conditions, ownership of land, political power, and establishment of agricultural organizations all served to change the farmers' self-image and attitude toward the outside world. They became more receptive to improving techniques and creating finer strains, to new methods of cultivation and new ideas. The demand for agricultural goods in general aided Denmark's development from a backward to a prosperous economy in the mid-nineteenth century. The growing competition of the United States and Russia in wheat production was foreseen by some farsighted wealthy cultivators. They encouraged the early shift from wheat to livestock which spared Denmark the worst effects of the 1870s depression.[47]

Danish produce had earned a bad reputation in England, its major market, because of its unequal quality. This condition prompted an Aarhus trader, Hans Broge, to suggest that cooperative dairies be set up in each village. The cooperatives would cut costs of production while maintaining a uniform level of quality—something individual farmers would not be able to attain. They would be run on democratic principles: one farmer, one vote, regardless of the size of the individual farm.[48] Profits, on the other hand, were to be shared according to the amount delivered by each farmer to the dairy. The idea took hold, and by 1885, eighty-four cooperative dairies were operating; by 1895, the number had swelled tenfold. The concept of cooperatives spread to pig farming and purchasing cooperatives for fodder, seed, machinery, and cement. By 1900, there were 900 cooperative stores for the benefit of the rural communities.[49]

The success of these cooperatives diminished the need for governmental intervention in all aspects of farming life in Denmark—acquisitions, production, or marketing. The state did take an interest in salvaging the good name of Danish produce, however, and provided quality inspectors both in Denmark and in England. It also issued a seal (*lur*) which testified that the product had passed governmental standards. By the end of the century, though, the government's role was largely supervisory. Having created and enforced the conditions for an efficient, egalitarian system of agricultural production, the Danish government receded to the background and allowed market forces to determine the direction of Danish agriculture.[50]

Conclusions

This consideration of the different experiences of England, France, and Denmark in their agricultural development yields a few fairly simple conclusions. Firstly, the timing of the break from feudalism does not seem to be an important factor in determining the course of later development; the fact that both France and Denmark endured several centuries of implicit or explicit feudalism gives an idea of the variety of legacies passed on by feudal systems. Secondly, innovations—technological or otherwise—led to modernization in the agricultural sector only when the farmers, the economy, and the society as a whole were ready to accept the changes. The story of the potato, accused for decades of all sorts of maleficent effects and therefore shunned in Europe as a poison, illustrates the importance of societal acceptance of change. Adoption of technological improvement depends not only on economics and availability but also on dissemination of information about the new methods in some kind of "public relations" program (whether formal or informal) which will "sell" the innovation to the general public.

My main conclusion is that the course of agricultural development is determined in large part by the actions of the governments involved and that the policies of the French, English, and Danish governments go far in accounting for the different agricultural trends and experiences of these countries. In Denmark, the case is clear: the government played a pivotal role in reforming agriculture. It is as if the eighteenth century policy makers there read from a book entitled "How to Be a Good Social Democrat," initiating a series of profound and effective reforms. It seems as though someone, somewhere, had a long-term vision of a healthy economy based on agriculture. The careful establishment of the various mechanisms to aid agricultural development, plus the creation of the web of cooperatives, set up an agricultural system in which governmental intervention was no longer necessary for a smoothly functioning and profitable agricultural sector. Perhaps the greatest surprise is that the government recognized its own superfluity and withdrew quietly.

The case of France is equally clear. The two major instances of governmental intervention in the agricultural sector, which the government used to achieve its own political and philosophical ends, actively prevented agricultural modernization. Certainly, the post-Revolution government did not oppose change; indeed, it used the massive weapon of land reform to promote its goal of equality. However, it inadequately thought out the consequences of its actions, and they were to hobble agricultural development for nearly two centuries. Consequently, it is hard to say, in the long run, whether the well-intentioned policy of land reform actually improved the general welfare. And the later governments' policies of protectionism, aimed at shielding French agriculture from foreign competition, simply served to shield the farmer from the challenges and innovations that might have revolutionized French farming. The result was that France really did not begin a program of agricultural modernization until after World War II. And the War wreaked sufficient havoc to necessitate a long-term plan for agricultural development.

The English case is not as straightforward, for it presents ambiguous evidence. It is important to consider the actions of the government over the long centuries of improvement in order to develop a sense of the timing of the government's various policies and of their effects on the agricultural sector. First, the land redistribution policies of the Reformation set the stage for the evolution to large farming estates; second, mercantile policies allowed for the establishment of a strong agricultural sector—which could survive into the period of little governmental intervention. Unlike the situation in France, the farms protected by the mercantile policies were increasing in size and wealth as land was concentrated in a few hands, hands which showed an inordinate interest in new ideas. Thus, governmental policies served to nurture the agriculture industry as it took shape in the seventeenth century and were continued until their usefulness had come to an end. This agricultural sector, however, was not based on the solid, equitable network that Denmark enjoyed, and proved, in the end, susceptible to the shocks of Russian and American competition.

Mercantile protectionism and *laissez-faire* policies worked only as long as the economy was growing and foreign competition was not severe. As a result of both policies, the individual landlords assumed great amounts of responsibility: at first to bring the winds of change to a sheltered sector, and later to absorb the fluctuations in supply, demand,

and price brought about by competitive foreign produce. That they were willing to act on their own and had the resources to do so accounts in large part for the success of British agriculture. But, paradoxically, it also accounts for its later failure. It was not until it was too late, until the landowners proved incapable of protecting themselves, that they and the government recognized the dangers of the system.

This exploration of agricultural history is not meant to leave the impression that had England or France followed the Danish government's lead, they would have sustained or developed healthy, active agricultural sectors during the nineteenth century. There are too many other variables involved in development, including a recognition of one's comparative advantage in the global economy, to support such an idea. My purpose was merely to point out the vital role that government plays in development and the necessity of appreciating its position in analyses of the modernization process. Whether it acts as a rampaging bull that charges everything in sight or as a reluctant dragon that prefers to retire from the scene, we on the outside must recognize that the policies a government chooses to follow are an essential determinant of the course of economic modernization.

Notes

1. There are many general theories about the causes and courses of agricultural modernization, the best of which recognize the complexity of the subject. For a sampling, the reader may wish to consult D. Gale Johnson, *World Agriculture in Disarray* (London: St. Martin's Press, 1973); Bruce Johnston and Peter Kilby, *Agriculture and Structural Transformation* (London, Toronto, New York: Oxford University Press, 1975); and Immanuel Wallerstein, *The Modern World System: Capitalist Agriculture and the Origins of the European World Economy in the Sixteenth Century* (New York and London: Academic Press, 1974).

2. For a thorough description of medieval life, see Marc Bloch, *Feudal Society* (Chicago: University of Chicago, 1964), and Guy Fourguin, *Lordship and Feudalism in the Middle Ages* (New York: Pica Press, 1976).

3. S. B. Clough and Charles W. Cole, *Economic History of Europe* (Boston: D. C. Hutton and Company, 1952).

4. R. H. Tawney, *Religion and the Rise of Capitalism* (Middlesex: Penguin Books, 1938), pp. 76-89.

5. This acceptance of communality reflected a broader belief in the sanctity of social order.

6. B. A. Holderness, *Pre-Industrial England: Economy and Society from 1500 to 1750* (London: Jim Dent and Sons, 1976), pp. 61-62.

7. M. M. Postan, *The Cambridge Economic History of Europe* (Cambridge: Cambridge University Press, 1966), pp. 660-741.

8. Harry A. Miskimin, *The Economy of Early Renaissance Europe 1300-*

1460 (Englewood Cliffs, N.J.: Prentice Hall, 1969), pp. 32-72.

9. Wallerstein, *The Modern World System,* pp. 27-31.

10. Geoffrey Barraclough, *The Crucible of Europe* (Berkeley and Los Angeles: University of California Press, 1976), pp. 124-142.

11. Maurice Powicke, *Medieval Europe 1066-1485* (London, Oxford, New York: Oxford University Press, 1969), pp. 18-23.

12. G. M. Trevelyan, *A Shortened History of England* (Baltimore: Penguin Books, 1959), pp. 198-200.

13. This is a conclusion reached by Donald Puchala and Jane Staveley in "The Political Economy of Taiwanese Agricultural Modernization," included in this volume. However, their hypothesis seems equally applicable here.

14. Harold J. Laski, *The Rise of European Liberalism* (London: Unwin Books, 1936), pp. 11-58.

15. Wallerstein, *The Modern World System,* pp. 27-31.

16. Christopher Hill, *Reformation to Industrial Revolution: The Making of Modern English Society,* vol. 1 (New York: Random Books, 1967), pp. 45-53.

17. Ibid., p. 119.

18. Wallerstein, *The Modern World System,* p. 110.

19. Hill, *Reformation to Industrial Revolution,* pp. 93-96.

20. Ibid., pp. 115-122.

21. Ibid., pp. 173-183.

22. Tawney, *Religion and Capitalism,* pp. 229-230.

23. E. L. Jones, "English and European Agricultural Development 1650-1750," in *The Industrial Revolution,* ed. R. M. Hartwell (New York: Barnes and Noble, 1970), pp. 42-76.

24. For a description of the aftermath of the Russian and American grain onslaught, see Michael Tracy, *Agriculture in Western Europe: Crisis and Adaptation Since 1880* (London: Jonathan Cape, 1964).

25. Wallerstein notes that agricultural transformation in northern France came to a halt in the sixteenth century and cites an argument of Marc Bloch that the English legal system permitted more flexibility to the landlords in drawing up arrangements for their land than the rigid, centralized French system, which favored the retention of a feudal relationship. *The Modern World System,* pp. 25-30.

26. Miskimin, *Early Renaissance Europe,* pp. 51-57.

27. See Alexis de Tocqueville, *The Old Régime and the French Revolution* (Garden City, N.Y.: Doubleday and Company, 1955).

28. Georges Lefebvre, "The Peasant on the Eve of the French Revolution," in *The Shaping of Modern France,* ed. James Friguglietti and Emmet Kennedy (London: Collier-Macmillan, 1969), pp. 25-30.

29. Barrington Moore, Jr., *Social Origins of Dictatorship and Democracy: Lord and Peasant in the Making of the Modern World* (Boston: Beacon Press, 1967), pp. 71-72.

30. Jan de Vries, *The Economy of Europe in an Age of Crisis, 1600-1750* (Cambridge, London, New York, Melbourne: Cambridge University Press, 1976), pp. 63-69.

31. Moore, *Social Origins of Dictatorship and Democracy,* p. 41.

72   *Pamela R. Aall*

32. Lefebvre, "The Peasant," p. 29.

33. Moore, *Social Origins of Dictatorship and Democracy*, pp. 43-44.

34. Ernest Labrousse, "The Fiscal and Economic Crisis at the End of the Ancien Régime," in *The Shaping of Modern France*, pp. 93-97.

35. Ibid, pp. 95-97.

36. Stanley Hoffman, "Paradoxes of the French Political Community" in *In Search of France: The Economy, Society, and Political System in the Twentieth Century* (New York: Harper and Row, 1963), pp. 1-117.

37. Georges Lefebvre, *The French Revolution from 1793 to 1799* (New York: Columbia University Press, 1964).

38. Moore, *Social Origins of Dictatorship and Democracy*, pp. 107-108.

39. Guillaume de Bertier de Sauvigny, "French Society under the Restoration," in *The Shaping of Modern France*, pp. 207-212.

40. Georges Pradalié, "The Economic Transformation of France under the Second Empire," in *The Shaping of Modern France*, pp. 265-273.

41. The major source for this section on Denmark has been W. Glyn Jones, *Denmark* (New York, Washington: Praeger Press, 1970).

42. G. M. Trevelyan suggests that the Danish devotion to trial by jury, which was practiced in the Danelaw villages in England, paved the way for English adoption of the jury system after the Norman invasion. See *A Shortened History of England*, pp. 81-82.

43. The coalescence of land was accompanied by a tendency toward specialization in agriculture based on serfdom, and, as Wallerstein attributes to Marion Malowist, this reduced any opportunity for the serfs to engage in independent commerce. See *The Modern World System*, p. 307n.

44. K. B. Andersen, "Political and Cultural Development in Nineteenth Century Denmark," in *Scandinavian Democracy*, ed. J. A. Lawerys (Copenhagen: Det Danske Selskap, 1958), pp. 153-156.

45. Franklin D. Scott, *Scandinavia* (Cambridge, Mass., and London, England: Harvard University Press, 1975), pp. 129-130.

46. Andersen, "Political and Cultural Development," pp. 151-152.

47. For another example of a crusading reformer in Scandinavia, see Franklin D. Scott, *Sweden: The Nation's History* (Minneapolis: University of Minnesota Press, 1977). Agricultural modernization in Sweden owes much to Rutger Maclean, who, learning from the Danish example, decreed reforms on his land and spread revolutionary techniques by example.

48. Andersen, "Political and Cultural Development," pp. 156-157.

49. Scott, *Scandinavia*, pp. 114-122, 129.

50. For a brief recent description of the state of agriculture in present-day Denmark, see Andrew Boyd, "Denmark in the World," *The Economist Survey* 3 (January 28, 1979):1-30.

4
The State and Collective Farming in the Soviet Union and China

Thomas P. Bernstein

Introduction

Today, sixteen states are ruled by Marxist-Leninist parties. In addition, several states, mainly in Africa, have leaders with Marxist-Leninist commitments. How the leaders of such countries modernize their agriculture and deal with their food problems is of obvious importance given their number and population. This is true first and foremost of the subjects of this essay, the Soviet Union and the People's Republic of China. In the case of China, whether its government can continue to feed its nearly one billion people without relying to a much greater extent than previously on grain imports is of fundamental importance to world food security. In the case of the Soviet Union, large-scale imports from the United States in 1972 and after have already had a vivid and disruptive impact on world grain markets and are blamed for the tripling of prices from 1972 to 1974.

Whether Marxist-Leninist states have the capacity effectively to modernize agriculture and solve their food problems has long been doubted. A powerful school of thought insists on the fundamental incompatibility of Marxist ideology on the one hand and the realities of peasant life and requisites of rural development on the other.[1] This school points to the Stalin era in Russia, to the troubles with collectivization of agriculture in Eastern Europe in the 1950s, and to the failures of the Chinese Great Leap Forward (1958-60) to substantiate its case. At the same time, other studies suggest that such East European countries as Hungary have succeeded in bringing about prosperity and growth through collective farming.[2] Similarly, the literature on China shows that with such exceptions as the Great Leap Forward,

I am indebted to the Fairbank Center for East Asian Research at Harvard University for financial support and to William Fierman for research assistance.

considerable successes have been attained in increasing agricultural output. Even the Soviet Union, whose agricultural system has had the worst reputation of all, has scored significant successes in agriculture since Stalin's death in 1953.

The problems that have arisen in the agricultural sectors of communist regimes have had a common source; namely, the tendency of Marxist-Leninist elites to define their role with regard to agriculture in highly interventionist terms. Guided by a sense of mission and urgency largely derived from ideology, they have embarked on intensive programs of societal reconstruction along socialist lines. In agriculture, they have not been content to use the conventional tools available to the state to influence rural life. Not content with the redistribution of rural property, they have largely abolished private property altogether—by organizing collective and state farms. Similarly, displeased with indirect inducements and sanctions as means to guide the agricultural economy, they have often used the collective farms to take on direct responsibility for the planning of production, the management of productive processes, and the disposal of agricultural products. In the process, the state's power vis-à-vis agriculture has expanded enormously. If in many less developed countries the problem is that the state is ineffectual in penetrating the villages to implement change, then in Marxist-Leninist systems the problem is that the state has had too much power.

State power can, of course, be used in any number of ways; the point is that in Marxist-Leninist systems it tends to be used in ways inimical to efficient agricultural growth. For instance, there is a tendency to overcentralize decision making. Effective farming requires a modicum of local autonomy, local involvement, and local initiative, fundamentally because the variability of agricultural tasks requires on-the-spot decision making. Typically, bureaucrats at administrative levels high above the farms lack the information and the flexibility to adjust plans to local circumstances, which vary greatly and can change as rapidly as the weather. Or, these states may override peasant interests to the extent that (as the Chinese press sometimes puts it) "the peasants' enthusiasm for production is dampened." The damaging effects of communist states' dominance over agriculture have been such significant features of these regimes that it is not unfair to say that the central problem of Marxist-Leninist states in relation to agriculture has been the state.[3]

In all Marxist-Leninist systems, the state has exerted strong domination over agriculture. There are crucial differences, however, among the systems. Communist states have differed in the severity and rigidity of the controls they have imposed, in part because the mix of goals that they have sought to attain by gaining control has also differed. Moreover, communist states have changed over time. In some cases, substantial accommodation between the state and the peasantry has been attained—as strict control has given way to partial autonomy on the collective farms and as economic levers have replaced administrative commands. Such differences are by no means trivial, since it is likely that agricultural performance is associated with the willingness of a Marxist-Leninist state to moderate its domination. To be sure, agricultural performance—as measured, say, by grain output— is a function of many variables. These range from climate to environmental conditions, but of particular importance is the capacity and willingness of the communist state to supply modern inputs. Thus, the point about accommodation to local needs and interests is only a partial explanation for agricultural performance, but it is an important one, as will emerge in the course of this chapter.

In comparing the Soviet Union and China, it is fair to say that the PRC has generally succeeded in striking a better balance between the state's claims and local interests than the Soviet Union has. The reasons for this difference are very complex; they are rooted in the interplay of historical legacies, situational variables, and policy choices. The brief historical analysis that follows is obviously in no sense exhaustive. It is organized into three sections: First, we will compare the collectivization of agriculture in the two countries (1929-32 and 1953-56). This will be followed by a section on the Stalinist agricultural system and the efforts by the two successive regimes, those of Khrushchev (1953-64) and Brezhnev (1964-), to cope with the legacy that Stalin left. The third section will examine Chinese agricultural development from the Great Leap Forward (1958-60) to the present in the light of the Soviet case.

Collectivization of Agriculture

In both countries, the revolutions that brought the communist parties to power entailed the breaking up of larger agricultural units and their distribution among land-hungry peasants. The result was the over-whelming predominance of small-holder agriculture, farming being done largely with traditional technology and methods. Yet, in the course of a few short years in both countries, small-holder farming was replaced by collective farming. The 25 million Soviet peasant households were organized into roughly 240,000 collective farms, and the 110 million Chinese peasant households into about 750,000 higher-stage producers' cooperatives. The process by which this dramatic change came about differed dramatically. In the Soviet Union, it was in the nature of a violent confrontation between state and peasantry. Relying heavily on force, the state imposed its will on the peasants. In China, the process was far less violent, and although there were elements of conflict and coercion, these were balanced by elements of peasant participation and cooperation in the process of change.[4]

Why did the two ruling elites decide to embark on programs of collectivization? In both countries, economic development goals were prominent, but these were conditioned by ideological assumptions. Their Marxist-Leninist beliefs led both elites to identify modernity with large-scale farming. Both believed that small-holder agriculture was inherently not viable and would inevitably be replaced either by large-scale capitalist or large-scale socialist farming. In either case, backward, inefficient, scattered, irrational petty-bourgeois peasant farming would give way to modern, efficient units that would benefit from economies of scale and would be able to make use of modern inputs, release labor for industry, and raise output far above the prevailing levels.

The beliefs of these elites predisposed them to favor change in a socialist direction, but ideology alone cannot account for the adoption of state promotion of collective farming. In the case of the Soviet Union, Leninist ideology in the mid-1920s offered a much wider range of choice than the policies adopted a few years later would indicate. Of particular note was Bukharin's evolutionary program of building rural socialism with marketing cooperatives.[5] China adopted the Stalinist model that emerged from the late 1920s, thus constricting her choices to some extent. But actually, the Chinese significantly modified Soviet practice.

It is necessary to look at the collectivization decisions in the context of the economic development programs adopted in the first five-year plans of both countries. These programs gave absolute priority to industrial growth, particularly heavy industry, but also envisaged significant agricultural growth linked to large-scale farming. In the Soviet Union, plans called for the state to supply machinery, especially tractors, to the key grain-producing regions. Here, collective farms and state-owned "grain factories" would be established. The rising output would provide the state with a reliable source of grain with which to feed the industrializing cities and buy modern equipment abroad.[6] In China, whose industrial capacities were significantly smaller than those of the Soviet Union (if 1928 is compared with 1953), the idea of relating growth in collective farming to the supply of modern inputs was not at all feasible. Hence, amidst considerable debate, a decision was made to promote collective farming even in the absence of modern inputs, on the grounds that the reorganization of traditional inputs itself would lead to large increases in output.[7] The Chinese believed that the merger of scattered holdings would by itself raise efficiency and permit the introduction of more modern farming practices. They believed the collective units would permit mobilization of underemployed rural labor on projects such as irrigation networks, thereby raising yields. In the Soviet Union, too, as the pace of collectivization gained momentum in 1929, with a consequent lag in the supply of machinery, similar rationales were offered to justify collective farming.

In both countries, collectivization was supposed to lead to increased output, but in the Soviet Union this goal was eclipsed by another goal related to economic development: that of maximizing the extraction of marketable grain and other agricultural products. Soviet leaders assumed that a substantial surplus above and beyond rural minimum needs existed, held primarily by "rich peasants" (kulaks) and middle peasants. They assumed these peasants were not prepared to sell at prices the state was willing to offer. The state defined its interest as the acquisition of that surplus at low prices. Then, because peasant incomes would be kept low, industry would not be required to manufacture goods to satisfy increasing rural demand, but could concentrate on producers' goods. Acquisition of the surplus would make it possible to feed a growing urban labor force and to export grain in exchange for modern technology. As Stalin put it in 1928, the peasants would be required to pay a "tribute" for industrialization. The collective farms became the institution for the collection of the tribute, since government control of the output of the collective farms was obviously much easier to achieve than control of millions of individual peasant households.[8]

Indeed, during the collectivization years, the proportion of the grain crop procured by the state rose precipitously—more than doubling—even when the harvest fell or remained stagnant.[9] Enforcement of the state's delivery quotas on terms highly disadvantageous to the peasants became the hallmark of the Stalinist collective farm system. During the early years, the procurement system was enforced in extremely arbitrary and chaotic ways, and toward the end of the period, in 1932-33, it contributed to a famine that claimed an estimated five million lives.[10] Stalin's extraction program was the central reason why the imposition of collective farming on the peasantry virtually took on the form of a civil war.

The thesis that Stalin's rigorous "pumping out" of resources from the agricultural sector made a decisive contribution to industrialization has been widely accepted, but has actually come under sharp challenge in recent years. The fact of the exploitation of the agricultural sector is not in dispute; whether it made much of a contribution is. The issue is whether the extremely high cost of collectivization did not in fact outweigh the benefits. Peasants opposed to collectivization slaughtered millions of farm animals; the cattle population of the country dropped by half between 1929 and 1933, as did the number of horses. This destruction compelled the state to step up the manufacture of tractors to replace lost draft animals. Thus, during the collectivization years, there was apparently a net flow of resources from the urban to the rural sector, contrary to what has been believed. For the later Stalin period, inadequate data have not made it possible to resolve the issue, but scholarly debate as to the economic rationality of the entire Stalinist program of industrialization at the expense of agriculture continues.[11]

In China, the goal of gaining control over agricultural output and over the marketing of surpluses at state-determined prices also played a major role in collectivization. But the extent to which state acquisition of surpluses was pushed was sharply constrained by the state's goal of stimulating increases in output. In Stalin's Russia it was possible to sustain a growing urban population on the surplus squeezed from a largely stagnant agriculture, but in China this was not the case. The problem, as K. C. Yeh put it, was to "create a large surplus in the first place."[12] In order to spur production, the willing cooperation of the peasants was required. Hence, care had to be taken both to limit the size of state purchases of grain and other products and to pay reasonable prices. In fact, considerable conflict developed between the regime and the peasants over this issue, particularly in 1954-55, when state prices were lower than they have been since and when administrative pressures to make up for shortfalls in disaster areas caused excessive state purchases. In sharp contrast to the Soviet case, however, the Chinese state immediately responded by lowering the delivery quotas slightly and by attempting to rationalize the program. This is one instance of repeated Chinese willingness to restore a balance between the interests of the state and those of the peasants.[13]

In both countries, the operative goals of collectivization emerged in the context of sharply differing elite perceptions of the peasants. To be sure, their common ideology did provide some shared perspectives, such as the assumption that small-holder agriculture, if left alone, will give rise to a politically threatening class of rich or "capitalist" farmers. But the formative experiences of the two elites imbued them with fundamentally differing views of the peasants as a whole.[14]

In the Russian case, the peasants' spontaneous rising in 1917 played a major role in propelling the urban-based Bolsheviks to power. But already in 1918, as the Civil War broke out, conflict arose between peasants and Bolsheviks, since the latter were compelled to rely on grain requisitioning to sustain the Red Army and the famine-stricken cities. This experience convinced much of the Soviet elite that the only way to deal with the peasants was to subject them to tight state control. During the era of the New Economic Policy (1921-27), antipeasant attitudes were to some extent submerged as alternate currents, such as Bukharin's conception of cooperative regime-peasant relations, came to the fore. Yet, with the onset of grain delivery crises in the late 1920s, Civil War attitudes reemerged as many Bolsheviks seemed ready to believe the worst about peasant sabotage. There was a readiness among committed Communists to accept the proposition that peasant independence had to be crushed, by force if necessary, in order to build a new, socialist society. In contrast, Chinese elite values had formed under the different conditions of a rural road to power. The success of the Chinese Communists had rested, to a significant extent, on the development of elite capacities to secure the cooperation and participation of peasants in the revolutionary enterprise. The distrust and hostility toward peasants found in the Soviet elite was thus largely absent in China.

The process of collectivization reflected the differences in elite attitudes and the different goal-mixes, but they were also shaped by significant differences in organizational strength and support within the villages. On the eve of collectivization, proregime leadership forces were quite weak in the Soviet countryside. This was a product both of the urban-centered revolution, which had not entailed the kind of protracted village-level organization-building characteristic of the Chinese case, and of the long hiatus between revolution and onset of socialist transformation in the late 1920s. During this period, economic recovery had given rise to a measure of social differentiation within the small-holder village. More prosperous peasants often occupied positions of leadership and economic power, exercising informal authority in the old village communes, which had gained a new lease on life since the revolution, and holding formal posts in the village soviets. Since they had the most to lose from collectivization and its associated policies, they became political targets. The decision of the Soviet government forcibly to deport hundreds of thousands of kulak families was, in part, a decision physically to remove this village leadership. At the same time, it was difficult to recruit and maintain new leaders, because loyalty to the village was not easily reconciled with loyalty to the regime. Consequently, much of the burden of organizing collective farms fell on higher-level officials and urbanites sent to the villages.

More broadly, the deprivations with which Soviet collectivization was associated undercut the regime's ability to mobilize village-level social

80 Thomas P. Bernstein

support. In principle, formation of a village-wide collective farm has a redistributive effect: poor peasants benefit from the superior means of production contributed to the collective by better-off middle peasants and, in this case, confiscated from the expropriated rich peasants (kulaks). But as it became clear that the prime beneficiary of collectivization was not the poor peasantry but the state, this incentive to support the change lost its force. Inadequate horizontal social support and leadership reinforced the dominant reality that collectivization was a change imposed on the village by the state.

The Chinese revolutionary process, which included the violent overthrow and partial killing of the old rural elite, yielded a base of organization and support within the village. Because the completion of land reform was followed almost immediately by the onset of socialist transformation—particularly the formation of simple forms of collective farming—there was no long hiatus during which the small-holder economy could take hold. Village leaders recruited for struggle against landlords were converted to the tasks of socialist transformation even before they had opportunities to prosper under the small-holder system. Besides, their responsiveness to the new tasks was not undercut as much as in Russia by harsh extractive policies. In addition, significant recruitment and training of cadres and activists took place. As as result, the change could be mediated through local leaders, whose active support was a crucial element in the relatively smooth transition.

Social support for collectivization came mainly from poor peasants, who, despite land redistribution, lacked draft animals and tools to farm on their own and could benefit from the redistributive effect. This incentive created a conflict of interest with middle peasants, who naturally wanted to be compensated for contributing their superior assets. A large, distinct class of rich peasants had not developed in China; in Russia (it is worth adding), the kulaks, though more numerous, were also differentiated from middle peasants only in degree.[15] The state worked out a strategy to protect middle-peasant interests by having the collectives pay them for inputs other than labor, since it was anxious to keep them producing. During the "high tide" of 1955-56, when most peasants were collectivized, the regime threw its weight behind the poor peasants, who constituted its social base. They did so by largely abandoning this scheme, fearing middle-peasant dominance of the collectives. The latter had to be pressured into joining, resulting in a good deal of resentment and discontent. But the point is that in China, collectivization was accomplished by the effective mobilization of intravillage pressures rather than by simply unleashing the power of the state on the village.

Finally, a word about the scope of the change. When Marxist-Leninist systems initiate campaigns of social transformation, enormous pressures for advance are generated in the hierarchies as the prospect of breaking through some hitherto intractable social problem takes hold. In the collectivization breakthrough campaigns of 1929-30 and 1955-56, intensive pressures to go "left" were generated. These, unless restrained by the top-level authorities, could easily get out of hand. In both countries' campaigns these pressures translated themselves into rates of collective farm establishment that far exceeded all plans. In China, the rapid changes could be absorbed (with some difficulty) because of the structural foundations of local leadership and already existing smaller collective units. In Russia, the strains proved so great that Stalin was forced to call a temporary halt. One reason was that limits to the advance had not been set. As a result, completely unmanageable, giant collective farms were set up under the motto "the bigger the better." In the new *kolkhozy* (collective farms), all property was socialized. Yet, from the peasants' point of view, a private sector—a private plot of land and livestock—was absolutely essential as a source of minimum subsistence, given the uncertainties associated with income from the collective sector.[16] But a private sector was not guaranteed until much later; and, in the meantime, the chaotic implementation of radical change magnified peasant anxiety and resistance. In China, similar leftist tendencies were generated in 1955-56, but, by and large, they were held in check by restraints imposed by policy makers.

What is particularly noteworthy about the Chinese case is that the establishment of collective units was often aligned with natural social units. As Parish writes, "Using local political activists and shaping new collectives around prerevolutionary villages and village neighborhoods, the regime built on existing community strengths."[17] The alignment of old with new collectivities gave strength and substance to the new, facilitating the difficult process of consolidation. In Russia, because of the wide rift between the peasants and the regime, preexisting natural solidarities could not be mobilized on behalf of the change. The traditional village communes seem to have disappeared during collectivization. Natural villages survived and became part of or even coextensive with the new collective farms, but whatever the potential for local initiative of the old villages, it was crushed in a process that Lewin calls "statization." Collectivization, he writes, resulted in the loss of the "regulators and stimulants of previous peasant life."

> The peasants' usual urge to save and accumulate was replaced by an equally strong urge to consume everything. His usual care and worry about his farm was replaced by apathy and "production nihilism." The

peasant was waiting to be guided, expecting to be told what to do.... The government was forced, or felt itself forced, to undertake salvage operations that led it ever deeper into the trap of growing interference in all phases and details of agricultural production and organization.[18]

These different patterns of collectivization are reflected in a variety of economic indicators. Two of these are presented in Table 4.1, namely grain output and per capita grain consumption in the rural areas.

The Stalin Era and Its Long-Term Legacy

Having passed through the trials of the collectivization campaigns, the Stalinist collective farm system settled into a pattern that persisted until the dictator's death in 1953. This pattern was defined by the obligation of the collective farms (literally labeled the "First Commandment") to meet the state's procurement quotas. Throughout the Stalin era, these quotas were characterized by unreasonably large size, by prices that did not cover the cost of production, and by irrational management that penalized successful collectives with additional quotas.[19] As Khrushchev put it in 1953, "No sooner does a kolkhoz rise above the level of its neighbors than the procuring agencies proceed to trim it, just as a gardener trims bushes in the garden with his shears."[20]

Limited accommodation of the peasants to this exploitative system was made possible by the existence of the private plot, privately owned livestock, and a collective farm market, at which peasants could sell part of their privately produced output (at high free-market prices) to town dwellers.[21] Since income in kind or money from the collective sector was minimal, peasants were compelled to put in prescribed amounts of time on the collective fields. These arrangements enabled the collective farm peasantry to survive, but left them in a resentful, sullen, and alienated state of mind.[22]

The conditions under which the collective farms functioned required a high degree of centralized bureaucratic control. Because of the zero-sum nature of the conflict of interests between the peasants and the state, the former had to be deprived of any and all initiative. Hence, the process of "statization" that originated during the collectivization period became institutionalized. The collective farm officials themselves were deprived of significant power. Early on, ownership of machinery was vested in machine-tractor stations, which functioned as agencies of control. Higher-level organs tightly circumscribed the powers of the kolkhoz chairman, inundating him with orders and demands. Even the simplest farming processes had to be prescribed from above. The result

TABLE 4.1
Grain Output and Rural Per Capita Consumption During the Collectivization Years
in the Soviet Union and China

	Soviet Union			China	
Year	Output	Consumption	Year	Output	Consumption
	(million MT)	(kg.)		(million MT)	(kg.)
1928	73	250.4	1952	161	n.a.
1929	72	245.1	1953	164	218
1930	84	241.5	1954	166	227.3
1931	66	233.9	1955	180	239.4
1932	63	214.6	1956	188	258.9
1933	67	n.a.	1957	191	n.a.

Sources: (1)Grain Output; U.S., Congress, Joint Economic Committee, Comparisons of the United States and Soviet Economies, 86th Cong., 1959, p.231. R. M. Field and J. A. Kilpatrick, "Chinese Grain Production: An Interpretation of the Data," China Quarterly, no. 74, June 1978, p.380. (2)Soviet grain consumption; Iu. Moshkov, Zernovaia Problema v Gody Sploshnoi Kollektivizatsii Sel'skogo Khoziaistva (The Grain Problem in the Years of Mass Collectivization)(Moscow: Izdatel'stvo Moskovskogo Universiteta, 1966), p.136. (3)Chinese grain consumption; N. R. Chen, Chinese Economic Statistics: A Handbook for Mainland China (Chicago: Aldine Publishing Co., 1967), p.437. (4)The Soviet consumption data are from an archive source. The Chinese data, which include soybean consumption, are not as reliable; cf. Peter Schran, The Development of Chinese Agriculture, 1950-1959 (Urbana: University of Illinois Press, 1969), pp.136-37.

was the growth of a vast and unwieldy bureaucratic apparatus, which
Lewin characterizes as "incompetent, capricious, and often self-
seeking."[23] Because of the prevailing distrust of the peasants and of local
cadres, a "work style" (as the Chinese would put it) developed in which
higher-level officials descended on the kolkhozy to "knock heads
together, tighten the screws, and straighten things out."[24] Rigid orders
from above had to be followed; if the plan prescribed that the harvest was
to begin on July 1, it began on July 1, even if the grain was still green.[25]
Above all, for an entire generation, the rural bureaucracy was imbued
with the "deeply rooted feeling that the kolkhozes and the peasant exist
to be exploited, to be prevented from using for their own purposes
produce which officials are obliged to secure for the state. There is no
equivalent of this in other sectors of the economy."[26]

At the level of the kolkhoz itself, the chairman, brigade leaders, and
other cadres were sharply differentiated from ordinary peasants by
higher pay. Some were outsiders; others were locals—often younger,
educated peasants coopted into the system. Among these cadres, a work
style of submissiveness to higher authority developed. The rare
exceptions were those who sought to protect, to the extent possible, the
interests of the ordinary kolkhoz members who had nominally elected
them. Post-Stalin Soviet literature describes the dilemmas in which such
officials found themselves.[27] More generally, the peasants were excluded
from any and all participation in decisions affecting their lives; the
result was to inculcate in them a sense of complete irresponsibility.[28]
Conversely, officials looked upon the kolkhoz peasant "as a child who is
hard to educate or as a lazy simpleton, who must be taught truths, which
the peasant of course knows from childhood on."[29]

So, of course, the Stalinist agricultural system was not very
productive, as Table 4.2 indicates. In evaluating it, two additional
factors must be kept in mind. One is that in the Stalin era as a whole,
apart from machinery supplies, investment in agriculture was seriously
neglected (e.g., with respect to fertilizer, irrigation installations, roads,
etc.). The other factor is the devastating impact of World War II.
Scholars agree, however, that the Stalinist system itself was largely
responsible for the fact that in the early 1950s, Soviet agriculture was
performing at precollectivization levels with regard to such indicators as
yields, livestock holdings, and per capita agricultural output.[30] Table
4.2 shows gross output of grain as well as yields during the Stalin years.

Post-Stalin Revitalization Policies

Stalin's successors recognized the deep-seated crisis of agriculture.
Economically, a growing urban-industrial sector could simply not

TABLE 4.2
Grain Output and Yields in the Soviet Union
During the Stalin Era

Year	Output	Yield
	(million MT)	(centners/hectare)
1928	73	7.9
1934	67	n.a.
1935	69	
1936	60	
1937	92	9.3 ⎫ 7.07
1938	71	
1939	n.a.	n.a.
1940	83	8.6
1941-44	n.a.	n.a.
1945	47	5.6
1946	40	4.6
1947	66	7.3
1948	67	6.7
1949	70	6.9
1950	81	7.9
1951	79	7.4
1952	92	8.6
1953	83	7.8

Sources: U.S., Congress, Joint Economic Committee, op. cit., p. 231. Data for 1945-48 are reported in M. Gardner Clark, "Soviet Agricultural
Policy," in Harry C. Shaffer, ed., Soviet Agriculture (New York: Praeger Publishers, 1977), p.25.
Clark gives higher figures for 1937 and 1940 than
those used in this table, 97 and 96 million tons,
respectively. Grain yield figures are in
Sel'skoe Khoziaistvo SSSR--Statisticheskii
Sbornik (Agriculture of the USSR--Statistical Collection) (Moscow: Statistika, 1971), p.26, except
for the 1935-38 average, which is in U.S., Congress, Joint Economic Committee, op. cit., p.211.

coexist indefinitely with a stagnant and depressed agricultural sector. Politically, popular demands for a higher standard of living had to be at least partially met, if only because the new leaders rejected heavy reliance on terror.

The two post-Stalinist regimes of Khrushchev and Brezhnev made a transition from extractive to growth-oriented agricultural strategies. One turning point is 1953, but Khrushchev's efforts faltered after 1958, and new difficulties in agriculture contributed to his downfall in 1964. Some observers believe that it is only since 1965, under Brezhnev, that the most decisive and sustained efforts have been made to revitalize agriculture. The fundamental problem has been how to convert the coercive, extraction-oriented bureaucratic apparatus into one oriented to growth and efficiency. A full solution still eludes the Soviet system. An optimal accommodation between the state and the agricultural producers has still not been attained.

Other major changes have occurred, however. The oppressive procurement system of the Stalin period has been decisively reformed since 1953. Quotas were rationalized, and state prices increased sharply. Between 1952 and 1964, the money flow from state procurements increased six times, from 2.5 billion rubles to 15 billion.[31] Khrushchev had already incurred a "small deficit" in the state budget, resulting from discrepancies between prices paid by the state to growers and retail prices. Under Brezhnev, the Soviet Union came to enjoy "the dubious distinction of paying the largest subsidy in the world for a still irregular and uncertain supply of inferior foodstuffs." In 1974, the annual subsidy amounted to 16 million rubles, or about 85 to 90 percent of the overt defense budget![32]

These changes have made possible very substantial increases in the income of collective farmers. "A revolution in household income" has occurred.[33] According to one Soviet survey, by 1967, the proportion of peasant income derived from the private plot was reduced to 47 percent (from 71 percent in 1953). Undoubtedly, significant further reductions have taken place since then as collective income has risen.[34]

Peasant security has increased. Until the mid-1960s, the peasants were residual claimants to variable farm income; since then, regular wages have been paid and a social security system has even been begun. According to one author, kolkhoz wages and bonuses have risen faster than urban incomes; if income from the private plots is taken into account, rural-urban income differentials may now be similar to those of other industrialized countries.[35] This is not meant to imply that the level of services and availability of goods in the rural areas come even close to those in the cities.[36]

Subsidization of prices paid to farmers is only one aspect of a pattern of vastly increased state expenditures in the agricultural sector. Investment in agriculture financed by the state tripled under Khrushchev and has since experienced still greater growth. "The Soviet Union is now investing about five times as much as the United States in agriculture."[37] Agriculture's share in total fixed investment has grown to over 25 percent; it amounts to the equivalent of $45 to $50 billion per year. A "massive transfer of resources" has been taking place since 1965 to implement "an intensified program of mechanization, chemicalization, land improvement, price support, material incentives, and industrialization of agriculture."[38] Vast land improvement projects are in progress, and the level of mechanization of agriculture has risen enormously.[39]

The resources poured into the agricultural sector since 1953 have produced substantial results. Between 1953 and 1976, agricultural output grew at an annual average rate of 3.4 percent, while the rate of population increase was only 1.4 percent.[40] Yet, as Table 4.3 shows, grain output has not been stable. It has suffered from sharp fluctuations. Poor harvests, such as those of 1964, 1972, and 1975, have necessitated massive imports. The purpose of these is not so much to prevent bread shortages as to maintain livestock herds, whose decimation is politically unpopular.[41] One indication of the fact that the Soviet Union is now among the developed nations is this rising consumer demand for high-quality agricultural products, such as meat, fruit, vegetables, and dairy products. It is in meeting these demands that chronic difficulties exist. But perhaps the most important performance judgment made by western economists is simply to point to the "inordinate absorption of current resources in Soviet agriculture to produce a still inadequate and highly costly output."[42] There appears to be a consensus among observers that much more could have been achieved. Why this gap?

One explanation is basically unfavorable climatic and soil conditions.[43] Another explanation is that, despite enormous investments, Soviet agriculture is still undercapitalized in comparison with the United States. In particular, there is an acute shortage of all-weather roads and of storage facilities that leads to enormous spoilage and waste. A Soviet economist suggests that the "annual shortfall in the grain harvest as a result of the shortage of agricultural machinery, which prevents execution of basic production processes within optimal agrotechnical time limits, is 35-40 million tons."[44] This shortfall appears to be caused not so much by a shortage of machinery as such as by inadequate repair facilities, which are a chronic and severe problem. This difficulty would seem to suggest that the "traditional (i.e.,

TABLE 4.3
Grain Output in the Soviet Union in the
Post-Stalin Era

Year	Grain Output	Percent Change Previous Year
	(million MT)	
1953	83	
1954	86	+ 4%
1955	104	+21%
1956	124	+19%
1957	103	-17%
1958	135	+31%
1959	120	-11%
1960	126	+ 5%
1961	131	+ 4%
1962	140	+ 7%
1963	108	-23%
1964	152	+41%
1965	121	-20%
1966	171	+41%
1967	148	-13%
1968	170	+15%
1969	162	- 5%
1970	187	+15%
1971	181	- 3%
1972	168	- 7%
1973	223	+33%
1974	196	-12%
1975	140	-29%
1976	224	+60%

Sources: U.S., Congress, Joint Economic Committee, op. cit., p. 231; USDA, Economic Research
Service, Agricultural Statistics of Eastern Europe
and the Soviet Union, 1950-1970 (1973), p.31;
U.S., Congress, Joint Economic Committee, Soviet
Economy in New Perspective, 94th Cong., 1976,
p.582; and J. R. Millar, "The Prospects for Soviet
Agriculture," Problems of Communism, vol. 26,
no. 3, May-June 1977, p.7.

Stalinist) low priority of the rural-agricultural sector in the planning process" has still not been overcome.[45]

The Stalin Legacy

What, then, of the hypothesis that Stalinist bureaucratic structures and habits are imposing constraints on more efficient agricultural growth? To begin with, one can ask to what extent higher administrative levels still arbitrarily interfere with farm-level decision making. Early on, in 1955, a decree was issued to give those in charge much more independence. But certainly during the Khrushchev era, high-level interference continued, in large part because of Khrushchev's own interventionist style of leadership. Thus, when he launched a campaign to plant corn (maize) and sugar beets, sowings of these crops were forced on areas with unsuitable conditions, "without thinking of the consequences, without economic analysis."[46] As Volin puts it, in evaluating the Khrushchev era, "Once again we come up against a crucial failing of agricultural operations—excessive regimentation and interference with managers of farm enterprises selected by the government itself."[47]

With the ouster of Khrushchev in 1965, the new leadership announced reforms which prompted the Minister of Agriculture of the Russian state to boast that for the first time in more than thirty years no outside authority was trying to impose cropping schemes and methods on farm managers and agronomists.[48] Yet in 1976, the economist Alec Nove referred to "constant interference from planners and ministerial and party officials, who tell (managers) what and how to sow."[49] Officials of the Ministry of Procurements are still charged with seeing to it that farm sowing plans are "adequate to meet contractual obligations."[50] Thus, while the Brezhnev era has been characterized by a more predictable, consistent, and rational style of leadership, farm officials continue to be under the direction of bureaucratic hierarchies that have, if anything, become more elaborate and complex in recent years.[51]

Aside from continuing higher-level tutelage, the operating units themselves suffer from inherent inefficiencies. In the view of western specialists, the primary cause is their excessive size, which evidently stems from an ideological faith in unlimited economies of scale. During the Stalin era, the collective farms were actually fairly small, averaging 70-80 households. But since 1950, amalgamations have led to enormous increases in size. In 1970, a kolkhoz consisted of an average of 431 households with 3,000 hectares of land. A *sovkhoz* (state farm) was at least twice as large in terms of land and often far larger still.[52]

The subdivisions of these huge units are often as big as the kolkhozy of the 1930s and usually lack autonomous decision-making power. The central problem, according to the economist Gardner Clark, is that of supervising labor. Particularly because of the sequential nature of the agricultural production cycle, the quality of performance at the beginning of the cycle is not apparent until the harvest, but by then it is difficult to fix responsibility. Thus, careful supervision is essential, but the huge size and dispersion of the labor force make this difficult to achieve. In the United States, Clark suggests, the owner-operator, bearing responsibility for profit and loss, will exercise unsupervised initiative. If rain threatens to damage hay left in the field, he will work at night; an initiative "almost unheard of in the Soviet Union." Despite the sharp rise in material incentives, Soviet agriculture has not solved the problem of supervision because of "uneconomically large units" worked by "relatively labor-intensive production methods." In the United States, the problem of supervision has been solved by largely eliminating the hired labor force.[53] In Russia, detailed norms are set but often backfire: the tractor driver is paid for the area plowed; hence, he will plow in a shallow manner unless a supervisor tells him to plow more deeply.[54] As Yanov, a former Soviet journalist says, "One kolkhoznik tills the soil, another sows, a third cultivates, and a fourth reaps—and not one of them is responsible for anything."[55] Extremely elaborate structures of supervision have been erected: "Who does not keep an eye on the work of the plowman! The accountant, the supervisor, the brigade-leader, the representative of People's Control, the Village soviet, the agronomist, the agitator, and even the volunteer quality controller."[56] Yet shoddy work is apparent everywhere.

For many years, an alternative mode of decentralized farming has been available in the Soviet Union—the "unsupervised link" (beznariadnoe zveno). The idea is simply to entrust a small group of farm workers, usually ten to twenty persons, with equipment and land and to make them responsible for the entire production cycle. Their reward would come from the end-result rather than from the performance of specific tasks. Instead of being told what to do, they would exercise their own initiative. Such independent "link" experiments began during the late Stalin era. According to their proponents, dramatic improvements result, both in labor and productivity per unit of land. They have argued that the autonomous link system gives its members the sense of being "masters of the land" that was lost during collectivization. Under the link system, "we would be able to work efficiently and productively without any controllers and auditors. . . . If only permanent plots were given to us, we would guarantee you, even in the worst drought years, a minimum of five quintals of wheat per hectare."[57] But the autonomous link system has not gone beyond the experimental stage and has, at times, been repudiated. There are some real problems with such a reform, one being the adaptability of a largely elderly, female, and unskilled labor force. It is difficult to escape the conclusion, however, that distrust of unsupervised local initiative, fear that the link system bears too close a resemblance to private farming, and fear for their jobs by supervising bureaucrats are the real obstacles to widespread adoption of this reform.[58]

In the absence of a more decentralized, participatory mode of farming, the gap that arose during the Stalin era between the rural elite and the ordinary peasants and farm workers persists. Even Soviet sociologists have documented the apathy, low involvement, and low participation of ordinary kolkhoz members.[59] The present system has other adverse consequences: it is one factor in the massive flight to the cities of the "educated, the technically trained, the young."[60] The reasons for this do not lie in the superior material attractiveness of cities alone. According to a Soviet study, rural youth leave because they feel that they are "hired laborers" rather than "masters of the land." Young people have "a need to make independent decisions on production problems," and if this were met by adoption of the link system, it would "radically change the attitudes of young workers toward farming, making their labor interesting and appealing."[61] As it is, the rural educated leave, forcing the regime to send managers and specialists from the urban area to the farms. They often try to get away as quickly as possible, and their outsider status deepens the gap between them and the locals.[62]

In sum, then, a need exists for structural reform that will increase grassroots autonomy and participation. Whether a future Soviet leadership not socialized in the Stalin era will implement such a change remains to be seen. But one factor that may force them to do so is that the economy is increasingly beset by a labor shortage—more efficient, labor-saving ways of farming must be found.

Chinese Rural Development
in Comparative Perspective

In both China and Russia, agriculture underwent severe crises after collectivization, forcing each ruling group to respond with new policies. The sources of the crises were different. As we have seen, in the Soviet Union, the crisis stemmed from twenty-five years of a ruthlessly enforced state extraction policy. In China, the crisis came about in the Great Leap Forward (1958-60) and was the result of the state's attempt to achieve a breakthrough in agricultural production. In China, the crisis was brief and intense; in Russia, prolonged and sustained. In Russia, the leadership responded from 1953 on by switching to a growth-oriented strategy in agriculture; in China, the leadership responded in the early 1960s by radically adapting its growth-oriented policies.

In China, collectivization had been accompanied by increased agricultural output, but the increase was not as great as the leaders had hoped. Agricultural growth lagged in comparison with industrial and urban growth, barely keeping up with population growth generally. The lagging agricultural sector constrained industrial growth—not only because the food supply was not increasing rapidly enough, but because light industry, a major source of capital accumulation in China, was dependent on agricultural raw materials. It was in this context that Chinese leaders embarked on the Great Leap. They felt unable to accelerate agricultural growth by supplying modern inputs. Instead, they believed that the ever more massive application of available traditional inputs, chiefly rural labor, could lead to substantial increases in agricultural output. Surplus labor could be mobilized and converted into capital—building irrigation networks, reclaiming land, and making new tools using local resources in village industries. Other labor-intensive innovations such as close planting or expansion of multicropping could raise yields.[63]

The goals of the Leap were not irrational; implementation was.[64] The Chinese leaders forgot that a measure of restraint and of respect for local interests and social alignments had been keys to successful collectivization. Now, they upset the balance between the regime and the peasants, not by massive coercion and the imposition of a bureaucratic straightjacket, as in Russia, but by overmobilization.

To elicit an outpouring of effort, leaders aroused utopian expectations of "3 years of hardship, 100 years of happiness," and of instant leaps into communism. Partly, the collective commitment to an all-out advance resulted from a climate of intolerance toward "rightist" doubters and skeptics, especially technically trained experts. The general orientation of the movement was that it is "better to be left than right."

The peoples' communes were created in this heady political climate. Rural labor mobilization had begun in the fall of 1957 with work on water conservation projects. As the scale of the effort rose, it was felt that the existing collective units were too small to handle large-scale mobilization of labor. Pressures to enlarge the collective farms led to a movement, sanctioned by Mao in the summer of 1958, to merge the 750,000 collective farms into 25,000 peoples' communes. At least for a time, centralized management was attempted. It gave rise to even greater problems of labor supervision than those that beset Soviet collective farms. In many places, a high degree of specialization was introduced by organization of functionally specific labor brigades that cut across village boundaries. As a result, the alignment between socialist collective and natural kin and neighborhood ties was disrupted. Often, the peasant was thrown in with people from villages that did not even participate in his particular market network.[65] The communes of 1958 were highly egalitarian institutions. Richer and poorer villages were merged for income-sharing purposes, thus penalizing the former. Private plots, an important source of peasant income, were largely abolished as a "communist wind" swept through the countryside.[66] For a brief period, free distribution of food was attempted, buffered by the good harvest of 1958. But as shortages arose, so did peasant anxieties and resentments. As in the Soviet collectivization era, the peasant's minimum subsistence was being endangered.

The Leap suffered from overextension, overcentralization, and major planning errors. Commune resources proved inadequate to handle the many assigned tasks. Manpower was misallocated, upsetting timely performance of agricultural tasks. The statistical system collapsed; euphoric but false reports of bumper harvests led authorities to divert acreage to nonagricultural purposes or to raise delivery quotas to unrealistic levels. Innovations introduced without adequate testing for suitability to local conditions, such as deep plowing and close planting, did more damage than good. The "explosive growth of irrigation" in North China, prone to droughts and floods, led to "rapid and drastic elevation of the water table, and thus to potential or actual alkalization of large areas of land."[67]

The Leap precipitated a deep depression. It was aggravated in agriculture by three years of very bad weather. Grain output plummeted by more than 20 percent down to the level of the early 1950s. Severe food shortages ensued. Food imports and the distribution system prevented famine on a national basis, but how much local starvation occurred is still not clear. The collapse of the Leap also precipitated a severe crisis of morale among the leadership and the peasants. The authority of village cadres was badly shaken, endangering one of the strengths of the system: the ability to tap the initiative of responsive and respected local leaders. In some places the collective system collapsed.

China's rulers responded by retreating from the extremes of the Leap. On the local level, communes were scaled down in size. Within each commune the lowest subdivision, the production team (consisting of 20-40 households) was designated the unit of distribution and production. The private sector was restored. Projects for which resources were lacking were scrapped and irrational innovations undone. Steps were taken to combat poor cadre morale.[68]

On the national level, a drastic revision of development strategy took place when agriculture was accorded much higher priority. The regime recognized that labor mobilization alone could not develop agriculture, but that it was essential to supply large quantities of modern inputs, such as chemical fertilizer, electric pumps, varieties of agricultural machinery, and hybrid seeds. Since 1962, a substantial industry oriented to agriculture has in fact been established. Production of chemical fertilizer rose rapidly in the 1960s, and, with the purchase in 1972 of thirteen of the world's largest ammonia-urea complexes from abroad, it will rise even more rapidly in the years ahead.[69] In addition, a very important network of small-scale rural industry has been widely established in the countryside, geared to local needs of modernizing agriculture.[70] It is worth noting by way of comparison that this is one aspect of industrialization that has traditionally been neglected in the Soviet Union. Only in the Brezhnev era have collective and state farms been encouraged to organize their own processing and manufacturing enterprises.[71]

As in the Soviet Union after 1953, investment in modern inputs has made substantial growth possible. This has been achieved in China primarily by increasing yields rather than by expanding acreage, which played a much larger role in the Soviet Union. Table 4.4 provides data on grain output since 1957. Field's and Kilpatrick's finding that between 1964 and 1977 grain output grew at an average annual rate of 3.4 percent indicates a respectable rate of growth, well above that of the population. Largely because of the lost years of the Great Leap Forward, however, grain output has grown at only 2.3 percent since 1952, barely keeping ahead of population growth. In 1952, 576 million people had 279 kilograms per capita of grain; in 1977, 994 million had 287 kilograms.[72] Thus it is that China has not yet solved the problem of increasing the grain supply much above subsistence levels: to this day grain must be rationed. Grain imports, which have ranged between 4 and 8 million tons in the 1970s, play a role in feeding coastal cities and maintaining peasant incentives by enabling the government to keep procurements at a reasonable rate.[73]

One can ask to what extent the problem of accelerating agricultural growth in China is technological and to what extent sociopolitical in nature. As in Russia, the answer is mixed. Unquestionably, one cannot help being impressed by how far China has to go in fully modernizing agriculture. As of 1973, for instance, China used 57 kilograms of chemical fertilizer per hectare of land, plus "at least" 40 kilograms of organic crop nutrient; Japan, in contrast, used 425 kilograms.[74] Very

TABLE 4.4
Grain Output in China from the Great Leap Forward
to the Present

Year	Grain Output	Percent Change Previous Year
	(million MT)	
1957	191	
1958	206	+ 8 %
1959	171	-17 %
1960	156	- 9 %
1961	168	+ 8 %
1962	180	+ 7 %
1963	190	+ 6 %
1964	194	+ 2 %
1965	194	0 %
1966	215	+11 %
1967	225	+ 5 %
1968	210	- 7 %
1969	215	+ 2 %
1970	243	+13 %
1971	246	+ 1 %
1972	240	- 2 %
1973	266	+11 %
1974	275	+ 3 %
1975	284	+ 3 %
1976	285	+ .4%
1977	285	0 %

Source: Field and Kilpatrick, China Quarterly,
op. cit., p. 380.

substantial progress has been made in raising the proportion of
cultivated land that is irrigated—from 20 percent in 1952 to 46 percent in
1975—but at this rate, "it will take more than thirty years to irrigate the
entire country."[75] In the mid-1960s, the Chinese concentrated their
modernizing efforts on those areas where the potential for raising yields
was greatest; now, they are tackling areas where much more difficult and
expensive projects are required to make higher and more stable yields
possible. As Dwight Perkins noted in 1975, "The main reason why
agricultural growth has not been faster appears to be simply that China
is attempting to achieve large farm output increases under basically
unfavorable conditions."[76]

In the Soviet case, we saw that unwillingness to grant sufficient local autonomy appeared to be a constraint on more effective agriculture. In China, a balance between state control and local initiative was restored after the Great Leap Forward. By and large, it is correct to say that more participatory, decentralized approaches to collective management have prevailed in China than in any of the phases through which the Soviet Union has moved. Undoubtedly, this has made an important contribution to the successes achieved since the Great Leap Forward. At the same time, it is important to keep in mind that "Soviet-style" bureaucratic abuse has recurred in China since the Leap. Let us first sketch what appears to be the normal situation.

To begin with, rural China has not suffered from the absence of a "stable nucleus of local leadership," a problem that has beset the Soviet Union ever since collectivization.[77] The two lowest subdivisions of the communes, the team and the brigade, are staffed by local leaders, and peasants have considerable input in the selection of team leaders. At the commune and county levels, one may find outsiders, but they usually stay in office for many years, thereby becoming integrated into the local system.[78] Moreover, a sustained effort has been made to cultivate a "style of work" among higher-level officials that emphasizes consultation, discussion, and involvement of village-level cadres and peasants in decision making. Higher-level officials are expected to go down to the grassroots to investigate conditions and to listen to what the locals have to say. Much of the Maoist style of leadership is, in fact, aimed at overcoming the status gap between officials and peasants. This is exemplified by the requirement that officials regularly do manual labor. The gap between elite and peasants has by no means been closed in China, but persistent efforts to close it have led to a more rational problem-solving approach to rural development than has characterized the Soviet case (certainly during the Stalin era and, to a significant extent, since then as well).

The center of gravity of the collective system in China is much closer to the actual farm working level than in Russia. In the 1960s, the average collective farm in the Soviet Union consisted of about 400 households, but its subdivisions had little power. In China, the commune itself is far larger in terms of households, but it's lowest subdivision, the production team (consisting of 20-40 households), is less than a tenth the size of the kolkhoz. Yet as the unit of production and distribution, it plays a significant role. The autonomy of the team is, to be sure, carefully circumscribed. The higher-level agencies hand down plans that specify the amount of land to be sown to grain and sold to the state. There is flexibility in the way these targets are determined, and, normally, efforts are made to take local variation into account. The rigid ruthlessness with which targets were imposed in the Stalin era is normally not present. Higher levels monitor team compliance carefully, since there is a conflict of interest between the teams and the larger system. It is usually more profitable to grow certain cash crops than to grow grain or to invest in sideline productive activities. But within these controls, the team is free to arrange its resources, and the evidence suggests that peasants take a vigorous part in the economic decision making of the teams.[79]

As an income-sharing unit, the production team is much larger than the experimental autonomous link in the Soviet Union. But it is small enough to sustain a relationship between individual effort and the final harvest, on which collective income depends. As a natural unit whose boundaries coincide with and are reinforced by kin and neighborhood solidarities, the production unit makes it possible to bring social pressure to bear on those who lag behind. Still, even within the team, members are normally not prepared to distribute income in an egalitarian manner. Time or piece rates are used; and team members normally have some choice as to which they prefer.[80]

As in Stalin's and Khrushchev's Russia, the peasants are the residual claimants to the collective harvest, since taxes, state quotas, investments, and welfare funds are first deducted. China has not reached the stage of the Brezhnev era in which it became possible to pay a guaranteed wage and to provide a genuine social security system. But in sharp contrast to the Stalin period, when peasants had to rely on their private plots for most of their income, the collective sector in China has provided most income for peasants. Thus, private plots and private sideline undertakings provide an estimated 10-30 percent of peasant incomes.[81] According to a recent Chinese report, state purchase prices for farm products have doubled since the 1950s, while the prices of industrial goods sold in the rural areas have risen by only 28 percent. The same report also notes that the disparity between farm and industrial prices is "still fairly large at present." This affects the willingness of production teams to invest in expensive modern inputs, which may raise yields but not peasant incomes. It is thus becoming "increasingly acute as an issue."[82] Provision of adequate incentives to work for the collective has continued to constitute a significant problem. As in Russia, a built-in conflict of interest exists between the household and the collective over the size of the private sector and the time to be spent on it. By all accounts, though, Chinese peasants do work hard and effectively for the collective. Modest increases in household income as well as increased collective welfare are important reasons for this.[83]

Another distinguishing feature of the Chinese rural system is its receptiveness to innovation and the introduction of new technologies such as hybrid seeds. Since the Great Leap Forward, stress has been placed on local testing and experimentation in order to adapt innovations to local conditions. A research network has been established in many parts of the country in which scientists, technicians, and peasants cooperate to test new seeds and try out new methods.[84] Once a generally applicable technology has been found, China's rural organizational network makes its widespread adoption possible in a short time. The economist Wiens points to the "extraordinary speed with which hybrid rice went from breeding to full-scale production (as) the most spectacular example of a facility which gives China several years' edge over other countries in the rapidity with which plant breeding results can be applied."[85]

In this connection, it is important to take note of a major characteristic of rural Chinese development that differentiates it sharply from the Soviet case and also from other LDCs. This is the retention of educated peasants in the village. China has long maintained rigid and coercive controls over migration to the urban sector. As education has spread, those with primary and secondary education have remained in their home communes. This may have an important impact on the capacity to absorb new technology.[86] At the same time, one must take note of the disruption of higher education in China since the Cultural Revolution of 1966 which has deprived China of a younger generation of trained scientists. The disruption of basic research caused by the ideological and political upheavals of the Cultural Revolution is one factor that is holding up further agricultural modernization; it is an issue the post-Mao leadership is addressing vigorously. In the Soviet Union, it may be noted, biology and genetics were dominated for a generation (from the mid-1930s to 1964, when Khrushchev was ousted) by quacks such as Trofim Lysenko, whose perscriptions promised quick fixes for Russia's ailing agriculture.[87] Because of Lysenko's influence, the Soviets failed to introduce hybrid corn in the 1930s, despite its success in the United States.[88] On the other hand, the Soviet Union has trained a much larger cadre of university-level agricultural scientists and agronomists than has China. But this strength has been offset by unwillingness of specialists to stay in agriculture and because "limitations on decentralized decision making must have impeded adoption of a sequence of innovations well adapted to local circumstances."[89] The latter is precisely one of the strengths of the Chinese system.

The accommodation between the Chinese state and local interests and needs sketched in the preceding pages rests on higher-level officials rather than on legally enforceable rules. Given the hierarchical nature of the system, officials under pressure to accelerate the rate of change or to abide by "leftist" ideological definitions, may upset the balance, disregarding local interests. In the aftermath of the Cultural Revolution, for instance, efforts were made to promote a greater level of egalitarianism by merging production teams, as had happened during the Leap. Slowdowns by peasants apparently contributed to a reversal of this trend and to the constitutional affirmation of the status of the production team as the basic unit of account.[90]

Recently, in 1978, the Chinese press has again detailed a series of severe abuses in a campaign that called for reducing "unreasonable burdens on the peasantry." A variety of abuses was described, especially violation of the autonomous rights of the production teams by forcing them to adopt new methods. The first party secretary of Hupei province said:

> It is incorrect to force people in those places [where conditions are lacking] to transplant double-crop rice, plant early rice before the season, or eliminate mid-season rice. It is also incorrect to struggle against people who plant mid-season rice as though they were enemies and pull up rice seedlings which have been transplanted. The production team is the basic accounting unit. If its production falls, the peasants will go hungry and their income will decline. . . it is essential to act in light of local conditions and follow the mass line. You cannot issue compulsory orders and infringe on the production teams' right of self-determination."[91]

Other articles described arbitrary requisitioning of team resources both for unproductive construction (e.g., office buildings or guest houses for officials) and for farmland capital construction, which is a major part of the rural development effort. The result of these "unreasonable" exactions was that many production teams suffered severe losses in income.[92] A *People's Daily* editorial suggested that the "irrational burdens" placed on the peasants were the "main obstacle" to the rapid development of production, thereby implicitly attributing the stagnation in output from 1975 on to this factor (see Table 4.4). In stern terms, the editorial called for the restoration of team autonomy and for dealings between the production teams and the higher levels based on equal exchange, so "peasant income increases with the rise in production."[93]

It is not altogether clear just how widespread the abuses were, nor when they began. Quite possibly, the deterioration in the quality of government that took place in connection with the prolonged struggle for the succession to Mao Tse-tung had a role in occurrences that are strikingly reminiscent of the Stalin period. Whatever the cause, the campaign to reduce irrational burdens on the peasants suggests that the accommodation between the state and the peasantry is not a stable one. In order to put it on a sounder footing, influential voices in 1978 called for the institution of legal, contractual relations between production units:

> Why is it possible for certain leading bodies according to their own whim to order the peasants to uproot crops they have planted and grow other crops instead, without being responsible both legally and economically for the ensuing losses? . . . we need to enact special laws and set up special law courts . . . a contract system should be established.[94]

Whether such a fundamental change will take place remains to be seen; but even without it, the current campaign will undoubtedly serve to restore greater official respect for peasant interests.

In sum, the fundamental difference between Russia and China with regard to the role of the state in collective agriculture is that in China, the dominant reality has been one of comparative restraint. This has made possible a fairly decentralized, participatory approach to development, with recurring episodes of arbitrary imposition of policies from the top down. In the Soviet Union, the state has played a much more overpowering role. This has resulted in a centralized, bureaucratic approach, even while ongoing experimentation with more decentralized approaches has taken place. The problems facing the two states in defining their relations with the agricultural sector are thus quite different. In Russia, the problem is how to alter the dominant reality of an overpowering state; in China, how to prevent abuse of state power from recurring. The former requires systemic change; the latter requires the institutionalization of established norms and practices. The latter is likely to be easier to attain than the former. This essay has suggested that a restrained role of the state in agriculture is an essential requirement if socialist farming is to be effective. If this is so, then China would seem to be in a better position than the Soviet Union has been to solve her still immense agricultural problems.

Notes

1. The classic statement is David Mitrany, *Marx Against the Peasant* (London: Weidenfeld and Nicolson, 1951).

2. See Ivan Volgyes, "Hungary's Rural Transformation," *Problems of Communism* 25, no. 5 (September-October 1976):82-86.

3. Cf. K. A. Wittfogel, "Communist and Non-Communist Agrarian

Systems, with Special Reference to the USSR and Communist China: A Comparative Approach," in W. A. Douglas Jackson, ed., *Agrarian Policies and Problems in Communist and Non-Communist Countries* (Seattle and London: University of Washington Press, 1971), pp. 3-60.

4. This part of the chapter is based on my unpublished dissertation, "Leadership and Mobilization in the Collectivization of Agriculture in China and Russia: A Comparison" (Columbia University, 1970). An early published version of key points appeared in *China Quarterly*, no. 31 (July-September 1967), pp. 1-47.

5. The major work is Stephen F. Cohen, *Bukharin and the Bolshevik Revolution* (New York: A. Knopf, 1973), especially chap. 6.

6. For plan discussions, see M. Lewin, *Russian Peasants and Soviet Power* (Evanston: Northwestern University Press, 1968), chap. 13.

7. See Benedict Stavis, *The Politics of Agricultural Mechanization in China* (Ithaca: Cornell University Press, 1978), chap. 3.

8. J. V. Stalin, "Industrialization and the Grain Problem," July 9, 1928, in *Works*, vol. 2 (Moscow: Foreign Languages Publishing House, 1954), p. 167. See also Alexander Erlich, "Stalin's Views on Economic Development," in Franklyn D. Holzman, ed., *Readings on the Soviet Economy* (Chicago: Rand McNally, 1962), p. 117.

9. See Naum Jasny, *The Socialized Agriculture of the USSR* (Stanford: Stanford University Press, 1949), p. 794.

10. Dana G. Dalrymple, "The Soviet Famine of 1932-33," *Soviet Studies* 15, no. 3 (January 1964).

11. A convenient summary of the issues is in James R. Millar and Alec Nove, "Was Stalin Really Necessary? A Debate on Collectivization," *Problems of Communism* 25, no. 4 (July-August 1976):49-62.

12. K. C. Yeh, "Soviet and Chinese Industrialization Strategies," in D. W. Treadgold, ed., *Soviet and Chinese Communism: Similarities and Differences* (Seattle: University of Washington Press, 1967), p. 334.

13. See T. P. Bernstein, "Cadre and Peasant Behavior under Conditions of Insecurity and Deprivation: The Grain Supply Crisis of the Spring of 1955," in A. D. Barnett, ed., *Chinese Communist Politics in Action* (Seattle: University of Washington Press, 1969), pp. 365-399.

14. For a fine analysis that links prerevolutionary social and political structure both to revolutionary processes and to postrevolutionary change, see Theda Skocpol, "Old Regime Legacies and Communist Revolutions in Russia and China," *Social Forces* 55, no. 2 (December 1976):284-315.

15. For an acute analysis that sharply disputes the validity of Marxist-Leninist rural class analysis, see Teodor Shanin, *The Awkward Class* (Oxford: Clarendon Press, 1972).

16. It is worth noting that subsistence appears as a central determinant in peasant choices, as analyzed in James C. Scott, *The Moral Economy of the Peasant* (New Haven: Yale University Press, 1976).

17. William L. Parish, "China—Team, Brigade, or Commune?" *Problems of*

Communism 25, no. 2 (March-April 1976):65.

18. Moshe Lewin, "Society, State, and Ideology during the First Five-Year Plan," in Sheila Fitzpatrick, ed., Cultural Revolution in Russia, 1928-1931 (Bloomington: Indiana University Press, 1978), p. 63.

19. Lazar Volin, A Century of Russian Agriculture (Cambridge: Harvard University Press, 1970), Part II.

20. Ibid., p. 379.

21. High prices paid by town dwellers for privately produced agricultural products are one reason why Millar believes that a substantial flow of urban resources to the village took place during the Stalin era. See n. 11. The state also imposed delivery quotas and high taxes on such produce.

22. "The peasantry is outstandingly the most disaffected group in the Soviet system," according to a study based on post–World War II emigré interviews. See Alex Inkeles and Raymond Bauer, The Soviet Citizen (Cambridge: Harvard University Press, 1961), p. 171.

23. Moshe Lewin, Political Undercurrents in Soviet Economic Debates (Princeton: Princeton University Press, 1974), p. 220.

24. Karl-Eugen Waedekin, Fuehrungskraefte im sowjetischen Dorf (Leader-ship forces in the Soviet village) (Berlin: Duncker & Humblot, 1969), p. 159, quoting a Soviet source.

25. Richard Lorenz, Sozialgeschichte der Sowjetunion, 1917-1945 (Social history of the Soviet Union) (Frankfurt: Suhrkamp Verlag, 1976), p. 202, quoting a Soviet source.

26. Alec Nove, "Peasants and Officials," in Jerzy F. Karcz, ed., Soviet and East European Agriculture (Berkeley: University of California Press, 1967), p. 58.

27. See Fyodor Abramov, The New Life: A Day on a Collective Farm (New York: Grove Press, 1963).

28. Lorenz, Social history of the Soviet Union, p. 213.

29. Waedekin, Leadership forces in the Soviet village, p. 82, quoting a Soviet official.

30. For data and discussion, see Volin, Century of Russian Agriculture, chaps. 11 and 13.

31. Ibid., p. 399.

32. Quotations and data are from M. Gardner Clark, "Soviet Agricultural Policy," in Harry G. Shaffer, ed., Soviet Agriculture (New York: Praeger Publishers, 1977), p. 37.

33. D. W. Bronson and C. B. Krueger, "The Revolution in Soviet Farm Household Income, 1953-1967," in James R. Millar, ed., The Soviet Rural Community (Urbana, Ill.: University of Illinois Press, 1971), pp. 214-258.

34. Ibid, p. 225.

35. Clark, "Soviet Agricultural Policy," p. 38.

36. For comments on rural backwardness, see especially Theodore H. Friedgut, "Integration of the Rural Sector in Soviet Society," Research Paper no. 15, Soviet and East European Research Centre, The Hebrew University of Jerusalem, January 1976.

37. Clark, "Soviet Agricultural Policy," p. 31.

38. Keith Bush, "Soviet Agriculture: Ten Years under New Management," *Radio Liberty Research Supplement*, May 23, 1975, p. 1.

39. For data, see Bush, "Soviet Agriculture," and Thane Gustafson, "Transforming Soviet Agriculture: Brezhnev's Gamble on Land Improvement," *Public Policy* 25, no. 3 (Summer 1977):293-312.

40. James R. Millar, "The Prospects for Soviet Agriculture," *Problems of Communism* 26, no 3 (May-June 1977):7.

41. Ibid., p. 5.

42. Ibid., p. 10. Keith Bush also concludes that "so much more could have been done with the existing labor and capital resources" than was actually accomplished, in "Soviet Agriculture," p. 45.

43. For the demoralizing impact of such conditions, see Friedgut, "Integration of Rural Sector," pp. 7-9.

44. V. Tikhonov, "On the Industrialization of Agriculture," *Voprosy Ekonomiki*, no. 10 (1977), translated in *Problems of Economics* 21, no. 2 (June 1978):17.

45. Millar, "Introduction," *The Soviet Rural Community*, p. xiv.

46. Nove, "Peasants and Officials," p. 58, quoting the Soviet journal *Novyi Mir*.

47. Volin, *Century of Russian Agriculture*, p. 543.

48. David Joravsky, "Ideology and Progress in Crop Rotation," in Karcz, ed., *Soviet and East European Agriculture*, p. 171.

49. Alec Nove, "Will Russia Ever Feed Itself?" *New York Times Magazine*, February 1, 1976.

50. Bush, "Soviet Agriculture," p. 27. See also Alec Nove, "Soviet Agriculture under Brezhnev," *Slavic Review* 29, no. 3 (September 1970):388-390.

51. Ibid., and Robert F. Miller, "The Future of the Soviet Kolkhoz," *Problems of Communism* 25, no. 2 (March-April 1976):34-50.

52. *Sel'skoe Khoziaistvo SSR* (Agriculture in the USSR) (Moscow: Statistika, 1971), p. 11. Since the 1950s, many collective farms have been converted into state farms, which now farm about as much land as the kolkhozy.

53. Clark, "Soviet Agricultural Policy," pp. 6-16.

54. Alec Nove, "Will Russia Ever Feed Itself?"

55. Alexander Yanov, "Behind the Soviet Union's Grain Purchases," op-ed article, *New York Times*, December 31, 1975.

56. Alec Nove quoting a Soviet journal, in "Will Russia Ever Feed Itself?"

57. Quoted in Dimitry Pospielovsky, "The 'Link System' in Soviet Agriculture," *Soviet Studies* 22, no. 4 (April 1970):419.

58. Cf. Yanov, "Behind the Grain Purchases," and Bush, "Soviet Agriculture," p. 37. But experiments are continuing. See "Stavropol Farmers Are Paid for Results," *Ekonomicheskaia Gazeta*, no. 20 (May 1976), in *Current Digest of the Soviet Press* 28, no. 27 (August 4, 1976):7.

59. See Iu. V. Arutiunian, "The Distribution of Decision-making among the Rural Population of the USSR," in M. Yanowitch and W. Fisher, eds., *Social Stratification and Mobility in the USSR* (White Plains, N.Y.: International Arts and Sciences Press, 1973), pp. 106-118. For a much bleaker analysis of

the sense of powerlessness among peasants, see Friedgut, "Integration of Rural Sector," p. 13.

60. Ibid., p. 16.

61. Quoted in David E. Powell, "The Rural Exodus," *Problems of Communism* 22, no. 6 (November-December 1974). See also Friedgut, "Integration of Rural Sector," pp. 27-28, for a case of local efforts to retain the educated young.

62. Ibid., pp. 18-19. For discussion of kolkhoz chairmen sent from towns in the 1950s, see Waedekin, *Leadership forces*, pp. 172-173.

63. For a recent summary of Great Leap Forward economic development strategy, see Alexander Eckstein, *China's Economic Revolution* (Cambridge: Cambridge University Press, 1977), pp. 54-58 and 200-202.

64. For a valuable discussion of the GLF as a process, see Ezra Vogel, *Canton Under Communism* (Cambridge: Harvard University Press, 1969), chap. 5.

65. Cf. G. W. Skinner, "Marketing and Social Structure in Rural China," *Journal of Asian Studies* 24 (February 1965):195-228.

66. These excesses were condemned by Mao himself as early as February 1959. See "Mao Tse-tung: Speeches at the Chengchow Conference (February and March 1959)," in *Chinese Law and Government* 9, no. 4 (Winter 1976-77):22-24.

67. Thomas B. Wiens, "The Evolution of Policy and Capabilities in China's Agricultural Technology," in Joint Economic Committee, 95th U.S. Congress, *Chinese Economy Post-Mao* (Washington, D.C.: U.S. Government Printing Office, 1978), p. 690.

68. See Byung-joon Ahn, *Chinese Politics and the Cultural Revolution* (Seattle: University of Washington Press, 1976), chaps. 3 and 4.

69. For data, see Joint Economic Committee, 94th U.S. Congress, *China: A Reassessment of the Economy* (Washington, D.C.: U.S. Government Printing Office, 1975), pt. 2.

70. See Jon Sigurdson, *Rural Industrialization in China* (Cambridge: Harvard University Press, 1977).

71. Clark, "Soviet Agricultural Policy," p. 40.

72. R. M. Field and J. A. Kilpatrick, "Chinese Grain Production: An Interpretation of the Data," *China Quarterly*, no. 74 (June 1978), pp. 378, 380. China's population is not known with certainty and could well be somewhat lower.

73. See Dwight Perkins, "Constraints Influencing China's Agricultural Performance," in *China: A Reassessment of the Economy*, p. 364.

74. Christopher Howe, *China's Economy: A Basic Guide* (New York: Basic Books, 1978), pp. 90-91.

75. Ibid., p. 86.

76. Perkins, "Constraints Influencing Agricultural Performance," p. 365.

77. Friedgut, "Integration of Rural Sector," p. 26.

78. Cf. William Parish, "Political Participation in Rural China," unpublished, December, 1973.

79. For an excellent recent study of these relationships, see Steven Butler, "Agricultural Mechanization in China: The Administrative Impact," *Occasional Papers of the East Asian Institute*, Columbia University. See also John

P. Burns, "Peasant Interest Articulation in China" (Ph.D. dissertation, Columbia University, 1978), for extensive documentation on peasant participation.

80. For extended discussion, see William L. Parish and Martin K. Whyte, *Village and Family in Contemporary China* (Chicago: University of Chicago Press, 1978), chap. 6.

81. Ibid., p. 119.

82. Hu Chiao-mu, "Observe Economic Laws, Speed Up the Four Modernizations," *Peking Review* 21, no. 47 (November 24, 1978):18.

83. See Parish and Whyte, *Village and Family*,chaps. 5 and 6, for detailed discussion.

84. For extensive discussion, see Benedict Stavis, "Making Green Revolution," Rural Development Committee, Cornell University, 1974.

85. Wiens, "Evolution of Policy," p. 680.

86. In addition, the Chinese have sent educated urban youths to the countryside, mainly to alleviate urban unemployment, but also to make contributions to rural development. This program has had mixed success. See the author's *Up to the Mountains and Down to the Countryside: The Transfer of Youth from Urban to Rural China* (New Haven: Yale University Press, 1977), especially chap. 5.

87. The standard work is David Joravsky, *The Lysenko Affair* (Cambridge: Harvard University Press, 1970).

88. Ibid., especially p. 286ff.

89. "The absolute majority" of cadres trained for agriculture work elsewhere, according to N. I. Moskalaeva et al., "Podogotovka kvalifitsirovannyikh kadrov i migratsiia sel'skogo naseleniia," (The training of qualified cadres and the migration of the rural population), in *Problemy Sel'skokhoziaistvennoi Nauki v Moskovskom Universitete* (Problems of agricultural science at Moscow University) (Moscow: Izdatel-stvo Moskovskom Universitete, 1975), p. 491. The quote is in Bruce F. Johnston and Peter Kilby, *Agriculture and Structural Transformation* (New York: Oxford University Press, 1975), p. 287.

90. Parish and Whyte, *Village and Family*, p. 124.

91. *Radio Wuhan*, November 16, 1978, in *Foreign Broadcast Information Service*, no. 224, November 20, 1978.

92. The main issues are detailed in a lengthy article about Hsiang-hsiang county, Hunan Province, in *Jen-min Jih-pao*, July 5, 1978.

93. *Jen-min Jih-pao* editorial, July 5, 1978. One of many other articles on this campaign was entitled, revealingly, "We must have faith that the peasants can till the land" (Yao hsiang-hsin nung-min hui chung-ti), *Jen-min Jih-pao*, October 15, 1978.

94. Hu Chiao-mu "Observe Economic Laws," pp. 19-20.

5
The Political Economy of Taiwanese Agricultural Development

Donald J. Puchala
Jane Staveley

The story of agricultural development on Taiwan is rather impressive. Production statistics compiled from 1895 onward show steadily rising outputs, specifically: an early attainment of self-sufficiency in dietary staples, the accumulation of surpluses in food and cash crops, continuing gains in export earnings, widespread assimilation of modern technologies, rising returns to farmers, improving rural standards of living, a decreasing labor force in the rural sector, and the ultimate transformation of Taiwan into a rurally healthy, modern industrial economy. The problem we address in this chapter is straightforward: what factors explain agricultural development on Taiwan during the first two-thirds of the twentieth century?

Our purpose in analyzing Taiwanese agriculture is twofold. First, we seek to understand the Taiwanese case. In many ways it is a rather positive, and therefore refreshing, example of what can be accomplished agriculturally in a less developed country (LDC), a country, incidentally, that is not atypical in its endowments of agronomic resources. What happened on Taiwan contrasts markedly with what happened (or did not happen) in other LDCs where agricultural stagnation and declining outputs per capita have been the orders of the day. Our second purpose is to try to explain some of these contrasts. By abstracting from the Taiwanese case, we hope to shed light on some of the general conditions for rapid and successful agricultural development. In particular, we shall seek to relate elements of political setting to elements of agricultural growth. Indeed, our major hypothesis is that politics and economics must attain certain "key and lock" relationships if agricultural development is to succeed. The thrust of our analysis is to test this hypothesis on the Taiwanese case. Our conclusions suggest an even more general applicability.

TABLE 5.1
Index of Total Food Production on Taiwan,
1911-1960

Period	Year	Index of Food Production[a]
Japanese Colonial	1911-15	100
	1916-20	116
	1921-25	137
	1926-30	172
	1931-35	211
	1936-40	237
	1941-45	188
Chinese Nationalist	1945-50	184
	1951-55	272
	1956-60	338

Source: Teng-hui Lee, Joint Commission on Rural Reconstruction, Economic Digest Series, #17.

[a]1911-15 = 100

Agricultural Development on Taiwan, 1895-1960: An Overview

Before we move very deeply into our analysis, let's review the phenomenon that we shall seek to explain, namely, agricultural development on Taiwan. This is most efficiently done with a statistical mapping of the domain. Tables 5.1-5.4 show the growth of total food supply, the production of principal crops—rice, sugar, and sweet potatoes—Taiwan's land productivity, and labor productivity, respectively, during the first six decades of the twentieth century.

The combination of production and productivity figures paints a rather impressive picture of agricultural progress on Taiwan under both the Japanese colonial regime, 1895-1945, and the Chinese Nationalist regime, 1945 to the present. Total food production doubled between

TABLE 5.2
Production of Principal Crops on Taiwan,
1900-1960

Period	Year	Rice	Sugar	Sweet Potatoes
		(00	MT)	
	1900	307	--	205
Japanese	1910	598	133[a]	642
Colonial	1920	691	263	836
	1930	1053	--	1330
	1940	1129	916[b]	1512
Chinese	1950	1492	529	2104
Nationalist	1960	1912	816	2979

Sources: T. H. Shen, <u>Agricultural Development on Taiwan Since World War II</u> (Ithaca, New York: Comstock, 1964), pp. 29-30. A. J. Grajdanzev, <u>The Economic Development of Formosa</u> (Shanghai: Kelly and Walsh, Ltd., 1941), pp. 41-72.

[a]1909
[b]1938

1911 and 1931 under the Japanese regime; then, after a falling off during the war years, it nearly doubled again under the Chinese Nationalist regime by 1960. In terms of specific crops, Taiwanese farmers produced nearly four times as much rice, almost seven times as much sugar, and about seven times as many sweet potatoes in 1940 as they did in 1900. By 1960, rice production was up 70 percent over 1940 levels, sweet potatoes were up by 97 percent, and sugar, though not produced in quantities characteristic of the colonial era, nonetheless increased by 54 percent between 1950 and 1960.

Productivity figures shown in Tables 5.3 and 5.4 begin to account for the production figures of Tables 5.1 and 5.2. Table 5.3 suggests that increased harvests were gained under the Japanese both by expanding lands under cultivation and by adding other agronomic inputs in quantity. Land area under rice increased by 96 percent between 1900 and 1940, and production per hectare went up nearly threefold. Under

Donald J. Puchala and Jane Staveley

TABLE 5.3
Land Productivity on Taiwan, 1900-1960
Rice and Sugar

Period	Year	Area (000 hec.)	MT/ hec.	Area (000 hec.)	MT/ hec.
	1900	325.6	.94	--	--
Japanese	1910	456.3	1.31	33.7	28.9
Colonial	1920	500.2	1.38	104.0	24.2
	1930	514.4	1.71	97.5	43.8
	1940	638.6	1.77	128.8	67.5
Chinese	1950	782.0	1.91	80.0	89.6
Nationalist	1960	783.0	2.58	95.0	154.6

Sources: See Table 5.2

the Nationalist regime, land under cultivation increased slightly for rice and decreased for sugar, but production per hectare nearly doubled for both crops. Moreover, while the productivity of land was rising, so too was the productivity of labor. As Table 5.4 makes clear, labor productivity had almost doubled between 1911 and 1940, and it then rose another 61 percent between 1940 and 1960. In all, we have a rather remarkable record of growth in the Taiwanese rural sector. This, in essence, is what we shall try to account for.

Explanations for these patterns of agricultural growth and modernization on Taiwan are manifold. Some range from the simplistic generalization that "the Taiwanese are Chinamen after all; nothing less is to be expected from these wizened, creative, and energetic people." Other, more sophisticated interpretations take account of farmers' receptivity to technological change, the availability of capital for the development of infrastructure and the modernization of farms, the existence of rural extension networks and the transmission of the results of research through them, the attention to agronomic research itself, timely land reform, and the early emergence of modern markets and credit structures. We subscribe to all of these interpretations, including the compliments to the Chinese. However, we are most struck by the frequently overlooked fact that Taiwanese agricultural development

TABLE 5.4
Productivity of Labor in Taiwanese Agriculture,
1911-1960

Period	Year	Production Per Worker (T$ 1935-37)	Production Per Worker (Index, 1911=100)
Japanese Colonial	1911	156	100
	1920	172	110
	1930	258	165
	1940	290	186
Chinese Nationalist	1950	278	178
	1960	385	247

Source: Teng-hui Lee, Intersectoral Capital
Flows in the Economic Development of Taiwan,
1895-1960, p. 13.

took place in response to agricultural policies conceived, formulated, and indefatigably executed under two political regimes. Although it is less than fashionable nowadays to compliment either of these regimes, least of all Japanese colonialism, it is nonetheless difficult to escape the fact that their public policies, applied on Taiwan, framed and fostered agricultural development.

Japanese Colonialism and Taiwanese Agriculture, 1896-1945

Prior to 1895, Taiwan was a province of China. From 1683 onward, however, the island can best be described as a colony of the mainland. Space limitations here do not permit extensive examination of this pre-Japanese period. Yet, to grasp the significance of changes under Japanese rule, it is important to point out that, agriculturally, traditional Taiwan had many of the familiar earmarks of colonial and early postcolonial economic underdevelopment. Most of the labor force was engaged in subsistence agriculture, and most of the peasants lived in abject poverty, untouched by the cash economy. Resources in peasant hands were siphoned off via rents, oppressive taxes, and exorbitant credit regimes, which commanded interest rates ranging above 100 percent.[1] The largest tracts of arable land were in the hands of landlords who either planted their estates with export cash crops like sugar and tea or rented to peasants on a share-crop basis to bring in exportable rice. Enclaves connected with the export sector, including some basic processing industries, warehouses, and shipping facilities, were controlled by mainland merchants or Westerners. Neither the Chinese government (the land-owning elites) nor the exporters exhibited interest in general agricultural development. As a result, food production on Taiwan stagnated for two centuries, technology in the subsistence sector remained constant, and per capita well-being declined as population expanded.

Although the Japanese gained Taiwan in 1895 as part of the terms of the treaty concluding the Sino-Japanese War (fought by the Japanese to gain political influence in Korea), the colonizers were quick to recognize the agricultural potential of their newly acquired colony (called Formosa by the Japanese). One-third of Taiwan is flatland; the soil is moderately rich, low in organic matter and nutrients, but easily fertilized; rainfall is ample, although irrigation is necessary to produce more than one rice crop a year; the subtropical climate permits double or triple cropping; this same climate is hospitable to a diversity of temperate zone, subtropical, and tropical crops, including sugar. Even in this early period, the Japanese saw limits to their home-island agriculture; Taiwan's potential promised answers to imminent food problems. In addition (again, even by the 1890s), large proportions of Japan's import bill (upwards of 60 million yen annually) were allocated to foodstuffs,[2] and exploiting Taiwan promised "within empire" cheap food relief. The regime's capacity to supply food from Taiwan to the home-island population hedged against social-political unrest linked to scarcity, and increased food production supported urban industrialization on the home islands, the perceived pathway to world power. Availabilities of cheap food saved foreign exchange and liberated resources for investment. Notably, Japanese motivations for developing Taiwanese agriculture were little concerned with living conditions, income, or well-being on Taiwan. This is a point that we shall return to in a moment.

As perceived by Japanese administrators the task was to unleash Taiwanese agricultural potential for the benefit of the Japanese people and the glory of the Empire. This was undertaken systematically over a period of decades via a multiphased program designed (1) to structurally integrate the Taiwanese peasantry into the imperial cash economy and to motivate farmers to respond to incentives in this economy, (2) to diffuse modern agricultural technology through the peasantry and to heighten incentives for technological innovation, and (3) to provide investment capital at times and in sums appropriate to maintain the momentum of agricultural development.

Restructuring the Taiwanese Countryside

Integrating the Taiwanese peasantry into the imperial economy initially meant sweeping away the feudal system of land tenure that characterized the pre-Japanese era. As a matter of course, the Japanese sought to eliminate absentee landlords and keep remaining landowners on their land in the expectation that their attentions would be directed toward enhancing productivity rather than simply taking rents. In particular, the Japanese sought to rationalize and control land rents in such a way that farmers' profits would not be wiped out by rent increases, as was typically the case under the former regime. The object here was to increase rural savings (i.e., farmers' profits) and then channel them into agricultural reinvestment. Furthermore, the Japanese sought to eliminate the excesses of sharecropping, the disincentives to productivity that such practices entailed, and the vicious circles wherein farmers' obligations as tenants and their family food needs discouraged the retention of good seeds. Finally, the Japanese wanted to establish a base for rural taxation from which they could manipulate the rural economy through fiscal incentives and sanctions. For this, they needed accurate data on ownership and land productivity.

Land reform was the primary means to these ends. Through a program of comprehensive and meticulous land surveys conducted between 1898 and 1904, under the auspicies of the Bureau of Land Surveys, Japanese authorities ascertained the ownership of all land parcels, standardized measures, fixed boundaries, and ultimately went so far as to define the productivity of each field. On the basis of the surveys' data, colonial authorities revised land taxes to accord with productivity, aligned the rental system with productivities, and adjusted rents downward. The immediate result of these measures was to squeeze landowners (especially large landowners) between higher taxes and lower rent receipts. The new regulations, however, offered escape from the squeeze to those who could increase the productivity of their holdings; inasmuch as permissible, increases in the rents of more productive tenants exceeded mandated increases in taxes to landlords. Meanwhile, tenants' incentives to produce were enhanced by the margins left for profits.

Concurrent with the reorganizations in rents and taxes went the Japanese drive to eliminate the traditional class of absentee landlords, the *ta tsu*. By most accounts, including the documents of the Japanese land survey, at the turn of the century there were about 40,000 families, many of whom wielded much power in local communities) who accumulated income and fortune by levying rents on tenant farmers on Taiwan[3] (and, incidentally, by evading taxes through false representation and bribery). Their activities posed disincentives to farmers inasmuch as they typically penalized productivity by raising rents. Nor were they prompted as a rule to reinvest their profits in their estates, since this amounted to a rent subsidy which they were not predisposed to pay. After concluding that this absentee class was dysfunctional to agricultural development, Japanese authorities penalized them heavily in the "rent/tax squeeze," thereby forcing some ta tsu to sell their estates. Subsequently, they obliged all remaining ta tsu to sell any rights of ownership of the land to the government, exchanging the ta tsu's rents for income-bearing bonds. At a stroke, this removed the unproductive landlords and diverted the capital they had been accumulating through rents into productive investment channels. Thus, freed land titles were made available to tenants, in particular the most influential class of tenant farmers, the hsiao tsu, who moved to full ownership.

The Japanese-directed land reform on Taiwan conducted between 1904 and 1910 achieved most of its goals. Land was transferred to the hands of resident owners; controlled rents became instruments of modernization (and tax corruption was all but abolished); rural savings began to accumulate; and capital was generated for reinvestment. However, *this land reform did not significantly alter the unequal distribution of land on Taiwan.* It was not a populist reform and was not intended as one. Absentee landlords were eliminated, but landlords per se were not. Land was transferred to the former tenants who could afford to buy it—the hsiao tsu—and they, by and large, were major operators in their own right. After the reform, 33 percent of the Taiwanese farmers were landlords and 67 percent were tenants. Ten percent of the farm households still controlled 60 percent of the land.[4] As far as the Japanese were concerned, this outcome was wholly acceptable. Their experience on the home islands during the Meiji period had suggested that a small, wealthy landowner class was a most appropriate medium through which to diffuse new agricultural technologies, as long as the responsiveness of such a class could be counted on. It was the Japanese intent, then, not to destroy rural hierarchy on Taiwan, but simply to replace an unproductive aristocracy with a productive squirarchy. The new structure was then to be used as an engine of modernization.

The Mobilization and Modernization of the Peasantry

By simplest definition, agricultural modernization is accomplished by innovating technologies whose application enhances productivity.

But innovating technology is a "key and lock" phenomenon inasmuch as new techniques must be tailored to the environment that is to receive them. In many ways, the Japanese assault on agricultural backwardness in Taiwan can be thought of as a working out of a "key and lock" problem. From their own experience of the last half of the nineteenth century, the Japanese were keenly aware of the necessity to shape technologies to local conditions; they were also conscious of the need to structure the environments into which the new technologies would be injected. They carried their experience with them as they moved to modernize Taiwan.

Tailoring agricultural technology is usually the object of locally based research and development, and so it was with Taiwan. One of the first moves of the Japanese colonial administration on Taiwan was to establish an infrastructure for agricultural research and development. The Central Agricultural Research Bureau was set up in Taipei in 1903 "to conduct scientific studies of Taiwan's agriculture." Immediately afterward, six experimental stations were opened on different parts of the island, and Japanese agronomists were brought to Taiwan in substantial numbers to staff the research establishments. Later, farmers' associations (discussed in a different context below) were encouraged to develop experimental plots, and more specialized associations dealing in particular crops were encouraged to do likewise. The goal of the scientific effort was to adapt new technologies to Taiwanese conditions, much as the Japanese had earlier adapted European technologies to home-island conditions. The quadrupling of sugar production and the doubling of rice output during the first three decades of the twentieth century are due in no small measure to the intensive efforts in fertilizer development and seed breeding undertaken at the Japanese-administered experimental stations on Taiwan.

But by far the largest challenge to Japanese colonial administrators on Taiwan was the task of disseminating research results among the farmers. Accomplishing this was a most ingenious achievement of Japanese colonial administration. Since innovation could only come from above (or, at least, so it was perceived by the Japanese), the rural sector of Taiwan had to be structured in such a way that the government could reach directly into every farm family. The Japanese believed that this had to be done not only to facilitate the transmission of information but also to monitor behavior. Their procedure was to organize the entire society in a hierarchical transmission belt from the top downward and to parallel this with an upward-flowing surveillance system. Needless to say, the regimented system that the Japanese established sacrificed many liberal values cherished in the West. We make no apologies for it. Our only point is that it functioned effectively to transform the technological basis of Taiwanese agriculture in a remarkably short time. Structures that transmitted agronomic information and demands for innovation downward were of three kinds. The first and least formal was a structure of network interactions between officials of the Japanese central administration in Taipei, or within the twenty administrative provinces (cho), and the large Taiwanese landowners. Contact was direct, frequent, sometimes on an individual basis, and usually unidirectional. The landowners were told what to grow, how much to grow, and how to grow it (i.e., what new techniques to apply), and they were instructed to pass directives to their tenants. Second, there was the system of farmers' associations. Initially, these were provincially based and organized by Japanese officials and wealthy landlords in accordance with rules handed down by the colonial administration. Officers of the associations were appointed by the Japanese government, and, since there were ultimately 341 township and 5,000 village chapters,[5] most farm families were members at one level or another. The associations sold fertilizers, seeds, and tools to members, kept experimental plots, and maintained close liaison with research stations. Eventually, associations were formed on a crop basis as well as by locality. By the 1920s, the associations had entered into agricultural training, land surveying, disease prevention, and crop and equipment storage.[6] The first association was formed in 1900, and by 1915 at least one functioned in each administrative district.[7] Finally, there was also an official extension service that provided technicians to aid local farmers. Each household was instructed to avail itself of extension services; each was assessed required fees. Extension services were first administered via the political-administrative system, but were later taken over by the farmers' associations. Buttressing all of the information-disseminating mechanisms was the Japanese-implanted educational system. It systematically overcame illiteracy in the Taiwanese countryside at the primary level and opened opportunities for higher-level technical agronomic training to selected Taiwanese students.

Paralleling the information-disseminating system was the political-administrative system itself. As noted, this served as a surveillance mechanism to monitor compliance with Japanese demands for innovation. In its police functions it also served as an instrument of enforcement. Upon occupying Taiwan, the Japanese subdivided the island into twenty provinces, these into counties, these into townships, villages, hos of 100 families, kos of 10 families, and finally, family units. Each unit in the system had either an appointed leader or one "elected" and then approved by the Japanese. Each leader, from family head to the

Governor-General of Taiwan, was held responsible before higher authority for the behavior of his group. At the same time, the police network was woven through the administrative structure; often, it overlapped it directly—where Japanese appointees to leadership positions were policemen. It is estimated that at least during the latter part of the Japanese colonial period there was one policeman for every 580 Taiwanese,[8] and, according to at least one analyst, the "policeman" was the most prominent symbol of government to the Taiwanese.[9]

Once the rural environment had been structured to receive information and commands for innovation, the Japanese activated the system they had created and promoted technological change from above by combining incentives and sanctions. Those who accepted Japanse directives for innovation received subsidized seed and seedlings, tax reductions and exemptions, water allocations from the public irrigation system, access to government-controlled marketing facilities, price and rent subsidies, freedom from police harassment, and a variety of other material and less tangible benefits. Contrariwise, those who resisted or dallied could expect tax penalties, denials of water, problems in marketing, promises of trouble with Japanese authorities, or fines and imprisonment. The system worked well to enhance production and productivity. In fact, it worked remarkably well, considering that the Taiwanese farmers themselves benefited from it only marginally.

Capital in the Right Place at the Right Time

Agricultural development on Taiwan during the colonial era was never starved for capital; the Japanese saw to this. In a systematic manner (similar to that employed in the diffusion of technology), the Japanese government prepared the Taiwanese rural sector to receive and distribute capital while pumping capital into the system. First, a rural credit system was established. The Cooperative Society Act of 1913 made credit accessible to farmers who wished to borrow for productive purposes. This was provided through agricultural cooperatives. More than 500 of these were established to offer credit services during the colonial era.[10] Farmers' associations also carried on lending activities, and landlords' associations funneled credit to tenants. The Irrigation Association channeled public funds into water projects. Banks backed the associational structure, and government regulations controlled interest rates and attacked usury in the countryside.

Early investments up until 1905 were largely from Japanese public coffers and were channeled into infrastructure development[11]— irrigation works, roads, research, and education. Later investments, particularly farm modernization and technological innovation, came mostly from tax revenues on Taiwan and partly from the Japanese private sector. The costs of government on Taiwan amounted to about half of public revenues through the 1920s and 1930s, leaving the remaining half to be reinvested in the island's economy.[12] During the same period, about a third of the Taiwanese government's development expenditure was allocated to agricultural research, extension services, and price subsidies on crops that were being promoted by central authorities. In all, this amounted to about 10 percent of the Taiwanese government's total yearly expenditure.[13] In addition, private funds were directed into Taiwanese agriculture by alluring programs sponsored by Japanese banks, and promising returns were made credible by Japanese tariffs. Between 1895 and 1905, the Japanese government subsidized the Taiwanese government in the form of huge grants. In 1896 they provided 75 percent of Taiwan's public revenue; in 1897, 34 percent; in 1899, 15 percent. Grants were suddenly terminated in 1905 at the outbreak of the Russo-Japanese War.[14] Increasing productivity in the island's economy easily rewarded early Japanese investment efforts.

Agricultural Modernization and the Taiwanese

In this perspective of flattering statistics and well-planned, well-administered programs, it is easy to lose sight of what the Japanese-directed program was actually accomplishing. The costs of the colonial programs are also easily blurred unless they are analyzed. As noted, the purposes of Japanese efforts to increase productivity in Taiwanese agriculture were: first, to enhance food security on the home islands; and second, to relieve balance-of-payments burdens by developing "within empire" supplies, especially sugar supplies. Taiwan, then, was developed as an agricultural export economy, mainly a sugar and rice economy. By the 1930s, 90 percent of the annual sugar crop and 40-50 percent of the rice crop were shipped to the home islands.[15] Prices awarded to producers of these export crops were relatively high and resulted in profits. Most profits were either returned directly to Japanese companies, especially in the sugar sector, or siphoned off in taxes, in particular, high consumption taxes, or they were reinvested or consumed in the repayment of credit obligations. In short, the bulk of returns from modernizing agriculture was recycled into the Japanese "growth machine." As for the Taiwanese farmers, various analysts, including Samuel Ho (most prominent among them), have concluded that their agricultural real wages remained constant from 1895 to 1945. Their diets deteriorated as pressures to grow export crops reduced local food crop outputs and as obligations to sell rice forced peasants onto sweet potato diets.[16] Japanese economists writing in the 1930s indicated improvements in housing and other factors of material well-being on Taiwan (even rises in Taiwanese bank deposits) and generally higher standards of living than those attained on the Chinese mainland.[17] But Taiwanese society remained sharply stratified with Japanese overlords on top. The social, economic, and political patterns persisting into the 1940s remained typically colonial: there was a lack of higher education and upward mobility for the Taiwanese and an imposition of Japanese culture, particularly language, on the upper strata of the Taiwanese population.

Agricultural Development under the Chinese Nationalist Government, 1945-1960

The world cataclysm of the 1940s affected Taiwan dramatically. Mobilization for war between 1939 and 1945 effected negative rates in the island's economy.[18] The destruction caused by the war cast the island into depression. Regime changes—from Japanese colonialism, to Chinese administration, to revolutionary turmoil, to Chinese Nationalist control—not only interjected great tension and instability in Taiwanese society in general but also effectively undermined the pattern of institutionalized rural development that the Japanese had constructed and used with such impressive effect. Preoccupied with the struggle against the Communists, the Chinese government largely ignored Taiwan between 1945 and 1949. Chinese officials took positions on Taiwan as political rewards and personally enriched themselves in their domains. The Taiwanese revolted in 1947 and were crushed. Order finally returned after 1949, and normalcy gradually set in as Chiang Kai Shek shifted his government (and army) to Taiwan and the island became, de facto, the Republic of China.

Agricultural reconstruction and development were high among the Nationalist regime's priorities. They had to be for several reasons, none of them linked to development per se. First, Chiang Kai Shek brought with him an army of one-half million. Maintaining this force required food and money. Agricultural growth meant increased food, and, as a leading sector in economic development, it also meant money for the Nationalist regime. Second, inflation had to be brought under control, not only for economic reasons but also for political ones. Unrest was widespread on Taiwan, a Chinese alternative to the Nationalist regime was close at hand, and Taiwanese peasants were well aware of it. Declining real income on Taiwan had to be controlled, therefore, and Chiang Kai Shek had to demonstrate that growth and prosperity were possible under a noncommunist Chinese regime. Moreover, since disenchanted tenant farmers were excellent candidates for communist subversion, the Nationalist government had to address the cause of their disenchantment, which was poverty. We give strong emphasis to these motivational factors underlying Nationalist agricultural policies on Taiwan because they have a general and theoretical relevance that we will discuss in our conclusions. For the moment, let it suffice to say that one important factor explaining the success of agricultural development under the Chiang Kai Shek regime was that the regime was highly motivated toward developing agriculture from 1949 onward.

Nationalist policies accomplished a good deal more than simply rebuilding the rural structures that the Japanese had created, though they did, indeed, accomplish this. The Nationalist approach to rural development had several elements or phases; they can be examined one at a time. Actually, though, many of these occurred simultaneously, in mutually supportive ways, and it must be remembered that the convergence of programs was itself an important element of development. In a manner reminiscent of the Japanese case, the Chinese Nationalists began with land reform. They then established and activated a set of organizational networks that linked the government to the countryside. Research continued several steps ahead of development, and massive and freely flowing capital rapidly transformed laboratory findings to productivity in the fields. Notably, much of the capital that flowed between 1949 and 1965 was provided by the foreign assistance programs of the United States. This was a result of the happy coincidence in Chinese Nationalist and American anticommunist goals. As in the Japanese case, farmers' responses to the regime's developmental initiatives followed as a result of rewards perceived and sanctions dreaded. But the emphasis in Nationalist policy was much more on rewards, and most notable among these was the promise and realizaton of improved well-being in the countryside.

Land Reform under the Chinese Nationalist Regime

Assessing the failures that produced their humiliation on the mainland, Nationalist leaders concluded that their procrastination on land reform was an important factor. Disaffected peasants had swelled communist ranks. A land reform program for the mainland was planned and drafted, but it could not be effectively executed, since landlord support was a basis of Kuomintang political power. When this support was rendered largely irrelevant with the move to Taiwan, the way was cleared for land reform. First steps were taken in 1949 in a series of measures designed to provide rent relief to tenants. Some rents were reduced directly and others were stabilized by setting quotas on production per field. Above-quota surpluses remained with farmers and could not be made a basis for raising rent. Written leases were obligatory. They set rents for periods of three to six years. Additionally, rents were to be decreased in years of poor harvest, and no rentals were to be paid on subsidized crops.

Meanwhile, the Nationalist government launched a series of land surveys; by 1953 these had become the bases for a comprehensive program of land re-distribution. The aim of the government was to create a system of small owner-operated farms (i.e., to eliminate the Taiwanese landlord class). Under their Land to the Tiller program, the Nationalists required sale to the government of all land worked by tenants in excess of a certain limit. By way of compensation, landowners received payment partly (30 percent) in the form of stock shares in government enterprises and partly (70 percent) in land bonds redeemable in twenty semiannual installments. Land acquired by the government was resold at the purchase price to the tenants who paid for it in kind in semiannual installments.

Overall, the results of the land reform were far-reaching. Between 1949 and 1965, the number of owner-operators in Taiwanese agriculture increased from 34 percent to 65 percent and the number of tenants declined from 36 percent to 15 percent.[19] The envisioned system of small owner-operators was thus approximated. Theories concerning heightened productivity in an owner-operator system appear to be validated in the production statistics from 1953 onward. At the very least, contentions that land redistributions into smaller plots threaten productivity were contradicted.

Organizing the Countryside, 1949-1965

While the land reform had its intended effects of defusing rural tensions without affecting productivity, the fragmented small-farmer system that it created compounded the Chinese government's problems in reaching into the rural sector. The former Japanese system of working through the large landowners was no longer feasible, and, if modernizing cues were to be passed to farmers, some surrogate for the Japanese transmission belts had to be devised. This was accomplished by reorganizing and revitalizing the farmers' associations, by assigning these associations manifold tasks, and by enmeshing virtually every farm family in one or more of them.

Organizationally, the Taiwanese rural structure was topped off from 1949 to 1965 by the Joint Commission on Rural Reconstruction (JCRR), a Chinese-American body that we shall discuss more elaborately in a moment. The JCRR overlapped the Department of Agriculture of the Republic of China as well as other departments responsible for

122   Donald J. Puchala and Jane Staveley

economic planning and development. These operated above the Provincial Department of Agriculture and Forestry (responsible for the Province of Taiwan), which was linked to the farmers' associations through its Farmers' Organizational Division. The farmers' associations themselves operated on four levels: the provincial, the county and city, the township, and the level of "small agricultural units." Membership in the farmers' associations was open to landlords, owner-operators, tenant farmers, farm hands, and graduates of agricultural schools. At the township level, each farm family was represented by one individual. In a marked and meaningful departure from the Japanese system, all officials of the farmers' associations were elected, and government officials were prohibited from holding positions of responsibility. The significance of this rests in the fact that the greater autonomy permitted to the reconstituted farmers' associations guaranteed that they would function as transmitters of information and appeals upward and not solely as transmitters of directives downward. In effect, the new structure was more democratic than its colonial predecessor (though we do not want to push this point too hard).

The farmers' associations were all-purpose structures. They transmitted information about technological innovations in agriculture, distributed seeds and fertilizers, supported research and development on their experimental plots, provided storage facilities, facilitated cooperative marketing and purchasing, extended credit, channeled capital, offered education and extension services, developed and allocated water resources (irrigation associations were a special variant), and participated directly in the drafting and execution of government development plans.

Lubricating the System with American Money

Although the organization of the countryside provided the milieu for agricultural development in postwar Taiwan, it cannot be emphasized too strongly that farmers' responses within this milieu followed most directly from the incentives and sanctions that the Chiang Kai Shek government commanded. Among incentives, money was undoubtedly most important. Because of American interest and generosity, money for agricultural development was abundant on Taiwan for the better part of fifteen years. To go deeply into the motivations behind U.S. aid to the Republic of China is well beyond the scope of this chapter. For our purposes, it must suffice to say simply that the independence of Taiwan, its strength in free-enterprise economy, and the anticommunist orientation of its regime were deemed vital to U.S. global security, especially after the outbreak of the Korean War in 1950. More important for the purposes of this paper is the fact that the United States deemed agricultural development vitally important to successful national development on Taiwan, and American aid was allocated accordingly. Between 1951 and 1965, the United States allocated roughly $1.5 billion in aid to Taiwan.[20] With regard to total capital investment, U.S. aid provided for 58.7 percent of all investment in agriculture, but for only 13 percent of that which was invested in industry, the largest share being invested in farm-related industries.[21]

There might be some temptation to argue that "American money did it all," which is not the case, but American contributions should not be underestimated. Following are some facts and figures.

- The United States allocated more than $2.5 million to develop irrigation projects on Taiwan.[22]
- Indigenous fertilizer and pesticide industries on Taiwan were developed with strong American financial backing.
- Between 1951 and 1965 the rural credit system on Taiwan functioned largely on American funds channeled through JCRR.
- Nearly every development and modernization project initiated on the island between 1953 and 1965 was at least partially funded by U.S. aid through JCRR.
- Hundreds of Chinese agronomists and agricultural technicians were trained in the United States between 1951 and 1965, representing an investment of hundreds of thousands of dollars.[23]
- Hundreds of American agronomists and technicians worked on Taiwan between 1951 and 1965, representing an investment of millions of dollars.[24]
- U.S. military aid to Taiwan between 1951 and 1961 released resources for the Nationalist government that could not otherwise have been invested in agriculture or general economic development.

For the purposes of this study, it is more enlightening to examine the ways in which American capital was channeled into the Taiwanese countryside than it is to marvel at the aggregate aid flows. For the most part, aid was distributed in the form of loans for projects, and distribution was carried out via the farmers' associations discussed above. As noted, agricultural development on Taiwan was organized and overseen by the binational Joint Commission on Rural Reconstruction. The JCRR was operated jointly by the prevailing economic and technical assistance agency of the United States. As of 1961, this was the agricultural division of the United States Agency for International Development (USAID) and the Department of Agriculture of the Republic of China (ROC). Power in the JCRR rested with a semiautonomous five-member commission composed of two Americans and three Chinese. All decisions had to be unanimous.[25] In its binational form, the JCRR enjoyed a significant degree of autonomy, since it could resist direct pressures from either national government. This autonomy permitted it to focus on its tasks of agricultural modernization efficiently and expeditiously.

By and large, and especially in the early years, the JCRR allocated funds on the basis of requests for project loans and grants originating in local agencies. Project requests were reviewed for their feasibility, responsibility for implementation was assigned to a local sponsoring agency usually drawn from local associations, and funding formulas were worked out. As a rule, financing obligations were shared by the JCRR (American funds), the National government (ROC funds), and the local initiating bodies. Procedures for inspection were developed, terms for repayment were specified in the case of loans, and capital was channeled to the project. In all, between 1951 and 1965, some 6,280 projects were approved by the JCRR.[26] According to T. H. Shen's analysis, only 1.1 percent of these were unsuccessful; in terms of resources, these amounted to 1.6 percent of the JCRR grants and 5.6 percent of its loans.[27]

Initiatives for agricultural development also came directly from the JCRR. For example, during the early part of the 1950-1965 period, the JCRR distributed fertilizers, encouraged the use of pesticides, and reorganized the farmers' associations. Efforts were also made in the area of irrigation. This was all in addition to JCRR funding for research directed largely toward heightening productivity and diversifying crops on Taiwan.

*The Role of the Chinese Nationalist Government in
Taiwanese Agricultural Development*

The JCRR can be credited with providing incentives that influenced agricultural development on Taiwan during the postwar era, but the Republic of China provided the constraints and sanctions that discouraged resistance and underachievement. Despite the climate of growth and improvement fostered in the countryside from the early fifties onward, there were strong elements in the Taiwanese population, especially the native Taiwanese, who did not share the goals of the Chiang Kai Shek regime, who were not inspired to work for the glorification of the Republic of China, who had no great interest in sustaining Chiang's army, and who, in any event, had little influence over the affairs of the Nationalist government. Resistance was not to be tolerated; the Nationalist government maintained and used the instruments of the police state to enforce compliance. Police surveillance was comprehensive, much as it was under the Japanese colonial system, and the army was omnipresent. The state of war that existed between Taiwan and the mainland government provided perpetual justification for denying civil liberties on Taiwan. To openly deviate from Nationalist goals was costly.

Nationalist goals for agriculture were embodied in successive four-year plans, the first of which was launched in 1953. This set out general production targets for the Taiwan Province as well as particular goals for each administrative subunit. All were fashioned in the context of assessments of domestic and export needs. The first plan placed special emphasis on self-sufficiency in food production and expansion of industries such as the fertilizer industry and included a special program to increase rice production. The second emphasized the more efficient use of natural resources and the coordination of industry and agriculture and set up projects for the development of irrigation and fishing industry. The third and fourth emphasized the development of irrigation, agricultural resources on the plains, marginal land, and fishing. Plans were worked out in consultation with local organizations and in coordination with the JCRR, and targets were set, by and large, within realms of feasibility. Many of the JCRR projects were prompted by the directions of these plans, and Nationalist government investments were geared specifically to their fulfillment. Even though the plans hardly created a command economy in the communist sense, they were ambitious in their growth assumptions, they clearly demarcated between reasonable performance and underachievement, they introduced a degree of regimentation in the rural economy, and they provided the Nationalist government considerable leverage against resistors.

Agricultural Development and the Taiwanese

There is little question that Taiwan benefited as a result of the Nationalist government's drive for rural development. Sugar productivity has increased dramatically, and Taiwan remains one of the world's important sugar exporters.[28] In addition, during the Nationalist period, Taiwan has attained the highest per hectare production of rice in the world.[29] Considerable crop diversification has also taken place. Wheat acreage, although decreasing in the early 1950s due to wheat exports from the United States, nearly tripled after 1957. Corn acreage greatly increased, and soybean acreage has more than doubled in the last decade.[30] Pineapples and bananas are now important export items, hog raising has become a new industry, and a wide variety of vegetable crops are now of significance beyond family plots. Most important, Taiwanese agriculture now supports a progressively modern industrial society. In 1965, only 54 percent of the population remained in agriculture, as compared to 63 percent in 1951.[31] Most notably, whereas only 7 percent of Taiwanese exports were in industrial goods in 1954, a full 55 percent fell in this category by 1967.[32] Agricultural development is no longer a major public policy problem on Taiwan; agriculture has developed!

But what of the Taiwanese farmer? The consensus of a number of analysts, Neil Jacoby most prominent among them, is that the benefits of economic growth on Taiwan have been relatively widespread.[33] There is no great disparity between rich and poor as in many other less developed countries.[34] Food consumption is shifting from rice and even poorer staples to meat, dairy products, fish, fruit, and vegetables. Per capita income and real wages have increased. Differences between urban and rural conditions persist, but these are far less dramatic than in the past. In many ways, the typical Taiwanese rural inhabitant looks like a modern farmer. Materially, at least, he has benefited from his country's agricultural development.

The Political Economy of Taiwanese
Agricultural Development: Conclusions

In many ways, the story of development on Taiwan is a narrative of accomplishment. Our research has been motivated not by the desire to lavish praise on the Taiwanese and their governments for a job well done, but by the desire to analyze the makings of agricultural modernization in a less developed country. We hypothesized that the explanation would have to do with the interplay of political and economic factors, and, indeed, it apparently does. However, as it turns out, our explanation for what happened on Taiwan also has to do with some philosophic factors of critical import, and it is to these that we turn first in our conclusions.

1. *Agricultural development on Taiwan progressed in an authoritarian political environment under both the Japanese and Chinese Nationalists.* In both systems, there was a high degree of regimentation, a considerable degree of forced mobilization (especially under the Japanese), and a tendency to forcefully prevent noncooperation and underachievement. Moreover, police surveillance was an integral part of

each system, as was hierarchical accountability. While we might like to say that all of this was unfortunate, we must honestly add that it was apparently quite functional. It did contribute to bringing about developmental outcomes that might not otherwise have come about. Clearly, the cases we studied involved some obvious value trade-offs. Democracy, civil liberties, and a considerable degree of individual autonomy were traded for agricultural productivity and economic growth. The trade-off was less marked under the Chinese Nationalist government, but it was there nonetheless. At this point, we are left wondering whether it is possible for a society to have it both ways. Certainly, these kinds of value trade-offs were not made in a number of historical cases of agricultural development, as in North America, for example. But are nineteenth century North America and twentieth century Asia and Africa at all comparable in the political economies of their development? More bluntly, is agricultural development possible in the majority of contemporary less developed countries without a considerable degree of forced mobilization and regimentation? Ultimately, are democracy and rural development compatible in our day and age?

2. *Agricultural development on Taiwan progressed under both the Japanese and the Chinese Nationalists because it was assigned highest priority among regime goals.* More simply, one of the reasons why agricultural development happened was because the respective governments genuinely wanted it to happen. This point is too easily overlooked. We deliberately made an issue of the governments' motivations to be certain that it would not be missed. The irony, however, is that neither regime pushed agricultural modernization for its own sake or the sake of the farmers who were furthering their goals. Japanese emphasis on agricultural development on Taiwan was linked to concerns about domestic stability in the home islands, balance-of-payments savings, and imperial aspirations for power. Nationalist efforts were linked to anticommunist goals and concerns for political stability in the Taiwan Province. The questions that these observations raise concern the conditions under which governments are likely to assign high priority to rural development programs. The answer that our study suggests is that official priorities are linked to perceived "high political" outcomes. Governments want rural development when the opposite course starts directly affecting either their tenure in office or their pursuit of external security or autonomy. By contrast, when rural nondevelopment simply presents the problem of a poor peasantry or an underfed lower class, priorities for enhanced food production are likely to slip.

3. *Agricultural development on Taiwan was in no small measure a function of respective governments' capacities to reach into their rural sectors.* Although we have dwelt on the structures that the Japanese and then the Chinese Nationalists built to reach the countryside in this chapter, the real point is not that they did reach the farmers, but that they could. Both regimes exhibited a highly sophisticated degree of administrative capacity—an extraordinary degree, if we compare them to typical governments in Asia, Africa, and Latin America today. This capacity evolved, in part, from long traditions in public administration in both Japan and China. What seems even more important in the Taiwan case is that the respective governments were willing to allocate scarce financial and human resources to the rural development task. Large allocations of public funds and first-rate public servants were poured into the rural development task. This, too, is in rather stark contrast to what we find in many other countries today.

4. *Technological innovation and change in the countryside followed after the rural sector had been prepared structurally to receive information and incentives.* This finding has been registered many times already. Our study merely adds further confirmation. Change came to the Taiwanese countryside well after the traditional society had passed (or perhaps "been swept away" is a better term). Information about modern agriculture on Taiwan was diffused within an educated, functionally organized population, and the better educated and more highly organized they became, the faster and more effectively this information diffused. Similarly, price and investment incentives were grasped only after their meaningfulness and promise were understood. This understanding was in itself a function of the associational structure of the farm society and the links between this structure and governmental bureaucracy. Even though there is something to be said for the wisdom and energy of the typical Chinese, precious few of these virtues were seen on Taiwan from the seventeenth to the twentieth centuries. But they were unleashed with gusto after peasants became farmers and were integrated into modern society.

5. *Money made a great deal of difference in Taiwanese agricultural development.* This conclusion hardly needs to be articulated. Agriculture on Taiwan was not starved for investment capital, public or private, save perhaps during Japanese mobilization for war in the late thirties and during the war itself. What is perhaps worthy of note is that neither regime used its agricultural sector primarily as a support for industrialization. By and large, rural savings were not directly scooped up and directed into industrial ventures, and farmers were not squeezed so urban workers could eat cheaply. Certainly, the Japanese and the

Nationalists were interested in industrial growth. Some rural savings, especially during the land reforms, were directed to industry, and there were price controls on rice under both regimes. In addition, there was a rice-fertilizer barter system. But these were not especially harsh or overly exploitative policies, and they certainly did not have the effect of blunting rural incentives. On the contrary, under the Japanese, the largest portions of rural savings on Taiwan were directed back to agriculture. The largest portions of tax revenues from the island were likewise recycled. Under the Nationalists, government investment in agriculture remained sizable, and equally sizable portions of American aid went to the countryside. Paradoxically, but understandably, all of this actually contributed to bringing about a structural transformation of the Taiwanese economy. This ultimately produced a thriving industrial state founded on a thriving, healthy agriculture, yet agriculture was developed first!

6. *Finally, land reform seems to have influenced the course of rural development on Taiwan, but its direct impact on productivity remains indeterminate.* Since this conclusion at least partially "flies in the face of conventional wisdom," we shall try to be as precise as possible. Inasmuch as both the Japanese and the Nationalist land reforms were essentially political moves intended to rid rural society of unproductive or obstructionist classes, they succeeded and were functional for rural development. Traditional landlord power was not a constraint on development, because the land reforms broke this power (the Nationalist reform broke it almost completely). But the land reforms of the two different countries were very different. The Japanese redistributed very little land; before and after their reform, the bulk of farmers were tenants. By contrast, the Nationalists redistributed a great deal of land and created a rural population composed mainly of owner-operators. Yet both reforms were followed by significant increases in both production and productivity. Therefore, it is difficult to conclude whether reforming by eliminating landlords is any better or worse for agricultural growth.

In addition, one is tempted to ask whether the land reforms in and of themselves had very much to do with subsequent rises in productivity and production. As the land reforms proceeded, many other elements in the technological and economic bases of Taiwanese rural society were also being changed. Farmers' associations were being created, research results were being diffused, extension services were operating, and capital was being poured into development. As a result of these changes, we are led to conclude that it was the land reform *plus* many other modernizing programs that accounted for agricultural growth, and we are led to suggest that the land reform by itself would not have been especially consequential. All of this leads to the more general conclusion that *land reform is essentially a political instrument of class warfare.* Agricultural development very often demands that such class wars in the countryside be fought and won by modernizers. But winning the class war is most often the prelude to agricultural development, not the essence of it.

Notes

1. Ramond Myers and Han-Yu Chang, "Japanese Colonial Development Policy 1895-1906: A Case of Bureaucratic Entrepreneurship," *Journal of Asian Studies* 22, no. 4 (August 1963):433.

2. Yosaburo Takekoshi, *Japanese Rule in Formosa* (London: Longmans, 1907), p. 271.

3. Myers and Chang, "Japanese Colonial Development," p. 559.

4. Ibid., p. 562.

5. Fred W. Riggs, *Formosa under Chinese Nationalist Rule* (New York: Macmillan, 1952), p. 87.

6. Samuel P. S. Ho, "Agricultural Transformation under Colonialism: The Case of Taiwan," *Journal of Economic History* 28, no. 3 (September 1968):330.

7. Myers and Chang, "Japanese Colonial Development," p. 562.

8. N. S. Ginsberg, *Economic Resources and Development of Formosa* (New York: Institute of Pacific Relations, 1953), p. 170.

9. Takekoshi, *Japanese Rule,* p. 147.

10. Ginsburg, *Economic Resources,* p. 29.

11. Neil H. Jacoby, *U.S. Aid to Taiwan* (New York: Praeger, 1966), pp. 75-76.

12. Riggs, *Formosa under Chinese rule,* p. 107.

13. Samuel P. S. Ho, "Development Policy of Japanese Colonial Government in Taiwan 1895-1945," in *Government and Economic Development,* ed. G. Ranis (New Haven, Conn.: Yale University Press, 1971), p. 315.

14. Jacoby, *U.S. Aid to Taiwan,* p. 76.

15. Ho, "Development Policy of Japanese Government," p. 340.

16. Ho, "Agricultural Transformation under Colonialism," p. 336.

17. Ching Yuan Lin, *Industrialization in Taiwan, 1946-1972: Trade and Import Substitution Policies for Developing Countries* (New York: Praeger, 1973), p. 24.

18. T. H. Shen, *The Sino-American Joint Commission on Rural Reconstruction* (Ithaca, N.Y.: Cornell University Press, 1970), p. 203.

19. T. H. Shen, *Agricultural Development on Taiwan Since World War II* (Ithaca, N.Y.: Comstock Publishing Associates, 1964), p. 43.

20. Shen, *Sino-American Joint Commission,* p. 42.

21. Jacoby, *U.S. Aid to Taiwan,* p. 51.

22. Ibid., p. 53.

23. Shen, *Sino-American Joint Commission,* p. 42.

24. Jacoby, *U.S. Aid to Taiwan*, p. 165.
25. Shen, *Agricultural Development on Taiwan*, p. 38.
26. Shen, *Sino-American Joint Commission*, p. 33.
27. Ibid., p. 242.
28. Ibid., p. 35.
29. Shen, *Agricultural Development on Taiwan*, p. 195.
30. Ibid., p. 175.
31. Shen, *Sino-American Joint Commission*, p. 147, 165.
32. Anthony Y. C. Koo, "Economic Development," in *Taiwan in Modern Times*, ed. Paul K. T. Sih (New York: St. John's University Press, 1973), p. 417.
33. Jacoby, *U.S. Aid to Taiwan*, p. 279.
34. Ibid., p. 101.

6
Politics and Agrarian Change in South Korea: Rural Modernization by "Induced" Mobilization

Young Whan Kihl

This chapter is concerned with agrarian change in South Korea and the role of the central government in guiding the process of agricultural development and rural modernization that began to transform the rural landscape in Korea in the 1970s. The principal characteristics of change in South Korea during this period have been: (1) food production has steadily increased, so that by 1976 the country attained the goal of self-sufficiency in rice and barley, the main dietary staples; (2) government programs have been effective in modernizing the rural areas through increased investment and "induced" mobilization; and (3) support of farmers and the public at large is important for the government to carry out its politics of agricultural and rural modernization. For these reasons, agricultural development and rural modernization in South Korea may be said to provide a "success" story that has some application to other rapidly developing countries.[1]

Korea is a country that is poor in agricultural endowment. The land is mountainous, except in the southwest, so only about one-fifth of the area is cultivable. In spite of the meager resources of the land, agriculture traditionally provided the lifeline for the population for many centuries, including the period of the Yi dynasty (1392-1910). Between 1910 and 1945, Korea was a Japanese colony. Together with Taiwan it produced enough rice to support the Japanese empire. During this time a measure of agricultural development—albeit to serve the interest of the Japanese—was attained. Nevertheless, the land tenure system operated solely to the benefit of Japanese landlords.[2] Toward the end of the colonial period, roughly three-fourths of all farm operators were tenants or at best part-owners, sometimes paying as much as 80 percent of their crops as rent.[3]

The division of Korea by World War II into the industrial north and the agricultural south handicapped the national economy. Nonetheless,

133

a series of land reforms were carried out in South Korea, first in 1948 under the American military occupation, then in 1950 under the newly established government of President Syngman Rhee.[4] These measures abolished the land tenure system, establishing in its place the principle of tiller-ownership. Under the provisions of the Farm Reform Law of April 1950, a ceiling of three hectares (or about 7.5 acres) was placed on most of the farmland ownership. One source indicates that by the early 1970s, nearly 70 percent of all farm families owned all of the land they worked, while about 7 percent still remained full tenants.[5]

The ensuing Korean War, 1950-53, and the efforts at reconstruction in the 1950s did not help the cause of economic development. During the Rhee administration (1948-60), the government had neither a coherent policy on agricultural development nor any blueprint for an overall measure of economic development.[6] Only after the military coup of 1961 did the government develop a sensible plan of economic development. Throughout the 1960s it concentrated on the strategy of industrialization by giving only lip service to the policy of agricultural development. Nevertheless, agricultural productivity maintained a steady growth rate of 3.5 percent (admittedly unimpressive as compared with the overall economic growth rate of 10 percent), which was ahead of the population growth rate. Government statistics indicated a growth of 40 percent in value added to the GNP by agriculture (including forestry and fishery) between 1961 and 1971.[7]

Throughout the 1960s, the government relied on the strategy of industrialization and agricultural development via resource, not technology, utilization.[8] Only in the early seventies did it decide to follow the technology-based strategy of agricultural development, as will be shown shortly. For this reason, the experience of South Korea since 1961 may be taken as a case of a delayed but rather successful response by the government to the main problems of agriculture associated with a rapidly growing economy. These are the increasing discrepancies between the industrial and agricultural sectors of the economy and the rural and urban areas in society. The role played by the central government in agricultural development, though not as domineering and pervasive as that of a centrally planned economy, was important in skillfully steering and directing the economy through the difficult period of uncertainty and imbalanced growth.[9]

Before proceeding any further, let us place South Korea in its proper comparative perspective. The Green Revolution came to South Korea only in the early 1970s. The pursuit of the resource-based strategy of agricultural development prevalent in the sixties was a reflection of the fact that human resources were abundant in Korea. The traditional, subsistence-level agriculture employed more than two-thirds of all the households, and agricultural production and productivity were relatively good (the Korean farmers were planting varieties of fertilizer-responsive rice introduced by the Japanese half a century earlier).[10] In this sense the experience in South Korea is different from that of other Asian countries like the Philippines and Indonesia, which had earlier adopted the technology-based strategy so as to upgrade agricultural production and productivity. South Korea's experience was more like that in Taiwan and Thailand and less like the experience in the communist Asian countries North Korea and China.

Timed with the completion of the Second Five Year Economic Plan in 1971, South Korea adopted a strategy of agricultural development that is both technology-based and resource-based. The introduction of high-yielding seeds (short-grain rice seeds called *T'ongilpyo* and *Yushinpyo*) and the inauguration of the new community movement called the *Saemaul Undong* marked the beginning of the shift in the strategy of agricultural development and rural modernization in Korea. The Third Five Year Economic Plan (1972-76) and the Fourth Five Year Economic Plan (1977-81) reflect this shift in government priority in the implementation of plans for economic development.

To achieve the task of economic development, South Korea also relied on the principle of "guided capitalism" whereby the government plays an active leadership role and pursues the strategy of authoritarian-technocratic rule in nation-building. In this sense, South Korea shares characteristics with other Third World countries, such as Brazil and Chile, where the government is run by civilianized military leaders and civilian technocrats in the bureaucracy.[11] South Korea has generally manipulated economic interdependence to her benefit, notably in securing substantial multinational business investments and in pursuing export-led industrialization. Unlike many Third World countries with authoritarian-technocratic rule, however, South Korea has brought about a reasonable degree of equity in the redistribution of national wealth. A World Bank study in 1974 revealed that South Korea ranked as one of the "growth and distribution" countries whose equity is reasonably good. This is a notable achievement, since South Korea suffers from the adverse conditions of scarce land and low concentration of land ownership plus a high degree of urbanization.[12] The Gini coefficient of income distribution in South Korea has decreased from .3045 in 1968 to .2718 in 1971; while the top 20 percent of the population enjoyed 45 percent of the wealth, the bottom 40 percent enjoyed 18 percent and the middle 40 percent enjoyed 37 percent of the wealth.[13] According to the government, in 1976, the annual income for the rural household surpassed that of the urban household.[14]

The overall lessons of South Korea in agricultural development and rural modernization are clear. South Korean experience demonstrates that (1) the resource first and technology second strategy of agricultural development works, (2) government policy can make a difference between success and failure in agricultural modernization, and (3) the support of the rural population is essential for achieving the goal of rural modernization. In the subsequent discussion, we shall proceed to discuss facets of agrarian change in South Korea in terms of (1) agricultural development policy making and (2) rural modernization policy making during the decade of 1960 and in the early 1970s. In describing the agricultural development policies, we will first identify some characteristics of Korean agriculture, then discuss the agricultural policy making environment, agriculture and planned economic development, and agricultural sector development, and finally offer some explanations of agricultural development in Korea.

Agricultural Development Policy Making

Korean Agriculture: Some Characteristics

What is the state of agriculture in South Korea in the 1970s, and how do the policy makers evaluate agriculture development problems in Korea? A study by a team of agricultural experts from Korea and the United States in 1971 concluded that because of rapid industrialization and increased off-farm migration, Korean agriculture was faced not "with a lack of effective demand for staple foodstuffs," but "with a lack of modern technology and meager, fragmented land resources which currently mean high production costs for staple foods."[15] The same study listed the following as the main characteristics of Korean agriculture in the 1970s:

1. It is based on small holdings controlled by individual entrepreneurs.
2. It possesses only limited and nearly fully developed arable land resources in a relatively harsh, temperate zone climate.
3. It uses mainly human and animal power.
4. It relies on moderately well-developed irrigation systems which often lack adequate drainage.
5. It researches and innovates new biological technology at less than an optimum rate while using substantial fertilizer and plant protection chemicals.
6. It depends on government-dominated markets for the supply of most modern production factors.

7. It is commercialized to the extent that about half the total production of the farm is sold.[16]

A government publication in 1975 similarly mentioned low agricultural production and uneconomic organization of farming as two of the major problems confronting agriculture in South Korea.[17] Of the total area of 22 million hectares of the Korean peninsula, South Korea below the demilitarized zone occupies approximately 10 million hectares, and only 23 percent of this land (or 2.24 million hectares) is cultivated for farming. The paddy land suited for rice plantation is about 13 percent of the total area and is located mainly in the four main river valleys and in the small plains along the western and southern coasts. Most of the arable land in Korea is used quite intensively; there is even double cropping, particularly in the southern plains, where rice is the main summer crop and barley or wheat is grown in the winter months. Despite large efforts for the expansion of irrigation and drainage facilities, only 85 percent of the total cultivated area was irrigated in 1975. Agricultural crop production still depends heavily on weather conditions.[18]

Furthermore, the small size of farms, heavy concentration of rice farming, and low supply of agricultural capital make it difficult for the Korean farmers to switch from a traditional to a more modern and commercial farming.[19] The small size and poor organization of the farms are evident from the fact that in 1975 the per farm household landholding in Korea was only 0.94 hectares.[20] Also, the land plots are so scattered as to require an average of four different plots per household. Since a supplementary nonfarm source of household income for Korean farmers is also meager, 18.1 percent in 1975 as compared with 71.1 percent for an average Japanese farm household, it is reasonable to conclude that agriculture has a long way to go in modernization in South Korea.[21]

In view of the narrow agricultural base and its meager natural resources, the government of South Korea early in the 1960s committed itself to the intensive development of its still-primitive industrial sector and, more specifically, of labor-intensive and export-oriented industry. This unorthodox and risky strategy has paid off, however, as a result of a combination of favorable conditions external to Korea. Some of these are the liberal trade policy of the United States and an ever-expanding world market despite the energy shortage and the oil price hike of 1973. In current dollars, the values of manufactured exports, for instance, rose more than 55 percent per annum from 1962 to 1975; this growth explains why Korea is seen as a model of export-led economic growth.[22] Before discussing the contribution of the agricultural sector to the overall economic development performance of South Korea in detail, however, we need to consider some aspects of agricultural policy making.

Agriculture Policy-Making Environment

Agricultural policy making in South Korea, like public policies in general, follows the pattern of policy making in command systems—decision making takes place in formal, hierarchical situations in accordance with specified rules and procedures.[23] In a command system, decisions are rarely subject to bargaining and negotiation among autonomous actors; rather, they reflect the will and desire of the leadership in an elaborate chain of command that is based on the explicit differentiation of superior and subordinate roles.[24] Agricultural policy in Korea generally is not made, therefore, as a result of political competition among various autonomous groups, as in the United States.[25] Although grassroots participation has occurred frequently in specific projects of rural development,[26] the principal shapers of policy at the national level are the top political elite and their technocratic staff.

In an executive-dominant command system, such as that in South Korea today, the role of representative institutions like the National Assembly and the political parties, both ruling and opposition, is minimal in its policy input and impact. Instead, the president and his special assistants in the Blue House—the name for the Office of the President—exercise dominant power and authority. The policy intent of the chief executive is carried out down the hierarchical structure of the governmental system.[27] The Ministry of Agriculture and Fisheries (MAF) and the Ministry of Home Affairs (MHA) are the cabinet-level offices in charge of the day-to-day operations of the agricultural production program. In formulating and implementing policies on agricultural development, however, the agricultural ministry is guided by the Office of the Prime Minister and the Economic Planning Board (EPB). Headed by a deputy prime minister, this board acts as a coordinating body for the formulation and implementation of economic development plans.

The Ministry of Agriculture and Fisheries is in charge of agriculture, livestock, sericulture, farm lands, irrigation, and fisheries. Its subunits include: the Agricultural Administration Bureau, the Food Administration Bureau, the Land Administration Bureau, and the Agricultural Production Bureau. It also controls and supervises the Office of Rural Development (ORD) and the Office of Marine Fisheries (OMF). The former consists of two bureaus, the Research Bureau, directing the various experiment stations, and the Rural Guidance Bureau, performing the functions of an extension service, with sections dealing with agricultural improvement, home improvement, community development, and rural youth.[28]

The Ministry of Home Affairs has responsibility for field supervision and coordination because of its authority over local government units rather than because of a substantive responsibility for agricultural production. Although the MHA handles a variety of matters unrelated to agriculture, such as elections, internal security, and fire prevention, its principal duty is to perform functions assigned by the central government. There is a provincial ORD in each of the nine provinces, supervised by the governor directly. Administratively, the nine provincial governors and the mayors of Seoul and Pusan are directly responsible to and supervised by the MHA. Thus, occasions arise wherein the implementation of developmental programs such as research and extension work necessitates coordination and consultation between the two ministries of agriculture and home affairs.[29] One of the bureaus of the MHA, the Local Affairs Bureau, was given the task of monitoring the program implementation of rural development policies, the Saemaul Movement.

The National Agricultural Cooperative Federation (NACF) is a government-organized credit institution that assists the implementation of agricultural development policies and programs. It acts as the sole agent of the government in handling commercial fertilizer supplies and insecticides, either through sale or on credit, and also in purchasing grains from the farmers at harvest time. The NACF has nine provincial branch offices aiding 132 special cooperatives and 139 county cooperative federations, which, in turn, are comprised of 17,600 cooperatives, with a total membership of well over 2.2 million farmers.[30] These government ministries and semiofficial organizations are the institutional basis on which the agricultural development policies are formulated and implemented.

Agriculture and Planned Economic Development

The current emphasis on agricultural development and rural modernization in South Korea is relatively recent in origin, dating to the year 1971, when the so-called *Saemaul Undong* (New Community Movement) was inaugurated and the guidelines for the Third Five-Year Economic Plan (1972-76) were contemplated. Agricultural development policy in South Korea is, thus, an integral part of an overall strategy of economic development and modernization that is vigorously pursued by the government of President Park Chung Hee. The fact that President

Park himself is rural in origin may partially explain why he has had a special concern about the plight of the rural population in Korea and a dedication to the cause of rural modernization. In his proclamation following the military coup of May 16, 1961, Major General Park solemnly pledged, as chairman of the Revolutionary Committee on National Reconstruction, that the welfare of the farmers would be protected and enhanced. Park said that as a farm boy he had known how difficult life could be in rural Korea and that he would therefore seek advice to improve the status of the farmers.[31]

Among the early measures adopted by the military-turned-civilian government of President Park was the upgrading of the Office of Rural Development (ORD) by placing it outside the Ministry of Agriculture and Forestry (subsequently Agriculture and Fisheries). As an independent agency, mainly concerned with extension activities (including distribution of improved seed and information on new crops and cultivation techniques), the ORD has become a major instrument for agricultural development in South Korea. It has some 8,000 workers scattered all over the country at the county level. Each of the 139 counties, called *gun*, has a rural guidance section that supervises the work of these extension workers. Thus, both the home ministry and the agricultural ministry became actively involved in the operations of the ORD at the grassroots level. At the provincial level, the activities of the ORD are placed under the direct supervision of each governor of the nine provinces, thus maximizing administrative efficiency and coordination. The governors, in turn, are placed under the jurisdiction of the Ministry of Home Affairs.

The government also made a major effort in 1961-62 to assist the poor farmers in replacing private debts by giving low-interest government loans through the National Agricultural Cooperative Federation (NACF), a semiautonomous government agency involved in the marketing of farm products. As a result of this policy, the ratio of farm household debt was reported to have declined slightly—from the high of 82 percent in 1956 to 70 percent in 1964.[32] But subsequent inflation, together with the farmer's tendency to misuse the loans for purposes other than farming, made the government downplay the measure of credit-giving through the NACF.

Agricultural policy considerations took a back seat in the scheme of priorities adopted by the government of President Park during the decade of the sixties. The First Five-Year Economic Plan, initiated in 1962, gave heavy emphasis to strengthening the industrial and manufacturing sectors of the economy. The Second Five-Year Plan (1967-71) continued the policy of industrialization. It was only in the Third Five-Year Plan (1972-76) that policy measures were adopted to correct the urban-rural imbalance and the excessive industrialization of the economy. The thinking of government planners in the initial stage appears to have been based on the assumption that although agriculture and industry are closely interrelated, agricultural development has to be preceded by industrial growth. What seems at first to be risky proved to be a farsighted decision in that it helped to redirect the economy—away from the traditional pattern of subsistence-level agricultural economy and toward the new pattern of industrial economy and urbanizing society.[33]

Although the industrial sector of the economy developed much faster than the rural sector, the politicians continued to give lip service to the need for a balanced growth of industry and agriculture. In spite of this rhetoric, the government has emphasized industrialization. Strengthening the heavy and petrochemical industry, for instance, is given priority over agriculture in the Fourth Five-Year Plan (1977-81). In this strategy favoring industry, South Korea deviates significantly from the approach adopted by many developing countries: that is, that agricultural "surpluses" are seized upon to finance the investments needed to develop the nonagricultural sector.[34] A discussion and analysis of agricultural development in Korea must reflect the overall emphasis on industrialization in economic development policies pursued by the central government since 1961. The logic of policy planners in the early years of making economic development plans was that the marginal savings to be realized through agricultural modernization and import substitution would not be sufficient to generate the surplus and investment capital required for sustained economic growth.

To finance the development programs of the five-year economic plans, the Park government made several bold political decisions in the 1960s. The decision to normalize diplomatic relations with Japan in 1965 was partially motivated by the desire to raise investment capital through reparation payments by the Japanese government. Diplomatic normalization subsequently led to the arrangement for further government grants and private loans by the Japanese.[35] The decision to send Republic of Korea troops to Vietnam in 1966 was also politically motivated and contributed to the task of financing economic development. This measure earned foreign currency through direct payments by the United States to Korean troops and through contract awards to Korean firms in Vietnam. These important political decisions were necessary because of declining economic assistance by the United States. It is a well-known fact that the process of industrial growth in the Korean economy was assisted by the increase in the amount of foreign loans and direct private investment by multinational firms, mostly from the United States and Japan.[36] The economic climate for development was thus created by the political moves of President Park.

Agricultural Sector Development

As the economy continued to grow in the 1970s, South Korea emerged as an industrial and urbanized society. Between 1962 and 1975, the mining and manufacturing sector of the economy expanded, in constant terms at more than three times the pace of the agricultural sector. While the GNP share of secondary industry (mining and manufacturing) increased from 17 percent to 30 percent between 1962 and 1975, the share of primary industry (agriculture and fisheries) declined from 37 percent to 27 percent in the same period.[37] The urban population exceeded the rural population by 1970, and in 1973 the value of manufactured goods surpassed that of all primary industries, including agriculture, combined. During the sixties, a large number of rural people left the farm to migrate to urban centers to seek better economic opportunities. This resulted in an absolute as well as a relative decline in total farm population. The share of farm population decreased from 57.6 percent of the total population in 1962 to 38.2 percent in 1975. This trend is expected to continue in the future; the farm population is projected to be only about 30.5 percent of the total population by 1981.[38]

The progress in agriculture, although less dramatic than that in the manufacturing sector, was steady. Between 1963 and 1975, the average annual gains in output and labor productivity in agriculture (combined with forestry and fisheries) increased at an annual rate of 4.8 and 3.5 percent respectively. The 4.8 percent rate is slightly above the minimum for food production increase (4.0 percent) recommended by the 1974 World Food Conference in Rome. In 1976, South Korea became self-sufficient in the production of rice, thanks largely to the utilization of high-yielding varieties of rice called *T'ongilpyo* and *Yushinpyo*. First introduced in 1972, the new rice seedlings were gradually adopted, and the area under such cultivation increased from 7 percent in 1973 to 15 percent in 1974, then to 23 percent in 1975 and 44 percent in 1976.[39] In 1977, the government ended the requirement that rice be mixed with other cereals in restaurants and lifted the ban on brewing rice wine, thrift measures adopted in the early years.[40] During the new year's news conference in 1977, President Park proudly announced that South Korea was ready—allegedly on humanitarian grounds—to extend food aid to North Korea, which, he said, was experiencing food shortage from a bad harvest in the preceding year.[41] Table 6.1 shows an overall increase in the production of cereals in the year between 1961 and 1976.

The increase in food production is not sufficient, however, to meet the minimum food and nutrition requirements of the expanding population in South Korea. Food shortages are still acute in Korea, since the

TABLE 6.1
Main Food Production for Selected Years, 1961-76[a]

Crop	1961	1966	1971	1976
	(in thousands of metric tons)			
Rice	3,463	3,919	3,998	5,215
Barley & Wheat	1,389	1,845	1,714	1,847
Pulses	190	195	263	354
Potatoes	383	972	707	671
Misc. cereals	96	107	110	119
Fruits	150	331	404	615
Vegetables	1,235	1,716	2,908	3,217
Special Crops[b]	47	60	89	85

Source: Nongchong Such'op, 1977 (Handbook of Agricultural Policy) (Seoul: Ministry of Agriculture and Fisheries, 1977), pp. 35-43.

[a]During the time periods the land use pattern has changed due to the pressure of urbanization and industrialization. Some paddies and croplands were used as industrial sites, while river and tidal basins were reclaimed for agricultural use. Nonetheless, overall hectares of the land under cultivation remained constant.
[b]Include sesame, mushrooms, tobaccos, etc.

amount of total grain production is far short of the demand for food. As Table 6.2 indicates, South Korea is not self-sufficient in food production, except for rice and barley. Approximately one fourth of its food requirement in 1976 had to be met by imported grains. Moreover, as the living standard improved, the food and dietary habits of the population also changed in Korea. More proteins, fruits, and processed foods are consumed in large quantities, and less starch and rice products are demanded. Food policy in Korea must reflect the changing nutrition requirements of the population. These, in turn, are affected by an economy that is becoming increasingly industrial and urban in character. It is no surprise that national grain policies in the Third Five-Year Plan included the three primary goals of achieving self-

TABLE 6.2
Food Consumption, Production and Import, 1961-76

Year	Consumption	Production	Imports	Self Sufficiency
(in thousands of metric tons)				
1961	5,463	4,993	536	91.4%
1962	5,976	5,429	482	90.8
1963	6,138	4,637	1,223	75.5
1964	6,408	5,996	84	93.6
1965	7,313	6,864	634	93.9
1966	7,089	6,715	525	94.7
1967	8,014	6,947	1,100	86.7
1968	7,976	6,486	1,496	81.3
1969	8,573	6,307	2,389	73.6
1970	8,820	7,097	2,115	80.5
1971	9,856	6,842	2,883	69.4
1972	9,626	6,807	3,210	70.7
1973	9,715	6,538	3,249	67.3
1974	9,470	6,674	2,732	70.5
1975	9,561	7,295	3,147	76.3
1976	10,271	7,692	2,849	74.0

Source: Nongchong Such'op, 1977 (Handbook of Agricultural Policy) (Seoul: Ministry of Agriculture and Fisheries, 1977), pp. 66-67.

sufficiency in rice production, increasing availability of livestock
products for dietary improvement, and increasing production of
agricultural products in order to enhance farm income.

By the middle of the 1970s, South Korea had transformed itself from a
nation with a marginally subsistent agricultural economy into one of
Asia's emerging industrial nations. Economic indicators of performance are all impressive. For instance, the GNP increased at an average
annual rate of 9.8 percent between 1962 and 1975, while the rate of
population growth declined from 2.9 percent in 1962 to 1.7 percent in
1975. With the growth in per capita income, from $87 in 1962 to $532 in
1975 (in current prices),[42] and the expansion of employment opportunities for the millions, the standard of living for average Koreans has
increased and the quality of life has also improved.[43] As Table 6.3 shows,

TABLE 6.3
Annual Household Income for Urban and Rural
Residents, 1962-75[a]

Year	Farm Household	Salary and Wage Earner Household	Farm Income as a Percent of Salary and Wage Income
	(Unit:	Won)	
1962	206,300	293,600	70.3
1963	234,700	201,900	116.2
1964	244,500	166,600	129.3
1965	192,100	192,700	99.7
1966	199,000	247,000	80.6
1967	206,200	343,000	60.1
1968	222,000	354,800	62.6
1969	245,600	376,100	65.3
1970	255,800	381,200	67.1
1971	317,300	402,400	78.9
1972	341,900	412,000	83.0
1973	371,200	424,900	87.4
1974	421,300	402,600	104.7
1975	431,700	425,000	101.6

Source: The Korean Economy: Growth, Equity and
Structural Change (Seoul: Economic Planning Board,
September 1976), p. 16.

[a]In 1970 prices, deflated by consumer price index.

the ratio of farm to urban household real income has steadily declined since 1965. But in 1974, the farm household income attained parity with the urban worker household and, given the continuous efforts of the government to improve the terms of trade for agricultural products, farm income will likely forge ahead of the salary and wage earners' real income in the cities in the years ahead.

Some Explanations for Agricultural Development

How do we explain the success story of South Korea in view of its rapid economic development and increased agricultural production? In their study of economic takeoff in the 1960s, Cole and Lyman attributed the interplay of economics and politics as the main cause for the success of Korean development.[44] They claim that the trade-offs between political stability and economic progress led to the "breakthrough" of the Korean economy in the mid-1960s.[45] Economic development was generated by the convergence of three additional factors: (1) a comparatively well-educated and highly motivated population; (2) an industrial structure based largely on light and relatively labor-intensive industry, and (3) policy changes that maximized the advantages of these and other factors in the Korean scene.[46] The last of these factors probably was the most important: the quality and effectiveness of political leadership in guiding economic development. The government leaders subscribed to the notion of rational economic planning and committed themselves to the belief that development could be brought about or accelerated by government intervention.[47] The civilianized military leaders of President Park's administration adopted an ideology of economic planning and had the will and the skill to carry it out by mobilizing all available means.

Many reasons are given for the agricultural production and rural development improvements in Korea. The input of technology and capital—such as adoption of high-yielding miracle seedlings, increased use of fertilizer and pesticides, and improvement of the irrigation system—are all very important factors in improving agricultural output. A rice strain called T'ong-il IR 667 was successfully developed in 1969 (although it was not planted by farmers until 1971) and increased the yield by more than 30 percent compared with common varieties. In the case of barley, the single-crop system was changed into a double-crop system in central and northern areas by cultivating a new variety, SB 6920, which yielded 17-23 percent more than common varieties. Some twenty-one improved varieties of rice and twenty varieties of barley were made available for farmers to choose from.[48] In 1975, the World Bank extended a loan to the Seoul government to spur the seed improvement campaign in South Korea. South Korea claims to be third-ranking among the countries of the world in rice production per unit area, following Spain and Japan. With current Korean unit productivity equal to 100 percent, Taiwan stands at 81 percent and the Philippines at 32 percent, and Indonesia and Vietnam at 40 percent.[49]

The increase in the productivity of land in Korea is also due to the infrastructure building efforts by the government that include: conducting basic agricultural research, increasing spending on agriculture and rural education, waging a mass campaign for increasing the efficiency of farm production, and upgrading the quality of rural life.[50] Also important in the Korean context, however, are the psychological factors of self-assurance and self-help that the government was able to instill in the minds of the farmers through a careful program of indoctrination and education. The means of political mobilization by the so-called *Saemaul Undong*, which will be discussed in the second half of this chapter, produced an agrarian revolution in the Korean village in the form of modernizing the attitudes and value orientations of the farmers.

Equally important for agricultural development in Korea were the spin-off effects accruing from industrial gains, which, in turn, resulted from the successful implementation of economic development policies. Increased fertilizer consumption and use of pesticides, for example, were made possible because of the construction of chemical and fertilizer plants as part of the overall industrialization program. There is a trade-off, therefore, between agricultural development policy and industrialization policy. The total quantity of plant nutrients used per hectare of planted crop, for instance, increased from 72 kilograms in 1962 to 260 kilograms in 1975. The total amount of fertilizer consumption also more than tripled in the same period, from 225,000 metric tons to 837,000 metric tons. The quantity of pesticides was almost eighteen times as large in 1974 as in 1962.[51] The demand for increased fertilizer and pesticide consumption was financed domestically by a steady increase in domestic supply rather than by externally relying on foreign sources of supply.

South Korea has thus implemented an agricultural development policy that is an integral part of the overall strategy of its economic development plans. Agricultural production is regarded as an important sector of the economy insofar as it generates enough surplus or savings to be used for investment elsewhere in the economy. Since South Korea is not self-sufficient in food and relies continually on foreign import of grain, the increased production of food at home will no doubt alleviate somewhat the pressure on foreign reserves for the purchase of grains.⁵² The savings thus obtained can be used as investment capital to finance more productive development projects. In achieving its development goals in agriculture, the government has taken a number of important steps and policy measures. They can be grouped into four broad areas: (1) infrastructure and institution building, (2) solicitation of policy recommendations, (3) rural modernization through mobilization strategy, and (4) farm price support policy.

Infrastructure building. The government supports the productive capability of agriculture through an increased investment in infrastructure building in this sector. Some examples are such broad measures as the building of highways to improve transportation between rural and urban areas and the modernizing of the banking and credit system to ease the terms of trade between villages and cities. Government investment in infrastructure building also includes such specific measures as support of activities and programs of the Office of Rural Development, the National Agricultural Cooperatives Federation, the Water Management Federation, The Soil Improvement Cooperative, the Agricultural Development Corporation, and the National Agricultural Economics Research Center. To finance a series of large-scale development projects, such as the river-basin development and irrigation project, the Seoul government also relies heavily on external sources of financing.

The success of South Korea in obtaining international loans to finance its development projects is testimony to how skillful and competent the development bureaucracy is in grantsmanship. It is said that South Korea has received the largest amount of bank loans from the Asia Development Bank. This is no mean accomplishment, given the keen competition for financial resources among the member nations involved. Most of the international loans are made through such multilateral international agencies as the World Bank and such bilateral channels as the U.S. Agency for International Development. Between 1967 and 1973, the Seoul government received international loans amounting to $68.9 million to finance the completion of nine projects. From 1973 to 1977, it successfully negotiated $517.7 million in loans to finance some twenty-three additional projects aimed at agricultural development and infrastructure building. In 1977, fifteen additional projects were proposed, for which the government is trying to acquire international loans. The estimated cost to complete these projects is listed as $568.8 million.⁵³

International loans have been used to finance a multitude of development projects, ranging from the construction of dams and highways to food refrigeration and farm mechanization. In illustration, we can cite an award made by the World Bank in December 1977 to assist the increased food-grain production in South Korea. The bank agreed to lend some $36 million to the Agricultural Development Corporation for a term of sixteen years with interest at 7.9 percent per annum. The specific development project for which the money is earmarked has to do with the $76 million Ogseo Area Development project, some 160 kilometers south of Seoul, which will provide irrigation facilities including pumping stations and canals on 7,090 hectares of newly irrigated lands. When this project is completed, it is estimated that some 23,400 farm families, or approximately 130,000 people, will be the beneficiaries and that there will be a net foreign exchange savings of some $8 million a year (which would otherwise be spent to purchase food grains from abroad.)[54]

Solicitation of policy recommendations. Recognizing the need to modernize farm operation and management in line with the changing structure of the Korean economy, the government seems to be searching for advice and recommendations from various sources in order to formulate agricultural development policies for the 1980s. It is listening seriously to a recommendation made by a study group of professors who were appointed by the Office of the Prime Minister to evaluate government policies. Their recommendation has to do with amending the existing law so as to allow a separation of ownership and the use of the land.[55] Ostensibly, this would promote the consolidation of small, divided landholdings and thereby enable the farmer to improve his output. It has also been reported that a group of agricultural scientists has advocated a comprehensive food and nutrition policy for Korea as part of the report adopted in 1976 by the Korea FAO Association entitled "Recommended Dietary Allowance for Koreans." Involved in producing this report were thirty professors and specialists organized into seven subcommittees.[56] The ruling Democratic Republican Party is reported to be interested in introducing a bill before the National Assembly to prohibit absentee ownership of the land and to lift the ban on the upper limit of land ownership, which is currently fixed at three hectares, so as to allow commercialization of agriculture well beyond the 1980s.[57]

The government also utilizes the research capability of various agencies for developmental tasks. Thus, the Ministry of Agriculture and Fisheries approved a joint research project between the National Agricultural Economics Research Institute and Michigan State University, through a U.S. AID grant, to develop a computer-simulated model of Korean Agricultural Sector Study (KASS). The project, undertaken between July 1, 1971, and June 30, 1976, was intended to provide policy makers with a comprehensive study and analysis of the components comprising the agricultural sector and of related policy strategies such as investment priorities.[58] The government also relies on the research capability and resources of the Korea Development Institute, a government agency composed of economists and other social scientists. In 1978, the government announced the establishment of a new research institute, called the Korea Rural Development Institute, which will be patterned after the Korea Development Institute but specialize in the study of agricultural problems.

In conclusion, the Korean experience of agricultural development shows that the pursuance of an industrialization policy and an agricultural development policy need not be mutually exclusive and that, given the proper policy guidance and leadership, the two policies can be made mutually reinforcing. Underlying the effort to harmonize the two policies, however, was the political will and skill of the government of President Park Chung Hee in transforming the rural environment through the mobilization of human resources in the agrarian sector.

Rural Modernization Policy Making

In this section, rural modernization policy in South Korea will be examined in three steps. First, the nature and characteristics of the New Community Movement will be discussed as mobilization strategy. Second, the factors responsible for the adoption of this policy will be reviewed. Third, an effort will be made to assess farm price-support policies and some of the consequences of adopting these policies on rural modernization in Korea.

The Saemaul Movement as Mobilization Strategy

The policy of rural modernization in South Korea, inaugurated in late 1971, is called *Saemaul Undong* or "New Community Movement." It is said that the idea originated from the staff of the Blue House with the special blessing of President Park Chung Hee.[59] An analysis of the making and implementation of the policy of the Saemaul Movement in Korea can provide a good example of the authoritarian character of Korean decision making and the need to use mobilization techniques to implement policies of rural modernization. All important policy decisions, including agricultural development and rural modernization, are made by the chief executive and his staff in the Blue House, rather than by the interaction of various actors in the political arena, including legislative leaders in the National Assembly and party politicians working closely with the spokesmen of various interest groups.

To implement the Saemaul Movement, a comprehensive economic self-help program for the rural villages, the chief executive worked closely, sometimes directly, with the village leaders, thereby often shortcutting or even bypassing an intermediary structure of various provincial, county, or subcounty-level government units. The formal responsibility for overseeing the Saemaul Movement is placed with the Ministry of Home Affairs, not the Ministry of Agriculture and Fisheries. This arrangement has a definite advantage in a highly centralized and authoritarian system. It makes sense to utilize the Home ministry because it enjoys a nation-wide system of communication, control, and surveillance that extends to the provincial, county, and village levels. The national police, part of the Home ministry, can always monitor the activities related to rural development. For similar reasons, the Bureau of Forestry was transferred a few years ago from the Agricultural ministry to the Home ministry. (Under national emergency measures, certain designated mountains and hills in Korea are made off-limits to civilians, allegedly to protect national security and to protect the environment from human damage.)

As a mobilization strategy of rural transformation, the Saemaul Movement is thus politically motivated. As stated by the Korean government, the movement has three main objectives: (1) "spiritual enlightenment," that is, the modernization of thinking and social patterns in the villages; (2) physical and environmental improvement of the villages, and (3) increased productivity and income, principally through the creation of more nonagricultural jobs in the rural areas.[60] Underlying the rationale of the Saemaul Movement is the assumption that the Korean farmers are basically backward in their attitudes and thinking, but that they can be modernized by improving the physical environment in the villages and enhancing the standard of living with increased income. To achieve the policy objective of rural modernization, government guidance is deemed essential, at least in the initial stage. Once the project is launched, however, local participation and self-help measures are encouraged, so the government will gradually be able to decrease the level of its financial support and supplies of material. The target date for completing the Saemaul projects is set at 1981, after which the rural population in Korea will presumably be self-reliant and require minimum government assistance.[61]

To achieve these developmental goals, the government initially provided supplies of cement and steel reinforcing rods. The villagers were encouraged to use these materials to improve the physical environment of roads, bridges, wells, and sanitation facilities.[62] A major program was also launched simultaneously to persuade farmers to replace their thatched roofs with tile, metal, or composition, especially in the villages along the elevated national highways. The policy intent here was to maximize the demonstration effect of the beautification efforts. There are numerous accounts of an excessive and coercive use of government power to carry this plan through. Eyewitness accounts of such excessive measures as these have been reported:

> If several farmers in a village were reluctant to replace the traditional brush fences around their houses with cement walls, jeep loads of men from the county seat might arrive and simply tear down all the brush fences. Similarly, there were occasions when house owners who were unwilling to make the substantial investment necessary to replace their thatched roofs with composition or tile might return home from a market trip to find the thatch gone and their homes open to the sky.[63]

These excesses, according to anthropologist Vincent Brandt, reflected "the obvious concern of local officials with producing quick results to please their superiors." They also "generated a lot of resentment and cynicism during the first two or three years of the movement."[64] The government planners seemed to think that through participation in projects having an immediate impact on the village environment, farmers would realize the benefit of working together during the off season, and a cooperative spirit of progressive community activism would be fostered. It seems that the logic of social engineering, or environmental rather than hereditary determinism, characterizes the thinking of these policy makers.

Under the circumstances, it is not too difficult to understand why many farmers were less than enthusiastic about the idea of the Saemaul Movement during its initial stage. Some farmers "distrusted the motives of officials and resented the constant interference in village affairs. . . . After all, nothing good had ever happened to rural society before as a result of closer contacts with the bureaucracy."[65] The government countered the resistance of farmers, however, by further increasing its effort through a mass campaign of indoctrination. The entire bureaucracy of the government was utilized to promote the cause of the Saemaul Movement. Some forward-looking and youthful village leaders were chosen as so-called Saemaul leaders and sent to the training center near Seoul for indoctrination. These cadres of the Saemaul Movement, who are decorated and rewarded for their leadership role, are used as agents of the central government in the villages to carry on the task of modernization. The extent of mobilization to fulfill the Saemaul Movement is vividly described by Vincent Brandt:

> Because of unrelenting pressure from the top, bureaucratic efforts to achieve the movement's goals were intense. Saemaul became the main focus of activity for all local administrative agencies, and thousands of other officials from the capital descended on the provinces to inspect, exhort, direct operations, and—to some extent—compete with local officials. The result initially was often confusion and bureaucratic overkill, while the astonished villagers struggled to comply with mounting and sometimes conflicting demands for compliance with various aspects of the overall plan.[66]

What seems astonishing, however, is that the Saemaul Movement has changed its character over a period of time—from the coercive mobilization campaign in the early years to a more persuasive, voluntary effort of self-help in subsequent years. In spite of initial setbacks and resistance, the policy goals of the Saemaul Movement have come to be accepted by most of the rural population in Korea. Of course, an important question still remains; that is, whether the rural transformation in South Korea is due primarily to the Saemaul Movement, as the government claims it is, or to some other extraneous factors, such as the maturation process that the changed value orientation of the farmers brought about. We may be able to answer this question more readily if we first examine the background and circumstances of the Saemaul Movement's adoption as the rural modernization policy in Korea.

Factors Responsible for Rural Modernization Policy

The decision to institute the Saemaul Movement in late 1971 was designed to solve two of the serious developmental problems in South Korea: the large-scale exodus of rural migrants to the cities and the increasingly apparent disparity between urban and rural conditions of living. According to a United Nations study, South Korea is one of the developing countries that exhibited the largest urban-rural growth differential (URGD) in the years between 1950 and 1970.[67] The population of Korea living in urban areas of 20,000 or more was only 3.1 percent in 1915. This increased to 16 percent in 1940. The urban population (living in administrative *sis* of more than 50,000 population) increased to 24.5 percent in 1955 and to 48.4 percent in 1975. Seoul illustrates the point of rapid urbanization. Its population grew from

240,000 in 1915 to about 1,250,000 in 1950 and to nearly 7 million in 1975.[68] There are indications that development strategists were ill prepared to cope with an ever-expanding population in the cities and the attendant socioeconomic problems. In 1969 agents from the Ministry of Health and Social Affairs attempted—out of desperation—to meet young migrants at bus and train stations in Seoul in order to dissuade them from contacting pimps or labor *gangpae* and to try to persuade them to return home.[69] In 1971 there were many complaints by young migrants of abuse at the hands of police and military police at checkpoints outside Seoul.[70]

The rural exodus to the cities was not necessarily objectionable from the perspective of developmental planning. According to one report, some economic planners are even pleased over the prospect of a continuous supply of excess rural labor that can be channeled into the manufacturing, industrial, and service sectors of the economy.[71] Thus, the introduction of the Saemaul Movement in the winter months of 1971-72 seems to have been well timed and planned to harmonize the rural development strategy with the overall strategy of economic development. The Saemaul Movement goals of rural modernization have thus become an integral part of the Third Five-Year Economic Plan, which began in 1972.

The Saemaul Movement has adopted the slogan of "self-help, cooperation, and diligence" symbolizing the nature of the cooperative village improvement projects initiated in the winter of 1971-72.[72] As a government-guided, economic self-help program, the Saemaul projects are aimed at contributing to the enhancement of the quality of life in the rural area. This is accomplished by improving the village environment through such projects as the expansion of rural roads and water supplies, rural electrification, and the establishment of rural medical clinics. The program also attempts to increase farm income through local cooperative projects, such as land reclamation, irrigation, reforestation, planting of fruit trees, and raising of livestock. The movement started as a mass mobilization campaign directed by the government to beautify the environment in the rural area. Subsequently, it expanded its scope and task to include sponsoring rural industries so as to utilize seasonally idle labor and thereby raise the off-farm income of rural households.[73] In this sense, the Saemaul Movement is considered to be an integral part of the overall plan of economic development that urges utilizing farm labor during the off season to increase the export of manufactured goods. The extent of financial investment in Saemaul projects is shown in Table 6.4.

TABLE 6.4
Investment in Saemaul Projects to Raise Farm Income, 1972-77
(In Millions of Wons)

	1968-71	1972	1973	1974	1975	1976	1977[a]
Number of Households	410	487	564	659	867	873	--
Total Investment	47,103	12,669	13,343	14,747	23,330	22,958	20,548
Nat'l. Govt. Contribution	2,192	474	681	691	628	875	1,002
Local Govt. Contribution	3,673	795	766	636	638	1,231	917
Medium-term Loan	23,500	6,667	7,151	8,402	10,007	10,998	12,550
Short-term Loan	1,030	93	154	--	628	4,769	98
Development Fund	4,502	170	665	646	--	145	1,644
Self-Contribution by Residents	12,206	4,183	3,926	4,372	11,429	4,940	4,337

Source: Nongchong Such'op, 1977 (Handbook of Agricultural Policy)
(Seoul: Ministry of Agriculture and Fisheries, 1977), pp. 184-185.

Note: The conversion of the Korean currency into the U.S. dollar is:
1 US$=400 Korean Won.

[a]tentative

There is an effort to expand the scope of the Saemaul Movement to include urban regions and communities as well. However, the movement remains largely a rural-based cooperative effort. Economic planners are concerned about the heavy centralization of industrial facilities in regions close to the cities (such as the Seoul-Inchon corridor) and the attendant problems of urban congestion and land use. As a remedy, the government is sponsoring measures of industrial dispersion and also of reversed migration from the cities to the rural areas. Planned industrial sites in remote regions and small-scale rural industries have been expanded. They are expected to contribute to internal economic development by the generation of additional exports. It is anticipated that the agricultural development programs will encourage the growth of commercial agriculture, and especially the export of processed foods that will earn foreign currencies. This line of thinking once again reflects the industrial orientation of South Korean agricultural development planners.

Political considerations also figured in the timing for instituting the movement in the winter of 1971-72. Traditionally, the incumbent president has always received a greater rural support in national elections than the opposition, and President Park could count on the rural votes, as shown in the national elections held in 1963 and 1967.[74] In the 1971 presidential election, however, he suffered a decline in rural support generally and was defeated in the southwestern region by the opposition, Kim Dae Jung of the New Democratic Party.[75] Alarmed by the deteriorating trend of political support, especially in the rural villages, President Park responded by instituting the mass mobilization programs of rural development and also by carrying out the so-called Revitalization Reform of October 17, 1972.[76] As a result of this political reform, the system of direct election of the president was replaced by an indirect method—through an electoral college that Park effectively controlled, thereby assuring himself of a life-long tenure of presidency. The result of the 1971 election was interpreted by many as an affirmation of voter diaspproval of governmental emphasis on industrialization and urban development at the expense of slow-paced agricultural and rural development.

Once inaugurated, the government quickly moved to implement the Saemaul program with vigor, discipline, and unrelenting pressure from the top. No village in South Korea was immune from government pressure. As of 1975, South Korea's 13.2 million farm population lived in 2.4 million farm households located in about 35,000 villages, although there were some scattered farm households in hilly and mountainous areas. These villages are designated by the government as "Saemaul villages." They are undergoing three stages of development. The first is initiation, with the government's moral support. These villages are called "basic villages." In the second stage, the village, now called a "self-help village," undertakes Saemaul projects with government support and supply of material and loans. Villages in stage three, now called "self-reliant" or "independent villages," are those that have implemented Saemaul programs and thereby significantly raised rural income and retained a degree of financial viability. The government's target is to have all of Korea's nearly 35,000 villages in the third stage by 1981,[77] as shown in Table 6.5.

The implementation of the Saemaul Movement, except for initial

TABLE 6.5   Actual and Projected Number of Saemaul
Villages

Stage	Actual		Projected	
	1973	1974	1976	1981
Basic	18,415	10,665	--	--
Self-help	13,943	20,000	20,165	--
Independent	2,307	4,000	14,500	34,665
Total	34,665	34,665	34,665	34,665

Source: Parvez Hassan, Korea: Problems and
Issues in a Rapidly Growing Economy (Baltimore:
Johns Hopkins University Press, 1976), pp. 160-61;
Hahn-been Lee, Korea: Time, Change and Adminis-
tration (Honolulu: East-West Center Press, 1967).

setbacks, appears to be proceeding far better than expected. There is
evidence to suggest that through government inducements some farmers
have been motivated to adopt modern farming practices. What is
amazing is that these government-initiated projects have been integrated
into the village life and that the myth of Saemaul has come true to a
certain extent. Even though it is difficult to know how genuinely the
Saemaul Movement has been carried out in the rural villages of Korea—
we have to rely on government propaganda—the fact is that the rural
population in Korea is constantly saturated with the Saemaul ideology
of cooperation in order to solve village problems. This incessant
government pressure may, as time goes by, bring about the intended
result. The following excerpt from a report of the *Hankook Ilbo,* dated
December 15, 1977, is a typical example of how a government decision is
made by the chief executive in a command system that is both
authoritarian and charismatic. During one of his frequent working-
lunch meetings, President Park decorated several Saemaul Movement
leaders and carried on the following conversation:[78]

President Park: I believe Korea is one of the few countries in the world
where farmers keep household records and I am glad to see this practice.
How about the case where children of the farm family are [sent] away to
the cities for employment and are sending some money back home? Do
you include or exclude such an extra income to an overall household
income?

Home Minister Kim: We exclude such an extra income from the total, sir.

Agriculture and Fisheries Minister Choe: In my opinion we should include such money in the total farm household income.

President Park: The Home ministry and Agricultural ministry appear to be at odds in computing statistics. Which one is more accurate? I think the extra earnings by farm children [which are] sent home from the city ought to be included, *and this will be the practice from now on.*

Deputy Prime Minister Nahm (who is also minister of the Economic Planning Board): Although it is correct that each government agency tends to differ slightly in its statistics, we do employ a uniform and scientific criterion for the purpose of a designated statistical survey. It is the usual practice to admit 5 percent margin of error in any survey undertaking.

President Park: A few days before on the way back from a visit to Chonju I noticed a rest area on Honam Expressway which was recently renovated so nicely that I sincerely felt that the surrounding area looked more beautiful than a European farm house I happened to see some years ago. I heard that as the village becomes beautified some elderly people frequently climb up the hills and they become very nostalgic about the past and impressed by the changing scenery of the area. *If the village is beautified, the consciousness of the farmers will also change* and they will be anxious to keep up with the plan of environmental beautification, including the planting of new trees, improving the sewage system, environment work, etc. In your village, Mrs. Park, tell me how many television sets and refrigerators are available as of now.

Mrs. Park: In our village there are sixteen TV sets and three washing machines.

President Park: Do many households in your village use an electric rice cooker?

Mrs. Park: Almost all the families in the village use one now. It certainly is convenient and saves fuel too.

President Park: If villages are to be developed, agricultural cooperatives must be run more efficiently. Men of ability or Saemaul Movement leaders must be encouraged to work for the cooperatives. Since I recently heard about an improper outside request being made to the Agricultural Cooperative Federation on matters of personnel, I have directed an attorney to look into the matter thoroughly. Pressures for personal favors will undermine the cooperatives. Follow, I beg you, a fair personnel practice. The same applies to water management cooperatives and to soil improvement cooperatives. When I asked some county chiefs at the regular monthly meeting similar to this one how long they thought it would take the average farm household income to reach 1,400,000 won (about 2,900 U.S. dollars), most of them said that we would not reach that goal until 1978. But the fact is that the target has already been achieved this year in 1977 despite a very conservative estimate by the Ministry of Agriculture and Fisheries.

The real problem, as I see it, is the increase in consumption expenditures by farmers when they receive additional income. I urge you to advise the farmers to save the income and to invest it in such projects as household improvements. Sightseeing projects (which I hear have become very popular among many farmers recently) can be accomplished rather slowly in the future. This kind of luxury can certainly wait until the 1980s when farm income will be much larger than now and more sightseeing areas will also be available. By 1981 I can assure you that 92 percent of all the roads in our country will be paved and this will certainly ease travel, too.

Farm Price-Support Policy and Its Effect

Closely related to the measures of the Saemaul Movement in enhancing the rural welfare is the government policy of price support for grains. The fluctuation of the price of rice in the market is perceived and interpreted by many as a barometer that reflects the health of the national economy. For this reason, the government is more than anxious to stabilize the price of grain in the market, especially during the preharvest season.

South Korea has employed two extreme types of food price policy. Up until 1968, food prices were kept purposefully low by price controls and, although relatively large quantities of food were imported from abroad, it was necessary to control distribution through consumer rationing and other measures. The shift in policy effective with the 1968 harvest had the major initial objective of improving production incentives for farmers. Subsequently, larger annual grain price increases were employed by the government to help restore balance between the rural and the urban incomes. To achieve this objective, a dual-price policy was adopted in 1968. The government purchased barley and wheat from farmers at high prices and sold it to consumers at lower prices. Through price supports, the government attempted to increase the farmers' income, stabilize prices for consumers, and substitute barley and wheat for rice. In view of the self-sufficiency in rice that has recently been attained, the dual-price policy for barley and wheat may need readjustment and modification. (Koreans prefer rice over wheat and barley in their everyday diet).

The government's major emphasis in rice policy, according to one expert, was to maintain low prices for urban consumers and prevent wide seasonal price fluctuations, rather than maintain adequate prices to support farm incomes.[79] Because of the major role of rice in the Korean economy, low rice prices were regarded as one of the most effective tools in achieving general price stability. Thus, the government purchase price was always below market prices, and rice was, in effect, requisitoned from farmers through local administrative channels. The situation changed after 1968. In that year, the government raised the purchase price of rice by 17 percent over the 1967 price. The rate of annual increase since 1968 has been substantial, as shown in Table 6.6. The ratio of purchase price to market price of rice was generally favorable between 1970 and 1973. This was a belated response by the government to face the growing income disparity between urban and rural households and the increasing food shortage. As one observer noted, "Policy makers were obliged to give serious consideration to a more equitable income distribution and expansion of food-grain production, and, in particular, to the achievement of self-sufficiency in rice production."[80] To solve the food shortage, more specific measures included the adoption of the dual price system for barley (to discourage rice consumption) as noted above. As a result, the price of barley was about two-thirds the price of rice prior to 1968. Since 1969, the price of barley for urban consumers has lowered to about half that of rice. Also, as noted, restaurants were required to serve a mixture of 75 percent rice and 25 percent barley and to serve noodles and nonrice food grains. Lunches carried by school children also had to contain a similar mixture of grains.[81]

The government policy of high prices for grains, intended to increase production incentives for farmers, had both positive and negative effects. It generally contributed to the attainment of self-sufficiency in rice production and the achievement of a closer balance between rural and urban household incomes. The dual price policy necessitated deficit financing, which became a major cause of general inflation. The fact that the selling price of barley and wheat was set below their purchase price (it was 90.3 percent of the purchase price in 1968 and 68.6 percent of the purchase price in 1973) resulted in a considerable burden on the national treasury. In 1973 alone, the government reportedly spent 8.9 billion won (approximately 22 million U.S. dollars) to subsidize grain prices.[82] Government efforts to phase out the difference between the two prices and to shift more of the costs directly to consumers brought pressure on the salaries and wages of the urban dwellers.[83] Thus, the grain support policy appears to have been less than a complete success. The continuous rise of grain prices in the market created inflationary pressures on the economy and caused a constant increase in the purchase price of grain in order to keep up with inflation.

TABLE 6.6
Rice Purchase Prices and Market Producer Prices, 1960-76

Crop Year	Purchase Price Won/80 kg polished rice	percent increase	Market Price[a] Won/80 kg polished rice	percent increase	Purchase Price as a percent of Market Price
1960	1,130	0	1,340	38.8	84.3
1961	1,550	46.4	1,404	4.8	110.4
1962	1,780	14.8	1,792	27.7	99.3
1963	2,056	15.5	2,635	47.0	78.0
1964	2,967	44.3	3,032	15.1	97.9
1965	3,150	6.2	3,000	-1.1	105.0
1966	3,306	5.0	3,140	4.7	105.3
1967	3,590	8.6	3,642	15.7	98.6
1968	4,200	17.0	4,937	35.9	85.1
1969	5,150	22.6	5,354	8.4	96.2
1970	7,000	35.9	6,596	23.2	106.1
1971	8,750	25.0	8,462	28.3	103.4
1972	9,888	13.0	9,750	15.2	101.4
1973	11,377	15.1	11,000	12.8	103.4
1974	15,760	38.5	16,652	51.4	94.6
1975	19,500	23.7	19,632	19.5	
1976	23,200	19.0			
1977	26,260	13.2			

Sources: Grain Statistics Yearbook (Seoul: Ministry of Agriculture and Fisheries, December, 1974), as cited in Pal Yong Moon, "The Evolution of Rice Policy in Korea," Food Research Institute Studies, 14-4 (1975), p. 393; Nongchong Such'op, 1977 (Handbook of Agricultural Policy) (Seoul: Min Ministry of Agriculture and Fisheries, 1977), pp. 287, 291; Hankuk Ilbo, October 15, 1977.

[a]November-January average prices at local markets..

Who benefits and how much from the policies of rural modernization and food price support? This is an important question to ask because the answers may provide the basis for assessing the success or failure of the agricultural policy of rural development and modernization in South Korea. Since the early 1970s, rising food prices and inflation probably hurt the urban dwellers the most, because salaries and wages did not increase proportionally. Real nonfarm incomes lagged far behind those of farmers. The government reports that there has been a significant increase in incomes of rural workers relative to those of urban workers during the 1970s.[84] An aggregate comparison is misleading, however, because the rural household is larger in composition than the urban household, in a ratio of five to four. The result is that on a per worker basis, the urban industrial worker is still ahead of the rural agricultural worker. Also, and more importantly, one should account for the structural element in Korean agriculture: farmers with large land-holdings (i.e., those who own more than two but less than three hectares) are likely to benefit more from the price support measures than farmers with small landholdings.

The possibility of differential effect on farm income was pointed out in a study by H.C. Kriesel of Michigan State University. It was evident, as summarized in Table 6.7, that "increases per person in income from agricultural sources were smallest for the households with less than 0.5 hectares; gains for larger farms ranged from 167 to 400 percent of those with the smallest of farm households."[85] What is evident from these statistics is that "Most households with larger landholdings undoubtedly have had greater opportunities to improve their material well-being or total quality of life. Among the lower-income components of the population, on the other hand, not only have the average gains been smaller, it is probable that many households with smaller landholdings experienced no per-member gains at all in real terms."[86] Kriesel believes that this situation came about because small farmers were "producing crops that did not benefit as much from price increases or technological advances, having larger households, or having limited access to nonfarm earning opportunities."[87]

Upon completion of the Saemaul projects by 1981, the government is contemplating a number of structural reform measures to modernize Korean agriculture. First, it wants to lift the ban on the upper limit of landholding, currently set at three hectares. The intent here is to allow commercial agriculture to take hold in South Korea. The government hopes this will improve the productivity and efficiency of farm operation. Second, it plans to amend the land law so as to prevent absentee ownership of the land. Third, it will separate the practice of land ownership and land-use rights. It is too early to predict what the consequences of these measures will be on the economy and rural structure. Nevertheless, it is interesting to note that the government agricultural policy makers are of the opinion that only through rationalization can Korean agriculture improve its productivity and meet the increasing challenge in the days ahead. Here again, the growth-oriented thinking and philosophy of the economic planners in the government is evident.

Conclusion

Relentless pressure from the top echelons of Korean government, together with the use of government bureaucracy to mobilize human and material resources in the land, brought about a gradual transformation of the rural landscape in Korea. This took shape in environmental beautification, improvement of the material condition

TABLE 6.7
Rural Households by Land Areas and Agricultural Income Increases, 1970-76
Unit: 100 won

Hectares	Proportion of Total, 1974[a]		Increases: 1976 over 1970					
	Rural House-holds %	Arable land %	Per Household		Per Worker		1970 Won/ Worker as % of Farms under 0.5 Hectares[b]	Per Worker Income, Current Won, 1976 as % of 1970
			Current Won %	1970 Won %	Current Won %	1970 Won %		
under 0.5	29.7	10.0	296	45	128	21	100	483
0.5–1.0	35.7	28.3	604	99	220	35	167	481
1.0–1.5	19.2	25.2	894	143	291	51	243	502
1.5–2.0	8.6	16.0	1,160	177	343	52	248	461
over 2.0	6.8	20.5	1,817	344	477	84	400	527
Total or average	100.0	100.0	627	116	261	43	205	490

Source: H. C. Kriesel, "Food and Nutrition Policies in Agricultural Development," in Papers on Agricultural Development Policy Seminar (Seoul: Ministry of Agriculture and Fisheries, 1977), p. 24.

[a]From data in "Population and Food in Korea," by Sung Hoon Kim and Dong Min Kim, (1975), p. 29. All other basic data are from annual "Reports on the Results of Farm Household Economy Survey."
[b]Per worker income for households of different land sizes as percentage of income per worker in households with less than 0.5 hectares.

of life and, more importantly, a gradually changing perspective and orientation of the rural population toward life in general. In my opinion, however, the real test of the success of agrarian change in South Korea will come when the farmers are freed from stringent government intervention and left alone to rely on their own judgment. Government intervention and guidance, however well-intentioned it initially was, may prove to be counterproductive in the long run if it stifles the farmers' incentive to produce and if it cultivates the habit of dependency on government support. Centralized control and authoritarian decision making, which have thus far been successful, may not prove to be the ultimate solution to the problems of agricultural development and modernization in Korea.

The prospect for South Korea in the 1980s and beyond is that the country will continue to face the problem of food deficits and the necessity of fashioning an agricultural development policy that is most appropriate for rapidly industrializing and urbanizing society. Some valid questions are: How much national resources should be allocated to the agricultural sector of the economy? Is the goal of food self-sufficiency realistic and viable, given the changing economy of Korea? Should the government continue to subsidize farm income through the hitherto successful export-oriented program of industrialization? To what extent should the country depend on the foreign supply of grain in order to feed its growing population?

As the living standards improve, the dietary habits of the population will change and the consumption of rice will decline. More animal proteins and dairy products, together with wheats and other cereals, will be in demand. This will necessitate large-scale animal husbandry and the importation of feed grains to sustain the dairy industry. Under such circumstances, the policy makers must decide to what extent resources should be set aside for the purpose of purchasing additional grains and food items from abroad. So long as South Korea continues to depend on the foreign import of grains to feed its population, its agricultural problem will be similar in many respects to that of Japan. Food policy in South Korea, like Japan, is conditioned by the fact that its agricultural land base is limited and its political leadership is determined to continue the strategy of export-led growth of the economy.

We must realize that we cannot settle the question of the relevance of South Korea as a model of agricultural development and rural modernization for other developing countries in the Third and Fourth worlds, since the experience of each nation is unique. Nevertheless, the Korean case may prove valuable to other nations in evaluating the effect of a centrally directed and induced strategy of agricultural development and rural modernization pursued as part of an overall economic development program whose goal is to upgrade the quality of life for the population at large.

Notes

1. As used in this chapter, *agricultural development policy* refers to the setting of economic goals and targets by the government to increase the efficiency of food production (promote self-sufficiency in food production). *Rural modernization policy,* on the other hand, refers to specific courses of action pursued by the government in improving the income and employment of the rural population (such as electrification of villages). Whereas *policy* is a deliberate design and course of action offered by the government to achieve a set of objectives, *program* refers to "a set of procedural steps" for implementing policy objectives, and *project* refers to a self-contained activity usually involving investment in a capital structure. A project (such as the building of an irrgation system) is typically location-specific and is usually terminated after a number of years. For a discussion of these differences, see Willard W. Cochrane, *Agricultural Development Planning: Economic Concepts, Administrative Procedures, and Political Process* (New York: Praeger Publishers, 1974), especially pp. 44-49.

2. On the economy of Korea as a Japanese colony, see Andrew Grajdanev, *Modern Korea: Her Economic and Social Development under the Japanese* (New York: Institute of Pacific Relations, 1944). See also Hoon Koo Lee, *Land Utilization and Rural Economy in Korea* (Shanghai: Kelly and Walsh, 1936).

3. *Area Handbook for South Korea* (Washington, D.C.: American University, Foreign Area Studies, 1975), p. 255.

4. Land reform in South Korea, delayed in its implementation, was stimulated by similar measures in practice in North Korea in 1946 under the Soviet occupation and in Japan under the U.S. military occupation. For a criticism of the lack of plans, including land reform, by the U.S. military government in Korea in 1945-48, see Gregory Henderson, *Korea: The Politics of the Vortex* (Cambridge, Mass.: Harvard University Press, 1968).

5. *Handbook,* p. 247.

6. See Hahn-been Lee, *Korea: Time, Change, and Administration* (Honolulu: East-West Center Press, 1967).

7. *Handbook,* p. 247.

8. On the resource versus technology-based strategy of agricultural development in Asia, see Richard Gable and J. Fred Springer, *Administering Agricultural Development in Asia: A Comparative Analysis of Four National Programs* (Boulder, Colorado: Westview Press, 1976).

9. On the performance of the Korean economy and its prolems of rapid growth, see Parvez Hasan, *Korea: Problems and Issues in a Rapidly Growing Economy* (Baltimore: Johns Hopkins University Press, 1976); Gilbert T. Brown, *Korean Pricing Policies and Economic Development in the 1960's*

(Baltimore: Johns Hopkins University Press, 1973). See also Paul W. Kuznets, *Economic Growth and Structure in the Republic of Korea* (New Haven: Yale University Press, 1977).

10. Gable and Springer, *Administering Agricultural Development*, pp. 320-321.

11. On bureaucratic authoritarianism as a model of nation building in Latin America, see Guilermo A. O'Donnell, *Modernization and Bureaucratic Authoritarianism: Studies in South American Politics* (Berkeley: University of California, Institute of International Studies, 1973). See also David Collier, "Industrialization and Authoritarianism in Latin America," *Items* 31/32, no. 4/1 (March 1978):5-13.

12. Hollis Chenery et al., *Redistribution with Growth* (New York: Oxford University Press, 1974).

13. As quoted in Gabriel Almond and G. Powell, *Comparative Politics*, 2nd ed. (Boston: Little, Brown and Co., 1978), p. 382. See also *The Korean Economy: Growth, Equity and Structural Change* (Seoul: Economic Planning Board, September 1976).

14. Ibid.

15. Ministry of Agriculture and Forestry and Michigan State University, *Korean Agricultural Sector Analysis and Recommended Development Strategies*, 1971-1975, Summary 3-4. (Hereafter noted as KASS.)

16. Ibid.

17. *Korean Agriculture: Present and Future* (Seoul: Ministry of Agriculture and Fisheries, 1975), p. 32.

18. Ibid.

19. Ibid.

20. An average per farm landholding is 1.13 hectares in Japan and 1.06 hectares in Taiwan, as reported in *Nongchong Such'op* (Agricultural Policy Handbook) (Seoul: Ministry of Agriculture and Fisheries, 1977), p. 116.

21. Ibid., p. 106.

22. *Korean Economy*, p. 9.

23. On policy making in command systems, see Robert A. Dahl and Charles E. Lindblom, *Politics, Economics, and Welfare* (New York; Harper and Row, 1953), especially chaps. 8-9; Joyce M. Mitchell and William C. Mitchell, *Political Analysis and Public Policy: An Introduction to Political Science* (Chicago: Rand McNally, 1969), pp. 452-59.

24. Ibid.

25. T. A. Stucker, J. B. Penn, and R. D. Knutson, "Agricultural-Food Policy-Making: Process and Participants," in *Agricultural-Food Policy Review* (Washington, D. C.: USDA Economic Research Service) (A-FPR-1), January 1977, pp. 1-11. See also Don F. Hadwiger and Richard Fraenkel, "The Agricultural Policy Process," in James E. Anderson, ed., *Economic Regulatory Policies* (Lexington, Ky.: D. C. Heath and Co., 1976), pp. 39-50.

26. More will be mentioned on this point in connection with the New Community Movement inaugurated in 1971.

27. Among the recently published books on the politics of Korea written in English, see C. I. Eugene Kim and Young Whan Kihl, eds., *Party Politics and Elections in Korea* (Silver Spring, Md.: The Research Institute on Korean Affairs, 1976); Se-Jin Kim and Chang-Hyun Cho, eds., *Korea: A Divided Nation* (Silver Spring, Md.: The Research Institute on Korean Affairs, 1976); Dae-Soon Suh and Chae-Jin Lee, eds., *Political Leadership in Korea* (Seattle: University of Washington Press, 1976); Edward R. Wright, ed., *Korean Politics in Transition* (Seattle: University of Washington Press, 1975). Also, for earlier publications on Korean politics, see Gregory Henderson, *Korea: The Politics of the Vortex* (Cambridge: Harvard University Press, 1968); Hahn-Been Lee, *Korea: Time, Change, and Administration* (Honolulu: East-West Center Press, 1968); and Pyong-Choon Hahm, *The Korean Political Tradition and Law* (Seoul: Hollym Corp., 1967).

28. For a brief discussion of the government ministries, see Gable and Springer, *Administering Agricultural Development*, pp. 111-18.

29. Ibid.

30. Ibid., p. 120.

31. Park Chung Hee, *Our Nation's Path: Ideology of Social Reconstruction* (Seoul: Dong-A Publishing Co., 1962). See also Chung Hee Park, *To Build a Nation* (Washington, D.C.: Acropolis Books, 1971).

32. David C. Cole and Princeton N. Lyman, *Korean Development: The Interplay of Politics and Economics* (Cambridge: Harvard University Press, 1971), p. 147.

33. For a discussion of the recent development in the Korean economy, see Hasan, *Korea* and *Korean Economy*.

34. This is also McNamara's argument in his *Address to the Board of Governors* [of the World Bank Group], Nairobi, Kenya, Sept. 24, 1973.

35. Kim Kwan Bong, *The Korea-Japan Treaty Crisis and the Instability of the Korean Political System* (New York: Praeger Publishers, 1971).

36. Kim Seung-Hee, *Foreign Capital for Economic Development: A Korean Case Study* (New York; Praeger, 1971).

37. *Korean Economy*, p. 10.

38. *Korean Agriculture*, p. 57.

39. *Nongchong Such'op*, p. 204.

40. *Hankuk Ilbo*, October 15, 1977.

41. Ibid., January 13, 1977.

42. In the 1970 constant prices, however, the per capita GNP increased from $150 in 1962 to $377 in 1975.

43. According to a recent World Bank study, *Redistribution with Growth*, South Korea compares favorably, in terms of equity, not only with developing nations with comparable per capita incomes but also with a number of the richer and more developed nations. As cited in *Korean Economy*, p. 8.

44. Cole and Lyman, *Korean Development*.

45. Ibid., p. 8.

46. Ibid., p. 122.

47. On the ideology of planning, see: Gunnard Myrdal, *Asian Drama: An Inquiry into the Poverty of Nations* (New York: Pantheon, 1968), p. 709. Myrdal observed that: "the basic principle in the ideology of economic planning is that the state shall take an active, indeed the decisive, role in the economy: by its own acts of investment and enterprise, and by its various controls—inducements and restrictions—over the private sector, the state shall initiate, spur, and steer economic development."

48. *Korea's Economy: Past and Present* (Seoul: Korea Development Institute, 1975), p. 138.

49. Ibid., p. 142.

50. Interview with the spokesman of the Ministry of Agriculture and Fisheries, Seoul, Korea, on August 17, 1977.

51. Statistical data are from *Korean Agriculture.*

52. The amount of money spent for imported grains increased from $45 million in 1966 to $273 million in 1971, then to $550 million in 1976. *Nongchong Su'chop*, p. 52.

53. Ibid., pp. 132-42.

54. *World Bank News Release*, no. 78/30, December 23, 1977.

55. *Hankuk Ilbo*, December 8, 1977.

56. As cited by H. C. Kriesel in "Food and Nutrition Policies in Agricultural Development," in *Papers on Agricultural Development Policy Seminar* (Seoul: Ministry of Agriculture and Fisheries, 1977), p. 37.

57. *Hankuk Ilbo*, December 13, 1977.

58. KASS.

59. Interview with director of the Saemaul Yonsuwon (Training Center), Suwon, Korea, August 1973.

60. Hasan, *Korea*, p. 159.

61. Ibid.

62. Vincent Brandt, "Why Rural Korea was Transformed," *The Asia Wall Street*, January 14, 1977.

63. Ibid.

64. Ibid.

65. Ibid. See also Vincent Brandt, *A Korean Village* (Cambridge: Harvard University Press, 1971).

66. Ibid.

67. United Nations, *Urban-Rural Projections from 1950 to 2000*, October 9, 1974. As cited in Herbert R. Barringer, "Some Social Consequences of Developmental Strategy," mimeographed, 1977.

68. Yoon Jong-Joo, "Population Concentration in Seoul: Characteristics and Prospects for the Future," *Korea Journal* 16, no. 9 (September 1976):13-27.

69. As cited in Barringer, "Social Consequences."

70. Ibid.

71. "Asia Survey," *The Economist*, May 7, 1977, p. 42.

72. *Korean Economy*, p. 17.

73. Ibid.

74. For the presidential elections of 1963 and 1967, see C. I. Eugene Kim,

"Patterns in the 1967 Korean Elections," *Pacific Affairs* 41, no. 1 (Spring 1968):60-70; and C. I. Eugene Kim, "Significance of the 1963 Korean Elections," *Asian Survey* 4, no. 3 (March 1964):765-73. See also Kim-Kihl, *Party Politics*.

75. On the 1971 presidential election, see C. I. Eugene Kim, "The Meanings of the 1971 Korean Elections: A Pattern of Political Development," *Asian Survey* 12, no. 3 (March 1972):213-24. See also Kim-Kihl, *Party Politics*.

76. On the Yushin reform of October 17, 1972, see C Eugene Kim, "Korea at the Crossroads: The Birth of the Fourth Republic, *Pacific Affairs* 46, no. 2. (Summer 1973):218-31.

77. Hasan, *Korea*, pp. 160-61.

78. *Hankuk Ilbo*, December 15, 1977. Translated by the author; italics mine.

79. Pal Young Moon, "The Evolution of Rice Policy in Korea," *Food Research Institute Studies* 14, no. 4 (1975):392.

80. Ibid.

81. Ibid., pp. 392-93.

82. *Korea's Economy*, p. 158.

83. Kriesel, "Food and Nutrition Policies," pp. 20-21.

84. On the details of this claim, see Table 6.3.

85. Kriesel, "Food and Nutrition Policies," p. 22.

86. Ibid., p. 24.

87. Ibid.

7
Food in Iran:
The Politics of Insufficiency

Ann T. Schulz

In 1977, Iran's expenditures on food imports reached $2 billion, an unprecedented sum for that country. Iran's food production had not kept pace with rapidly rising demand, and the shah's government was held responsible. No public policy in that year was so controversial as the consumption of foreign food—Danish cheese (manufactured as an imitation of Iranian goat cheese), American rice, Rumanian sugar, and Australian lamb. "How is it that this 'powerful, 2500-year-old empire' cannot produce its own cheese?" asked one Iranian sarcastically. Conspicuous consumption politicized the issue of food imports even more. In September 1978, a week after the demonstrations that brought martial law to Tehran, international bankers who were in Iran to celebrate the National Bank's fiftieth anniversay dined at the Tehran Hilton's Chez Maurice restaurant on thirty-two tons of meat from the Boucherie de Paris.[1] The luxury of the bankers' entertainment was a harsh reminder of the state of political order at this time (when inflation *halved* real wages every four to six years).

In the final analysis, Iran's expensive but superficial industrialization, inflationary pressures on middle and lower class incomes, and political repression combined to bring the downfall of the monarchy. The regime's agricultural policies contributed to the dissatisfaction with the shah's rule both because they relied on imported food to meet demand and because they disrupted Iranian farming. Although Iran is known as an oil-producing state, it also has a rich agricultural tradition, from the animal husbandry of its tribal population to the tea and rice farms of the Caspian Sea littoral. Although it was through oil politics that Iran attracted international concern about its political stability, it was the politics of food that dominated political debate within Iran.

Throughout his thirty-seven-year rule, Iran's head of state, Mohammad Reza Shah Pahlavi, made decisions that ultimately contributed to the country's present food deficit. In a world increasingly conscious of the political significance of abundant food, this was possible because the regime was not politically dependent on its peasantry. And in the 1970s, domestic commercial agriculture was still a weak political force. Instead, the regime depended for its security on competition among urban groups and foreign interests, using state power to preserve a balance.

The Iranian regime essentially consisted of the shah and his close advisers. Their chief concern was how to invest the country's oil revenues against the time when its oil supplies would be depleted. Industrialization appeared to offer the best assurance of sustained economic growth and a competitive position in international markets. As a consequence, food production took second place in development planning.

The Iranian regime's conclusion that agricultural investments would not be as productive as investments in other sectors—consumer and heavy industry, energy, communications, defense, and social welfare, for example—was based, in part, on the geographic and climatic conditions that prevail in Iran. Soil salinity, desertification, and water shortages have all been major obstacles to increasing the productivity of agriculture. Even more than some countries in the Near East and North Africa, Iran would need to make enormous investments in land reconstruction in order for its agriculture to be competitive internationally.

The political framework within which agricultural development and food policies have been formulated has strongly reinforced the effects of geography and climate. Food policies raised fundamental questions of state security. The shah's decision not to give more emphasis to food production was intimately related to his state-building strategies in the historical context of Iran's ethnic pluralism, international insecurity, and bureaucratic politics. His decision to emphasize industrialization and defense grew from his determination to consolidate the territorial state by integrating rather than opposing U.S. intervention in the structure of his regime. The bureaucratic state was to be consolidated by making the private sector dependent on the state bureaucracy.

These two approaches to state building came together in the agricultural sector, allying Iranian and foreign investors in large-scale commercial farming enterprises. The shah's regime gave wide scope to private-sector agribusiness despite strong criticism from proponents of peasant agriculture. Ayatollah Khomeini's economic adviser, Abolhassan Bani-Sadr, foresaw the land reform program by creating agricultural collectives and mechanizing agriculture. None of the successive regimes recommended less restructuring and more investment as a tonic for the faltering agricultural sector.

Clearly, the peasant "ethic" was more likely to remain a nostalgic image than it was to become a political force. The most serious obstacle to increased food production in Iran in 1978 was the discrepancy between the peasants' substantial role in agricultural production and their simultaneous lack of political leverage. The shah had not relied on them for political support, and the eventual outcome of the revolution that overthrew his government was being decided in the cities. Iran's food deficits were rooted in the structure of the state and in the ways in which political regimes used the state apparatus to maintain their own power.

Food Production Trends

Historically, food production in Iran has been insufficient to meet the biological needs of the population. Iranians never have been well-fed. In the period of 1964-1966, the average Iranian consumed 300 calories less than the minimum daily requirement of 2300 calories. Approximately 28 percent of the Iranian population was suffering from malnutrition in those years.[2]

The higher incomes that the oil price rise brought increased the effective demand for food within a short period of time. Estimates of the annual rate of increase in the demand for food in 1977-1978 range from 8 to 11 percent.[3] With growth in agricultural production estimated at 5 percent for that year, food imports had to increase if the demand were to be met. In the two years between 1975 and 1977, the bill for food imports rose from $1.4 billion to $2 billion.[4]

Indices of agricultural production in Iran should not be regarded as highly reliable. Still, all except the most recent government statistics show agricultural production increasing only very slowly over the past several decades. Often, production has not kept pace with Iran's population growth rate (roughly 3 percent per year). According to one set of figures, shown in Table 7.1, per capita agricultural production was significantly lower in 1960 than it was in 1935.

Other figures published by historian Elwell-Sutton indicate that Iranian farmers produced 2 million tons of wheat in 1940.[5] By 1970, wheat production exceeded 4 million tons.[6] Production had doubled, but it had taken thirty years for it to do so. In 1975, shortfalls in wheat production below consumption were estimated to be from 15 to 25 percent.[7] Again, imports would fill the gap between supply and demand.

Food and Political Protest

The low priority given to agricultural productivity was a result of the

TABLE 7.1   Indexes of Agricultural Production (AP)
and Per Capita Agricultural Production (PCAP) for
Iran

Year	AP	PCAP
	(1952-1954=100)	
1935-1939	85	118
1957-1958	117	106
1958-1959	119	108
1959-1960	123	106
1960-1961	118	96

Source: Merip Reports, 43 (1976), p. 6.

fact that the regime identified political stability more with commercial prosperity and Iran's territorial integrity than with food security. Unlike many Third World countries, commercial agriculture has historically been in the hands of Iranian nationals, which meant that commercial cash-crop interests were not identified with foreign investors or colonial regimes.[8] For centuries, the commercialization of agriculture had been underway under the management of Iranian farmers. As a result, shifting resources from cash crops to food production was politically more difficult, because it came up against Iranian, not foreign, commercial interests. Political resistance to foreign investment in agriculture also came from domestic commercial interests, not from small-scale food producers.

The clearest polarization of Iranian and foreign agricultural interests was in the Tobacco Boycott of 1890, often cited as the major event leading to Iran's Constitutional Revolution (in 1906). The boycott was organized in protest over a concession made by Nasiru'd Din Shah Qajar to the (British) Imperial Tobacco Corporation of Persia. By the terms of the concession, the company had exclusive rights to purchase, process, and sell all the tobacco grown in Iran. In response to the concession, religious authorities issued a *fatwa* (edict) that forbade Iranians to use tobacco as long as foreigners controlled it; according to the *fatwa*, the infidel tobacco was impure.[9] The population responded, and the resulting tobacco boycott became an example of the influence of alliances between the clergy and the bazaar. Faced with their united opposition, the government was finally forced to cancel the concession in 1892. The British corporation was indemnified at 500,000 pounds to cover its losses, and the regime fell further into the debt of international financiers.

The Tobacco Boycott illustrates the market-oriented character of food politics in Iran. By contrast, the unequal distribution of food has been a more common source of political protest in the history of many other countries. Most of these episodes, as the ill-fated Marie Antoinette's "Let them eat cake" so ominously implied, were class upheavals that were further exacerbated by the maldistribution of food. Food riots were not an uncommon phenomenon as Britain industrialized. In fact, one historian has connected Britain's food riots with the creation of its national police.[10]

In India in 1974, the army was sent to the State of Gujarat to put down a food riot. The state police, the Border Security Force, and the Central Reserve Police had all failed to quell it. The state's allotment in the national food distribution system had gone down, and local farmers hid their stocks from procurement agents.[11]

Iran's class conflict was historically more contained than that in India, although in the continuing revolution of 1979, radical and conservative groups had become increasingly polarized. The Tobacco Boycott of 1890 was instigated and organized by the bazaar guilds and the clergy, whose object it was to eliminate foreign commercial competition. The possibility of growing food in place of tobacco did not become an issue. The bazaar had enough political influence that the merchants and their clerical allies did not look to the food-poor rural population for additional support.

Nearly a half-century later, the invasion of Iran by British and Soviet troops in the course of World War II led to what was probably the severest food shortage in Iran's recent history.[12] With foreign troops occupying the country from 1941-1946, the demands on Iranian food production increased enormously. As a result, food prices soared and many Iranians went hungry.

Still, there were no organized "hunger strikes." In national politics, the issue of foreign troops on Iranian soil took precedence over food shortages. Parts of Iran had been made virtually inaccessible to the government with the occupation. In the north, Soviet troops held the Caspian provinces, Azerbaijan, and Khorassan (all agricultural provinces). In the south, the British ruled. Only Tehran and its immediate environs were controlled by the present shah, who had come to power at the beginning of the occupation.

Sporadic attempts were made, nonetheless, to reform the structure of

Iranian agriculture during that period, but the succession of weak governments made it impossible to accomplish any major reforms. Few prime ministers could keep their support in parliament for more than a few months under the wartime conditions.[13] By 1946, removing the Soviet troops from Iranian soil was the highest political priority for the shah, the cabinet, and parliament. The continued interference of Britain and the Soviet Union in domestic politics had contributed to armed confrontations between the government and *Qashqa'i* (tribal) troops in southern Fars province and to the potential secession of Azerbaijan in the north. Foreign intervention during the war ensured that preserving territorial integrity would supersede class politics in the post–World War II period, as it had during other crises.

Even though national strategic interests often took precedence over domestic food concerns, government intervention in agriculture for the purpose of strengthening the state apparatus has regularly occurred. Under Reza Shah (1925-1941), the government became directly involved in the production and distribution of food and food products—mostly in foreign trade and processing sugar. These politics were aimed principally at raising revenue for the state, not at assuring adequate levels of investment in agriculture. Reza Shah put tea and sugar imports under state control and used the revenues for financing a railroad construction program that he viewed as critical for state security.[14]

With eight state-owned sugar refineries, Reza Shah established a precedent for further state participation in processing and marketing food. In addition to providing revenue, other demands of the growing machinery of the state had to be met. In 1941, for example, the army had collapsed in the face of the British-Soviet invasion. The new shah determined that his army would be well-fed as well as well-trained. So, one of his first "defense contracts" was with the U.S. firm Foremost Dairy to provide the army with milk and other dairy products.

In the end, the intervention of the state bureaucracy in agriculture contributed to the revolution, although the issue was not food shortages—a situation the regime had carefully avoided. By 1978, Iran's agricultural sector was in disarray and urban migration had created a sizable population of young city dwellers who were recognized as potential supporters of the anti-shah religious movement. The polarization of revolutionary groups during Khomeini's regime was one between more educated and skilled urban leftists and migrants whose "only ties are with religion, the mosques, [and] the mullahs." The two-headed revolution gave one of the shah's former cabinet members occasion to reflect that "if we had done one thing differently, it would have been to strike a balance between urban industry and agriculture."[15]

Land and Political Stability

State intervention in agriculture has historically been most pronounced in landownership. This history makes it impossible to separate policies designed to promote political stability from those designed to promote agricultural development. Historically, rights to land were used to control the political fortunes of potential opponents of regimes in power. In addition to being a landowner itself, the state periodically controlled lands held in charitable trust (*waqf*). In that way, state elites were able to control the power of those religious authorities who managed the *waqf* land.[16]

Second, state land (*khaliseh*) was strategically distributed to political allies. Land was a means for the crown to cement alliances and destroy the political fortunes of its opponents. Reza Shah's supporters in the army received valuable state lands around Tehran in that manner.[17] The state assumed proprietorship when it was politically necessary and abandoned it when that course was politically useful. Landowning was not secure; it was contingent on politics.[18]

When Reza Shah abdicated his throne in 1941, he had not initiated a land redistribution program, but he had promoted agricultural change in other ways. On his own extensive landholdings, he began using commercial methods of production. He had acquired personal title (through confiscation and purchase) to extensive landholdings in Mazandaran, Gilan, and Gorgan—three of Iran's most fertile provinces. Improvements on these lands were made through the government's agricultural bureaucracy at public expense—paying for seed, imported tractors, irrigation, hiring foreign agricultural consultants, improving roads to market centers, and so forth.[19]

Beyond developing his own land, Reza Shah also promulgated land registration laws that fostered private landownership.[20] But these laws by no means eliminated the role of politics in the agricultural economy. In 1942, for example, many of the personal lands of Reza Shah were returned to their former owners or were leased to private farmers and farm corporations through the Pahlavi Foundation. The Gordan Dry Farming Company was one beneficiary. It was founded by a former minister of Agriculture (Mahdavi), the minister of Labor (Alam), and an Iranian manager of the Anglo-Iranian Oil Company.[21]

In 1950, Reza Shah's son and successor began to dispose of some of the crown lands that he controlled, stating that he expected other landowners to follow his example. Several other approaches to land redistribution were put forward by successive governments over the next twelve years, including one during Mossadegh's premiership that would

have improved landlord-tenant contracts. None of these was implemented, however. It was not until 1962, while the landlord-dominated
parliament was closed, that a serious redistribution program was finally
initiated.

Over the decade following passage of the redistribution law, rural
welfare was not improved, but the commercialization of agriculture
gained a little momentum. The land redistribution program, as it was
conceived and subsequently evolved, was conservative. Landowners
were compensated for the land that they gave up, enabling them to
become "capitalists" by investing in other sectors of the economy. In the
late 1960s, by the "third stage" of the land redistribution program, two
options had been made available to landlords who did not want to sell
their excess holdings. One was to mechanize their farms, thus making
them exempt from redistribution—a development favoring greater
inequality, as Herring and Kennedy show for Pakistan (Chapter 8). The
other was to sign long-term leases with their tenants, affording both
tenant and landlord greater security.

Unlike the massive redistribution of land in China that accompanied
the transformation of state power (see Bernstein, Chapter 4), breaking
up landed estates in Iran was a conservative strategy to preserve the
monarchy. In China, the inseparability of the Communist revolution
and land redistribution made it more imperative for revolutionary
leaders to follow through on the initial phases of redistribution by
creating political institutions that would link the peasant to the state.
This was not the case in Iran, where former landowners held new power
as industrialists. An entire class was not uprooted. Instead, the tactics for
balancing power among influential groups and individuals—a
traditional approach to state security—were simply changed.[22] Technology and financial capital replaced land as a quid pro quo for
political support.

The land redistribution program that was initiated in 1962 can be seen,
historically, as yet another episode in the shah's efforts to create a strong
bureaucratic state, although his continued resort to traditional political
balancing tactics simultaneously undermined those efforts. One
historian of contemporary Iran wrote that the emergence of a "landed
class" in Iran was a relatively recent phenomenon, making the Pahlavis
the first dynasty that had to assert its power over landed interests.[23]
Another saw the interference of state elites with land ownership as
characteristic of the way that new regimes had established their rule
throughout Iranian history.[24] Both agreed, however, that state building
and land policies were closely related.

Foreign advisers encouraged land redistribution for a variety of reasons. When Arthur Millspaugh, an American financial adviser, came to Iran in 1922, he recommended a tax reform, without which he doubted that the state could become financially solvent.[25] The primary source of taxes at the time was land. The tax was set at 10 percent of production. But it was not a reliable source of income as long as landowning records were unreliable and as long as the landowners stood between the state and those who farmed the land.

After land redistribution, parastatal cooperative organizations and farm corporations provided a more direct link between the new peasant landowners and the state. The cooperatives were to provide agricultural inputs, sell basic consumer goods to their members, and collect a 2 percent tax on farm produce. Still, however, Millspaugh's objective was not realized. The cooperatives foundered on the regime's limited commitment to peasant agriculture. By 1975, cooperatives covered approximately two-thirds of Iran's villages.[26] Three years later, the Ministry of Cooperatives and Rural Development had been absorbed by the Ministry of Agriculture; the cooperative movement had been declared a failure by a prominent cabinet member; and the 2 percent tax had been abolished. According to one provincial development administrator, it was not worth the effort to try to collect the tax.

While they were trying to create a more solid structure for the state, the Pahlavis officially justified their continuing interference with land-owning on the basis of increased agricultural productivity. State interference was to stimulate productivity by putting land in the hands of those who would invest in machinery, irrigation, and improved crop technology.[27]

Those official objectives were limited by the changing structure of the Iranian economy, a process that the government did little to reverse. Even before oil revenues had quadrupled, investors found higher rates of return in construction than they did in agriculture.[28] By 1968, industry was growing at a rate of 15 percent annually, as contrasted with a government figure of 5 percent for agriculture—providing still another profitable sector for investment.[29]

In subsequent years, both public and private investors channeled decreasing proportions of their capital into agriculture. Between 1968 and 1970, agricultural credits had dropped from 11.5 percent of total credit to 8 percent.[30] At the beginning of the twentieth century, agriculture provided an estimated 80 to 90 percent of the gross national product; in 1973, agriculture provided no more than 13 or 14 percent.[31] The pattern of investment credit reflected the secular economic transformation of Iran.[32]

The Agricultural Development Bank of Iran (ADBI) was created in

1968 to help reduce that discrepancy. The ADBI concentrates its capital in the large-scale sector of agriculture. The minimum loan that the ADBI was legally authorized to float was 1 million rials, or about $150,000. The average size of the ADBI's loans was 15 million rials.[33]

The alternative to the ADBI was the Agricultural Cooperative Bank, a holdover from Reza Shah's reign. It made smaller loans, and it made only half of its loans to cooperatives. The other half went to farmers outside the cooperative organizations. Its capital was limited, too. The majority of funds lent to agricultural enterprises still came from noninstitutional money lenders, at interest rates reaching 50 percent.[34]

With so much of agricultural financing taking place outside formal capital markets, realistic estimates of agricultural profits have been difficult to establish. Based on the assessments of Iranian agricultural economists, commercial agriculture has not been sufficiently profitable to attract private investment without government incentives. The government has not invested heavily in agriculture, however. Ironically (from a nonpolitical perspective), just when land redistribution raised the potential for agricultural development, public and private capital moved into other sectors, and the regime committed its development efforts to industrialization.

Farmers were not eager to see government loans put on a commercial basis either (resistance to involvement with state institutions was one factor in the farmers' attitudes toward government lending). As the revolutionary regime of Khomeini began to sort out the demands for reform put forward by various groups, one farm spokesman called for the cancellation of farmers' debts to state banks.[35]

Part of the suspicion concerning the government's approach to agriculture was a direct result of the earlier land redistribution program. Land redistribution had been undertaken more to eliminate the landed upper class than to increase food production. In a survey of several contemporary land redistribution programs, Hung-chao Tai argues that political regimes use redistribution as a means to eliminate their opponents.[36] This has been particularly true for the Iranian regime. The availability of foreign exchange gave the shah insurance against declining food consumption while the agricultural sector was being reconstructed.

The Peasant Ethic and Agricultural Development

In deemphasizing peasant agriculture, the shah has encountered opposition, although it did not successfully change the regime's approach to agriculture. No regime can make agricultural policy without impinging on the values and interests of some of its rural population. Iran is no exception. In the past decade, two schools of thought developed concerning how best to promote agricultural growth. One was grounded on the principle that peasant-based agriculture would provide the solution to Iran's lagging agricultural sector if given enough resources. The other wanted to see rural Iran fundamentally changed.

These same debates can be heard in other countries. The Iranian regime, for example, could scarcely be more different from that of Tanzania. Yet both have used similar agricultural strategies and both have encountered similar resistance. Compared to Tanzania and to African states generally (see Bates, Chapter 9), a far lower proportion of the Iranian population is engaged in agriculture, the Iranian government has far more financial resources available for development projects, and the Pahlavi regime's ideological orientation evidences little of the philosophy of peasant socialism that President Nyerere espouses. Still, both regimes have tried to stimulate rural development by resettling farmers and consolidating agricultural holdings, and both have given particular attention to investing in regions that have a high growth potential.[37]

Iran's former minister of Agriculture, Mansur Ruhani, began a village consolidation program in 1972 as part of his "Policy for Agricultural Development at the Poles of Soil and Water."[38] The program was based on the belief that the populations of small villages in poor regions could be induced to move to places more favored with natural resources by receiving better public services in those villages. Villages chosen as magnet villages were to receive a disproportionate share of development funds for schools, clinics, roads, and extension services. The villages so favored would also give the regime a more solid base of political support in the countryside.

Few agricultural policies since land redistribution stimulated so much controversy as did Ruhani's. His "poles policy" received the strongest criticism from agricultural economists in the academic community and in the Plan and Budget Organization—the central planning authority that employs large numbers of highly trained social scientists. Their fundamental objection to the "poles policy" was that it ignored the extent to which agricultural production has depended on traditional forms of peasant production.

One of Iran's best known agricultural economists, Hushang Sa'edlu, argued that the basic unit of agricultural production was the village, not individual farmers.[39] Peasant *"boneh"* and *"nasaq"* organizations made production a collective activity. By relocating individual farmers, those collective organizations would be destroyed, and production would inevitably suffer. Sa'edlu's skepticism about the outcome of government intervention in peasant agriculture reflected an antimaterialist tradition in Iranian social science that emphasized village studies.[40] In the absence of reliable and comprehensive information about agricultural production, Sa'edlu's critique could only cite the unusually good performance of small-scale farming in Japan and the high cost of large-scale farming in Iran.[41] That skepticism was supported by the increasing disparity between rural and urban incomes that occurred during the 1970s—a disparity that could be statistically documented and had occurred while Ruhani's policy was being implemented.[42] The differences between rural incomes in various provinces were strong as well—ranging from $8 per year in Baluchistan to $576 in the northern provinces of Gilan, Azerbaijan, and Mazandaran. From the standpoint of a prosperous agricultural sector, the regime's agricultural policies did not have a convincing record.

The central theme of the attack on Ruhani, who was removed from the cabinet in 1977 (and jailed in 1978), was that Iranian agriculture depended on a peasant wisdom that the state could ignore only at the risk of agricultural stagnation worse than it had already experienced. This view was institutionalized when Nader Afshar-Naderi, an anthropologist with a long-standing commitment to nomadic welfare, founded the Center for Peasant Studies in Tehran. Ten years before, Afshar-Naderi had predicted that the government's refusal to invest in nomadic sheep herds would lead to serious meat deficits—a prediction that was borne out by 1975. By 1978, the nomadic focus had been enlarged in scope to encompass all of peasant agriculture.

Proponents of peasant agriculture still faced formidable opposition, despite Ruhani's demotion. The amount of government investment in agriculture in the 1978-1979 development budget was expected to increase by 53 percent over that of the previous year.[43] But expectations were not necessarily realities. The cabinet appointed in the wake of the 1978 political crisis proposed a "new" agricultual strategy, but its emphasis still appeared to be on agro-industry and technological modernization.[44]

Most of Iran's farmland was held in small and medium-sized farms in the early 1970s (see Table 7.2). But most of the marketed agricultural output came from medium-sized and large farms. It was the marketed output in which the government was interested. The varied structure of the agricultural sector had inherent political value. Many peasants owned their own land, and tenants had more secure leases than they once had. So the regime felt politically safe supporting large-scale

.

TABLE 7.2   Structure of Iranian Agriculture, 1972

Farm Size	Percent Farm Area	Percent of Gross Output	Percent of Marketed Output
Large			
100 ha.	12	6	
Medium			77^a
51-100 ha.	4	36	
11-50 ha.	46		
Small			
6-10 ha.	21		
3-5 ha.	12	41	19
1-2 ha.	3		
1 ha.	2		
Pastoralists[b]			
Other, not land owners		17	4

Source: Condensed from Oddvar Aresvik, The Agricultural Development of Iran (New York: Praeger,
1976), p. 101.

[a]Large and medium-size farms combined.
[b]Estimated at 3.5 million persons.

commercial farming (1) to keep food coming to the market, (2) to discourage the flight of domestic capital from Iran by offering profits for investors in agriculture, (3) to improve Iran's technological capacity, and (4) to offer employment to managers and agricultural technicians who might otherwise be on the public payroll.

Food and Foreign Policy

Shortfalls in food production left the shah with four alternatives to politically dangerous food price increases. He could (1) try to increase domestic production at some cost to his vision of creating an industrial state; (2) bargain with foreign food suppliers for lower prices in return for concessions on oil prices; (3) underwrite domestic food prices with government subsidies; or, (4) invest in food production outside Iran.

The shah adopted a portion of each alternative as policy and the result was the internationalization of Iran's agricultural politics. In essence, the shah tried to postpone a political accounting for the decline of agriculture by creating a new dependency on foreign sources of food, food production systems, and investment capital for large-scale agricultural projects.

By 1978, Iranian officials had signed agreements for joint agricultural ventures in Syria, Egypt, India, and Rumania. The agreements were a means to develop amicable political relationships with a variety of regimes. They also had value because they created new potential food supplies. Until these projects matured, Iran was to be dependent on food imported primarily from the West.

Many of the contracts for Western food imports were concluded during Ruhani's term as Minister of Agriculture. Nonetheless, the contracts should be seen as one part of the regime's basic foreign posture during that period, not simply one bureaucrat's personal persuasion. Iran's food imports supported the regime's overall commitments to the West—its major food suppliers, oil customers, and arms suppliers.

Fortunately for the shah, Iran's foreign exchange position again gave his regime short-run political protection, this time against the most obvious signs of international political dependency. Iran last received subsidized food from the United States in 1973.[45] As a consequence, when, in 1975, a U.S. congresswoman wanted to question the politics of U.S. food aid to Iran, she was assured that the Iran "program" was "strictly a private trade arrangement, not a bilateral assistance program."[46] Because of this arrangement, Iran–U.S. relations were subjected to less congressional scrutiny.

While the Iranian regime gave considerable publicity at home to its independence from food aid, the Iranian food market was becoming increasingly dependent on food and food technology imports, especially from the United States. The Commodity Credit Corporation (CCC) financing of food exports to Iran increased dramatically between 1971 and 1973.[47] In 1971, Iran was the twelfth largest recipient of CCC credits; by 1973, it had moved into seventh place. The credits went mainly for wheat sales (Iran was one of the United States' five largest buyers), barley (one of the three largest buyers), and rice. In other commodity markets, the United States faced more competition. The Netherlands, France, and West Germany outsold the United States in animal feed and poultry.[48]

The attractiveness of the Iranian food market was partly a result of the government's policy of subsidizing food imports to keep consumer food prices down. Cereals and rice have been prime candidates for subsidies, and foreign sellers reaped the profits while the Iranian public paid the bill.

The government has also helped foreign firms sell whole food production systems to domestic businessmen. Government banks gave loan preferences to Iranian businesses that had contracts with foreign agribusinesses. For example, in order to qualify for government loans, prospective poultry producers had to prove that their firms possessed the requisite technical qualifications. The borrower could do this simply by showing the bank a contract with any foreign firm that could be assumed to have the highest technological capacity.[49] The contracts were typically franchise arrangements in which Iranian managers agreed to buy their stock, feed, and equipment from one supplier.

The franchising arrangement had several harmful effects on domestic Iranian food production. Firms that held franchises became linked to a particular brand name. If the franchiser changed the terms of the contract, or if the Iranian producer wanted to branch out on his own, it was difficult for him to develop his own clientele. Secondly, a franchise arrangement would affect many of the firms' purchases, even if they were not specifically enumerated in the contract. For example, only foreign poultry feed suppliers could meet the increased demand for particular kinds of feed in the short run. The size of the new poultry operations meant that demand increased in spurts, not in a gradual manner. The regime declared its intention to promote self-sufficiency in animal feed, but the kinds of production decisions—firm size, breed, and so forth— that it was making effectively prevented domestic feed producers from being able to respond to demand.

The most devastating effect of the dependent relationship between Iranian poultry and meat production and foreign suppliers showed up during the 1979 revolution. Because bank strikes forced the government to cut back on most imports, the animal feed necessary to sustain the poultry and cattle was not available; growers had to cut back drastically in the production of poultry. They were forced to slaughter dairy cattle as well.[50] The fear of being "at the mercy" of foreign food suppliers— voiced by critics of the shah's agricultural policies—was finally realized during the uprising that overthrew him.

Other foreign interests had invested directly in Iranian agriculture. The inauguration of these projects depended on governmental creation of infrastructure, yet private investors controlled the returns. A strong critic of agribusiness, Susan George, cites a foreigner involved in Iranian agribusiness: "They [the Iranian government] develop the water first and we come in and farm it [the irrigated land]. It's an attractive arrangement."[51]

One of the prime movers behind Iran's interest in multinational agribusiness was David E. Lilienthal, chairman of Development Resources Corporation and former director of the Tennessee Valley Authority. For years, Lilienthal enjoyed the confidence of the shah. In the late 1950s, he suggested a TVA-like model for Khuzistan, a province directly north of the Persian Gulf. By 1971, that project had become Iran's major experiment with agribusiness.[52] The investors, both Iranian and American, decided to produce sugar beets, wheat, and other cash crops. Small peasant farms were bought out below the huge Dez dam, and the World Bank and the International Finance Corporation bought in. In the manner in which Lilienthal's plan was implemented, it offered (1) investment opportunities to firms involved in other sectors of the economy that were willing to prove their commitment to Iran's development, (2) planning scope to government bureaucrats in the new and powerful Khuzistan Water and Power Authority, and (3) a symbol for the people of the shah's determination to "modernize" Iran.

Bureaucratic Food

The Khuzistan project and subsequent large-scale commercial agricultural ventures have not yet made Iran self-sufficient in food. In fact, many Iranian economists thought that the Khuzistan agribusinesses were too large, that they were mismanaged from the beginning, and that the project opened the way for extensive misappropriation of funds and for high-level corruption.

The success of Lilienthal's model, for example, depended on reliable financial markets. It was widely believed in Iran that some government loans for agricultural projects were diverted to the construction sector, where profits were higher. Several stories circulated about the misuse of investment funds in agribusiness. One told of a sheep farm in northwest Iran, begun with government loans, that had no sheep. When alerted to the shah's impending inspection tour, the farm's managers hurriedly arranged for several thousand head of sheep to be flown in from neighboring Turkey.

Foreign businesses, too, have engaged in illegal practices in the food and agriculture sector; corruption is not a uniquely Iranian problem. In 1977, a British sugar exporter was taken to court for buying its way into the Iranian market by bribing government officials.[53] Other cases of bureaucratic corruption came to light during the revolution, when the parliament became more active. According to the deputy for Kerman, Ali Mazhari, he had received a letter from a Ministry of Agriculture official, who wrote that "His boss had told him to double the price of wheat in his invoices. When he protested in a letter to the minister, he answered that these interferences should be stopped. . . . Whoever spoke against any institution or person heard the stock reply 'Shut-up, you Marxist.'"[54]

Public policy has been erratic as well as corrupt on occasion. The Ministry of Agriculture, for example, was asked to issue a license to an American poultry company.[55] The Iranian Poultry Cooperative and Syndicate complained that domestic producers would eventually be driven out of the market. When the Ministry of Agriculture decided to support the domestic producers, the American company turned to the Ministry of Economy, which granted the license.

Similar uncertainty has surrounded the extent and conditions of the government's intervention in the private sector. It has wavered between intervening in food production and marketing and leaving those activities to the private sector. For example, a bankrupt private sugar beet processing plant in Khuzistan was taken over and run by the government. The government set up the Meat Organization of Iran as a wholesaling operation, but, by 1978, the Meat Organization was running "meat supers" that competed with private butchers. The government agreed to buy wheat from Iranian farmers at supported prices, but it cut off export licenses for domestic wheat when demand rose. At the same time, official statements about agriculture policy renewed the government's pledge that it would support private enterprise in agriculture.[56]

A major impediment to eliminating the system of influence peddling and, in turn, to implementing more consistent food policy was the lack of pressure for bureaucratic responsibility from a productive domestic farming sector. The Imperial Inspectorate, which investigates corrupt practices, reached into the agricultural sector, but it had little support outside its own organization. A larger commercial agricultural sector and more open politics would provide valuable bureaucratic overview.

Conclusion

The problem of limited government intervention in food affairs and the failure to press for greater equity and production was not entirely one of oversight. Iran's food deficit was immediately responsible for shifting public policies. In the situation in which the shah's regime found itself—one of rapidly increasing demand for food and not-so-rapidly increasing domestic food supplies—there were no obvious or politically safe guidelines for public policy.

In historical perspective, Iran's food deficit is an indication of the structure of power in the Iranian political system and of the strategies the shah chose to make his regime more secure. Policies designed to increase agricultural production had to compete with the regime's interest in cementing alliances with foreign investors and in trying to buy support of domestic elites. At the same time, they had to proceed with the shah's industrial development plans.

These strategies are not characteristics of a tightly run, authoritarian state. They were endemic to a regime that relied on balancing the particularistic demands of opponents against one another to conserve its own limited political resources. Given the constraints on the regime over time, the 1977 food deficit appeared to offer a politically safe alternative to structural reform. A vigorous assertion of domestic commercial agriculture interests and the realignment of Iran's foreign policy (away from the United States) could supply the impetus for a new calculus of agricultural politics in the revolutionary regime. But unless there is a fundamental shift in the balance of power between urban and rural Iran, Iran's food deficit is not likely to disappear.

Notes

1. *Kayhan International* (Tehran), September 12, 1978.

2. Susan George, *How the Other Half Dies; The Real Reasons for World Hunger* (Montclair, N.J.: Allanheld, Osmun, and Company, 1977), p. 150; Oddvar Aresvik, *The Agricultural Development of Iran* (New York; Praeger, 1976), p. 28.

3. Marvin G. Weinbaum, "Agricultural Policy and Development Politics in Iran," *Middle East Journal* 31, no. 3 (Summer 1977):43, gives a figure of 9-12 percent annual growth in consumer demand for food. Estimates of food production, imports, and consumption for the year 1977, made in this chapter, were based on interviews with agricultural economists in Tehran in June 1978.

4. The 1975 figure is from Weinbaum, "Agricultural Policy," p. 43. Most of the increase in agricultural production in recent years has been from the expansion of acreage under production. According to F.A.O. figures, for example, the annual increase in cereal production was 3.9 percent; the increase in hectares under production from 1972 to 1974 was 6.9 percent! International Agricultural Development Service, *Agricultural Development Indicators; a Statistical Handbook* (New York, 1978).

5. L. P. Elwell-Sutton, *Modern Iran* (London: George Routledge and Sons, 1941), p. 84.

6. Aresvik, *Agricultural Development*, p. 43 and p. 133. Aresvik provides a lower figure, 1,400,000 metric tons, for 1940-44 annual averages, but notes that the figures are not reliable. Elwell-Sutton's have been used here, because they were produced by field research during that contemporary period.

7. U.S., House of Representatives, *Food Problems of Developing Countries: Implications for U.S. Policy*, Hearings, Subcommittee on International

Resources, Food, and Energy, Committee on International Relations, 94th Cong., 1st Sess. (Washington, D.C.: U.S. Government Printing Office, 1975), p. 347.

8. Colin Leys, *Underdevelopment in Kenya* (Berkeley: University of California Press, 1975); and Michael F. Lofchie, "The Political and Economic Origins of African Hunger," *Journal of Modern African Studies* 13, no. 4 (December 1975):551-68.

9. Edward Granville Browne, "The Persian Constitutional Movement," *Proceedings of the British Academy* 8 (1917-1918):311-31; and M. L. Tom, "Ekonomischeskoi Polozhenie Persii" (published in St. Petersburg, 1895), in Charles Issawi, ed., *The Economic History of Iran 1800-1914* (Chicago: University of Chicago Press, 1971), p. 249.

10. Charles Tilly, "Food Supply and Public Order in Modern Europe," in Charles Tilly, ed., *The Formation of National States in Modern Europe, Studies in Political Development*, 8 vols. (Princeton, N.J.: Princeton University Press, 1976).

11. Dawn E. Jones and Rodney W. Jones, "Urban Upheaval in India: The 1974 Nav Nirman Riots in Gujarat," *Asian Survey* 16, no. 11 (November 1976):1012.

12. Donald N. Wilber, *Iran: Past and Present*, 8th ed. (Princeton, N.J.: Princeton University Press, 1976), p. 135; and Richard N. Frye, *Iran* (New York: Henry Holt and Company, 1953), p. 82.

13. Hoseyn, Key-Ostovān, *Siāsat-e movāzene-ye Manfi dar Majles-e chahardahom, yā Seyre-e tarirkhi-ye Mashrute-ye Iran* ("Negative Balancing Politics in the Fourteenth Majles or the Full History of Constitutionalism in Iran"), 2 vols. (Tehran: n.p., 1927-29/1948-50); and Frye, *Iran*.

14. Amin Banani, *The Modernization of Iran: 1921-1941* (Stanford: Stanford University Press, 1961), p. 140.

15. *New York Times*, November 16, 1978.

16. Hamid Algar, *Religion and the State in Iran* (Berkeley: University of California Press, 1969).

17. Shoko Okazaki, *The Development of Large-Scale Farming in Iran: The Case of the Province of Gorgan*, Occasional Papers no. 3 (Tokyo: The Institute of Asian Economic Affairs, 1968), p. 12.

18. A. K. S. Lambton, *Landlord and Peasant in Persia*, 2nd ed. (London: Oxford University Press, 1969); Banani, *Modernization of Iran*, p. 125.

19. Okazaki, *Development of Farming*, p. 11.

20. A. K. S. Lambton, *The Persian Land Reform, 1962-66* (London: Oxford University Press, 1969).

21. Okazaki, *Development of Farming*, p. 33.

22. Ervand Abrahamian, "Oriental Depotism: The Case of Qajar Iran," *International Journal of Middle East Studies* 5, no. 1 (January 1974):3-31.

23. Nikki R. Keddie, "The Iranian Power Structure and Social Change 1800-1969: An Overview," *International Journal of Middle East Studies* 2, no. 1 (January 1971):3-20.

24. A. K. S. Lambton, *Landlord and Peasant in Persia* (1953, reprint ed.,

London: Oxford University Press, 1969), p. 182.
  25. Banani, *Modernization of Iran,* pp. 124ff.
  26. "Land Reform and Agribusiness in Iran," *Merip Reports,* no. 43 (Washington, D.C.: Middle East Research and Information Project, 1976).
  27. Banani, *Modernization of Iran,* p. 123 describes the Land Development Act of 1937 as a "legislative landmark" in providing incentives to landowners for making improvements on the land, although this apparent intent was undermined by placing its implementation in the hands of landowners.
  28. Lambton, *Landlord and Peasant,* p. 264.
  29. *The Times* (London), July 19, 1975.
  30. Ali Parvizi, "Report to the Ministry of Agriculture, 1972," mimeographed (Tehran, n.d.).
  31. Ismail Ajami, "Agrarian Reform, Modernization of Peasants, and Agricultural Development in Iran," in *Iran: Past, Present, and Future,* ed. Jane W. Jacqz (New York: The Aspen Institute for Humanistic Studies, 1976), p. 138; and Imperial Government of Iran, Plan and Budget Organization, Statistical Center of Iran, *Statistical Yearbook of Iran 1352 (March 1973–March 1974)* (Tehran: June 1976), p. 487.
  32. Aresvik, *Agricultural Development,* p. 172. Eight percent of the government's development expenditures under the 4th Plan (1968-73) went to agriculture; 13 percent under the 5th Plan (1973-78). Perry Clark Carey and Andrew Galbraith Carey, "Iran Agriculture and Its Development: 1952-73," *International Journal of Middle East Studies* 7 (1976):363; Imperial Government of Iran, Plan and Budget Organization, *Iran's 5th Developent Plan 1973-1978* (Tehran, 1973). The 13 percent is unreliable; the 5th Plan was revised several times and still is unfinished.
  33. Aresvik, *Agricultural Development,* p. 172.
  34. Nikki R. Keddie, "The Iranian Village Before and After Land Reform," *Journal of Contemporary History,* July 1969, p. 75.
  35. *The Washington Post,* February 24, 1979.
  36. Hung-chao Tai, *Land Reform and Politics: A Comparative Analysis* (Berkeley: University of California Press, 1974).
  37. Juma Volter Mwapacha, "Operation Planned Villages in Rural Tanzania: a Revolutionary Strategy for Development," *The African Review* 6, no. 1 (1976):1-16.
  38. Mansur Ruhani, *Towse'e eqtesadi dar qotbharje manabe'-ye ab va khak* (Economic Development at the Poles of Soil and Water), Report to the Ministry of Agriculture, 1967.
  39. Hushang Sa'edlu, "A Critique of 'A Policy for Agricultural Development at the Poles of Soil and Water'," *Tahqiqat-e Eqtesadi* 9, nos. 25 and 26 (Winter and Spring 1972):54-80.
  40. Fatemeh Edemad Moqadam, "A Study of Some Selected Villages in Iran: Methodology and Empirical Results," mimeographed (Tehran: Iran Planning Institute, 1977).
  41. Sa'edlu, "Critique."
  42. M. Hashem Pesaran, "Income Distribution and Its Major Determinants in Iran," in *Iran: Past, Present and Future,* pp. 267-86.

43. An-Nahar, *Arab Report and Memo* 2, no. 7 (February 13, 1978):3.

44. *Kayhan International* (Tehran), September 11, 1978.

45. U.S., Senate, *U.S. Foreign Agricultural Trade Policy Hearings before the Subcommittee on Foreign Agricultural Policy,* Committee on Agriculture and Forestry, 93rd Cong. 1st Sess., (Washington, D.C.: U.S. Government Printing Office, 1973), p. 184.

46. U.S., House of Representatives, *International Development and Food Assistance Act of 1975 Hearings and Markup of the Committee on International Relations,* 94th Cong., 1st Sess. July 14-30, 1975 (Washington, D.C.: U.S. Government Printing Office, 1975), p. 122.

47. *U.S. Foreign Agricultural Trade Policy,* p. 149.

48. U.N. Statistical Office, *World Trade Annual* 6 (January-December 1975).

49. The observations on the politics of foreign investment in agribusiness draw on discussions with Iranian and foreign "agribusinessmen" in Iran in 1978, unless otherwise noted.

50. *The Washington Post,* February 10, 1979.

51. George, *How the Other Half Dies,* p. 150. See also Vahid F. Nowshirvani and Robert Bildner, "Direct Foreign Investment in the Non-Oil Sectors of the Iranian Economy," *Iranian Studies* 6, nos. 2-3 (Spring-Summer 1973):66-109. Nowshirvani and Bildner report tax holidays, subsidized water, cheap credit, exemption from import duties, and long-term leases at concessionary rates, and so forth, as inducements to foreign agricultural investors. (Many of these same inducements were used to encourage investments in the western United States decades earlier.)

52. David E. Lilienthal, *The Harvest Years 1959-1963: The Journals of David E. Lilienthal,* vol. 5 (New York: Harper and Row, 1971). In this volume, Lilienthal describes his efforts to get World Bank and Iranian government support for the Dez project. He was pleased with the shah's enthusiasm and writes of no concern about how its implementation will be affected by Iranian politics. For other descriptions of the Khuzistan project, see "Land Reform and Agribusiness in Iran," in *Merip Reports* and F. R. C. Bagley, "A Bright Future After Oil: Dams and Agro-Industry in Khuzistan," *Middle East Journal* 30, no. 1(Winter 1976):25-35.

53. *Etela'at* (Persian), October 8, 1977.

54. *Kayhan International* (Tehran), September 14, 1978.

55. Ray A. Goldberg, "Iran-America Poultry S.A.," Seminar in Agribusiness, Harvard School of Business Administration, Case No. 1CH 12G 24 AI242, 1966.

56. *Kayhan International* (Tehran), September 11, 1978.

8
The Political Economy
of Farm Mechanization Policy:
Tractors in Pakistan

Ronald J. Herring
Charles R. Kennedy, Jr.

Introduction

For many South Asians—farmers, urban elites, planners (and their American advisors)—the modernization of agriculture is symbolized by the introduction of tractors. The tractor epitomizes modernity and imparts to agriculture a new symbolic importance. Land has always conferred prestige; hierarchies of social status have closely paralleled hierarchies of land control, and relative position in such hierarchies is a central determinant of social stratification. But despite the hallowed status attached to land control, cultivation of the soil has in the Indic context denoted inferior social standing—the necessity to work with one's hands, to get dirty. Whereas the plodding bullock and plow are associated with drudgery and backwardness, with tradition and antiquity, the tractor is suffused with science, technical progress, and Western civilization. The tractor confers on its owner an aura of progressive, scientific agriculture. Sons of landlords who previously disdained agriculture in favor of "modern" (often urban) pursuits have returned to the land. Civil and military officers of high standing purchase tractors to retire to the land as a scientific and progressive gentry. As William Hinton remarked of China in the period immediately following World War II:

> There was no doubt that romance surrounded the very idea of tractoring. Tractors had become a symbol of all that was new and bright in the countryside. The "iron ox" would draw in its wake a whole new world. A shimmering aura of prestige and progress enveloped mechanized farming and drew young people as a magnet draws filings. In China there was no occupation, except flying, which carried with it such public interest.[1]

Of course, all is not symbol and romance in farm mechanization; there are considerable profits to be made, new power handles for landowners, tenant evictions, and violence. The image of village children pressing around a new tractor in the Punjab to take turns sitting in the cab is one reality; the blackened hulks of tractors burned by farm laborers in Kerala is another.

Far removed from the gritty reality of villages and field labor, in the model-strewn world of economic planners, the tractors symbolize something more than modernity. Farm mechanization has come to stand for a dynamic agriculture. This in turn provides an engine for economic growth—through export earnings and by freeing the national economy from crippling and destabilizing dependence on grain imports from abroad. Rapid farm mechanization in both the Soviet Union and the West has been associated with extension of cultivated area, increasing labor productivity in agriculture and generating ancillary jobs in the manufacture and maintenance of farm implements and machines. Modern agriculture is powerful agriculture; farming in the developed economies is mechanized farming.

Critics of farm mechanization have an equally compelling developmental case. They argue that a capital-intensive strategy such as tractorization* is inappropriate in a "labor-surplus," "capital-scarce" economy (the argument from factor endowment), that jobs will be destroyed, that the foreign exchange costs are too high, that agriculture can develop rapidly with traditional power sources or less costly, less capital-intensive "intermediate" technologies (such as power tillers or improved implements), and that the benefits of mechanization accrue to the privileged, whereas the "social costs" are borne by those least able to bear them. Critics fear the dependence on foreign credits, foreign firms, and foreign technology. They stress that, whereas the benefits of tractorization have a shaky empirical base, the negative externalities and direct costs are indisputable.

Thus, mechanization policy etches developmental dilemmas quite sharply. The strategy that has become official policy in Pakistan points toward introduction of large tractors as quickly as farmers can absorb them, even force-feeding mechanization through direct and indirect subsidies in the hope of transforming traditional agriculture rapidly. The vision is the North American plains. The model depends on assumptions that aggregate growth and agricultural modernization will generate more jobs than tractors destroy, that benefits will "trickle

*We recognize the inelegance of this neologism but will employ it because of its obvious efficiency and established status in ordinary and official language in the community of people interested in this issue. By tractorization we mean the introduction of large riding tractors, with a minimum horsepower rating of 45.

down" to the vast majority of rural people who are too poor to afford tractors or have no land of their own.

There are alternative models of farm mechanization, of course. They stress small riding tractors and power tillers, or "walking tractors," of less than 20 horsepower. When we speak of tractors in Pakistan, we mean *large* tractors (by Asian standards)—typically 45 horsepower and above. To be operated economically, the small tractors do not require large farms and have proved quite popular in the Indian Punjab and throughout Asia. Other models, such as the Chinese, stress the use of large tractors in some areas and small in others, but under conditions of collective ownership of both tractors and land. There are also models of "intermediate" technology employing bullock power with improved implements and scientific methods. These alternative models would produce quite a different pattern of consequences, in both class-specific and aggregate terms. But our focus is on Pakistan's strategy; it is critical to note that at no time were these alternative technical and institutional strategies seriously investigated in Pakistan's policy circles. This fact should be kept in mind as we explore the consequences of the model chosen.

Many observers have been struck by the similarity of Pakistan (agronomically) to the American Southwest. The four provinces of present-day Pakistan—Sind, Baluchistan, the Northwest Frontier, and the Punjab (collectively West Pakistan before the dismemberment of the country in 1971 with the traumatic separation of East Pakistan, now Bangladesh)—are relatively arid but receive a tremendous amount of sunshine. They contain some rich alluvial soils, and, under irrigated conditions, exhibit outstanding agricultural potential. This is particularly true of the heart of the Indus Valley, the provinces of Sind, and the Punjab, which altogether account for over 80 percent of Pakistan's rural population, farm area, and tractors. About three-fourths of the nation's agricultural land is irrigated—three times the ratio of India and an important colonial legacy. In the heyday of the "green revolution" of the 1960s, Pakistan's agricultural growth rate was remarkable, demonstrating the agronomic potential of bright sun and irrigated land.

But the resemblance to the American Southwest is only climatic and agronomic. Pakistan's almost 80 million people are overwhelmingly rural (about three-fourths of the population) and distressingly poor. Life expectancy for the country as a whole is forty-nine years, lower in the rural areas. Although the country is large (310,402 square miles), harsh climates and inhospitable terrains leave much of the land area (particularly Baluchistan) uninhabited waste. The large rural population is crowded on a relatively small agricultural base; crop land per member of the agricultural population is only about an acre and a half, compared to over fifty acres in the United States. A majority of the nation's farmers own less than 7.5 acres of land.

The lifeblood of Pakistan's economy is agriculture; the major exports are agricultural—*basmati* rice and cotton—and wheat is the mainstay of the subsistence economy. Although some see the future of Pakistan as a granary for the more arid and less developed oil states, at present food production is inadequate even for domestic consumption at painfully low per capita levels. These basic facts—a high labor-land ratio, extreme rural poverty, dependence of the national economy on agriculture, and tremendous agronomic potential on the irrigated alluvial plains—sketch the context within which tractor policy was formulated.

Pakistan's tractorization strategy evolved over decades in three distinct phases. Prior to Ayub Khan's military coup and long reign, the policy was one of caution. There was some fear about the huge costs of tractorization in terms of foreign exchange, unemployment, and "social tensions." The second period began with Ayub's decision in 1961 to make tractorization official policy. This was the period of "green revolution"—rapid growth in output and technological change under the technocratic martial law regime. The third period is one of acceleration and intensification of mechanization. It began with the Fourth Five-Year Plan (1970) and continues under the avowedly democratic and "socialist" regime of Zulfikar Ali Bhutto (1971-77). Our analytical task is to explain the reasons for policy changes and continuities and the ways in which policy decisions interacted with empirical assessments of the social, political, and economic consequences of farm mechanization.

The Analytical Perspective

The dominant conceptualization of "development" has undergone a shift of major proportions in recent years.[2] In the new definition of development in mainstream work, the "poorest of the poor" have received explicit attention. "Basic needs" and similar concepts have joined or replaced aggregate growth rates as indicators of development. The development community is more sensitive to questions of development for whom, at what costs, with what alternatives?[3]

This paradigm shift has been gratifying to students of agriculture and practitioners of critical social theory. First, the concern with the poorest of the poor focuses attention directly on rural areas and those at the bottom of the agrarian hierarchy. Secondly, the focus of analysis is necessarily disaggregated; wealthy landlords and substantial farmers are affected in fundamentally different ways from landless sharecroppers and field laborers by different strategies of agricultural modernization. The issue of tractors and farm mechanization in precapitalist and transitional societies raises the following concerns in a stark and direct manner: Who benefits from rapid, state-sponsored, subsidized technical change and who loses? What is the impact on the poorest of the poor, the "target groups" (to use the somewhat chilling institutional lexicon) who are supposedly the *problem* of underdevelopment?

Marxist scholars of development have always argued the fallacy of aggregate analysis, which does not differentiate developmental impact by class; but the paradigm shift in non-Marxist circles has produced a flurry of "new" scholarly activity. We now hear a great deal of concern with "equity-growth trade-offs," strategies for "redistribution with growth" and "appropriate technology." There is a new interest in issues of central concern to critical social theory—the impact of property institutions and distributions on the life chances of individuals and classes. The "dependencia" theorists have sensitized even conservative scholars to the process of "marginalization," in which certain growth processes, particularly those involving technical change, result in a net deterioration in the position of certain classes.[4] Farm mechanization is one such process. But it must be stressed that, although technical change is by no means neutral in its impact, neither is it determinative; it is the *interaction* between technical change and institutions governing relations of production and distribution that determines who benefits and who loses.

Just as critical theory has been concerned with the differential impact on various classes of different development strategies, it has focused attention on the class analysis of public policy: What classes are represented in the local and national power and authority structures? What are the *operative values* (as opposed to public professions) imbedded in policy outcomes? We have analyzed Pakistan's agricultural development strategy from these perspectives.

Public policy is demonstrably an interaction between politics and knowledge. Indeed, investigation of the knowledge-seeking process (what questions are asked? what information is collected?) and the knowledge-utilization process (what decisions are made when the evidence is ambiguous, contradictory, or absent altogether?) provides a means of understanding the operative political power structure. Our investigation illustrates clearly that certain critical questions about mechanization were not asked, that some decisions (and not others) were made in the absence of justifying evidence, and that empirical investigations that ran counter to certain interests were consistently ignored or unjustifiably discredited. Studying the assumptions—the unproven assertions—in the policy logic of the elites, and even the conceptual framework of policy studies, reveals the operative values of the political system. Such analysis also helps to elucidate the worldviews of policy and political elites; it helps us understand what elites believe about the way the world works and is important in understanding the politics and policy of the past, present, and future.

Tractor policy is particularly illuminating in this respect. The critical decisions were made when evidence to support the official rationale was lacking, ambiguous, or contradictory. Policy makers always operate in a world of empirical uncertainty; the choices made, when analyzed in terms of the knowledge available, add important evidence for understanding the real structure of political power. Modernization inevitably imposes costs. It also confers benefits, but as Sartre reminds us, society chooses its expendables.[5] The choices in the case of tractor policy in Pakistan have been clear. We now turn to an analysis of them.

The Initial Strategy:
A Selective and "Go-Slow" Approach

The initial strategy for agricultural mechanization was proposed well before Pakistani independence. In 1928, the Royal Commission Report on Agriculture "recognized the (long-term) need for replacing the bullocks with tractors," while simultaneously arguing that for a small farmer, "the use of large-scale machinery ... is obviously entirely outside his purview in present conditions." The Famine Inquiry Commission of 1945 saw the need for eventual mechanization in terms of reclaiming waste land and freeing scarce land resources from fodder production, but recognized, as well, the paradox of introducing labor-saving, expensive technology in a labor-abundant and extremely poor sector.[6] As a result, concepts of selective mechanization and a gradual adoption of mechanization became cornerstones of initial policy and foreshadowed the bimodal development policy of later years—modern technology on large farms, traditional technology on the vast majority of farms.

This policy model was clearly reflected in initial government policies in independent Pakistan. Realizing the importance of raising agricultural production, the government appointed an Agricultural Inquiry Committee in 1951, which concluded that:

It would be unwise to follow exactly the same pattern of rapid transition from animal to tractor power as adopted by U.K., U.S.A., and U.S.S.R. . . . [for] it is estimated that complete farm mechanization would displace two out of three laborers. Such a change in agricultural economy might create a serious problem of unemployment. Caution against too rapid mechanization is, therefore, needed.[7]

The Committee also suggested the selective use of available tractor power, which "should be confined to reclamations of canal irrigation projects in state lands which are not efficiently and quickly cultivable by animal power."[8] The cautions about unemployment typify the selective and go-slow approach to agricultural mechanization. They stem from fears that a widening of class differentials among farmers and deprivations suffered by the landless would result in an upsurge of social tensions.

The First Five-Year Plan, 1955-60, echoed these sentiments while supplying additional observations and recommendations. The Planning Commission observed:

> One possible way to increase the production is through the use of tractors, but this can only be economic for a larger holding than is normally feasible in the country. The question of how far tractor cultivation should be adopted cannot be answered until systematic investigations have been made to determine the economies of tractor use. . . . We feel that precluding such investigations, the following reasons prevent an expansion of tractor cultivation on a large scale: (a) Pakistan has a large labor force, the greater part of which is underemployed . . . ; (b) Existing individual holdings are small and fragmented . . . ; and (c) Foreign exchange involved in the import of tractors is considerable.[9]

The Second Five-Year Plan continued to support the same approach: tractor use should be limited to new irrigation projects, land reclamation, antierosion programs and flood-control purposes.[10] Such mechanization is arguably land-augmenting and not labor-displacing and adds to total production capabilities. During this period, the total importation of tractors was small and the growth rate slow; there were only 500 tractors in 1947 and fewer than 2,000 in 1959, despite advantageous import and tax policies.[11]

The government's reluctant policy towards rapid tractorization is understandable. As the First Plan admitted, the absence of "systematic investigations" and empirical evidence cautioned against the acceptance of a rapid mechanization policy[12]; the social, political, and economic consequences were unknown and potentially negative. Moreover, the pressure for increasing agricultural production was not yet critical. Historically, the area had been a net exporter of food, and virtually no foreign exchange had been spent on food imports during the years prior to the First Plan; the bad crop year of 1956 resulted in Pakistan's first major food imports.[13]

National, provincial, and local agrarian power structures may further explain this general lack of interest in rapid mechanization. The ruling political party, the Muslim League, was dominated by traditional landlords, who formed the largest occupational group within the League's National Council. Moreover, the proportion of landlords in the Interim and Second Constituent Assemblies during the 1950s were 64 percent and 69 percent, respectively; in fact, 68 percent of all West Pakistani legislators in the 1947-58 period were landlords.[14] On the provincial level, the two main agricultural regions of Pakistan, the Punjab and Sind, which account for 87 percent of the country's agricultural output and 85 percent of the rural population, were also dominated by landlord interests. In Sind, 90 percept of the 1955 Legislative Assembly membership was composed of landlords, and in the Punjab, the 1951 provincial legislature had a membership that was 80 percent landlord.[15] Most of these landlords were of the traditional type, owning large tracts of land and deriving their incomes almost solely from rent payments made by tenants and sharecroppers.[16] The 1960 Agricultural Census indicated that 40.5 percent of all farm holdings were tenant-operated on land that constituted 45.2 percent of the cultivated acreage; in addition, 17.9 percent of the holdings were operated by owner-cum-tenants on 23.1 percent of the cultivated land.[17] At the same time, a small group of landlords with large landholdings owned most of this tenanted land; according to the 1959 Land Reforms Commission, 30.4 percent of the total land in West Pakistan was owned by 1.2 percent of all landowners, with each landlord having over 100 acres.[18]

Based on these statistics, Dr. Azimusshan Haider has estimated that in the Punjab, 13,000 landlords, or about 0.5 percent of total landowners, owned 21.5 percent of the cultivated area, and in Sind, a mere 3,000 landlords owned 69 percent of the occupied land.[19] In other words, available data on the rural tenure structure show a highly skewed distribution of landownership, with large farms being operated primarily through tenancy and sharecropping arrangements. In most areas, agricultural laborers were a very small percentage of the rural population.

The reluctance of traditional landlords to adopt, or promote through government policy, an expensive and alien technology had both economic and political roots (in addition to the cultural incongruity). Politically, landlord power was based on the ability to mobilize dependents—tenants and village artisans (*kammis*) who occupied both houses and fields at the sufferance of the landlord.[20] Mechanization has the potential of fundamentally transforming those very agrarian relationships that formed the basis of landlord power, both locally and nationally. Economically, the sharecropping organization of production imposes constraints on capital investment; although the landlord bears the full cost of any major investment, any increases in output must be shared with tenants half and half (typically), *unless* rental shares can be altered (a move strongly resisted by tenants). Moreover, with grain prices low and technical knowledge of tractors alien to most traditional landlords, mechanization was a risky and unnecessary investment.

The Policy Shift to Mechanization: Entrepreneurs and Dynamism

With the military coup of Ayub Khan and the formal transfer of power to the military in 1958, a new model of agricultural development appeared. It was centered on promotion of agrarian entrepreneurs, transformation of parasitic rentier landlords, and creation of a "middle class" of modern, progressive farmers. One of the first acts and highest priorities of the new regime was to appoint a Land Reform Commission. The Commission's report exemplifies the new policy model; its recommendations were transformed into law almost immediately. Those classes that were important to the regime—urban professional groups, bureaucrats, industrialists, progressive farmers— felt that the traditional landlord-sharecropper organization of production stunted the modernization of agriculture and hindered the operation of incentives for increasing farm production. They felt that the new policies for pricing both inputs and farm produce and the 1959 land reforms were justified in encouraging the growth of a profit and production oriented capitalist farmer class. As the 1959 Land Reform Commission stated:

> What we thought prudent was to fix the ceiling at a level which will on the one hand eradicate the feudalistic elements from the existing tenure structure, and on the other, by causing the minimum of disturbance of the social edifice, lead to a harmonious changeover and at the same time, by providing incentives at all levels, conduce to greater production. . . . Farming as a profession should remain sufficiently lucrative to attract and engage suitable talent on a wholesale basis . . . and should offer opportunities for enterprise and leadership which, through precept and example, will be capable of influencing rural life and will provide a point of contact between rural conservatism and modern ideas and technology.[21]

A central symbol of modern agriculture, and a mechanism for abolishing "feudal" agrarian relations in favor of progressive capitalist relations, is the tractor. The first dramatic and public change in the government's attitude toward tractorization was pronounced by the Food and Agricultural Committee of 1960:

> The standard objection in Pakistan to the mechanization of agriculture is the fear of widespread unemployment, and it is a very valid one. Moreover, it is important to use to the fullest extent the one resource the country has in abundance, namely, human labor. Nevertheless, there are strong reasons for examining the case for mechanization. In judging its value there is need to assess whether its use may not earn or save far more foreign exchange than its importation costs, and, by increasing production, create more jobs in the long run than it displaces.[22]

The Agricultural Committee went on to say that if mechanization were ignored, "it may be to forfeit a valuable ally in the production war."[23] The protractorization model was thus being advanced by a governmental body for the first time; the committee claimed both production and employment advantages would accrue from a mechanization approach. It should be noted here that, as previous official policy statements emphasized, there existed no systematic evidence for these claims. Indeed, the empirical basis for these claims is still quite questionable.

This policy shift toward officially sponsored tractorization was cemented in 1961, when the president of Pakistan issued a directive to adopt farm mechanization in the country and appointed a "working party" to investigate and suggest means of implementation.[24] Tractorization was encouraged over the following years by complementary policies, including: high support prices for wheat and cotton (above world market prices); cessation of forced wheat procurement and government regulation of wheat movements; cessation of export duties on cotton; consolidation and funding of credit and investment in institutions such as the Agricultural Development Bank of Pakistan in 1960-61; higher subsidization for agricultural inputs; favorable exchange rate policies and the absence of any agricultural income tax; encouragement to large farmers to accumulate surplus and reinvest in agriculture.[25]

Indeed, because of extremely high support prices and artificially favorable exchange rates, American tractors were actually cheaper in Pakistan than in the United States. (At times tractors in Pakistan were undervalued by as much as 216 percent.) These policies dramatically increased profit opportunities for capitalist farmers and encouraged the adoption of mechanized agriculture. They also deflected scarce credit away from short-term and small-farm uses. Simultaneously, the rapid expansion of private and public tubewells and the introduction of high-yielding varieties of grain made double-cropping more feasible agronomically and more attractive economically, increasing the demand for tractor power.[26]

For the military/bureaucratic elite who formulated Pakistan's public policy after the coup (and for the industrial families to whom they were closely tied), stagnation in agriculture represented a serious obstacle to national development. Food shortages represented a political danger, and food imports diverted precious development resources. Food production in the 1950s not only failed to keep pace with population growth but turned the nation into a net importer of food grains. Indeed, total food grain production at the end of the First Five-Year Plan (1959-60) failed to equal levels achieved during the base years of 1948-55.[27] Consequently, imports of grain averaged one million tons per year during the First Plan.[28] The language of the Second Plan expressed the dilemma: "Food imports were higher than anticipated and other imports had to be cut correspondingly more. . . . This resulted not only in a cut in the development program but also in a serious distortion of the Plan priorities."[29]

Agricultural stagnation leading to food imports and diversion of valuable foreign exchange reserves adversely affected other areas of development, especially industrialization. That situation was clearly objectionable to government professionals, planners, and industrialists; transformation of the traditional agricultural sector became a high priority. The result was an entrepreneurial strategy of development that promoted the transformation of traditional landlords, rich peasants, and urban-based groups such as retired civil servants and military officers into progressive capitalist farmers.

The mechanisms for such a transformation were varied. Land reform was explicitly defended, but implementation of a radical land reform was beyond the administrative capability of the regime and was ruled out on tactical political grounds, in any event. Although the reform symbolically attacked the "feudal" landlords, in fact implementation disturbed few of the great landowning families and benefited only a tiny fraction of the nation's impoverished tenants. The real importance of the reform was symbolic: to serve notice to backward landowners (the "parasitic feudals" of official prose) that a new wave had come, that agriculture would, in the future, be dominated by the progressive and entrepreneurial landowners, not by the "drone-like" absentee feudals, whose factional manipulations and scheming had produced political chaos and allowed agriculture to stagnate. Simultaneously, newly developed state lands were being appropriated by bureaucrats and military officers—part of the "progressive middle class" farm community fostered by the regime.[30] If Ayub led a bourgeois revolution, it was a relatively bloodless one; the "feudals" survived quite well and were compensated handsomely for the little land they lost. They were, as Bhutto later said, "fattened" by the same policies meant to encourage the agrarian entrepreneurs.

The warnings to "feudals" via land reform were reinforced by the concrete policy inducements mentioned above: subsidized capital, easy and cheap credit, the absence of an agricultural income tax, favorable exchange rates, complementary public investment in electricity connections, tubewells, etc., promotion of high-yielding seed varieties, and so forth. Tractors were a part of this package, and the tractor population soared. From a base of only 2,000 tractors in 1959, the number of tractors jumped to 16,000 in 1968, an increase of 700 percent in nine years.[31] By contrast, in the period from 1947 to 1959, before the emergence of the farm entrepreneur strategy, tractors increased from 500 to 2,000.

How successful were these policies in converting feudals into rural capitalists? According to the government's 1968 study of mechanization, there were 1,495 tractor owners in Pakistan who owned more than 500 acres (the ceiling for irrigated land in Ayub's reforms) in 1968; these agriculturalists owned an average of 1,317 acres each and 15 percent of the private tractors in Pakistan.[32] Even though this is a significant concentration of mechanized capital, the number of tractors per owned acre on these huge farms was the lowest of any farm-size group. Whereas smaller landowners possessed a private tractor for every 21 to 150 acres, depending on size of holding, the great landowners averaged only a little more than one tractor per 1,000 acres owned, not a very intensive use of mechanization. Indeed, that level of tractorization suggests that most large landowners continued to cultivate the bulk of their holdings with tenants and bullocks. It was the smaller landowners who adopted the new tractor technology on a more intensive scale.[33] Owners of more than 200 acres held about 78 percent of all land held by tractor owners in 1968, but owned ony 34 percent of the tractors; owners of between 26 and 100 areas held only 9.5 percent of the land, but 35 percent of the tractors.[34]

These figures have limitations, since land quality and percentage of waste vary by size of holding, but they do suggest that the huge land owners have not been the most aggressive agricultural entrepreneurs. That conclusion is bolstered by data on tubewell ownership. Of the tractor owners, those with more than 200 acres of land possessed only 14 percent of the tubewells, but 78 percent of the land. Tractor owners with between 13 and 100 acres possessed 63 percent of the tubewells on only 21.5 percent of the land. It is thus difficult to argue that the 1959 land reforms and subsequent policy inducements fully succeeded in creating a class of progressive agriculturalists from the dronelike "feudal" landlords; on the other hand, the goal of creating an aggressive and progressive middle stratum of agrarian entrepreneurs was largely accomplished.

But what exactly was the policy logic of making tractors a central part of the agrarian entrepreneur strategy? What of the earlier official concerns—that tractors would increase unemployment and social tensions, that they were too costly and inappropriate in a "labor-surplus" economy? Was there new evidence to quiet these concerns? What was the role of knowledge about tractor impact on the formation of policy during the "green revolution" years of the 1960s? On what empirical base did the decision to jettison the cautious and selective approach to tractorization rest?

Knowledge and Policy: The Empirical Base of the Pro-Tractor Model

The most noteworthy answer to the questions in the preceding section is that there *was* no new evidence to justify a dramatic policy shift away from the go-slow, selective, land-augmenting tractorization policy. And, though the crisis in food production was an important justification for the new strategy, there was no evidence then (and none now) that tractors (particularly the large, 45-60 horsepower variety being utilized) are necessary or sufficient for increasing yields per acre or aggregate food production. A tractor supplies power for accomplishing operations that may otherwise be accomplished by utilizing power from other sources, human or animal.

It is hard to find evidence that shortage of power is the problem in Pakistani agriculture. The policy logic supporting tractorization must thus operate through more indirect channels—perhaps the tractors' impact on altering the traditional share tenancy organization of production, the attraction of more scientific and progressive individuals to agriculture, the raising of profits and encouragement of agricultural investment, increased crop intensity, and so on. As for the previously articulated unemployment and social tension concerns, the new policy logic assumed rapid industrial growth would siphon off the rural displaced (and a powerful military and police force would handle any residual "tensions"). The social morphology of the new policy logic was to be built around state-subsidized entrepreneurial capitalism in both urban and rural sectors, closely tied to the West and guaranteed by an authoritarian military government.

At the time of the decision to speed up the adoption of mechanized farm power (1960-61), no study, governmental or private, had been systematically undertaken in the field to determine the consequences of rapid tractorization. The transition to a rapid tractorization policy was made essentially on faith, borrowing heavily, as most development models of the time did, on the Western experience. The role of foreign experts and development paradigms was central. In fact, much of the initiative behind the mechanization and entrepreneurial approach (and its specific energy- and capital-intensive form) was supplied by U.S. government agencies and international develoment interests. As Carl Gotsch observed, "the U.S. Agency for International Development's agricultural program was influenced by a desire to show that the environment of the Indus Basin was quite capable of producing the same kinds of crops and yields that have been achieved in comparable areas in the southwestern part of the United States," and from USAID's viewpoint, this necessitated mechanized farming.[35]

The position of USAID, in turn, was based more on assumptions about the transferability of the American model (and the desire to open markets for American-made agricultural inputs) than on careful field studies of the impact of large tractors on Pakistan's rural economy and society.[36] At the same time, most development decisions during the early Ayub era were largely determined by a group of Harvard economists who often operated de facto as the Planning Commission. The decision to emphasize capital-intensive development strategies in both the rural and the urban sectors in particular, was influenced by American development experts and American institutions.[37]

In 1967 the International Bank for Reconstruction and Development (IBRD), whose funds and credit policies are largely controlled by the United States, advanced the first of three credit packages specifically earmarked for the purchase of tractors. The loan conditions directly targeted tractors for the tiny minority of large landowners: tractor loans on IBRD credit, which constituted the major source of tractor loans made by the Agricultural Development Bank of Pakistan, were originally not available to farmers owning less than 75 acres of land.[38] (Such farmers constituted less than 2 percent of the agricultural community.) The availability of such funds allowed the Pakistani government to stem the costly drainage of foreign exchange reserves that had developed under the Open General License system, and in 1966-67, that system was halted. Thereafter, tractor imports were obtained solely through foreign credits and barter arrangements, thus making the continued adoption and intensification of tractorization even more attractive.[39] Transactions the following year involved the use of a $23.2 million IBRD loan to import 8,000 tractors; 6,000 more were imported from Eastern Europe on barter arrangements. Almost 16,000 tractors had been purchased under IBRD loans by March 1972.[40]

Such developments were favorable, of course, to certain U.S. economic interests, since the vast majority of purchased tractors had been bought from U.S. firms.[41] (This is hardly surprising, since seven of the ten largest tractor firms, which control over 80 percent of all tractor sales in the non-Socialist world, are U.S. multinational corporations.)[42] Moreover, the same interests that promoted these policies also provided many of the empirical justifications for the tractorization approach, providing a rationale for the Pakistani government to discount those studies that cast doubts on the wisdom of the tractorization policy. In sum, it is not possible to discuss tractorization decisions of the government of Pakistan without reference to its particular position in the international system as a poor, client state with easily permeable policy membrances, suffused with foreign experts to whom there was no countervailing power.

Although there has been intense controversy and a great expenditure of intellectual labor on the tractor issue, the major decisions were made before empirical studies were completed. The first studies that justified the approach were done in 1967-68, long after the acceleration of tractor imports had been decided. The operative values—the pattern of assumptions and priorities—in these reports are particularly revealing.

The first such report was produced by the Ministry of Agriculture and Works and is entitled *The Survey Report on Farm Power, Machinery, and Equipment in Pakistan.* In the words of the survey, "It has been concluded that mechanized cultivation in West Pakistan is economical and more advantageous than bullock farming because per cultivated acre cost in case of tractor is Rs 96.00 and of bullock is Rs 131.82." In other words, tractorization should be adopted because it is more "efficient" (meaning less costly) and because it augments the profits of capitalist farmers, which in turn stimulates production and increases "the welfare of [the] rural masses" through high wages.[43]

The logic is curious for two reasons: first, the figures on cost of production ignore the subsidized nature of tractor costs, and second, the mechanisms whereby the rural masses are to be benefitted are barely adumbrated, much less demonstrated. Indeed, the report frankly admits that tractorization would displace an enormous number of tenants—32 percent of the bullock farm area studied was occupied by tenants, whereas tenants operated only 3.6 percent of the cultivated area on tractor farms.[44] At the same time, fully employed labor would be reduced by about one-half on tractor farms, even though wages were projected as increasing considerably for those permanent and casual laborers hired. Even more telling is the report's (rather curious) projection that unemployment of family labor would increase three times on tractor farms.[45] Thus, the assertion that tractorization would lead to an "increase in the welfare of rural masses" seems more a hopeful rationalization for a preferred policy than a result of rigorous empirical analysis.

Similar criticisms apply to the work of G. W. Giles, who prepared a report for the government of Pakistan under the auspices of the Ford Foundation (entitled *Towards a More Powerful Agriculture*) in 1968. Giles recommended a 12 percent increase in mechanization per annum and stressed the demonstrable private benefits of tractorization enjoyed by individual farmers. But as Carl Gotsch noted, Giles—like the official Farm Power Report—"failed to deal adequately with mechanization alternatives or with the concept of social costs and benefits."[46] The failure to consider alternative models of agricultural development was acutely evident in a report Giles wrote while on the President's Science Advisory Committee in 1967. In that report, Giles assumed the minimum mechanical requirement for agricultural development was at least 0.5 horsepower per hectare of land cultivated.[47] But as Robert d'A. Shaw observed, Giles's own data reveal that Asian and African nations could increase yields by "about 400 percent (to a level of Taiwan) with almost no increase in the use of horsepower per hectare."[48]

Thus, other alternatives for increasing yields and questions concerning *social* (as opposed to private) costs and benefits were not seriously considered. In this respect, both the Giles and the Farm Power reports ignored negative externalities associated with tractorization, justifying rapid mechanization by pointing to the private profits available to farmers wealthy enough to afford tractors. But of course what is a "cost" to the capitalist farmer—wage labor—is a means to a livelihood for the landless laborer.

An investigation of the relationship between private and social benefits of tractorization was first undertaken by Swadesh Bose and Edwin Clark in 1969; they concluded that there was a wide divergence between the two. Whereas Bose and Clark agreed with earlier findings indicating considerable net private benefits (higher farm profits), they argued that "Direct social benefits would be considerably smaller than direct social costs. Moreover, the indirect social costs, mainly arising from throwing large numbers of farm laborers out of employment, may be considered much greater than the possible indirect benefits."[49] After interviewing farmers who had mechanized their work, Bose and Clark estimated that the labor force per acre had decreased by about 50 percent from the premechanized period. After assuming an increase in cropping intensities and the mechanization of all farms over 25 acres by 1985, they calculated the displacement of between 600,000 and 700,000 laborers.[50]

Carl Gotsch demonstrated that even Bose and Clark underestimated the divergence of public and private benefits "by understating the potential private benefits to individuals who are able to both mechanize and to obtain access to unlimited supplies of groundwater."[51] In Gotsch's analysis, the preponderence of social costs over social benefits precludes the adoption of a tractorization policy. A modernization strategy stressing small-scale farming with improved agricultural implements, labor-intensive techniques, and modern non–labor-displacing inputs—such as high-yielding seed varieties, fertilizers, and tubewells—was recommended instead.[52]

In 1970, a USAID report by Roger Lawrence, *Some Economic Aspects of Mechanization in Pakistan*, disputed the findings of Bose and Clark by utilizing the same conceptual standard of private and social benefits and costs, but finding little divergence. Lawrence assumed farmers would reach cropping intensities of 200 percent as a result of mechanization. That assumption is totally untenable, however; scarcity of water alone limits the average potential cropping intensity in Pakistan to 150 percent.[53] And, of course, other factors prevent real-world cropping intensities from rising from their theoretical potential. It thus seems obvious, as Carl Gotsch concludes, that "the Lawrence analysis leads to an underestimate of the public-private divergence of the return on investments in mechanization because it overstates the net social benefits."[54]

The problem of unrealistic assumptions is endemic to cost-benefit analysis and has been a major source of disagreement among scholars of tractorization. Given the freedom to assume whatever we wish, it is possible to show any policy to be a good (or disastrous) one. Lawrence was quite correct, however, in raising the point that mechanical power does make possible certain crop rotations that are virtually impossible otherwise (and thus encourages multiple cropping under some agronomic and economic conditions). However, it has not been (and in principle cannot be) demonstrated that the large tractors being imported are necessary or sufficient for increasing labor demand through raising cropping intensities. As is frequently the case, cost-benefit analyses of tractorization vary in results as they vary in assumptions and smack more of ideology than science.[55]

Of perhaps more significance than these U.S.-sponsored reports are the surveys conducted by the government of Pakistan. The most important of these efforts was the study by the Farm Mechanization Committee for West Pakistan established in September 1968. (Its report was completed in 1970.) Serious dissension within the Agricultural Ministry precluded its publication. The report reads more as a rationale for mechanization than as an investigation into the desirability of the policy; its central theme is that "mechanization of agriculture should be accepted as inevitable and promoted on a planned basis to maximize benefits for the good of the farmers as well as for the country."[56]

The Mechanization Committee concluded that the need to substantially raise cropping intensities and yields was necessarily linked to tractorization. As a result (of tractorization) farm incomes would be raised, as would the employment of permanent and casual labor.[57] It was admitted that tractorization would cause an increase in tenant displacements, but it was assumed that they could be absorbed as wage laborers in industry and agriculture.[58] In addition, it was recommended that the benefits of mechanization should be extended to small farmers through the creation of tractor cooperatives and by persuading the IBRD to lower tractor loan requirements to 25 acres and to allow the limited purchase of tractors by cash.[59] Curiously, no empirical evidence was supplied to support many of these contentions, especially those regarding employment and the ramifications of tenant evictions. Indeed, almost all of the committee's conclusions and recommendations mirrored the findings of the 1967 Farm Power Survey and are completely consistent with the well-known pro-tractorization model. It is thus hard to avoid the conclusion that the committee entered its deliberations with certain fixed preconceptions, with foreknowledge of their ultimate verdict. The characterization in the report of tractorization as "inevitable" accurately reflected political reality and renders questions of the validity of the findings academic.

In sharp contrast to these official arguments are the findings of a study produced in 1973 by John McInerney and Graham Donaldson—*The Consequences of Farm Tractors in Pakistan*—under the auspices of the IBRD. This study was specifically designed to determine the socioeconomic and political ramifications of tractorization in view of the bank's strong support of tractor loans and its newly announced priority of funding projects that contribute directly to the welfare of the poorest people—specifically the rural masses.[60] One principal conclusion of the study was that tractors did not increase productivity in terms of yields per acre, a conclusion supported by other studies as well.[61] Tractor

5 jobs per tractor

owners tended to extend their operated holdings (by means of new purchases, renting-in, or tenant evictions) in order to efficiently utilize the new input and failed to intensify land use to any appreciable degree. This, of course, led to increased tenant evictions—4.2 tenant families per tractor farm—and a 40 percent decrease in labor use per cultivated acre, a figure close to the Bose and Clark estimate. In other words, the net destruction of full-time jobs is about five per tractor. Such conclusions contradict every finding of the Farm Mechanization Report and the major assumptions underlying the capital-intensive mechanized approach to agricultural development. Such a document was extremely controversial, given the significant IBRD involvement in tractor loans and its new policy of supporting rural uplift for the poorest of the poor. Because of this controversy, publication of the report was considerably delayed.

Similar conclusions emerged from an internal study conducted by the Agricultural Devlopment Bank of Pakistan (ADBP), the primary source of long-term tractor loans. Contrary to the assumptions of pro-tractor arguments, the bank's field survey found a negligible increase in cropping intensity after tractor purchase, and an extension of cultivation by large farmers through tenant evictions, purchase of land, land development, leasing, etc. The report put the tenant displacement figure at 6.1 families per tractor (using a rather odd methodology). Like the social costs, the private benefits of tractorization were again confirmed; the tractor recipients made enormous profits.[62] And like the report of the World Bank (the source of ADBP's tractor funds), the ADBP report evoked controversy within the bank and lay unpublished for years. The report covered the years 1966-67 to 1969-70, but, to the best of our knowledge, has yet to be published officially.

Given these contradictory findings, what should we conclude about the impact of tractors on the economy and social structure of rural Pakistan? In a sense, we have presented only the tip of the tractor dispute iceberg. With more sophisticated analysis, the question can be made even more complex. But it must be emphasized that (a) the sequence is important—tractorization decisions came before serious studies of the impact of tractors on the economy and society, despite early official fears that those effects would be negative and borne by the weakest sectors of rural Pakistan; and (b) uncertainty about the effects of tractorization varies—some effects are clearly established; others depend on a series of assumptions about future behavior. In the long run, the net effect on important variables is probably unknowable; it was certainly unknown when the tractorization strategy was launched. These points deserve some elaboration.

In the case of mechanization policy, we are faced not only with the usual problems of public policy analysis—how many and which of the variables and parameters should be considered changeable?—but also with a serious data constraint. The conclusion of K. N. Raj is gloomy, but accurate: To assess the real impact of mechanization requires information on the production and employment impact of all other technological parameters and inputs in the system (and their synergistic properties!), but

> such data are not available for the pre- and post-mechanization phases in any region (of South Asia) for even small samples of farms. The various statements made about the impact of mechanization on agriculture in these conditions rest therefore, almost without exception, on partial or suggested evidence—in some cases, on little more than casual observation. ... [Thus] since the data base for such analysis has been very meager, the case for and against mechanization (and different forms of it) has been discussed usually in general terms on *a priori* reasoning and on certain assumptions. ... But the weak empirical foundations of the assumptions made, and the oversimplifications on which they usually rest, make this kind of analysis an unreliable guide for either policy-making or for judging the correctness of the choices actually made.[63]

Fortunately, we are not left with analytical nihilism, however. There are points on which the empirical studies agree and points at which speculation produces divergent results. For example, it is certain that farmers who purchase tractors evict tenants; what is not certain is whether or not increased cropping intensities will provide for more jobs than mechanization destroys *or* if large-tractor mechanization is necessary to increase cropping intensities.[64] We will return to these questions. For the present, it is sufficient to note that official policy promoting tractorization *preceded* empirical studies of its impact. The most certain consequences have been higher profits for large landholdings and eviction or diminished plots for tenants, with net increases in demand for farm labor and higher yields remaining a matter of speculation. These facts clearly demonstrate the operative values of the planners of the 1960s and the distribution of effective political power. Farmers wealthy enough to mechanize—a tiny proportion of the rural populace—were important to the regime; the masses of unorganized sharecroppers and landless field laborers were not. Notions of "net employment," presented in all of the pro-tractor reports, likewise illustrate operative values by denying the importance of critical changes in the organization of production and labor processes, i.e., the structural transformation of tenant farmers into mere carriers of a homogeneous commodity—labor power.

But if the regimes of the 1960s showed little concern for the rural masses, what happened to tractor policy when the avowedly socialist and populist Pakistan People's Party came to power on a platform promising social justice and salvation to the rural poor?

The Bhutto Years: Social Justice
and Intensified Mechanization

In the elections of December 1970, Zulfikar Ali Bhutto's Pakistan People's Party (PPP) scored tremendous electoral successes in the Punjab and Sind through appeals to the rural and urban dispossessed and promises of redemption of the poor through creation of a socialist society. As a mass-based populist movement, the PPP was something new in Pakistani politics. Bhutto's fiery campaign rhetoric excoriated both capitalists and feudals and vowed to end the exploitative practices of both. Bhutto railed against the "favored few" and the traditional power structure that had "fattened them."[65] Given that existing empirical studies showed clearly that tractor owners were among the favored few, fattened by the high tax-free profits of mechanization, and that the clearest victims of mechanization were distressingly poor sharecroppers, it would seem reasonable to expect that official tractor policy would change. Instead, the Bhutto period witnessed an acceleration of farm mechanization.

The intensification process had begun in the 1960s. The Third Five-Year Plan (1965-70) promised implementation of the pro-tractor decisions made at the beginning of the decade. The Planning Commission stated that

> mechanization will play an increasingly important role in the agricultural sector during the Third Plan period. . . . The number of tractors in both the public and private sectors in West Pakistan will be further augmented. . . (and) the program started in West Pakistan during the Second Plan for distributing improved implements at subsidized prices will be expanded.[66]

Budget allocations supported these intentions. Compared to the First and Second Plans, which allocated only around 4 percent of the agricultural budget to mechanization, the Third Plan projected a 12 percent share of the agricultural expenditure.[67]

The same trends were reflected in the Fourth Five-Year Plan, 1970-75, which sought to "encourage expansion of farm mechanization in the private sector."[68] This would be accomplished through an expansion of institutional supports, such as training facilities that were started in the Third Plan to encourage the "adoption of farm mechanization on an increasing scale."[69] Budget allocations continued at a relatively high level; over 9 percent of agricultural expenditure was allocated to mechanization, with the percentage drop from the Third Plan largely due to the new availability of foreign credit for tractor purposes.[70] As a result, the tractor population nearly doubled between 1968 and 1972. In absolute terms, the growth of the tractor population during Pakistan's first twenty years (1948-68) was more than equaled by the growth in the next five years.

By the end of 1974, the Agricultural Inquiry Committee reported that 35,000 tractors were in use, an increase of 5,000 in two years.[71] Even more dramatically, tractor imports for 1975 alone were set at 15,000.[72] Additionally, tractor imports were to be allowed on a gift scheme as well as on foreign credit and barter arrangements; the scheme allows the use of foreign exchange earned by Pakistanis abroad to import tractors.[73] In 1976, 15,000 tractors were again imported; this acceleration was supported by a new "free sale policy for tractors," which abolished the permit system and all restrictions on individual purchases.[74] The 1977 target, moreover, was set at importation of 20,000 tractors.[75] If these import targets were reached, the tractor population would have increased by over 150 percent in the three years between 1975 and 1977.

The acceleration of tractor imports was not the result of any new evidence about the impact of mechanization. The Fourth Plan admitted that "practically no research is being carried out in the field of farm mechanization (including its impact on socioeconomic conditions)."[76] In the Planning Commission's Working Papers for the Development Perspective (1975-80), it was officially acknowledged that the effects of mechanization were disputed and uncertain. But given this uncertainty, the government's operative values were clear; the Planning Commission suggested that "research in this field should be carried on on a continuing basis as the mechanization proceeds."[77] The regime continually cited in public the increase in tractors as evidence of its commitment to the farming community, though 77 percent of that community owned less than the official "subsistence" holding of 12.5 acres. Even Sheikh Rashid (the radical in Bhutto's cabinet who steered the land reform and fulminated against the landlord class) publicly proclaimed the acceleration in mechanization as evidence of the bona fides of the regime vis-à-vis the farmers.[78]

Bhutto, Sheikh Rashid, and the Planning Commission all associated mechanization with the "break-through in the agricultural sector"—the tremendous increases in production of the Third Plan period.[79]

Whatever the empirical and theoretical problems of this position, it had become enshrined in policy logic and social lore. No distinctions were made between genetic innovation (for the high-yielding varieties of crops) and higher levels of inputs (water, fertilizer), on the one hand, and mechanical power innovations (tractors, threshers, etc.), on the other. The tractor was a symbol of progressive, scientific farming and all its successes; in an odd metonymy of policy logic, the part came to stand for the whole. And, as always, the regime could not afford to chance the dislocations of a stagnant agricultural sector.

More than social lore, symbols, and policy logic were at work, of course. Tractors were in great demand in Pakistan. Farmers were so eager to mechanize that a black market grew up around tractors, with prices often running nearly double the official rate. Bribes changed hands to secure access to scarce tractors; strings were pulled.[80] And despite the rhetoric of socialism and rehabilitating the dispossessed, it was this substantial capitalist farmer class that was courted and counted upon by the regime.[81]

This is not the place for a political analysis of the power base and politics of the PPP, but it should be noted that the populist and leftist impulses at the mass level were contradicted by the power of representatives of traditional elite groups, including large landholders, in the party hierarchy and the government. Over time, powerful landed families crossed over to the PPP ranks; in the Punjab for example, the landed gentry within the PPP included the Gardazi, Noon, Khar, and Qureshi families.[82] The land reforms that Bhutto had promised in order to crush the rural elite had, in fact, extremely limited impact, particularly in the areas of PPP strength, the Punjab and Sind. Indeed, the policy logic of the land reforms followed the Ayub Khan model precisely in distinguishing between the parasitic feudals, who were to be "eradicated" (excepting PPP stalwarts, of course), and the progressive capitalist farmers, who were to be encouraged.[83]

So committed was the Bhutto regime to rapid mechanization that elaborate negotiations were begun to establish indigenous tractor production. In May 1977, the federal minister for production announced an agreement with Massey-Ferguson for construction of a plant with an initial capacity of 10,000 tractors annually, rising to 20,000 annually in four years. Imports would have to continue for some time, since the current demand is between 15,000 and 17,000 tractors per year and growing at about 9 or 10 percent per year. (Consider this figure in light of the fact that it took twenty-one years, from 1947 to 1968, for the country to acquire its first 15,000 tractors!)[84] The machine to be built is a 45 horsepower model, though the chief minister of the Punjab argued that

larger machines were necessary for Sind because of the larger
landholdings there.[85] And, although the 45 horsepower tractor was
considered adequate for 150- to 200-acre farms, importation or
manufacture of larger machines is being considerd. This consideration is somewhat peculiar in light of the ceiling on landholdings (100-
200 acres). And the urgency of large tractor production seems curious
considering the size distribution of holdings; more than three-fourths of
Pakistan's farmers operate on less than 12.5 acres. Yet, the most recent
estimate from Planning Commission technicians is that within five
years the annual demand for new tractors will be 36,000.[86]

Costs, Benefits, and Structure: Winners and Losers

Despite the controversy surrounding mechanization studies, some
consequences are beyond doubt. Although there is dispute over the level
of aggregate benefits, there has never been any doubt about the private
benefits that accrue to farmers who can obtain tractors. The Pakistan
Agricultural Committee found that tractors could reduce the costs of
cultivation by one half.[87] A study by the Agricultural Development Bank
of Pakistan found that its customers who received tractors realized a
financial rate of return on the investment of 54.6 percent.[88] The private
profitability of tractorization was also manifest in the appearance of a
black market and the clamor of large landowners for higher levels of
imports. This profitability results not merely from altering production
relations on the farm (including changes in cropping patterns,
expansion of cropped area, eviction of sharecroppers, etc.) but also from
participation in a vigorous tractor rental market. Custom plowing and
short-term rental of the tractor and its implements are extremely
lucrative; in the ADBP study, the average tractor owner realized Rs 1,112
from such activities in the first year of ownership.[89]

As mentioned previously, the private profitability of tractor
ownership is dependent on ancillary public policies—exchange rates,
cheap official credit (made cheaper by the high rates of default,
especially by politically powerful tractor owners), irrigation development, support prices, etc. These policies, and hence private profitability,
change over time. The desirability of tractor ownership, however, is not
tied solely to profitability. The tractor owner is able to evict tenants (or
reduce plot size) and thus be rid of (or exert increased control of) an
increasingly troublesome class. The tenancy reforms of the Bhutto
period (though effectively unenforced) technically give tenants important rights vis-à-vis landowners,[90] and increasing tenant consciousness
inevitably creates difficulties for owners. The tractor also decreases the

dependence of owners on field laborers, another source of potential trouble. The tractor increases landowner control of the production process. In short, farm mechanization (including tractor complements such as harvesters and threshers) alters the rural class balance in favor of capital (against labor) and thus appeals to landowners independently of strict profitability concerns.

Just as all studies of tractors in Pakistan agree on the private benefits of tractor ownership, all concede that farm mechanization displaces share tenants. The disagreement comes in projections of the *net* impact on "demand for labor"—will more jobs be created than are destroyed? The aggregate focus denies the normative and political significance of the process of change. Whatever jobs are created, the tenant farmer (or village craftsman)[91] who is evicted loses his farm—his firm, his enterprise, his workplace—and often his home as well. The change in status and life prospects, security, and autonomy is significant far beyond the muddying concept of net employment effects. The share tenant who becomes a casual field laborer loses control of the labor process, becomes a carrier of labor power rather than a farmer. Indeed, the conceptualization of policy analysis in terms of net jobs created or destroyed lends legitimacy to that structural change, denying the validity of the normative framework of the agrarian underclass.

The significance of the structural change is evident politically. Tenant evictions, for whatever reasons, have produced militant peasant movements and local violence throughout South Asia, as elsewhere. Although there has been local and small-scale violence over this issue in Pakistan,[92] the absence of political organization among tenants and the isolated and sporadic character of the process have discouraged the emergence of mass movements. For example, Hamza Alavi reported from the Punjabi village he studied: "The militancy of sharecroppers is latent in their attitudes of bitterness and grievance because of farm mechanization and eviction. But this militancy is not yet reflected in political action."[93] Alavi notes that Rajput tenants in a nearby village were able, because of specific social and structural conditions, to organize against tractor-induced evictions.[94] The political and economic dynamics that will shape the future are in principle not predictable, but it seems inconceivable that class consciousness and class conflict will not develop further and vertical patron-client ties deteriorate. They will be driven by a number of factors, of which tractorization is decidedly one. Effective mobilization of the agrarian underclass is, of course, an entirely different and even less predictable matter; there are formidable obstacles to such mobilization.

Two qualifications must be added to the general conclusion that tractors cause evictions. First, landlords often find it convenient to retain some (often many) of their tenants in order to be assured of a labor force, particularly in times of peak labor demand, such as harvest. In this situation, the process involves reducing the size of the tenant's plot, an action that accomplishes several goals. The landlord is able to acquire more land for personal cultivation, increasing the area over which profits can be appropriated rather than having to share half and half with a sharecropper. Moreover, the tenant on a plot smaller than the generally agreed subsistence size (10-12 acres) is "underemployed" (has difficulty meeting subsistence needs) and thus readily available to work when needed by the landlord. The process thus allows the owner to extend the area on which capitalist relations operate (and on which profits can be appropriated), while securing an inexpensive and dependent labor force. At the same time, the net reduction in the amount of land available for sharecropping improves the bargaining position of owners vis-à-vis the landless.[95]

The dynamics sketched above from Hamza Alavi's village work were confirmed by the ADBP study of 207 sample tractor farms throughout Pakistan. After tractor purchase, the average sample farm reduced the acreage rented out to share tenants by about 27 percent (from 77.7 acres to 56.7 acres). The average tenant holding on these farms before mechanization was 10.5 acres, almost exactly the national average. After the tractor purchase, the average tenant holding fell to 7.2 acres.[96]

The second qualification to the tractor-induced eviction phenomenon is simply that evictions are caused by other factors as well. Tractors were introduced during a period of rapid technological change and high profitability, and these conditions will tend to produce transitions from share tenancy to wage labor for reasons already stated: under sharecropping arrangements, the landowner must share increments to production that could otherwise be appropriated exclusively (under a wage labor system).[97] The alternative is for landlords to raise rents, and though there are clearly instances of this in Pakistan (up to three-fourths of the gross produce), there are traditional resistances to raising rents. (It is also against the law, but that is not an important consideration; rental ceilings—usually 40 percent of gross produce—have never been seriously enforced.) The tractor does, however, add an independent impetus to the pressure for eviction, because of the microeconomics of utilizing an expensive capital item; landlords seek to reduce unit costs of operation by enlarging the self-cultivated area. The tractor also facilitates reorganization of the production process. But as Bashir Ahmed and others have shown, evictions proceed independently of tractorization.[98] In agriculture, technical change and newly profitable conditions pressure landowners to alter the terms and relations of production to appropriate the additional surplus. Simultaneously, land reforms and tenant militance contribute to evictions by making the traditional social organization of production more troublesome and less manageable.

The third phenomenon on which tractor studies agree is that mechanization increases concentration of landholding. Unit costs of operation are high on small areas, but fall as farm size expands (to a limit that depends on tractor size). Thus, tractor purchasers typically expand operations. The way in which they expand has important structural consequences. For example, in the ADBP study, the average self-cultivated area increased from 42.1 acres in the pre-tractor year to 106.4 acres the year after the tractor purchase, an increase of 153 percent. The average area *owned* increased only slightly, from 145.3 acres to 152.8 acres, with the greatest increase coming on the largest farms. The increase in self-cultivated area came from four sources: newly purchased land accounted for 11.7 percent of the increase, development of uncultivated land for 27.3 percent, land taken back from tenants, 32.6 percent, and area *rented in*, for 31.4 percent.[99] Thus, the pro-tractor model is correct in projecting new land development as a consequence, but even more significant as sources of new area were eviction of tenants and renting-in land. Although the tractors were to make capitalists of the feudals, in fact a large number of landlords became sharecroppers to better utilize their tractors.

The structural consequences are important. Further concentration of holdings defeats stated policy objectives of reducing rural inequalities and seems especially unacceptable, given the terrible pressure of poor, small-scale farmers on scarce land resources. About 44 percent of Pakistan's farmers *till* less than 7.5 acres; the average tractor owner in the 1968 Farm Mechanization Report *owned* 228 acres. Moreover, the entry of large-scale farmers into the leasing market increases the pressure on the share tenant class, which is already being squeezed by the reduction in available farm area for rent. And expansion of land area is done at the expense of *intensification* of cultivation, one of the primary justifications for tractor use; the ADBP tractor owners increased cropping intensely only marginally, by less than 4 percent, but increased cultivated area by 153 percent.[100] Both expansion and intensification lower unit costs of tractor ownership, but the former results in increased concentration of economic power and deprivation for the poorest rural classes. The result is a bimodal pattern of rural development, with substantial farmers increasing both their control of land and nonland capital and the surplus that flows from that control.

The point about intensification brings us full circle in the tractor controversy; greater cropping intensities are supposed to increase labor demand and thus allow the benefits of mechanization to "trickle down" to the have-nots. Projections and empirical studies disagree as to the amount of intensification of production. But the entire model suffers from analytical blinders. Whether or not cropping intensities increase is left to the whim of substantial landowners, yet the justification is in terms of the welfare of the "farming community." But there is no farming community; there are individuals and classes in competition for land and agricultural capital. Expansion of holdings or eviction of tenants is as likely as intensification; and following the tractors come the harvesters and threshers. Whatever the short-term net effect on labor demand, in the long run the Pakistani model points toward the West. Those who control the means of production—land, machines, working capital, and credit—will continue to control the process and reap the benefits of technical change. Those who own nothing will continue to count only as bearers of the commodity "labor power," for which the demand and conditions fluctuate according to forces beyond their control.

Marx noted the particularly cruel irony of capitalist growth and technical change; labor is confronted with (and threatened by) its own surplus product, transformed into the embodied capital of new machines. Rather than liberating the worker, the machine threatens displacement, loss of autonomy, an unfamiliar labor process. In one sense, this is the case with tractors in Pakistan. The sharecropper whose landlord accumulates and mechanizes watches the historic drama—his own labor, realized in the half-share rent of many harvests, perhaps several generations, being transformed into mechanized capital that alters his relation to both land and landlord, production and distribution, exchange and consumption. Such a scenario is sufficiently classical to be appealing, but it represents only one aspect of the process. Much of the capital that confronts the sharecropper in Pakistan comes directly from the state, through direct and indirect subsidies. The state in turn obtains credits of both a general and a specific sort (the IBRD-IDA loans) through international channels—credits that facilitate and accelerate the pace and determine the specific form of technical change in agriculture.

The logic of the preceding pages does not lead to a Luddite conclusion. Tractors have tremendous potential to liberate rural men and women from mind-numbing, back-breaking labor and, under certain conditions, to enhance production capabilities.[101] But the institutional framework is critical. Our analysis has shown that the

benefits of technical change in the development model pursued by
Pakistan accrue to those already privileged; the deprivations fall on ✓
those already relatively deprived. This outcome is the dynamic product
of complementary structures of political power and interests at the local,
national, and international levels. The privileged are well-organized
and have powerful international allies (not the least of whom are
traditional development economists); they also control the state. The
share tenants and laborers lack organization and political representation, are divided by structural isolation and factional politics, and are
often exacerbated by competition with one another. Although these
conditions characterize much of the subcontinent, there are enough
exceptions to demonstrate that they are not immutable.

Notes

1. William Hinton, *Iron Oxen: A Documentary of Revolution in Chinese
Farming* (New York: Vintage, 1970), p. 44.

2. For an interesting treatment, see Aidan Foster-Carter, "From Rostow to
Gunder Frank: Conflicting Paradigms in the Analysis of Development," *World
Development* 4, no. 3 (March 1976):167-80.

3. Illustrative examples of work that has had a major impact in
mainstream development circles include Dudley Seers, "The Meaning of
Development," *International Development Review* 11, no. 4 (December 1969):2-
6; and Mahbub-ul-Haq, "Crisis in Development Strategies," *World Development* 1, no. 7 (July 1973):29-31.

4. Much of the best literature remains inaccessible to those of us who do not
read Spanish. We have been guided to this literature through the work of Devora
Grynspan: "Structural Dependency and Marginalization in Latin America,"
manuscript, Northwestern University (April 1977).

5. Jean-Paul Sartre, *Search for a Method*, trans. Hazel E. Barnes (New York:
Random House, 1968), p. xvi.

6. Cited in Government of Pakistan, Ministry of Agriculture and Works,
"Farm Mechanization in West Pakistan," Report of the Farm Mechanization
Committee, Islamabad, March 1970, p. 39.

7. Government of Pakistan, Ministry of Food and Agriculture, *The Report
of the Pakistan Agricultural Inquiry Committee, 1951-52* (Karachi, 1952), p. 11.

8. Government of Pakistan, Ministry of Agriculture and Works, *Report on
Tractor Survey in West Pakistan* (Karachi, 1967), p. 1.

9. Government of Pakistan, National Planning Board, *The First Five-Year
Plan, 1955-1960* (Karachi, 1957), p. 232.

10. Government of Pakistan, Planning Commission, *The Second Five-Year
Plan, 1960-1965* (Karachi, 1960), p. 144.

11. *Report on Tractor Survey*, p. 3, and Bashir Ahmad, "Farm Mechanization
and Agricultural Development: A Case Study of Pakistan," Ph.D. Dissertation,

Michigan State University (1972), pp. 38-39.

12. *First Five-Year Plan*, p. 232.

13. Ibid., pp. 175, 187; and Gustav Papanek, *Pakistan's Development: Social and Private Incentives* (Cambridge: Harvard University Press, 1967), p. 146.

14. Tariq Ali, *Pakistan: Military Rule or People's Power* (New York: William Morrow and Company, 1970), p. 38; Azimusshan Haider, *Economic History of the Region Constituting Pakistan from 1825 to 1974* (Karachi: A. Haider, 1975), p. 64; and Talukdar Maniruzzaman, "Crisis in Political Development and the Collapse of the Ayub Regime in Pakistan," *The Journal of Developing Areas* 5, no. 2 (January 1971):226-27.

15. Haider, *Economic History*, p. 64.

16. Daniel Thorner, *The Agrarian Prospect in India* (Delhi: University Press, 1956), pp. 4-5; and Francine Frankel and Carl von Vorys, *The Political Challenge of the Green Revolution: Shifting Patterns of Peasant Participation in India and Pakistan* (Princeton: Center for International Studies, Princeton University, 1972), pp. 23-24.

17. Government of Pakistan, *Census of Agriculture, vol. 2, West Pakistan*, Tables 5-9; also, Leslie Nulty, *The Green Revolution in West Pakistan: Implications of Technological Change* (New York: Praeger Publishers, 1972), pp. 33-34.

18. Government of West Pakistan, *Report of the Land Reform Commission* (Lahore, January 1959), App. A.

19. Haider, *Economic History*, p. 63.

20. For excellent treatment from village studies, see Saghir Ahmad, *Class and Power on a Punjabi Village* (New York: Monthly Review Press, 1977), pp. 91-126. Also, Hamza Alavi, "The Politics of Dependence: A Village in West Punjab," *South Asia Review* 4, no. 2 (January 1971):111-25.

21. *Report of the Land Reform Commission*, p. 30. See also Ronald J. Herring, "Redistributive Agrarian Policy: Land and Credit in South Asia, Ph.D. Dissertation, University of Wisconsin-Madison (Land Tenure Center, 1976), chaps. 5 and 6 for a full exposition of the policy model and implementation results.

22. Government of Pakistan, *The Report of the Pakistan Food and Agriculture Committee* (Karachi, 1960), p. 106.

23. Ibid, p. 110.

24. *Farm Mechanization in West Pakistan*, p. 43.

25. See Hiromitsu Kaneda, "Economic Implications of the 'Green Revolution' and the Strategy of Agricultural Development in West Pakistan," Pakistan Institute of Development Economics, Report no. 78 (Karachi, 1969).

26. *Second Five-Year Plan*, p. 143; Hiromitsu Kaneda, "Economic Implications," p. 103; and Swadesh Bose, "East-West Contrast in Pakistan's Agricultural Development," pp. 86-88, both in *Growth and Inequality in Pakistan*, ed. Keith Griffin and Azizur Rahman Khan (London: Macmillan, 1972). See also Carl Gotsch, "Tractor Mechanization and Rural Development in Pakistan," *International Labor Review* (Geneva) 107, no. 2 (February 1973):158.

27. *Second Five-Year Plan*, p. 132.

28. Papanek, *Pakistan's Development*, p. 146.

29. *Second Five-Year Plan*, p. 82.

30. On implementation of the land reforms, see Herring, "Redistributive Agrarian Policy," and Saghir Ahmad, *Class and Power*, pp. 29-40. Also, Nimal Sanderatne and M. A. Zaman, "The Impact of Agrarian Structure on the Political Leadership of Undivided Pakistan," Land Tenure Center Paper no. 94 (Madison, Wisconsin, November 1973), especially pp. 14-15. On the ambiguity of the term "feudal" in the context of Pakistan, and the policy measures taken against the feudals, see Ronald J. Herring, "Zulfikar Ali Bhutto and the 'Eradication of Feudalism' in Pakistan," *Comparative Studies in Society and History* (forthcoming). For an argument that the Ayub years *did* see a rise of a new "middle class" agrarian entrepreneur at the expense of the feudals, see Sahid Javed Burki, "The Development of Pakistan's Agriculture," in Robert D. Stevens, Hamza Alavi, and Peter J. Bertocci, eds., *Rural Development in Bangladesh and Pakistan* (Honolulu: University of Hawaii, 1976). For a refutation of Burki, and an excellent treatment of official policy and its effects in this period, see Hamza Alavi, "The Rural Elite and Agricultural Development in Pakistan," in the same volume, pp. 317-53.

31. Shafi Niaz, "Agricultural Mechanization in Pakistan," *Journal of Rural Development and Administration*, 7, no. 2 (April-June 1960):61.

32. *Farm Mechanization in West Pakistan*, p. 60.

33. See also, Burki, "Development of Pakistan's Agriculture."

34. Our calculations are from *Farm Mechanization in West Pakistan*, p. 60.

35. Gotsch, "Tractor Mechanization," p. 139-40.

36. These facts were reinforced through conversations with AID officials in Islamabad in 1974 and, especially, in the fall of 1976.

37. Cf. Anwar Syed, "Foreign Aid: Case Studies in Recipient Independence," *Pakistan Horizon* (Karachi) 23, no. 1 (1970):20-21; Hamza Alavi and Amir Khusro, "Pakistan: The Burden of U.S.-Aid," in Robert Rhodes, ed., *Imperialism and Underdevelopment* (New York: Monthly Review Press, 1970), pp. 68-72.

38. For details of the credits and their conditions, see John McInerney and Graham Donaldson, "The Consequences of Farm Tractors in Pakistan," an unofficial draft of their report for the World Bank (Washington, D.C., March 1973); *Farm Mechanization in West Pakistan*, especially p. 125; *Annual Reports* of the Agricultural Development Bank of Pakistan (Karachi, yearly).

39. Gotsch, "Tractor Mechanization," p. 140.

40. Ibid., p. 135; Iftikar Ahmed, "The Green Revolution and Tractorization," *International Labor Review* 114, no. 1 (July-August 1976):89; and Saeed Hafeez, *Pakistan Agriculture* (Karachi: Press Corporation of Pakistan, 1972), p. 6.

41. By 1967, nearly 83 percent of all operating tractors in Pakistan were purchased from multinational firms based in the United States; *Report on Tractor Survey*, p. 4; and *Standard and Poor's Register of Corporations*, vol. I (New York, 1978), pp. 662, 1193, 1448.

42. Montague Yudelman, Gavin Butler, and Ranadev Banerji, *Technological Change in Agriculture and Employment in Developing Countries* (Paris: Center of the Organization for Economic Cooperation and Development, 1971), p. 145.

43. Government of Pakistan, Ministry of Agriculture and Works, *Survey Report on Farm Power, Machinery, and Equipment of Pakistan* (1967), p. 10.

44. Ibid., p. 6.

45. Ibid., p. 7.

46. Swadesh Bose and Edwin Clark, "Some Basic Considerations on Agricultural Mechanization in West Pakistan," *The Pakistan Development Review* 9, no. 3 (Autumn 1969):294; and Gotsch, "Tractor Mechanization," p. 140.

47. G. W. Giles, "Agricultural Power and Equipment," *The World Food Problem*, Report of the President's Science Advisory Committee (Washington, D.C., 1967), vol. 3, p. 183.

48. Robert d'A. Shaw, *Jobs and Agricultural Development*, Overseas Development Council, Monograph no. 3 (1971), p. 34. See also Eric Clayton, "A Note on Farm Mechanization and Employment in Developing Countries," *International Labor Review* 110, no. 1 (July 1974):58.

49. Bose and Clark, "Considerations on Mechanization," p. 294.

50. Ibid.

51. Gotsch, "Tractor Mechanization," p. 144.

52. Ibid., p. 162. See also Bose and Clark, "Considerations on Mechanization," p. 276; and Kaneda, "Economic Implications," pp. 114-16, on the feasibility of such a strategy.

53. Roger Lawrence, "Some Economic Aspects of Mechanization in Pakistan," USAID Memorandum (1970), as cited in Gotsch, "Tractor Mechanization," p. 143. On the water constraint on cropping intensities in Pakistan, see International Bank for Reconstruction and Development, *Program for the Development of Irrigation and Agriculture in West Pakistan: Comprehensive Report* (May 1968), pp. 26-27, 42-43.

54. Gotsch, "Tractor Mechanization," p. 144.

55. This is not the place for an elaboration of the problems in cost-benefit analysis, but it should be noted that the very notion of a "social cost" or "social benefit" is rooted in unstated and undefended premises about what ought to be the case. What is a "cost" from one normative framework (or class position) may well be a "benefit" from another.

56. *Farm Mechanization in West Pakistan*, p. 158.

57. Ibid., pp. 78-81; 51-53.

58. Ibid., p. 80.

59. Ibid., pp. 26, 94-95.

60. McInerney and Donaldson, "Consequences of Tractors." For the World Bank's new views on development, see The World Bank, *The Assault on World Poverty* (Baltimore: Johns Hopkins University Press, 1975).

61. McInerney and Donaldson, "Consequences of Tractors," p. 88; Ahmad, "Farm Mechanization," p. 79.

62. Agricultural Development Bank of Pakistan, "Survey Report on Impact of Tractor Loans in West Pakistan," typescript draft of Spring 1974 meeting in Islambad, pp. 66, 85-99; App. 1, 2, 4, 5, 6, and 11.

63. K. N. Raj, "Mechanization of Agriculture in India and Sri Lanka,"

International Labor Review 106, no. 4 (October 1972):317-18. For a similarly ✓ pessimistic conclusion as to the possibility of definitive results (but with different policy implications), see Ronald Ridker, "Employment and Unemployment in Near East and South Asian Countries: A Review of Evidence and Issues," in *Employment and Unemployment Problems of the Near East and South Asia*, vol. I, ed. Ronald Ridker and Harold Lubell (Delhi: Vikas Publications, 1971), p. 29.

64. We agree in this with William H. Bartsch, "Employment Effects of Alternative Technologies and Techniques—A Survey of Evidence," International Labor Office, World Employment Program (Geneva, August 1973).

65. See, for example, Herring, "Zulfikar Ali Bhutto"; Hasan Askari Rizvi, *Pakistan Peoples' Party: The First Place 1967-71* (Lahore: Progressive Publishers, 1973); Frankel and von Vorys, *Political Challenge*, pp. 33-37.

66. Government of Pakistan, Planning Commission, *The Third Five-Year Plan, 1965-1970* (Karachi, 1965), pp. 402-3.

67. *First Five-Year Plan*, p. 280; *Second Five-Year Plan*, p. 192; and *Third Five-Year Plan*, p. 443.

68. Government of Pakistan, Planning Commission, *The Fourth Five-Year Plan, 1970-75* (Karachi, 1970), p. 277.

69. Ibid., pp. 277-78.

70. Ibid., p. 310.

71. Government of Pakistan, Ministry of Food and Agriculture, *Agricultural Inquiry Committee Report of the Sub-Working Group on Mechanization* (Islamabad, April 1975), p. 1.

72. Government of Pakistan, Planning Commission, "Working Papers Relating to the Agricultural Sector—Fifth Five-Year Plan, 1975-1979," (Islamabad, 1979).

73. Embassy of Pakistan, Information Division, *Pakistan Affairs* (Washington, D.C.), July 16, 1975, p. 1.

74. "Towards Agricultural Breakthrough," *Pakistan Times*, September 13, 1976, p. 4.

75. *Pakistan Times*, November 4, 1976, p. 5.

76. *Fourth Five-Year Plan*, p. 278.

77. Government of Pakistan, Planning Commission, "Working Papers for the Development of Perspective (1975-1980) (Islamabad), vol. 2, p. 18.

78. *Pakistan Times*, September 25, 1974; November 8, 1974.

79. See, for example, *Fourth Five-Year Plan*, p. 275.

80. Authors' field notes, 1974-76.

81. For example, see *Farm Mechanization in West Pakistan*, p. 97; N. K. Chandra, "The Class Character of the Pakistani State," *Economic and Political Weekly* (Bombay), Annual Number, 1972, pp. 275-92; Hamza Alavi, "The Rural Elite"; Philip E. Jones, "Changing Party Structures in Pakistan: From Muslim League to People's Party," in Ahmed, ed., *Contemporary Pakistan*.

82. Cf. Feroz Ahmed, "Structure and Contradiction in Pakistan," in Kathleen Gough and Hari Sharma, eds., *Imperialism and Revolution in South Asia* (New York: Monthly Review Press, 1973), p. 185; Craig Baxter, "Pakistan Votes—

1970," *Asian Survey* 11, no. 3 (March 1971):209; Jones, "Changing Party Structures."

83. For details, see Ronald J. Herring and M. Ghaffar Chaudhry, "The 1972 Land Reforms in Pakistan and Their Economic Implications," *The Pakistan Development Review* 13, no. 3 (Autumn 1974). For a more recent, and accurate, evaluation, see Herring," Zulfikar Ali Bhutto" and Feroz Ahmed, "Land Reforms and Social Structure," *Pakistan Forum* 3, no. 4 (January 1973).

84. *Business Recorder* (Karachi), May 20, 1977; *Pakistan Times,* May 20, 1977.

85. *Pakistan Times,* May 21, 1977.

86. *Pakistan Affairs* 31, no. 8 (April 16, 1978).

87. *Farm Mechanization in West Pakistan,* p. 41.

88. ADBP, *Survey Report on Tractor Loans in West Pakistan,* p. 97.

89. Ibid.

90. See Herring and Chaudhry, "1972 Land Reforms," pp. 247, 267-69, 272-75.

91. Saghir Ahmad, *Class and Power,* p. 130, describes how tractorization deprives not only share tenants in the village but local artisans as well.

92. For example, see "Sarhad Peasants under Attack," *Pakistan Forum* 2, nos. 9-10 (June-July 1972).

93. Hamza Alavi, "The Politics of Dependence," in *Rural Development,* p. 127.

94. Ibid., p. 124.

95. Alavi, "Rural Elite and Agricultural Development," p. 324; Alavi, "The Politics of Dependence," p. 119.

96. *Survey Report,* App. 34.

97. See Keith Griffin, *The Political Economy of Agrarian Change* (Cambridge, Mass.: Harvard University Press, 1974) for a discussion of this well-known phenomenon.

98. Ahmad, *Class and Power,* pp. 63-129; Yudelman, Butler, and Banerji, *Technological Change,* pp. 48-49; Leslie Nulty, *The Green Revolution in West Pakistan* (New York: Praeger, 1972), pp. 79-80.

99. *Survey Report,* App. 1-6. This phenomenon is dramatically illustrated at the aggregate level in Government of Pakistan, *Pakistan Census of Agricultural Machinery, Final Report* (Lahore, 1975), Table 22.

100. *Survey Report,* pp. 98-99.

101. To end where we began, compare William Hinton's *Iron Oxen* to the account presented in our text.

9
The Commercialization of Agriculture and the Rise of Rural Political Protest in Black Africa

Robert H. Bates

Introduction

Throughout the developing world, the commercialization of agriculture has been highly ambiguous in its effects. On the one hand, it has brought prosperity to rural farm families. On the other, it has produced political grievances and generated social conflict. These paradoxical consequences have been as true in Africa as elsewhere in the developing world. In this essay, I look at the relationship between the commercialization of agriculture and the rise of political protest in that continent. And I do so by addressing the question: Why would rural dwellers, having sought to improve their lot by taking advantage of communal markets, demand political action in support of these efforts?

In answering this question, I will examine several of the major issues that arose in the countryside during the colonial period in Africa. These issues included protests over governmental regulation of agricultural production, protests concerning the structure of markets, conflicts over land tenure, and disputes over taxes. Taken together, confrontations over these issues made up much of the rural political agenda in Africa during the colonial period.

Some of these issues were more significant in some places than in others. Disputes over the structure of markets most frequently arose in the forest areas of West Africa and in the cotton-producing regions around Lake Victoria, whereas conflicts over land-use regulations most frequently arose in the savanah farmlands of East Africa. The relative significance of the issues varied over time as well. Disputes over land tenure were most important at the onset of the large-scale commerciali-

This essay was written with the support of the National Science Foundation, grant number NSF 4 SOC 77-08573. The foundation is in no way responsible for the contents of this essay.

zation of agriculture, that is, in the late nineteenth and early twentieth centuries. The conservation issue rose to prominence after intensification of agricultural production had begun to make a major impact on the environment and ecology of the farming areas—i.e., in the 1930s and 1940s. The importance of these issues thus varied over space and time. But, over the continent as a whole and over the colonial period in its entirety, these issues accounted for a large portion of the political grievances of the African countryside. The successful exploitation of these issues by nationalist politicians enabled them to mobilize rural political support for the movements which made Africa ungovernable by foreign powers and led to political independence throughout most of sub-Saharan Africa.

Historical Background

The rise of commercial agriculture in Africa was, in large part, a response to the nineteenth century growth of the economies of Europe. In the nineteenth century, Britain's industrial revolution neared completion, and Germany rapidly became a major industrial power. The economies of other areas of Europe offer a more ambiguous record, yet it is true that the nineteenth century saw the establishment of many of Europe's major industrial centers—centers of mining, heavy industry and manufacturing; centers of commerce, finance, and shipping; and major urban areas.

With the transformation of the European economy came a rise in demand for Africa's primary products. This demand found its origins in the new technologies employed by European enterprises; in the increased number and higher average incomes of Europe's population; in changes in taste, some of which were associated with a move to an urban and industrial lifestyle; and in shifts in the relative price of Africa's products by comparison with close substitutes—shifts accounted for partly by changes in transport technologies and partly by apparent inelasticities in alternative sources of supply.

It is obvious and important that Europe's industrial revolution was based on the use of machines. The machines required lubrication. Not until the 1860s were petroleum products available, however; and until that time, the oils and fats produced from animal and vegetable sources served as the basic source of lubricants. Although the fats and oils produced by animals appear to have provided most of the lubricants, the increased use of machinery drove up the price of these products to the point where vegetable oils, though technically inferior, became attractive as substitutes. A major result was a rise in the demand of palm products from West Africa.

The growth of Europe's urban population, the rise in average incomes in Europe, and the change in tastes associated with the move to an urban and industrial lifestyle—these too had important consequences for Africa's rural economies. Their effects are perhaps best seen in the growth of demand for candles and soap. Both products use animal and vegetable oils, but, for both products, vegetable oils soon displaced animal products. In part, they did so simply because of their technical superiority; in soaps, for example, the vegetable oils were less likely to discolor, and they produced an odor that consumers found more attractive.[1] Palm oil, palm kernel oil, cottonseed oil, and groundnuts— these were the major sources of vegetable oils for these products. And Africa, along with other tropical areas, became an important source of supply for these commodities.

Larger numbers of consumers and higher personal incomes also led to an increased demand for cotton. In the nineteenth century, Africa was seen as a particularly important source of supply for this commodity because alternative suppliers had proved unreliable. Lancashire "cotton famines" were periodic events in the nineteenth century. The American civil war in the 1860s and the spread of the boll weevil in the 1890s made for unpredictable and increasingly expensive supplies of cotton for the British millers and complicated efforts on their part to develop alternative sources. They therefore sought out new areas for cotton growing. Part of Livingstone's mandate was to search for sites for cotton production in Africa, and the reports from commercial and governmental sources in Africa convinced the British manufacturers that the interior of that continent offered good prospects. In league with the heavy steel industry—itself in recession due to the completion of orders for the manufacture of engines, bridges, and rails for the European, Russian, American, and Indian railways—the cotton manufacturers backed the building of railways into the interior of Africa and the promotion of cotton production therein.[2]

The rise in the average incomes of European consumers and shifts in taste also increased the demand for "luxury" products. Cocoa furnishes an example of such a commodity. First introduced as a beverage, cocoa then penetrated the confectionary market in the form of milk chocolate—a product first introduced in the late 1870s. Coffee, too, appears to have benefited from such changes in taste, but also important was the behavior of other suppliers. Thus, the attempt by São Paulo producers to force a price rise in the world coffee market in the early 1900s created favorable conditions for the establishment of a coffee industry in Africa.

Technological change also played an important part in the rising demand for African cash crops. In the mid-nineteenth century, the development of steamships, on the one hand, and the opening of the Suez Canal, on the other, dramatically lowered transport costs and enhanced the relative position of African producers in the European market. The development of hydrogenation in the 1920s also represented a major boon to African producers. The rising costs of animal products had made oleo an expensive ingredient in the manufacture of margarine; but vegetable oils tended to melt at room temperatures. With the development of hydrogenation, a technique for "hardening" vegetable oils, they became a technically feasible substitute for oleo, and the producers of vegetable oils won a new market for their output.

Changes in the basic factors of demand on the European market—the number of consumers, their average incomes, the technologies of production, and the behavior of alternative suppliers—thus led to an increased demand for the products grown in Africa. African farmers responded by producing crops for export to the European market: palm oil, palm kernels, cocoa, cotton, coffee, and groundnuts.[3] Tables 9.1-9.5 document this response.

The transformation of African agriculture was not confined to the production of cash crops for export. It also took place in the production of food crops for the domestic markets of Africa. The transporting, bulking, and shipping of export crops required the formation of basic infrastructure; among the facilities required were railways and harbors.

The first railways were completed in the early 1900s. Basic harbor facilities were also begun in the early 1900s. A major expansion in the railways, through the construction of spur lines, and a major upgrading of the harbor facilities, through the construction of deep-water berths, warehouses, and wharves, took place in association with the commodity boom of the 1920s. The construction of railways and harbors led to the growth of an African labor force. By 1920, the population of Dakar had reached 30,000; of Accra, 38,000; and of Lagos, 100,000. In the early 1930s, the mining companies of the Zambian copperbelt employed over 30,000 people.[4] The growth of wage labor in Africa entailed a rise in the demand for food. Maize, rice, cassava, meat, fish, millet—these and other commodities that the subsistence farmers had produced for themselves could now be sold for a profit.

The rise in demand for cash crops for export and the rise in demand for food crops for local consumption both generated opportunities for higher rural incomes.[5] The question we ask is why and in what way did the growth of economic opportunity lead to the rise of political protest? To answer this question we will examine some of the basic issues that arose in conjunction with the growth of commercial production in the African countryside.

The Structure of Markets

One of the primary issues that promoted agrarian protest in colonial Africa was the structure of the markets faced by the producers of cash crops. The commercialization of agriculture promoted significant economic gains, but, in some cases, the producers faced cartels that sought to appropriate these gains by engaging in price setting behavior. Collusion on the part of the purchasers of the cash crops furnished an incentive for the producers to combine and so achieve market power in an effort to increase their profits.

One example of this kind of behavior is provided by the cocoa producers in the Gold Coast. The major links between the cocoa producers and the European markets were provided by merchant houses; these merchant houses handled both the export of cocoa from the Gold Coast to Europe and the importation into the Gold Coast of consumer products from the European market. For a variety of reasons, there were significant economies of scale in the import-export business.[6] Consolidation took place within the industry, and the number of merchant houses declined. By 1937, the largest four of these firms marketed over two-thirds of the Gold Coast cocoa crop. Because they so dominated the market, these few firms could, by combining, effectively set the price of cocoa to their advantage and appropriate much of the gains to be made from the production of cocoa. The best documented of their attempts to do so comes from the 1930s.

Early in 1937, the major merchant houses began negotiations in an effort to collude in the purchase of that year's output; by autumn, they had developed a market-sharing agreement.[7] On September 18, the headquarters of the firms in England sent letters of instruction to their buyers in the Gold Coast outlining the procedures to be followed in purchasing the crop; the procedures, of course, were designed to remove incentives for competition between the local buyers and thereby depress the price they offered the cocoa farmers. Rumors were rife in the Gold Coast about the activities of the major firms; local newspapers speculated openly about the possibility of an agreement. In the words of the Nowell Report:

> By [mid-October] the formation of the so-called "Pool" was becoming widely known, and in a circular letter dated 14th of October, the President of the Provincial Council of Chiefs of the Central Province called an emergency meeting of the Council to "protest against the selfish and inimical policy enunciated by the trading firms."[8]

As landowners, cocoa farmers, holders of cocoa stocks, and political

TABLE 9.1
Exports of Palm Oil, Palm Kernel Oil, and Palm Kernels

(in thousands of metric tons)

Date	Zaire Palm Oil	Zaire Palm Kernel Oil	Zaire Palm Kernels	French West Africa Palm Oil	French West Africa Palm Kernel Oil	French West Africa Palm Kernels	Nigeria Palm Oil	Nigeria Palm Kernels	Sierra Leone Palm Oil	Sierra Leone Palm Kernels
1909	1.7	...	5.2	19.1	...	46.3	83.4	161.4	3.5	43.6
10	2.2	...	6.1	17.3	...	44.3	78.1	175.8	2.7	43.7
11	2.3	...	6.8		...		80.6	179.2	3.0	43.6
12	2.0	...	5.9		...		78.2	187.6	3.0	51.6
13	2.0	...	7.2		...		84.4	177.5	2.5	50.0
14	2.5	...	8.1		...		73.7	165.1	1.8	36.5
15	3.4	...	11.0		...		74.2	155.8	2.0	40.3
16	3.9	...	22.4	19.9	...	50.9	68.5	164.0	2.3	46.0
17	5.4	...	35.0		...		75.8	189.0	2.2	59.0
18	5.1	...	31.4		...		87.8	208.5	1.1	41.5
19	8.0	...	37.3		...		102.6	220.4	3.4	51.4
20	7.6	...	39.5	19.4	...	55.9	86.2	210.3	2.1	51.2
21	9.0	...	46.0		...		53.6	155.8	0.2	41.1
22	10.7	...	49.3		...		89.0	181.6	2.1	49.8
23	12.4	...	54.6		...		101.0	226.8	3.4	60.5
24	14.1	...	47.5	25.8	...	72.1	126.0	256.6	3.2	62.1
25	18.7	...	74.1	26.0	...	73.3	130.2	277.3	3.0	64.2
26	18.5	...	70.4	25.4	...	70.2	115.1	253.1	2.9	66.0
27	18.4	...	74.0	25.9	...	74.5	115.1	261.3	3.7	66.5
28	26.5	...	72.5	17.4	...	59.5	128.1	249.1	2.6	68.2
29	30.3	...	75.4	22.9	...	62.4	132.9	254.1	2.9	61.2
30	37.0	...	66.4	22.5	...	78.4	136.8	262.8	3.7	57.6
31	36.6	...	47.2	20.9	...	65.7	118.8	257.4	1.4	55.3
32	38.8	...	57.9	14.6	...	71.0	116.2	312.4	2.2	78.4
33	52.5	...	62.1	12.1	...	53.5	128.9	262.5	1.6	65.1

34	45.0	...		49.3	15.4	...	76.6		113.1	292.8	2.3	69.8
35	56.8	–		65.0	26.5	...	80.7		143.2	316.3	2.9	79.3
36	60.0	–		92.4	29.2	...	98.5		163.7	390.8	1.2	85.9
37	69.1	–		95.6	20.1	...	81.5		146.2	341.6	2.4	78.0
38	70.3	–		88.7	13.7	...	70.3		110.4	315.6	1.4	64.7
39	72.5	0.1		84.8	13.4	...	55.2		128.1	304.8	1.2	70.9
1940	65.3	0.2	44.9	45.3	11.9	...	51.6		134.9	239.2	1.4	54.1
41	60.3	0.5	30.2	31.1	15.7	...	46.5		129.8	384.2	0.1	37.8
42	79.4	4.8	52.5	63.2	7.8	...	41.7		153.7	350.1	0.3	20.9
43	99.1	6.8	63.2	78.3	7.8	...	50.5		137.4	336.6	–	37.0
44	86.9	5.6	56.9	69.3	10.6	...	50.1		126.8	318.6	–	46.4
45	77.9	7.8	43.5	60.8	4.8	...	46.3		116.0	298.2	0.1	48.1
46	88.1	9.4	48.9	69.8	0.7	...	35.4		102.5	281.7	0.6	47.5
47	84.9	11.1	48.1	72.8	0.7	...	40.0		128.0	321.5	2.2	64.0
48	110.4	17.6	83.4	121.7	10.8	–	63.3		141.5	332.4	3.4	67.5
49	117.8	12.2	80.0	106.5	9.8	–	85.5		172.9	381.9		77.8
50	125.0	12.8	85.8	113.6	11.2	0.6	84.5	85.8	175.8	416.8	2.0	72.4
51	128.1	17.2	86.2	123.6	14.5	–	75.3		152.1	352.6	3.2	76.3
52	137.5	11.2	92.5	116.8	9.5	0.4	64.2	65.0	170.0	380.2	0.8	77.6
53	131.8	15.0	87.6	120.2	16.3	–	85.7		203.9	406.6	0.4	70.0
54	136.8	24.3	71.3	124.1	14.4	–	81.3		211.8	471.6	0.9	69.2
55	149.0	34.6	62.8	138.0	18.3	–	63.5		185.1	440.2	...	58.6

Source: K. R. M. Anthony, Bruce F. Johnston, William O. Jones, Victor C. Uchendu, Agricultural Change in Tropical Africa, (Ithaca, New York: Cornell University Press, Forthcoming 1978).

...Not available
– None at all

TABLE 9.2
Cocoa Exports

Year	Cameroon	French West Africa	Ghana	Nigeria
		(in thousands of metric tons)		
1909	3.3	–	20.5	2.3
10	3.4	–	23.0	3.0
11	3.6	–	40.4	4.5
12	4.6	–	39.3	3.4
13	4.5	0.1	51.4	3.7
14	3.2	–	53.7	5.0
15	3.4	0.1	78.5	9.2
16	0.8	0.2	73.3	9.1
17	1.1	0.3	97.4	15.7
18	0.7	0.4	67.4	10.4
19	2.3	1.0	107.0	26.1
1920	2.6	1.0	126.8	17.4
21	3.3	1.5	135.3	18.2
22	3.5	2.4	161.9	31.8
23	3.5	3.6	200.8	33.3
24	4.5	4.3	226.9	37.8
25	4.9	6.3	221.6	45.4
26	5.4	6.9	234.5	39.7
27	7.6	9.8	213.3	39.8
28	7.3	16.5	228.7	46.3
29	10.0	16.5	241.9	53.1
1930	10.6	22.3	193.6	50.2
31	10.9	19.9	248.0	50.6
32	13.8	25.8	237.5	28.8
33	17.2	31.1	239.9	58.0
34	19.5	41.6	234.0	74.6
35	23.4	43.6	273.2	85.4
36	23.8	49.8	316.1	77.0
37	26.6	48.1	240.0	100.0
38	31.0	52.7	267.4	94.8
39	27.6	55.2	285.2	115.7
1940	24.4	45.5	227.5	91.2
41	20.4	43.0	222.4	106.4
42	15.0	28.6	125.9	60.9
43	32.4	0.5	190.4	88.9
44	35.1	14.7	206.1	71.2
45	34.8	26.9	236.0	78.2
46	34.0	28.4	240.0	101.8
47	33.7	28.1	183.1	112.6
48	47.9	41.2	217.7	92.9
49	48.0	56.1	267.8	118.0
1950	43.7	61.8	271.7	92.9
51	48.8	55.5	233.2	123.4
52	51.1	50.2	215.4	116.6
53	60.5	71.7	240.4	106.3
54	50.0	52.7	217.6	100.0
55	55.6	75.2	209.2	89.8

Source: See source Table 9.1.

leaders, the chiefs had a major interest in preventing a forceful reduction in the price of cocoa. They therefore combined with the farmers and attempted to form a producers' cartel to rival the power achieved by the merchant houses in the market for their products. By passing ordinances in their native authorities, issuing edicts, and even invoking traditional oaths, the chiefs, in league with the farmers, sought to withhold cocoa from the market until they had secured a price rise from the merchant houses. The resultant cocoa boycott led to the large-scale politicization of the rural interior of the Gold Coast and furnished one of the historical legends that shaped the nationalist consciousness of the colony's rural population.

A similar situation arose in East Africa, where the producers of cotton also faced a noncompetitive market—one that was used by the purchasers and processors of the commodity to lower the price they paid for the farmers' output. Again, the structure of the market furnished an incentive for the producers to combine. In the case of East Africa, the farmers' combinations took the form of cooperative societies—agencies that the farmers tried to use to break the power of the purchasers and thus to realize higher profits from cash crop production.

In the production and processing of cotton in East Africa, economies of scale tended to concentrate in the ginning, as opposed to the growing, of cotton. The ginners had relatively high fixed costs: the buildings and machinery of the gineries represented significant capital investments. Moreover, the machines, at least, could be used for no other purpose than ginning and so stood idle for much of the year. An important consideration for a prospective investor in ginning, then, was the certainty of a high volume of cotton for processing at the time of harvest.

To promote cotton production in East Africa, the governments of the area sought to promote investments in ginning capacity; and to secure such investments, they sought ways of guaranteeing to prospective investors a high volume of produce for each gin. In the case of both Uganda and Tanganyika, the major cotton growing areas, the governments therefore passed ordinances requiring ginning licenses, and they restricted the number of licenses that could be issued. Moreover, they formed marketing zones. In a specified area about each gin, only buyers who sold to that gin were permitted to operate, and no shipping across the zones was allowed. The curtailment of competition on the part of the ginners naturally led to a decline in the price offered the farmers for their produce.[9]

One result was protest on the part of the producers. Thus, for example, in 1934, "all the *saza* chiefs in Busoga signed a letter to the provincial commissioner expressing . . . their dislike of zoning, which 'gives an opportunity to the cotton buyers to reduce the prices of cotton, knowing

TABLE 9.3
Cotton Exports

(in thousands of metric tons)

Year	Zaire	French Equitorial Africa	Uganda	Mozambique	Nigeria	Sudan	Tanzania
1909	—	—	..	—	2.3	..	0.5
10	—	—	—	—	1.1	..	0.5
11	—	—	3.0	—	1.0	..	1.1
12	—	—	3.9	—	2.0	..	1.9
13	—	—	4.3	—	2.9	..	2.2
14	—	—	5.4	—	2.6	..	..
15	—	—	4.6	—	1.2	..	..
16	—	—	3.9	—	3.4	3.5	..
17	—	—	5.0	—	2.4	2.6	..
18	—	—	5.0	—	0.7	2.2	..
19	0.2	—	..	—	3.1	4.3	..
1920	0.2	—	9.5	—	3.3	3.5	1.0
21	0.2	—	14.8	0.2	5.8	5.0	1.1
22	1.0	—	8.8	0.2	3.0	4.4	1.6
23	..	—	16.0	0.3	3.2	5.1	1.5
24	1.3	—	23.3	0.4	4.7	8.4	2.6
25	2.2	—	35.6	1.4	6.7	7.8	4.6
26	5.2	—	32.8	2.0	9.1	22.2	5.0
27	7.5	—	23.9	1.3	5.1	28.9	4.0
28	9.6	0.1	25.1	1.2	3.8	23.5	5.0
29	10.0	0.2	37.0	1.6	6.0	30.5	5.0
1930	12.5	0.8	23.4	1.7	8.1	27.8	3.7
31	12.1	0.9	34.3	1.5	3.6	9.0	2.5
32	12.8	1.6	37.6	1.8	1.2	38.2	3.3
33		2.4	53.5	2.3	4.5	24.4	5.2

Year							
34	20.0	5.1	51.8	2.0	6.0	33.0	5.7
35	23.5	6.2	45.9	2.9	11.0	37.7	10.1
36	26.5	6.7	58.3	4.8	11.3	48.0	11.4
37	32.3	8.4	61.4	8.4	9.7	70.4	11.7
38	42.0	9.9	73.0	8.9	5.8	62.3	9.0
39	35.5	8.8	59.8	6.6	4.4	61.7	11.8
1940	23.0	8.8	55.1	5.2	9.5	37.6	10.8
41	25.7	17.7	66.4	6.6	10.4	84.2	13.3
42	32.3	17.5	42.9	14.3	18.8	50.8	8.1
43	41.3	10.0	22.3	15.4	7.3	9.5	7.1
44	30.0	17.5	34.3	23.9	4.4	22.7	6.0
45	38.3	20.0	48.0	14.3	1.1	73.8	7.3
46	48.0	24.8	39.8	10.9	6.7	52.9	4.3
47	45.1	21.1	45.9	5.9	5.3	52.7	7.2
48	51.2	32.3	31.6	26.0	4.7	50.8	6.8
49	46.8	23.6	70.8	28.1	10.1	65.2	11.0
1950	49.0	24.0	63.2	24.4	12.8	66.5	7.2
51	39.8	27.0	62.8	24.1	15.6	95.5	8.4
52	45.7	29.4	68.5	30.1	19.6	55.2	11.3
53	45.6	25.0	60.8	38.3	18.0	90.2	15.0
54	40.7	31.7	71.4	38.3	26.4	60.4	12.3
55	40.0	33.0	55.6	32.8	33.7	94.7	20.7

Source: See source Table 9.1.

TABLE 9.4
Coffee Exports

(in thousands of metric tons)

Year	Angola	Zaire	Cameroon	Ethiopia	Ivory Coast	Kenya	Uganda	Tanzania
1909	4.4	—	—	3.2 *	—	0.4	—	
10	6.1	—	—	*	—	0.6	—	..
11	4.4	—	—	*	—	0.7	0.1	1.0
12	4.0	—	—	*	—	1.0	0.2	1.2
13	4.8	—	—	*	—	1.3	0.6	1.2
14	4.4	—	—	3.1	—	1.5	1.1	1.1
15	4.0	—	—	3.4	—	1.1	2.2	..
16	3.2	—	—	4.7	—	4.4	2.6	..
17	4.1	—	—	4.2	—	5.0	1.0	..
18	4.2	0.1	—	3.1	—	8.5	4.5	..
19	6.2	0.2	—	3.1	—	6.2	3.0	4.0
1920	3.9	0.1	—	4.6	—	8.0	3.7	—
21	5.1	—	—	3.1	—	—	2.5	3.8
22	9.8	0.2	—	4.1	—	6.6	2.6	4.3
23	6.0	0.1	—	6.6	—	9.4	2.1	4.1
24	8.9	0.4	—	5.6	0.1	10.1	2.1	5.3
25	12.6	0.2	—	11.1	—	7.5	1.5	6.1
26	9.3	0.2	—	10.4	0.1	7.2	1.7	6.6
27	10.0	0.3	—	11.5	0.2	10.7	2.2	6.7
28	9.8	0.6	—	14.0	0.2	10.8	2.0	10.6
29	8.8	0.8	—	..	0.4	6.8	2.1	9.0
1930	11.8	1.5	—	14.1	0.5	15.8	2.5	11.7
31	11.8	2.9	—	18.1	0.7	12.5	3.6	9.4
32	9.5	5.4	0.1	11.1	1.4	14.0	4.4	11.5
33	12.0	8.5	0.5	12.5	1.8	13.1	5.1	12.9
34	11.7	12.4	0.8	17.2	2.7	9.5	7.8	15.0
35	10.3	13.2	1.4	15.2	5.3	18.2	6.4	18.9

* Ethiopia figure 3.2 shown with a brace grouping the years 1909–1913 in the original.

239

Year							
36	19.6	16.8	2.0	8.7	6.7	20.8	11.6	12.3
37	16.4	16.0	2.6	9.0	10.4	13.9	13.1	13.8
38	17.5	19.1	4.2	. . .	14.5	17.4	14.2	14.0
39	20.7	19.7	5.3	. . .	18.6	17.2	17.4	16.9
1940	15.8	13.2	4.2	{ 12.0	17.1	8.7	18.2	15.9
41	14.2	18.3	0.1		29.0	12.6	20.6	13.9
42	19.5	19.7	6.6		20.0	12.5	17.5	15.1
43	23.9	22.4	8.6	10.0	23.0	7.9	20.5	11.1
44	23.8	14.9	5.1	15.9	24.5	7.6	19.4	15.8
45	30.9	24.3	6.7	14.9	39.2	7.6	20.6	14.7
46	44.3	26.8	5.9	15.3	36.4	9.7	31.9	10.2
47	40.6	37.3	5.6	22.4	44.1	10.8	21.4	14.1
48	53.4	30.5	7.3	18.7	56.3	14.5	38.4	11.4
49	46.4	31.4	8.2	30.3	63.7	7.9	24.3	12.4
1950	37.6	32.7	7.7	21.4	57.7	10.4	32.4	15.2
51	64.4	34.5	8.7	43.1	62.9	10.1	44.3	16.8
52	47.7	30.3	9.2	37.2	71.4	17.0	40.1	18.9
53	71.6	33.5	9.6	41.8	56.4	15.0	36.3	15.5
54	44.2	35.4	11.4		94.9	10.9	35.2	19.7
55	57.9	43.7	13.9		85.8	19.7	75.6	18.8

Source: See source Talbe 9.1.

TABLE 9.5
Exports of Peanuts and Peanut Oil in Shelled Nut Equivalent

Year	Ivory Coast	Gambia	Nigeria	Sudan
		(in thousands of metric tons)		
1909	102.0	38.2	1.6	0.2
10	...	41.6	1.0	0.6
11	...	34.1	1.3	0.8
12	157.7	45.6	2.6	0.6
13	...	48.0	19.6	0.5
14	...	47.6	17.3	0.1
15	...	68.4	9.1	0.4
16	...	33.0	51.2	0.7
17	146.9	52.8	51.1	2.0
18	...	40.2	58.5	1.8
19	...	50.0	40.0	2.4
1920	...	59.8	46.1	2.0
21	...	41.4	51.8	2.9
22	207.8	44.8	24.3	1.9
23	...	44.5	23.3	4.2
24	...	43.1	79.5	7.3
25	317.6	34.6	129.3	8.3
26	343.9	43.4	128.8	6.9
27	288.3	48.4	92.2	1.1
28	304.7	54.6	104.8	1.3
29	312.5	41.3	149.7	2.6
1930	381.5	53.2	148.7	3.4
31	325.4	68.5	162.3	2.0
32	139.2	26.5	191.1	0.9
33	274.7	47.9	207.9	2.2
34	395.8	51.2	248.8	5.0
35	306.2	32.1	187.0	3.1
36	418.2	35.3	221.9	3.0
37	556.3	47.8	331.2	4.8
38	441.8	33.7	183.0	4.1
39	526.9	35.4	149.6	2.9
1940	372.9	30.7	172.2	5.7
41	425.5	31.4	251.1	2.7
42	107.1	12.0	197.3	1.8
43	56.9	14.1	144.8	−
44	191.0	21.3	156.7	−
45	172.1	30.7	179.1	−
46	248.8	28.8	290.3	−
47	275.6	40.0	260.0	−
48	357.0	49.7	249.9	−
49	339.2	43.6	385.3	9.1
1950	367.4	41.8	330.2	3.3
51	307.4	39.9	153.1	10.0
52	334.3	43.3	288.1	17.4
53	446.5	36.3	376.1	26.7
54	479.7	37.5	507.1	16.5
55	372.7	40.0	482.8	34.9

Source: See source Table 9.1.

that people cannot remove their cotton and sell it in other neighbouring districts.'"[10] Another result was the formation of the cooperative movement. The farmers sought to form cooperatives that would buy and gin cotton; by entering the market, they sought to insure for themselves better prices than those offered by the cartelized ginners and so reap more gains from cash crop production. One movement of this kind was the famous Victoria Federation of Cooperative Unions in Tanganyika—a society that helped to form the nucleus of the nationalist movement in the northeastern regions of that territory.[11] Another was the Uganda African Farmers Union. The Farmers Union made the grievances of the cotton producers a central issue in the 1949 disturbances in Uganda—disturbances that laid the foundation for the postwar period of national protest in that territory.[12]

Production Externalities, Government Intervention, and Political Protest

Producers of cash crops in Africa thus sometimes faced a market structure which threatened to divert much of the gains to be had from commercial agriculture to other parties in the industry. Collusion on the part of others served as an incentive for the producers themselves to combine. And attempts to achieve the power to influence prices in the marketplace motivated collective action in the countryside.

A second group of issues arose around externalities generated in the production of cash crops. Externalities occur when the activities of one producer directly influence the production possibilities of another. If the activity of one producer adversely affects the profits of another, in the absence of market mechanisms for creating incentives to adjust his behavior, the first producer will engage in more of that activity than is desirable; greater total profits could be secured by producers as a whole if the first producer reduced the degree to which he engaged in that activity. If the activity creates beneficial effects for the second party, in the absence of the proper market mechanisms, he will engage in less of the activity than is desirable. Under such circumstances, there are gains to be made if the government intervenes in the market and provides the incentives for the first producer to increase the activity that generates benefits to others. In the case of cash crop production in Africa, negative externalities appear to have been more common than positive ones; the colonial government had to frequently curtail activities that were privately profitable but socially undesirable. A major result was protest on the part of cash crop producers who benefited from the use of externality-producing production techniques and a willingness to turn against the colonial government.

One common source of production externalities was erosion. During World War II, the colonial government promoted the production of cash crops at a maximum rate, irrespective of the effects on the ecology or the environment. In East Africa, for example, they vigorously championed the production of maize, largely as a way of securing food for troops in the Mideast and North Africa. One result was extreme monocropping, with attendant depletion of the soils; another was the extention of cash-crop production into increasingly marginal lands. The result of both trends was increased soil erosion.

An important example of this problem arose in the Uluguru mountains of northeastern Tanzania. The mountains form an important watershed and are the source of several streams and rivers. In response to the increased demand for food, producers had moved into the mountains and cleared them of trees, shrubs, and groundcover so as to put them into production. According to government sources, the effect of increased production in the hills was decreased production downstream. With less ground cover, the soils in the hills retained rainwater for a shorter period than before. One result was downstream flooding and the loss of crops by those who planted alluvial gardens. Moreover, with the more precipitate release of the waters deposited by the rains, the dry-season level of the rivers declined. Salt water from the ocean moved further upstream; the result was increased salinization and a loss in the fertility of the soils near the rivers. As is true everywhere in Africa, the major concentrations of population were located along the rivers of northeastern Tanzania, and their loss of crops due to the increased runoff from the hills more than offset the increase in the production of foodstuffs by the mountain producers.

The colonial government was unable to devise mechanisms for the downstream producers to encourage the hillside producers to clear less land or for the mountain producers to compensate the downstream farmers for the damage that they inflicted by bringing the hillsides into production. Instead, the government had to attempt to use political power to alter the productive practices of the hillside farmers. Using its legal powers, it sought to compel the hillside farmers to make bench terraces to curtail runoff from the hills. The farmers resisted the government's efforts. At first, they attempted to bribe the government's agents; when that failed, they turned to violence. In 1956, riots broke out, troops were called in, and people were killed in the confrontation that followed. A new group of rural dwellers joined the antigovernment coalition formed by the nationalist movement.[13]

Erosion is one source of externalities, and measures taken to control it led to political protest throughout East Africa.[14] Another source of externalities are crop diseases. An important source of rural political protest in West Africa were the attempts of the colonial governments to control the spread of diseases through the cocoa industry of that region.

In 1936, officials of the Department of Agriculture of the Gold Coast first noted the abnormal deaths of cacao trees in the older producing areas, New Juaben and Akim Abuakwa. The officials were sufficiently concerned to investigate further. Upon doing so, they discovered that a significant infestation had taken place over an area of 200 square miles. Because of the physical evidence that it left on the trees, the disease was called "swollen shoot." At first it was misdiagnosed, and only after the completion of a new research station—the first agricultural research station to be built in the Gold Coast—were investigators able to recognize the disease as a virus whose vector was the mealybug. What made the virus so difficult to control was that ants served as hosts for the mealybugs and provided protective shelters for them—shelters that made the vectors inaccessible to sprays. The only viable control method was the destruction of diseased trees. Adjacent, apparently healthy trees had to be destroyed as well, for they might provide shelter for the infected insects. Following World War II, the government launched its control program.[15]

The major problem faced by the government was the resistance of the farmers themselves. A principal reason for the clash between the farmers and the government was that each farmer evaluated the control measure from the point of view of his own private gains and losses, whereas the government took into account the effects of his behavior on other cocoa producers. A farmer who kept diseased trees in production—and trees often would continue to produce for several harvests after infestation—would continue to earn profits, but he would be imposing costs on other farmers, in terms of increasing the probability of the infestation of their farms. Were there a way that other farmers could charge a farmer with diseased trees for the injury he inflicted on their healthy ones, then control measures could perhaps have been voluntarily implemented. Moreover, had the governments understood the externalities problem, they may have been more ready at the outset to reward the afflicted producers for lessening the probability of infesting the farms of others. But the West African governments did not understand this aspect of the problem, and they refused compensation; as one Nigerian official put it, why pay compensation when "the farmers are receiving the cutting out service for free."[16]

Instead, using their legal powers, the government simply coerced the farmers. Government agents would move from one farm to the next. Locating diseased trees, they would mark the farm. Then the work gangs would arrive, and, in the words of one farmer, "The farms became a plain field within an hour."[17] In the Gold Coast, the cutting-out program began in January 1947; by 1948, over 600,000 trees had been removed from over 2,500 acres;[18] and in that year, the farmers rose against the government's program. Protesting cutting out, they joined in the 1948 disturbances that led to basic constitutional reforms in the colony. Mobilized in large part through the issue of disease control, they joined the political coalition that brought an end to British rule.[19]

The problem of externalities arises in other settings—for example, under conditions of common property. Collective rights in grazing land promote mismanagement of land resources. Under conditions of collective grazing rights, if one producer restricts his herd size to a level that is socially optimal, given the carrying capacity of the land, he simply confers a benefit on the other producers who share in the rights to graze livestock on that land. The result is that private incentives fail to produce the correct choice of herd size, and, in the absence of government intervention, the lands are overgrazed. Attempts by the government to reduce herd sizes led, however, to clashes between the government's vision of the public good and the producers' perception of their own best interest. Destocking often became an issue that led to the mobilization of the arid land farmers against the colonial governments.[20]

Collective rights to fisheries also led to the politicization of rural populations. Thus, in Zambia, conflicts between the fishermen and the government, which imposed regulations in an attempt to prevent the depletion of the Lake Mweru fishery—issuing controls over net sizes, fishing during the spawning season, etc.—furnished a basis for incorporating the Luapula fisheries into the nationalist movement.[21]

Externalities also arose in the establishment of quality standards. The purchasers of many of the export crops of Africa were willing to offer only one price—one that reflected their appraisal of the average quality of the crop. Insofar as it was cheaper to produce a low-quality product, each farmer was better off marketing a low quality of output while being paid the price for an average-quality product. But when all farmers behaved in this way, then the average quality of output declined. The rational behavior of each farmer thus imposed costs on all farmers in the form of a lowering of the market price. In the absence of a willingness on the part of purchasers to offer a spectrum of prices for a variety of quality standards, the governments in cash-crop growing areas felt compelled to intervene and to maintain by administrative methods a high standard of marketed output. The result, once again, was conflict between cash-crop producers and the government.[22]

The colonial government's attempts to promote soil conservation, control crop diseases, and increase the quality of production thus led to increasing state intervention in the agricultural industries of Africa. In the absence of mechanisms that would secure voluntary compliance with rules to maximize the profits of producers as a whole, they felt compelled to constrain (by administrative means) the behavior of African farmers. Under the impact of government regulation, producers who generated negative externalities experienced a decline in their private profits. They resented being coerced into accepting a lower level of economic reward. And they were therefore willing to turn against the colonial governments and to back the efforts of nationalist politicians to overthrow the colonial regimes.[23]

Structure of Land Rights

With the prospects of profits from agriculture came an increase in the value of land. The allocation of these gains among competing claimants was largely determined by the allocation of land rights, and the ultimate adjudicator of that allocation was the state. Control over the state and its legal system was therefore sought by those who wished to gain economic benefits from commercial farming.

Struggles between indigenous peoples and highly capitalized foreign immigrants constituted one set of such disputes. Thus, in Kenya, for example, the colonial administration won a ruling from the legal officers of the crown that all waste and unoccupied land in the colony was crown land; the colonial government was the legal agent of the crown in the East African Protectorate, and it therefore became the legal owner of "waste and unoccupied" lands in that area. Both the indigenous human and livestock populations had declined precipitously as a result of famines and pestilence in the 1870s; and as indigenous agricultural technology depended, in any case, on long and extensive land rotations, much of the land in Kenya *appeared* to be waste or unoccupied. Employing the legal ruling as a basis for determining land rights thus transferred legal rights over vast acreages from the indigenous farm families to the colonial administration. And the administration rapidly transferred its rights to immigrant commercial farmers. Protests over the loss of land rights subsequently formed the basis for much of the nationalist movement in Kenya.[24]

In Ghana, disputes between the farmers and the state over rights to "waste" lands also gave rise to popular movements of political protest against the colonial order. In a series of ordinances in the late nineteenth century, the government of the Gold Coast attempted to transfer rights over waste and unoccupied lands to the crown. But the indigenous poulation, led by the rural chiefs and the legal and commercial elites of the coastal towns, vigorously opposed this action. They defended the rights of the native population to this resource, and argued that, though lands might presently be unexploited, rights over them were well defined under the traditional legal system. A major reason for their resistance to the transfer of land rights to the crown was that both the chiefs and the coastal elites had begun to profit from the exercise of their land rights. An active market in land and in concessions for its use had begun in the Gold Coast—a market that allowed the chiefs and the coastal elites to share in the economic benefits deriving from control over this valuable input into commercial cash-crop production.[25] To promote their resistance to the alienation of lands by foreign control, the chiefs and the coastal elites formed the Aborigines Rights Protection Association—the first nationalist political party in West Africa.

Disputes over the control of land also arose in the Congo, where the Belgian government gave large-scale concessions to foreign capitalists.[26] They also arose in Tanzania, Zambia, Rhodesia, and South Africa, where foreign settlers, backed by the colonial state, appropriated large acreages. In almost every area in Africa, these disputes formed a prominent basis for rural resistance to colonial rule on the continent.[27]

It should also be noted that disputes over land rights led to splits within the indigenous community; the way in which these political cleavages formed in any African territory gave a special character to the nationalist movement of that area. One of the major characteristics of the nationalist movement in several territories, for example, was that it sought as much to depose the indigenous political elites, the chiefs, as it sought to displace the foreign administration. Where such movements arose, they often did so in areas where the chiefs and the peasants were at odds over land rights. In the Gold Coast, for example, where there were waste and unoccupied lands they remained stool lands. That is, they remained the lands of the community, and rights to these lands could only be alienated by the administrative head of that community, the chief, who was said to occupy the stool or throne. With the rise of the demand for cash crops from Africa, there then arose a demand for rights to land; and the chiefs, in conformity with their traditional role, sold rights to the stool lands. The problem was that, rather than diverting the profits from their sale to the communal treasury, the chiefs diverted many of the profits to their private pockets. Increasing indignation over their corruption led to splits between the chiefs and the masses, and these conflicts lent a radical character to much of the nationalist politics of that territory. They also led to major cleavages within the nationalist forces. The chiefs and the commoners, having split over this and other issues, tended to back different factions of the nationalist movement. The chiefs tended to be drawn to the United Gold Coast Convention, while the commoners tended to support the more radical Conservative People's Party.[28]

A similar radicalization and polarization emerged in Uganda. In negotiating the final terms of their settlement with the encroaching colonial power, the Kabaka and his subordinate chiefs evoked a recasting of land rights in terms of freehold tenure. Each major chief secured freehold rights over large estates in exchange for acknowledging British sovereignty. The actual occupants of these lands then became tenants of the chiefs. With the growth in the commercial value of these lands—a growth which principally resulted from the spread of cotton production in Uganda—the chiefs were able to use their control over land rights to divert revenues from the producers to themselves. They did so by raising the rental fees on the land and by increasing the burden of services required of the tenants. The result was the emergence of a major cleavage between the traditional elites and the peasant farmers—a split that was only partially healed by the passage of rent control laws.[29]

Other kinds of political cleavages arose in disputes over land rights. Some occurred between communities, when major indigenous communities filed competing claims over lands.[30] Others took the form of conflicts between different levels of government; these, too, often appeared to be communal in nature. Groups which, in the past, had conquered others responded to the growing profits to be gained from agriculture by attempting to increase the extent and value of tribute obligations. As these obligations were paid from what amounted to property taxes at the local level, these disputes often arose in the form of differences concerning the allocation of jurisdiction over land.[31] So-called age-old disputes between different indigenous communities often revolved, fundamentally, around the allocation of legal rights to this productive resource. And those seeking to benefit economically from the growth of commercial production had good reason to invest in political efforts to seek a favorable determination of rights to land.

One last kind of dispute over land rights is of interest—conflicts over collective as opposed to individual forms of tenure. Collective rights assure access to land or to the profits to be realized from its use in commercial agriculture to all members of a community. In insuring everyone access to these benefits, however, such rights also reduce the ability of entrepreneurs to secure maximum returns from commercial agriculture. Collective rights increase the costs of securing credit; they also curtail the incentive of producers to invest in improvements that would increase the productivity of the land. Those who sought to maximize their private advantage in the emerging agricultural industries of Africa therefore sought private rights to land; those who were more concerned with securing guaranteed access to a subsistence level of production favored the establishment of collective rights. This conflict appears to have been the one most frequently generating interest in East Africa. In Uganda, for example, it took the form of the militant reassertion of traditional clan rights over the lands that had been given over to the chiefs under freehold tenure. The dedication to clan rights formed much of the basis of the Bataka Association—a movement of the farmers and the clan heads who opposed the power of the chiefs in general and their private rights over the *mailo* lands in particular.[32] Analogous disputes broke out among the Kukuyu. Prosperous farmers sought to advance their claims to individual tenure, while others sought to emphasize collective rights to *mbari* lands out of fear of losing their rights to land in the Kikuyu reserves.[33] The assertion of private rights over collective property by the chiefs of the Gold Coast underlay much of the rural politics in that area. In the contemporary period, the attempts by the state in Tanzania to promote collective rights to land in the cash-cropping regions of that territory have apparently found favor among the rural poor, for they fear the loss of land rights in the countryside. These attempts have met with resistance from the prosperous farmers, who naturally see such measures as threatening the gains that they hope to secure through cash-crop production.[34]

Taxation

There is a last set of issues that arose in conjunction with the commercialization of agriculture; these revolved around taxation. As is well known, taxation was repeatedly used by public policy makers to induce subsistence farmers to exchange produce or labor for cash; as such, its introduction met with resistance by African rural dwellers. More relevant to this chapter, however, was the behavior of the farmers once they had begun to produce for the market. For a variety of reasons, they continued to engage in political protest against the levying of taxes.

Leaving out of consideration for the moment the properties of public goods, we can view the payment of taxes as an exchange. The private citizen relinquishes the power to purchase a basket of commodities provided in the private marketplace in exchange for a collection of public goods and services provided by the state. In making this exchange, the rural dwellers in Africa have repeatedly protested that the rate of exchange was unfavorable, that the goods and services received from the state failed to equal in value the private commodities forsaken in the payment of taxes.

One example of this reaction arose in the early tax rebellions of the 1850s. In the Gold Coast, for example, the colonial administration convened a series of local assemblies to announce that in order to provide a variety of services—roads, schools, and hospitals, for example—the government would be imposing a capitation tax. For a brief period, the tax was successfully collected; but then, resistance broke out. Opposition grew to the point of large-scale rebellion, and no serious attempt was made to collect the tax after 1852. Upon investigating the resistance to taxes, the colonial administration determined that "only about one-fifth the amount collected . . . had been spent on the objects for which it was given."[35] A major grievance was that "the stipends and expenses of collection swallowed up nearly the whole revenue, and the people became restless at the failure to provide the promised benefits."[36] The people protested taxes because they felt that taxes made them worse off; the loss in income that they suffered from taxation had not been compensated for by public services of comparable value. So strong were their feelings on the matter, and so successfully did they act on them, that the Gold Coast government was unable to impose direct taxes until 1943.

A second major source of grievance over the collection of taxes often fed into and exacerbated the split between the chiefs and the masses that arose with respect to land rights. In the absence of an ability to provide satisfactory services, the colonial government's exercise of its power of taxation in the countryside led to a redistribution of income between tax-paying peasantry and the holders of public office. Protests over taxation frequently became protests against rural office holders, the most prominent of whom were the chiefs. Kilson's analysis of the rural basis of the nationalist movement in Sierra Leone emphasizes these dynamics.[37] So, too, do many of the studies of rural protest in Ghana. Thus, Tordoff notes that with the commercialization of agriculture in the inland areas of the Gold Coast, the chiefs used their powers of taxation to build up the public treasury; the funds of the native authorities were supposed to be used to provide public goods, but the rural public authorities largely failed to supply these amenities. The result was that "the number of destoolments increased rapidly and underlined the basic insecurity of the chief's tenure of office. Malcontents were quick to seize the opportunity of accusing their ruler of misappropriating stool money, and the failure of most chiefs to keep proper accounts made this charge difficult to rebut."[38] In his analysis of the changing role of the chief in the Gold Coast, Busia makes a similar point and provides data on local government finances which help to substantiate the argument. Busia's data show that during the early to mid-1940s, over 80 percent of the expenditures of the native authorities were for "administrative expenses" (i.e., for salaries, by and large), and less than 20 percent for education, medical services, capital works, and other improvements.[39] Because of the failure to provide services, the payment of taxes thus appeared to involve not a creation of public benefits but rather a redistribution of income between cash-crop producers and those who drew their incomes from the state. Naturally, the rural producers resented this transfer.[40]

Two other features of the taxation of cash-crop producers generated political protest in colonial Africa. One is the inherent nature of public goods. In the case of public goods and services, such as roads or law and order, it is reasonable for citizens to misrepresent the value they place on them and to protest that they are being charged too much for them. Being public goods, the goods provided by the state will be available for consumption by the taxpayer irrespective of the amount he actually pays for them. The taxpayer would, in fact, do best by letting others pay for the public goods, which he could then consume free. The African cash-crop producers, like taxpayers everywhere, were simply behaving in a way that maximized their own private welfare when they denigrated the value of the services that they received from the government or condemned the level of taxation as excessive. Political protest and taxation simply go together.

Secondly, the power of taxation is the power to coerce, and this power can be used to redistribute income. Redistribution makes some people better off by making some people worse off; the latter group will not, of course, voluntarily consent to redistributive measures. When taxes are used in this way, they lead to political protest, be it in rural Africa or anywhere else.

This pattern is clearly revealed in the political conflicts between small-scale subsistence farmers and large-scale commercial farmers in Kenya and in the emergence of anticolonial politics in that country. The commodities boom of the early twenties increased the commercial farmers' demand for labor. The government's recruitment of laborers for railway construction, the lingering effects of the loss of population in World War I, and the loss of population in the postwar outbreaks of influenza all had reduced the labor supply. The commercial producers were unwilling to increase the level of wages they paid and they therefore experienced a shortage of labor. In response to this shortage, they championed an increase in the level of taxes on subsistence farm families as a means of redistributing labor power from the subsistence to the commercial farm sector. In 1920, the government raised the tax rate;

because of a change in the budget year, the new tax was collected twice in a single calendar year. Largely in response to this tax, Harry Thuku organized the first African political party in Kenya: the Young Kikuyu Association.[41]

It was not labor alone that was forcefully redeployed between the two farming sectors. The costs of providing services were concentrated in one sector; the benefits from consuming them were reaped by the other. Thus, in 1920, the colonial government of Kenya passed an income tax and the commercial farmers resisted it. Forming a Taxpayers Protection League, they opposed the measure in the legislative council and organized the withholding of tax payments. Finally, in May 1922, they secured the repeal of the income tax and secured passage of a substitute financial measure: a schedule of customs rates that was designed to generate revenue by imposing duties on items consumed in large part by the native population and to provide protection for the commodities produced by the commercial farmers.[42]

The power of taxation was thus used in Kenya to facilitate the redistribution of resources between different sectors of the farming community; much of the politics of that area centered around efforts to alter the structure of taxes and the allocation of services that they financed. Similar patterns could be observed in West Africa. Thus, one of the main reasons for the taxpayers' revolt in mid-nineteenth century Ghana was that the rural communities perceived that the fiscal policy was being used to redeploy resources among different sections of the population. Explaining their resistance to taxes to which they had formerly assented, Kimble notes: "The original Assemblies had thought that they were taxing themselves for purely local purposes, and the Accras, for example, 'never could have conceived that their money was being applied in making roads and supplying medical aid for Fantees.'"[43] The Accras therefore joined the tax rebellion.

The redistributive nature of taxation emerged in another form, and it, too, promoted political unrest. Through public financial institutions, groups can achieve particular benefits while transferring the costs of supplying them to the political community as a whole. As each group can potentially secure all the benefits of a particular measure while paying only part of the costs, each group will therefore demand that the political community provide those services in which it has a particular interest, even though the total benefits of the measure are outweighed by the total costs. The result is an oversupply of public services. This dynamic appeared to underlie a series of financial crises that beset rural political institutions in Africa. I refer to the fiscal crises that bedeviled the native authorities of midcentury Ghana.

As we have discussed, the rise of cocoa production in the Gold Coast increased the tax base of the rural chieftancies. Through rents, tributes, special levies, and the sale of land, the chieftancies strengthened their finances by transferring funds from the cocoa farmers to themselves. The rise of cocoa farming also increased the demand for services from the chieftancies—in particular, the demand for secure rights to land. The cocoa farmers obtained their farmlands by purchasing land rights from the chiefs; where the jurisdiction of the chiefs was uncertain, it was in the interest of the farmers to demonstrate through a court of law the jurisdictional primacy of the chief that had sold them their lands. The disputes between the cocoa farmers thus became disputes between different local chieftancies.

With the increased density of farms in the cocoa-producing forest lands, the numbers of conflicting land claims multiplied and the cocoa farmers had more frequent occasion to seek clarification of their chiefs' jurisdictions. The costs of these disputes were borne by all of the taxpayers who fell under the jurisdiction of the chief; the benefits were reaped by a particular group of farmers. The result of these factors was apparently to increase the volume of litigation, both by raising the likelihood that disputes that had a low probability of winning would be pushed and by increasing the number of appeals against adverse rulings. It was therefore not surprising that the costs of litigation rose to an alarming degree in the cocoa farming areas. They, in fact, imposed a major fiscal burden on native authorities throughout the area.[44] Much of the political unrest in the cash-cropping areas of the Gold Coast reflected dissatisfaction with the mounting stool debts and the apparent mismanagement of public finances by local governments.

The rising stool debts, and the attempts to remove them through general levies, represented a transfer of resources to the farmers—who would benefit from the establishment of their rights to the full capital value of their lands—from present and future taxpayers—who would have to pay the costs of litigation involved in establishing their chiefs' jurisdiction over these lands. Farmers were not always the primary beneficiaries of the redistribution of resources through fiscal measures; indeed, they have become the victims of such measures. This has become increasingly true as ambitious political elites have sought to secure for public purposes the private resources being amassed by those making profits from commercial agriculture. The result has been political protest—protest mounted by the farmers against those who seek to use the state to deprive farmers of their earnings.

Political events in Ghana best illustrate this argument. In June 1954 Ghana became self-governing. The nationalist government sought to realize the ambitions that had fueled its attempts to wrest power from the hands of foreigners by mounting a major development program. This program would not only bring greater prosperity to the country as a whole but would, through the diversification of the economy, reduce the country's vulnerability to fluctuations in the price of cocoa. In August 1954 the government therefore enacted the Cocoa Duty and Development Funds (Amendment) Bill—a measure to freeze the producer price of cocoa for four years and to increase the rate of progression of the cocoa duty.

The effect of the first feature of this legislation was to hold the price paid to the farmer steady while allowing the Marketing Board, which purchased the crop from the farmers and sold it abroad, to sell at whatever price prevailed in the world market. As in the past, the board would accumulate the difference between the two prices; but at a time when people expected the world price to rise, the effect of fixing local prices at a level proposed by the government appeared to be the appropriation by the government of an increasing percentage of the earnings of the cocoa farmers.

The effect of the second feature of the 1954 legislation was to redistribute funds from the Marketing Board to the government itself. The trading surpluses of the Marketing Board were often used for purposes that little benefited the farmer. The high salaries it paid its officials, and its inflated costs of marketing, represented transfers from the farmers to the directors and managers of the state agency. Many of its trading surpluses were invested in low-bearing treasury notes. They were, thus, in effect, used to provide a subsidized loan from the farmers to the government. The trading surpluses also financed a price-stabilizing fund; but this was rarely employed to shelter the farmers from slumps in the cocoa price. Nonetheless, by law, the trading surpluses were at least *supposed* to be used to benefit the farmers. By employing these funds to investigate cocoa diseases and control their spread, to rehabilitate cocoa farms, to conduct research on behalf of the cocoa industry, and to provide scholarships for the children of cocoa farmers, the Marketing Board did, in fact, use a portion of its trading surpluses to provide benefits to the cocoa farmers. By increasing the cocoa duty, however, the government sought, for any pair of producer and sale prices, to reduce the amount of surplus accruing to the Marketing Board. It therefore sought to divert the funds from an agency mandated to use its trading surplus on behalf of the cocoa industry to the government, an agency whose constituency included all sectors of the economy and whose mandate was to bring prosperity not to the cocoa industry alone, but the nation as a whole.

The cocoa farmers reacted vigorously to the passage of the legislation. Most of the farmers resided in the Ashanti area; organized by dissenting politicians, many vigorously backed the development of a regionalist political movement. Named the National Liberation Movement, it called for greater autonomy for Ashanti and for a weakening of the central government's fiscal powers. As Beckman succinctly states, "From the point of view of Ashanti, the federal issue and the cocoa price were of course greatly related. Greater regional autonomy would serve to redirect a greater portion of cocoa revenue to its origin."[45]

Ambitious governments have thus designed fiscal measures to accumulate resources out of cash cropping and to use these to finance the development of other sectors. And cash-crop producers have vigorously resisted this redistribution. Opposition to publicly sponsored monopsonies has characterized the behavior of cash-crop producers throughout Africa. Most commonly, it has taken the form of smuggling. Governments, of course, have sought to curtail this activity. And resistance to government efforts to suppress illegal markets has become a muted form of political protest, analogous, perhaps, to the resistance to poaching laws in post-feudal Europe. More dramatic, but less frequent, have been open rebellions, such as those mounted by the cocoa farmers of Ibadan.[46] The use of taxation to redistribute income from country to town, from agriculture to industry, from farmer to bureaucrat, industrialist, or worker—the use of the power of the state in this manner—is one of the most potent sources of rural political protest in Africa.

Conclusion

In this essay, we have examined the relationship between the commercialization of agriculture and the rise of political protest in Africa. We have done so by asking why those who seek profits from the production of agricultural commodities should leave the marketplace and enter the political arena. We have seen that several considerations account for this behavior. The structure of the markets that producers confronted in their search for profits provided an incentive to combine. The existence of significant production externalities promoted public intervention in an attempt to secure greater profitability for the industry as a whole. Those who benefited from these externalities, and those who simply resented the use of coercion on African peasants by a foreign power, then turned to politics to alter the government's behavior. The allocation of land rights had a strong bearing on the ultimate allocation of the benefits produced by the commercialization of agriculture; this allocation was determined by the state. These considerations also provided a rationale for those seeking profits from agriculture to engage in political action. Lastly, the state influenced the distribution of profits from cash cropping through its use of the power to levy taxes. Through political action, African cash-crop producers sought to alter the structure of taxes and the allocation of the benefits that they financed. Increasingly, the political efforts of cash-crop producers have focused on attempts to prevent the confiscation of their earnings by the state and their redeployment to other sectors. Sporadic resistance against market controls, taxpayers' rebellions, and movements in support of regional autonomy all constitute attempts by rural dwellers to use coercion to safeguard the profits that they seek to realize from the commercial production of agricultural products.

Notes

1. Charles Wilson, *The History of Unilever*, vols. 1-3 (New York: Frederick A. Praeger, 1968).

2. Board of Trade, *Memorandum on Transport Development and Cotton Growing in East Africa* (Cmd. 2463) (London: His Majesty's Stationery Office, 1925).

3. For discussion of the rise of African exports, see Bruce F. Johnston, "Changes in Agricultural Productivity," in *Economic Transition in Africa*, ed. Melville J. Herskovits and Mitchell Horwitz (Evanston, Ill.: Northwestern University Press, 1964), pp. 151-178; Jan S. Hogendorn, "Economic Initiative and African Cash Farming: Pre-Colonial Origins and Early Colonial Developments," in *Colonialism in Africa 1870-1960, Volume 4, The Economics of Colonialism*, ed. Peter Guignan and L. H. Gann (New York: Cambridge University Press, 1975), pp. 283-328; Allan McPhee, *The Economic Revolution in British West Africa* (London: George Routledge and Sons, 1926); A. G. Hopkins, *An Economic History of West Africa* (New York: Columbia University Press, 1973); and Wilson, *History of Unilever*. See also some of the material contained in Richard D. Wolff, *The Economics of Colonialism: Britain and Kenya, 1870-1930* (New Haven and London: Yale University Press, 1974).

4. Elena J. Berger, *Labour, Race, and Colonial Rule: The Copperbelt from 1924 to Independence* (Oxford: At the Clarendon Press, 1974); Donald George Morrison et. al., *Black Africa: A Comparative Handbook* (New York: The Free Press, 1972); B. S. Hoyle and D. Hilling, eds., *Seaports and Development in Tropical Africa* (New York: Praeger Publishers, 1970).

5. In some instances—and they were important ones—the production of these commodities was secured at a loss of welfare. The use of coercion in the growing of cotton in French and German Africa, and to some degree in British

256   Robert H. Bates

Africa as well, is a case in point, as is the use of forced labor in palm oil production in the Belgian Congo. See, for example, G. C. K. Gwassa and John Iliffe, *Records of the Maji Maji Rising* (Dar es Salaam: East African Publishing House, 1967). But in the vast majority of cases, there can be no question but that the penetration of the market into the rural countryside generated new economic opportunities and the prospects of significant material gain.

6. P. T. Bauer, *West African Trade: A Study of Competition, Oligopoly, and Monopoly in a Changing Economy* (London: Routledge and Kegan Paul, 1963).

7. Josephine Milburn, "The 1938 Gold Coast Crisis: British Business and the Colonial Office," *African Historical Studies* 3, no. 1 (1970):57-74; United Kingdom, *Report of the Commission on the Marketing of West African Cocoa*, The Nowell Commission (Cmd. 5845) (London: His Majesty's Stationary Office, 1938).

8. United Kingdom, *Report of Commission on Marketing of Cocoa*, p. 54.

9. The magnitude of the monopsony rents is suggested in the rapidly rising price of options to purchase licensed gins. See G. Andrew Maguire, *Toward 'Uhuru' in Tanzania: The Politics of Participation* (Cambridge: At the University Press, 1969), p. 86.

10. Cyril Ehrlich, "The Uganda Economy: 1903-1945," *History of East Africa*, vol. 2, ed. Vincent Harlow and E. M. Chilver (Oxford: Clarendon Press, 1965), p. 466.

11. Maguire, *Toward 'Uhuru.'*

12. See Uganda Protectorate, *Report of the Commission of Inquiry into the Disturbances in Uganda during April 1949* (Entebbe: Government Printer, 1950). It should also be noted that the cooperative unions in fact bought into the cartel. Rather than breaking up the monopsony and securing a competitive market, they simply secured ginning capacity within the structure of the market as mandated by colonial law. The result was that the cooperative societies ended up accumulating monopsony profits on their milling operations from their own cotton-growing members. See, for example, Lionel Cliffe and J. S. Saul, "The District Development Front in Tanzania," *Socialism in Tanzania*, vol. 1, ed. Lionel Cliffe and John S. Saul (Nairobi: East African Publishing House, 1972), pp. 302-328; John S. Saul, "Marketing Cooperatives in a Developing Country: The Tanzanian Case," *Socialism in Tanzania*, vol. 2, ed. Lionel Cliffe and John S. Saul (Nairobi: East African Publishing House, 1973), pp. 141-152.

13. Roland Young and Henry Fosbrooke, *Smoke in the Hills: Political Tension in the Morgoro District of Tanzania* (Evanston, Ill.: Northwestern University Press, 1960).

14. Lionel R. Cliffe, "Nationalism and the Reaction to Enforced Agricultural Change in Tanganyika during the Colonial Period," *Taamuli: A Political Science Forum* 1, no. 1 (July 1970):1-15.

15. See materials contained in J. Brian Wills, ed., *Agriculture and Land Use in Ghana*, (London: Oxford University Press, for the Ghana Ministry of Food and Agriculture, 1962).

16. Christopher Beer, *The Politics of Peasant Groups in Western Nigeria*

(Ibadan: Ibadan University Press, 1976), p. 55.

17. Ibid., p. 60.

18. Kwamina Busamafi Dickson, "Cocoa in Ghana" (Ph.D. dissertation, University of London, 1960), p. 275.

19. *Report of the Commission of Enquiry into Disturbances in the Gold Coast 1948* (Colonial no. 321) (London: His Majesty's Staionery Office, 1948).

20. Cliffe, "Nationalism and Reaction," Peter F. M. McLoughlin, "Agricultural Development in Sukumaland," *Experiences with Agriculture Development in Tropical Africa*, vol. 2, ed. John C. de Wilde (Baltimore: The Johns Hopkins University Press, 1967); Maguire, *Toward 'Uhuru.'*

21. Robert H. Bates, *Rural Responses to Industrialization: A Study of Village Zambia* (New Haven, Conn. and London: Yale University Press, 1976).

22. See the discussion by P. T. Bauer and B. S. Yamey, "The Economics of Marketing Reform," *Journal of Political Economy* 62 (1954):210-235. They argue that there is, in fact, no problem here save that of the stupidity of the government, for if there were a demand for a high-quality product, then the purchasers would offer a premium for it. They are both right and wrong. They are right concerning the acuity of the governments; they are wrong in thinking that the purchaser would offer an appropriate spectrum of prices. For over the period in which the issue of quality control was most prominent, it was the governments themselves who were buying the output of the cash-crop producers. This period was the 1940s and, in some instances, the early 1950s, when the colonial governments purchased the full national output under terms of bulk buying agreements. Presumably, following the termination of these agreements, the market established price gradations reflecting the relative value of different qualities of output, and the need for public controls to secure high quality declined. This may account for the apparent reduction in the significance of this issue in the rural politics of Africa.

23. It should be noted that factors other than externalities made the imposition of regulations a political issue. The people did not like being coerced, plain and simple. They did not like the fact that the regulations were often imposed on them without prior consultation and without soliciting the input of producers in the planning process. Moreover, the regulations were often poorly designed. They were developed on the basis of the average producers, and, therefore, often made little sense. For example, imposing the same percentage reduction in herd size on farmers in the lushest grazing areas as on farmers in arid zones had little justification. The regulations were often insensitive to the interdependence of the production process. Building up herds served as a hedge on the production of good crops, which were periodically threatened by drought; limiting the production of cattle without adjusting for the increased risks to the farmer lowered his welfare. Lastly, some of the measures were simply destructive; digging bench terracing often brought sterile soils to the surface and reduced the productivity of the gardens. For all these reasons, then, in addition to the problems arising from externalities, the regulations were unpopular with the rural dwellers.

24. M. P. K. Sorrenson, *Origins of European Settlement in Kenya* (Nairobi: Oxford University Press, 1968); Carl G. Rosberg, Jr. and John

Nottingham, *The Myth of "Mau Mau": Nationalism in Kenya* (New York: Frederick A. Praeger, for The Hoover Institution on War, Revolution, and Peace, 1966).

25. David Kimble, *A Political History of Ghana: The Rise of Gold Coast Nationalism, 1850-1928* (Oxford: At the Clarendon Press, 1963).

26. Jean Stengers, "The Congo Free State and the Belgian Congo before 1914," *Colonialism in Africa 1870-1960, Volume 1, History and Politics of Colonialism 1870-1914*, ed. L. H. Gann and Peter Guigan (Cambridge: At the University Press, 1969), pp. 261-292.

27. Robert I. Rotberg, "The Rise of African Nationalism: The Case of East and Central Africa," *World Politics* 15, no. 1 (October 1962):75-90.

28. Terence J. Johnson, "An Analysis of Southern Gold Coast Riots 1890-1920," *Economy and Society* 1, no. 2 (1972):164-193; Jarle Simensen, "Rural Mass Action in the Context of Anti-Colonial Protest: The Asafo Movement of Akim Abuawka, Ghana," *Canadian Journal of African Studies* 8, no. 1(1974):25-41; Martin L. Kilson, "Nationalism and Social Classes in British West Africa," *The Journal of Politics* 20, no. 2 (May 1958):368-387; K. A. Busia, *The Position of the Chief in the Modern Political System of Ashanti*, (London: Oxford University Press, for the International African Institute, 1951); Dennis Austin, *Politics in Ghana 1946-1960* (London: Oxford University Press, for the Royal Institute of International Affairs, 1970).

29. R. C. Pratt, "Administration and Politics in Uganda, 1919-1945," *History of East Africa*, vol. 2, ed. Vincent Harlow and E. M. Chilver (Oxford: At the Clarendon Press, 1965); Cyril Ehrlich, "The Uganda Economy: 1903-1945," *History of East Africa*; C. C. Wrigley, *Crops and Wealth in Uganda, A Short Agrarian History* (Nairobi: Oxford University Press, for Makerere Institute of Social Research, 1970).

30. *Report of Commission of Inquiry into Expenses Incurred by Litigants in the Courts of the Gold Coast and Indebtedness Caused Thereby* (Accra: Government Printing Department, 1945); H. Conway Belfield, *Report on the Legislation Governing the Alienation of Native Lands in the Gold Coast Colony and Ashanti; With Some Observations on the "Forest Ordinance," 1911* (Cd. 6278) (London: His Majesty's Stationery Office, 1912); Polly Hill, *The Migrant Cocoa-Farmers of Southern Ghana: A Study in Rural Capitalism* (Cambridge: The University Press, 1963). As Busia has noted: "The earlier land disputes settled by Government clearly show the relation between litigation about land and the new industries which enhanced its economic value. Earlier settlements of boundary disputes are tabulated below. [They] indicate . . . that most litigation took place in the mining and cocoa areas in South Ashanti." Busia, *Position of the Chief*, p. 205.

31. One example of this is the struggle between the Ashanti Confederacy Council and other chieftaincies. The former sought to extend its fiscal jurisdiction over outlying areas and so centralize the revenues derived from the commercial utilization of land. John Dunn and A. F. Robertson, *Dependence and Opportunity: Political Change in Ahafo*, Volume 9, *The African Studies Series*, ed. J. R. Goody (Cambridge: The University Press, 1973). Another example would be Nana Ofori Atta's attempt to expand the power of the

Omanahene of Akim Abuakwa and thereby lay hold of the revenues being generated by the richest cocoa lands of his time. See Polly Hill, *The Migrant Cocoa-Farmers*, p. 148.

32. Pratt, "Administration and Politics in Uganda."

33. Gretha Kershaw, "The Land is the People: A Study of Kikuyu Social Organization in Historical Perspective" (Ph.D. dissertation, University of Chicago, 1972); M. P. K. Sorrenson, *Land Reform in the Kikuyu Country: A Study in Government Policy* (Nairobi: Oxford University Press, for the East African Institute of Social Research, 1967).

34. Lionel Cliffe, "The Policy of Ujamaa Vijijini and the Class Struggle in Tanzania," *Socialism in Tanzania*, vol. 2, ed. Lionel Cliffe and John S. Saul (Nairobi: East African Publishing House, 1973), pp. 141-152; John S. Saul, "Class and Penetration in Tanzania," *Socialism in Tanzania*, pp. 118-126; John S. Saul, "Marketing Cooperatives."

35. David Kimble, *Political History of Ghana*, p. 182.

36. Ibid., p. 190.

37. Martin L. Kilson, "Grass-Roots Politics in Africa: Local Government in Sierra Leone," *Political Studies* 12 (February 1964):47-66; Martin L. Kilson, *Political Change in a West African State: A Study of the Modernization Process in Sierra Leone* (Cambridge, Mass.: Harvard University Press, 1966).

38. William Tordoff, *Ashanti Under the Prempehs: 1888-1935* (London: Oxford University Press, 1965), p. 192.

39. Busia, *Position of the Chief*, p. 165.

40. See also Simensen, "Rural Mass Action."

41. W. McGregor Ross, *Kenya From Within: A Short Political History* (London: George Allen and Unwin, 1927), p. 153.

42. Ibid., p. 154.

43. David Kimble, *Political History of Ghana*, p. 182.

44. See Belfield, *Report on Legislation Governing Alienation of Native Lands; Report of Commission of Inquiry into Expenses Incurred by Litigants.* Several institutional changes were innovated in an attempt to ameliorate this crisis. One was the selection of wealthy persons as chiefs, the winning candidate being one who would pay off the public debt. Another was making the undertaking of a law suit contingent on the plaintiff's willingness to assume the stool and retire the debt it had incurred in clarifying its jurisdiction over his lands.

45. Björn Beckman, *Organising the Farmers: Cocoa Politics and National Development in Ghana* (New York: Africana Publishing Company, 1976), p. 196; Austin, *Politics in Ghana 1946-1960*, pp. 253ff.

46. Christopher Beer, *Politics of Peasant Groups; Western State of Nigeria, Report of the Commission of Inquiry into the Civil Disturbances Which Occurred in Certain Parts of the Western State of Nigeria in the Month of December 1968*, Honourable Mr. Justice Ebenezer Olufemi Ayoola (Ibadan: Government Printer, 1969).

10
The Politics of Food Scarcities in Developing Countries

Norman K. Nicholson
John D. Esseks
Ali Akhtar Khan

Introduction

The history of the food scarcity problem in the developing countries goes as far back as the colonial era, when these countries were made to serve the interests of their colonial powers. Therefore, the colonial economy has certain features in common, be it a case in Asia or Africa. In the case of India, the economy, which was basically agricultural, was marred by heavy land taxation, fluctuating and uncertain land tax assessment, remittance of larger portions of revenue to England (nearly 44 million sterling annually by the end of the nineteenth century), no investment in agriculture, and promotion of raw material production for British industries and consumption of British manufactures in India. Rapid expansion of the railway, for example, was preferred to irrigation development, because the former exposed the self-sustained economy to further and more intensive exploitation, while the latter would have provided the means to widen and secure the base of the economy. As a result, the economic situation at the end of the nineteenth century was dominated by constant famines.[1]

In Africa, there was minimal or no (foreign) investment on agricultural ("indigenous") development, except for the plantations with or without foreign settlers. Rapid industrialization in the West generated an effective demand for tropical raw materials. This led the internal colonial governments to invest in raw-material production and to exploit mineral resources. The external trade involved the exchange of mostly luxury items—ivory, gold, alcohol, textiles, and tobacco. The slave trade depopulated the continent and disrupted the natural growth

We are very grateful to the following for their helpful comments on an earlier draft of this essay: Edgar Owens, Rollow Erick, Tom Dobbs, Donald Puchala, and Raymond Hopkins.

261

of the economy. Consequently, the traditonal agricultural economy was destroyed.[2]

After independence, most development strategies could not redress the shortfalls of colonial Africa. The traditional sector continues to be neglected, and the agricultural population is underdeveloped and impoverished. The agricultural economy is stagnant, without any sign of transformation. India had some advantage over its independent African counterparts. It evolved relatively better developed institutional (especially bureaucratic) and physical infrastructures. India's postindependence investment in agriculture and the subsequent effects are encouraging for developing countries. But such achievements are concentrated mostly in small areas. We shall elaborate this point in a later section. "In many ways," however, "it is still a case of 'dual society,' in which an industrializing urban minority is drawing away from a stagnating traditionalist rural community."[3]

As it appears now, many less developed countries (LDCs) have become or will shortly be (a) incapable of increasing domestic food production as rapidly as demand rises from population growth and higher personal incomes and (b) unable to cover the consequent deficits with commercial imports. By the mid-1980s, the aggregate food-grain import needs of LDCs and other deficit countries (in Western and Eastern Europe) are expected to exceed the capacities of exporting states. In the resulting high-priced commercial markets, the many poor LDCs will tend to be outbid by rich importing countries.

Major exporting countries, particularly the United States, could help foreign-exchange-poor LDCs cover their grain deficits by providing them with food aid—i.e., grants or credits to enhance their buying power in grain markets or direct shipments from government-held stocks. Humanitarian concerns and/or national self-interest may persuade exporting states to budget the funds necessary to divert sizable quantities of grain away from cash buyers in Europe and Japan, who seek to improve on or protect their already relatively high consumption standards, to Asian or African countries, who have low effective demand and poor consumption levels. However, exporting countries face their own balance-of-payments problems, particularly from rising oil import bills. The prospects for handsome foreign exchange earnings from cash sales are likely to discourage them from putting much grain aside for concessional sales or grants. In the tight supply year 1973, U.S. food aid dropped in volume by about 40 percent from the 1972 level; and in 1974, shipments declined by a further 50 percent.[4]

Critics of food aid may applaud or be ambivalent toward this decline, since they believe that Public Law 480 and other aid programs have encouraged recipient LDCs to ignore or postpone solving their domestic food production problems. The argument runs: Lacking a severe food supply crisis, governments have not been shaken out of their typical absorption with urban-sector problems; and/or with food aid supplies dampening local market prices for food, farmers have lacked as much incentive to increase output as if there had been no aid.[5] On the other hand, in many LDCs future grain deficits may well be so large that, even with the deflationary impact of sizable food assistance shipments, local prices will remain more than high enough to attract increasing inputs into farming. Nevertheless, the preferred solution is increased domestic production rather than reliance on foreign food aid or some combination of both policy approaches that slights production.

In sum, with domestic production decreasing relative to population, commercial imports too expensive, and food aid probably scarce, many LDCs will see nutritional levels deteriorate, perhaps to the point of widespread starvation. In the process, there are likely to be such attendant political ills as mass-scale unrest from soaring domestic food prices, public-sector employees' demand for compensating wage hikes (which overstrain treasuries), and increased official corruption as government takes on rationing food and distributing relief supplies on a large scale.

Not all LDCs face this destiny. A 1974 food-production-demand study by the U.S. Department of Agriculture classifies developing countries in four groupings.[6] One comprises "countries which have traditionally produced food surpluses" (Thailand, Burma, Nepal, Kenya) and which, with reasonably high further investments and good management in the food-farming sector, should be able to continue to feed themselves, at least in basic foodstuffs. A second group consists of states (Algeria, Indonesia, Iran, Morocco, Nigeria) which have not been self-sufficient, but which, thanks to their high-demand export products (oil, phosphates) can expect to bid successfuly in the world grain market and cover their needs with imports. In a third group are states which cannot afford the import consequences of stagnant food production, but which either have already "made definite progress with the Green Revolution" (Pakistan, the Philippines, Turkey) or have unexploited potential in the sense of good climates and under-utilized land (much of Latin America). The fourth group, however, consists of severely disadvantaged countries whose limited foreign-exchange earning capacities combine with population pressures (India, Bangladesh, Sri Lanka) and/or unfavorable climates (the drought-prone states neighboring the Sahara) to threaten periodic or near-chronic food scarcities. They are hard pressed to come up with foreign exchange to cover both needed food imports and

TABLE 10.1 Indexes of Per Capita Food Production: 1961-75,
USDA and FAO Estimates

		1961-65 Average	1967	1969	1971	1973	1975	1971-75 Average
A.	**Stagnant or Declining Output (Africa)**							
Benin	USDA	100	95	91	90	95	99	95
	FAO	100	108	106	104	102	75	102
Ethiopia	USDA	100	101	102	99	87	77	88
	FAO	100	101	102	100	96	83	93
Ghana	USDA	100	100	92	92	86	88	87
	FAO	100	101	94	108	101	89	100
Guinea	USDA	100	101	109	108	107	104	106
	FAO	100	103	104	101	90	85	92
Kenya	USDA	100	105	95	90	95	96	94
	FAO	100	108	109	100	99	86	96
Liberia	USDA	100	86	84	85	92	89	89
	FAO	100	90	91	96	92	102	97
Madagascar	USDA	100	106	109	108	98	104	104
	FAO	100	102	101	95	88	91	91
Mali	USDA	100	95	96	80	60	65	68
	FAO	100	100	99	95	57	80	75
Niger	USDA	100	107	99	88	52	64	70
	FAO	100	108	101	84	57	60	70
Nigeria	USDA	100	88	102	94	89	93	93
	FAO	100	86	97	90	74	84	82
Senegal	USDA	100	107	92	93	73	102	84
	FAO	100	108	91	94	70	107	81
Sierra Leone	USDA	100	95	92	100	96	99	97
	FAO	100	105	109	107	105	104	106
Togo	USDA	100	106	111	100	91	94	95
	FAO	100	116	105	109	74	61	83
Uganda	USDA	100	106	108	101	87	78	90
	FAO	100	104	111	101	95	86	95
Upper Volta	USDA	100	92	82	71	64	74	71
	FAO	100	107	103	94	71	90	80
B.	**Increased Outputs (Africa)**							
Ivory Coast	USDA	100	108	113	119	118	133	122
	FAO	100	118	117	120	119	136	122
Malawi	USDA	100	144	127	120	104	118	117
	FAO	100	125	121	117	121	110	119
Rwanda	USDA	100	120	117	119	115	106	111
	FAO	100	116	114	118	113	119	111
Zaire	USDA	100	111	120	111	111	111	111
	FAO	100	106	118	110	121	89	112

TABLE 10.1 (cont.)

		1961-65 Average	1967	1969	1971	1973	1975	1971-75 Average
C.	Widely Divergent Indexes							
	Burundi — USDA	100	106	107	109	104	98	100
	Burundi — FAO	100	106	108	139	169	105	153
	Cameroon — USDA	100	105	101	100	91	94	95
	Cameroon — FAO	100	118	121	123	118	110	119
	Tanzania — USDA	100	99	99	102	98	95	97
	Tanzania — FAO	100	105	112	114	113	119	114
	Zambia — USDA	100	187	85	110	113	125	129
	Zambia — FAO	100	117	107	98	98	113	102
D.	South Asian Countries							
	Bangladesh — USDA	100	103	103	83	92	92	86
	Bangladesh — FAO	100	101	101	81	90	97	85
	Burma — USDA	100	94	92	89	90	100	90
	Burma — FAO	100	95	93	92	92	92	90
	India — USDA	100	94	103	107	104	105	102
	India — FAO	100	96	101	104	102	103	100
	Pakistan — USDA	100	107	127	121	121	114	119
	Pakistan — FAO	100	104	118	113	115	115	114
	Sri Lanka — USDA	100	100	109	107	92	82	102
	Sri Lanka — FAO	100	97	96	95	91	107	96

Sources: U.S. Department of Agriculture, Indices of Agricultural Production in Africa and the Near East, 1956-75 (Washington, D.C., 1976,
Statistical Bulletin No. 556); USDA, Indicies of Agricultural Production
for the Far East and Oceania, Average 1961-65 and Annual 1966-75 (Washington, D.C., 1976, Statistical Bulletin No. 555); and Food and Agriculture Organization, Production Yearbook, 1974 & 1976 (Rome, 1975 and
1976), Vol. 1, pp. 29-30 and pp. 73-74.

Green Revolution inputs (fertilizers, irrigation equipment) which could
eventually reduce import dependence. This chapter concentrates on the
two problem areas, sub-Saharan Africa and South Asia.

Tables 10.1-10.4 give indicators of the progress or lack of it, over the
years 1961-75, in increasing per capita food production and reducing
dependence on food imports. Since both food output and population
estimates for LDCs are often weakly based, we try for a greater measure of
reliability by referring to two separate time-series of per capita food
production for each of the twenty-eight countries surveyed—estimates
by the Food and Agricultural Organization (FAO) and those by the U.S.
Department of Agriculture (USDA).[7] For fifteen of the twenty-three

African states surveyed, the two series agree that food production either failed to keep pace with population (e.g., in Ethiopia, Liberia, Nigeria) or improved only a few percentage points above the 1961-65 base (Benin, Guinea, Madagascar); see the 1971-75 averages in group A of Table 10.1. Staying close to the baseline tended not to be much of an achievement, since African states were then and are now among the world's poorest nutritionally. According to FAO estimates for the early 1960s, the average daily supply of calories per person in Africa was below the level required for good health and about two-thirds the level prevailing in the developed world.[8] In nine of the fifteen problem countries, the loss or stagnation in food outputs per capita can be attributed in varying degrees to the multiyear droughts of the early 1970s.[9] However, in five of those nine cases, downward or stagnating trends began before the droughts.[10] Significantly upward trends—with per capita food outputs increasing by more than 10 percent—are displayed by only four of the sub-Saharan African countries surveyed: the Ivory Coast, Malawi, Rwanda, and Zaire (group B in Table 10.1). For another four states (group C), the FAO and USDA estimates diverge too greatly.

Among the South Asian states for which both FAO and USDA estimates were available, Bangladesh and Burma apparently failed to expand food production as rapidly as population growth. India's 1971-75 average was virtually unchanged from that of 1961-65. The indices for Sri Lanka are too divergent. Only Pakistan appears to have achieved significant progress, with the FAO and USDA estimates showing 14 to 19 percent increases in food outputs per person (Table 10.1).

Table 10.2's survey of food imports, 1962-75, by twenty-one sub-Saharan and South Asian countries (i.e., those for which data were available) indicates a general and substantial rise in the money value of food imports. If we compare averages for 1971-75 with the 1962-65 bases, we find a mean increase of 174 percent. Some countries could "afford" their increased food import bills in the sense that the latter did not represent a proportionately larger drain on export earnings. For eleven of the twenty countries covered in Table 10.3 (group B), the ratios of food import to export revenues were no higher in 1971-75 than in 1961-65; export earnings rose enough to offset the higher food bill. However, for the other countries (group A), the reverse was true; food imports became more expensive, relatively as well as absolutely. Relative increase or not, many countries in both groups continued to have high foreign food bills: India's food imports during 1971-75 averaged 21 percent of total export earnings; for Pakistan it was 22 percent; Zaire, 16 percent; Sierra Leone, 25 percent; Sri Lanka, 54 percent; and Senegal, 46 percent (Table 10.3).

TABLE 10.2   Indexes of Food Imports, 1962-75,
Based on Current Market Values

	1962-65 Average	1967	1969	1971	1973	1975	1971-75 Average
A. African Countries							
Cameroon	100	123	134	190	247	438	297
Ethiopia	100	159	110	174	152	280	174
Ghana	100	90	85	87	126	131	115
Ivory Coast	100	--	260	308	412	486	424
Kenya	100	67	165	224	247	195	227
Liberia	100	119	95	146	206	263	210
Madagascar	100	82	120	157	205	249	232
Malawi[a]	100	84	92	149	205	280	207
Mali	100	108	184	247	563	804	578
Nigeria	100	93	147	245	359	644	390
Senegal	100	106	136	131	237	283	221
Sierra Leone	100	130	118	151	246	232	225
Tanzania	100	135	222	268	411	1490	848
Togo	100	138	114	129	255	350	227
Uganda	100	170	517	561	551	378	553
Zaire	100	107	97	96	173	--	132
Zambia[a]	100	--	172	297	153	226	234
B. South Asian Countries							
Burma	100	--	29	43	20	42	37
India	100	158	103	67	118	276	138
Pakistan	100	131	60	67	136	223	135
Sri Lanka	100	103	90	93	125	237	148
All Countries							247

Source: Food and Agriculture Organization, Trade Yearbook (1968, 1974, 1976) (Rome, 1969, 1975, 1977).

[a] 1964-65 average.

While Tables 10.2 and 10.3 focus on monetary indicators of food import dependence, Table 10.4 looks at physical or volume dependence. The "problem" countries identified in Table 10.3—i.e., those that had relatively higher food import bills (group A)—tend to appear among the problem states also in Table 10.4. That is to say, they were more dependent in 1971-75 than in 1961-65 on imported grain relative to total volume consumed. They were concurrently paying more for imports relative to their total export earnings and consuming more imports relative to total domestic consumption. Such a situation may threaten consumption levels. The increased expensiveness of food imports makes them a conspicuous target for cutbacks by government action, such as licensing controls. And any cutback will obviously have an even greater impact on consumption levels where the latter are based on imports.

When production lags behind population growth and imports fail to

TABLE 10.3   Food Import as Percentage of Total Export Earnings, 1962-75

	1962-65 Average	1967	1969	1971	1973	1975	1971-75 Average
A. More Costly Dependence							
Sri Lanka	40.5	46.5	44.0	45.0	54.0	66.0	54.0
Senegal	43.6	41.0	58.5	55.0	64.5	33.4	46.0
Sierra Leone	18.0	30.1	16.5	22.1	23.5	26.0	25.0
Tanzania	5.2	5.5	8.0	9.0	35.0	36.3	21.0
Madagascar	14.3	10.2	14.0	14.0	13.1	15.3	15.0
Ivory Coast	11.0	--	15.4	18.2	13.0	11.1	14.6
Cameroon	9.4	11.0	7.0	10.4	8.0	11.5	10.0
Uganda	2.3	3.4	8.5	8.0	6.5	5.2	7.1
Zambia	4.2	--	4.0	9.1	2.8	6.2	5.6
B. Less Costly Dependence							
Pakistan	31.3	31.0	13.2	13.5	24.0	31.0	22.0
India	32.0	51.0	29.0	16.0	21.0	33.0	21.0
Zaire	18.2	17.3	17.0	18.5	21.6	11.5	16.0
Togo	19.0	19.1	11.5	11.4	18.2	--	13.0
Ghana	19.3	19.3	16.0	15.5	12.4	10.0	12.3
Malawi[a]	14.0	8.0	9.1	11.0	11.0	10.3	10.7
Kenya	14.0	8.0	11.6	14.0	10.0	6.3	10.1
Liberia	14.0	11.0	6.0	8.4	9.1	9.5	9.0
Burma	10.0	--	5.6	8.6	5.5	7.0	6.7
Nigeria	11.1	9.0	10.5	9.0	7.0	5.1	6.5
Ethiopia	6.0	9.1	5.3	8.0	3.6	6.7	5.1

Source: Same as Table 10.2

[a] 1964-65 average

fill the gap, per capita consumption will of course drop. This happened in at least seven African countries in that the averages for cereals, 1973-75, were below 1961-65 baselines (see Table 10.5); available data on the seven indicate both lower or stagnant ouput relative to population and import volumes that did not compensate.[11]

In addition to an imbalance between supply and need for food, LDCs tend to have the problem of inequitable distribution of income. Malenbaum suggests that in many Third World countries, one-third or less of the population consumes more than half of the available food.[12] Even in a country such as India, which has barely managed to match food production to growing population, there are large regional variations in consumption. Difference among economic classes are even more striking (see Tables 10.6 and 10.7). In the long term, of course, the absolute magnitude of the human population threatens to exceed our capacity to produce food. But in the short term, it is our inability to provide jobs and income to increasing numbers of the poor, and not the physical lack of food, that is the problem. It is a crisis of planning and

TABLE 10.4   Cereals Imports[a] as a Percentage of
Total Cereals Consumption (By Volume), 1961-75

	1961-65 Average	1967	1969	1971	1973	1975	1971-75 Average
A. Increased Import Dependence							
Ethiopia	.3	.7	.9	1.3	2.7	1.2	1.7
Ivory Coast	24.0	20.2	31.5	28.2	29.5	18.8	26.4
Liberia[b]	26.2	36.2	36.3	30.0	17.7	22.7	24.5
Madagascar	3.8	2.0	3.8	6.0	17.7	16.4	14.5
Nigeria	2.4	3.6	4.8	8.3	8.7	7.8	7.8
Senegal	76.7	68.3	67.8	79.1	90.0	60.2	77.7
Sierra Leone[c]	11.1	15.8	13.0	21.0	18.6	8.1	14.7
Tanzania	6.3	4.3	7.6	8.3	16.5	20.0	18.1
Upper Volta	1.8	4.4	4.0	7.0	10.5	4.3	6.9
Zaire	36.2	31.2	24.9	32.9	38.4	37.1	36.2
Zambia[d]	4.7	4.6	11.6	7.7	10.1	25.2	11.3
B. Decreased Dependence							
Ghana	25.3	19.0	23.9	21.6	25.7	12.9	18.7
Guinea	18.1	18.7	16.4	17.8	13.2	16.8	15.8
India	8.3	11.0	4.5	2.3	4.5	7.9	4.5
Kenya	5.8	.2	1.1	7.2	3.4	1.9	3.8
Sri Lanka	54.6	52.7	48.3	48.2	52.1	60/6	51.0
Pakistan	19.3	26.4	9.9	10.8	9.7	12.3	11.2

Sources: U.S. Department of Agriculture, Foreign Agriculture Circular:
Reference Tables on Wheat, Corn, and Total Coarse Grains Supply-
Distribution for Individual Countries (Washington, D.C., 1976); and
ibid., Reference Tables on Rice Supply-Distribution for Individual
Countries (Washington, D.C., 1976).

[a]Wheat, coarse grains, and rice unless otherwise indicated.
[b]Rice only.
[c]Wheat and rice.
[d]Wheat and coarse grains.

implementation when production grows, but not consumption. Poverty
is as much a part of the world food crisis as food shortages.

   In summary, we see in these two regions (South Asia and sub-Saharan
Africa) many countries whose production, import, and/or consumption
records are not encouraging. From the early 1960s to the mid-1970s, their
per capita food outputs declined or were stagnant; they remained
significantly dependent on costly food imports or food aid; and/or their
actual consumption levels (at least for cereals) declined. Some countries
were "problems" in all three respects (e.g., Ethiopia, Senegal, and Sierra
Leone.)

   What follows is a discussion of the kinds of policy adjustments and
related policy outcomes that can be anticipated as LDCs cope with the
threat of mass famine or chronic, widespread malnutrition. The
discussion is based largely on the experiences of India and selected

TABLE 10.5   Indexes of Per Capita Consumption of Cereals,[a] 1961-75

	1961-65 Average	1967	1969	1971	1973	1975	1973-75 Average
A. Lower Consumption							
Ethiopia	100	105	112	107	78	95	85
Kenya	100	91	86	69	88	82	83
Liberia[b]	100	81	80	79	77	76	76
Nigeria	100	78	93	71	69	79	75
Senegal	100	113	105	124	107	86	95
Sierra Leone[c]	100	95	90	117	94	98	99
Upper Volta	100	88	75	79	67	69	68
B. Higher Consumption							
Ghana	100	118	110	121	150	127	137
Guinea	100	128	115	114	106	101	104
India	100	100	105	103	107	105	104
Ivory Coast	100	121	139	141	121	122	119
Madagascar	100	112	103	106	108	118	115
Pakistan	100	107	123	111	117	114	115
Sri Lanka	100	104	110	115	108	102	108
Tanzania	100	87	86	105	126	131	122
Zambia[d]	100	146	154	135	116	123	121
Zaire	100	95	120	133	150	163	157

Sources: Same as Table 10.4.

[a]Wheat, coarse grains, and rice unless otherwise indicated.
[b]Rice only.
[c]Wheat and rice.
[d]Wheat and coarse grains.

African countries and is divided into two sections: problems and related policies concerned with (a) distribution and (b) food production. Among the problems investigated are:

- the tendency toward enormously high budgetary costs and political risks when governments try to manage food distribution directly;
- the tendency for political imperatives and administrative difficulties to bias food distribution programs towards urban centers to the neglect of smaller towns and rural areas;
- the lack, among many LDC governments, of the institutional capacity to detect incipient famine crises and to arrange for relief in time to prevent massive suffering;
- the production gamble of concentrating governmental assistance in relatively few areas with favorable climate, soil fertility, and other input factors;
- the political risks in emphasizing aid to "progressive farmers" to the neglect of the less efficient;

TABLE 10.6 Average Calorie Supply Per Consumer
Unit Per Day In Rural Areas of India, By State
1971-72

State	Calories Per Consumer Unit[a] Per Day
Andhra Pradesh	2,670
Assam	2,660
Bihar	2,730
Gujrat	2,820
Haryana	3,650
Jammu and Kashmir	3,490
Kerala	2,020
Madhya Pradesh	3,650
Maharashtra	2,570
Manipur	3,110
Mysore	2,840
Orissa	2,530
Punjab	3,710
Rajasthan	3,210
Tamil Nadu	2,390
Tripura	3,030
Uttar Pradesh	3,200
West Bengal	2,310

Source: Food and Agriculture Organization, The
Fourth World Survey (Rome, 1977), p. 31. Data
obtained by FAO from the Government of India
based on National Sample Survey of India, 1971-
72.

[a]Consumer Unit refers to "reference man," i.e.,
an individual standardized for age and sex.

TABLE 10.7 Average Calorie and Protein Availability Per Consumer Unit of Rural Households by Expenditure Groups, India, 1971-72

Expenditure (Rupees/ Capita/Month)	Percent of Households	Calories (per Consumer Unit/Day)	Protein (Grams/Consumer Unit/Day)
0-15	3.9	1,493	46
15-21	10.5	1,957	60
21-24	7.1	2,287	69
24-28	10.2	2,431	73
28-34	15.2	2,734	82
34-43	17.7	3,127	93
43-55	14.4	3,513	105
55-75	11.5	4,016	121
75-100	5.2	4,574	139
More than 100	4.2	6,181	182

Source: Same as Table 10.6.

- the political obstacles to higher productivity represented by conservatively controlled local institutions;
- the tendency of policymakers in LDCs to concentrate on short-term responses to food scarcity to the detriment of long-term structural changes;
- the difficulty of defining an effective balance between public- and private-sector activities in agriculture;
- the need for a system of international food reserves that will permit LDCs to risk radical departures in policymaking and the chance of short-term production losses in order to restructure their rural sectors for long-term gains.

The Politics of Distribution

In India, the distinction between short, intense periods of deprivation (famine) and the growing incidence of continuing destitution is fairly clear. Furthermore, India's institutional development for dealing with the facts of hunger goes back more than two decades and provides many lessons. The Indian case illustrates the capacity of even fairly minor shortfalls in production to escalate politically in the absence of effective management.

For nearly twenty years (1954-72), surplus American grain stocks provided developing nations (the friendly ones, at least) with an inexpensive and politically attractive solution to their food problems.[13] In terms of famine policy, the U.S. Commodity Credit Corporation stocks supplied the essential "insurance" against erratic weather. But that is not the only function those stocks performed. In India, they were used, somewhat ineffectively, as an antiinflation device to compensate for extensive deficit financing. It is also clear that, given the apparent stagnation in Indian agriculture and the difficulty of persuading subsistence farmers to part with their produce on the market, American grain was used by Indian planners to avoid the necessity of what they perceived to be fruitless investment in the agricultural sector. The uses of the American stocks varied, of course, from time to time. Clearly, they also varied from country to country. But whatever their uses, most Third World countries are now left largely to their own devices.

What was once done solely through import policy must now be accompanied by effective regulation of national food-grain supplies and markets. This involves the control of price levels, whether for famine, welfare, or antiinflation reasons. Restrictions on the physical movement of grains are likely to be necessary at least where areas of high demand and high income compete with areas of high need and low income for stocks. Stocks will also have to be maintained as reserves for famine and, once established, the system may prove useful for "buffer stock operations" to even out price fluctuations. Finally, given the collapse of income-earning capacity in certain regions due to weather, or within certain classes due to the structure of the economy, it may be advisable to target supplies specifically to the "vulnerable population." Each of these functions will require the development of new institutional capacity by the government. The total cost of this operation is likely to be high, and a number of difficult decisions must be made regarding the allocation of costs and the benefits of the system.

As a first step, it is important to recognize the magnitude of the task at hand. In 1973, Ali Khusro estimated that India required, at minimum, a buffer stock of about 5 million tons a year to provide adequate security.[14] Taking into account procurement costs, handling, storage costs, and storage construction, the total cost for each million tons was calculated to be about $119.6 million in nonrecurring costs and $3.1 million in recurring costs.[15] In fact, a stock of 8 or 9 million tons proved barely adequate to cover the deficits of the seventies. The operative costs of the public-sector Food Corporation of India, which handles these stocks, has proven higher than expected.[16] A careful analysis of the costs of the corporation indicated that for each quintal of grain, purchased at Rs 80, the necessary markup for the corporation was Rs 25, or 31 percent (one rupee equals thirteen cents). Furthermore, the longer a stock was held in reserve, the larger that figure would be. On a stock of 8.9 million tons handled in 1972-73, losses in storage and handling alone were estimated at a value of $28 million. In addition, rising foreign and domestic prices have forced the Government of India to subsidize the operation in the amount of $196.3 million in the same year. In comparison, the entire proposed central government expenditure on agriculture for 1971-73 was $584.2 million. This enormous expenditure and a staff of 38,000 at the central level alone (in many cases, actual procurement and distribution of grain is handled by state-level officials) is the price of a national system of food crisis management.

India's present massive system of food-grain management evolved slowly after the inflationary effects of the Second Five-Year Plan (1956-57 and 1961-62) led to a public outcry against rising prices. At that time, however, the state's role consisted of little more than allocating imported stocks and making the arrangements for their dispatch to the larger cities. Stocks were not maintained against emergencies, no buffer stock operations were attempted to stabilize prices, and there was no serious attempt to use food stocks as a device for economic planning.[17] There were certain left-wing politicians and Planning Commission economists who, even at that time, called for greater control over both imported and domestic stocks, but the flood of U.S. grain relieved the pressure and delayed institutional development for nearly ten years!

It was not until 1964 that the government of India accepted a proposal for the establishment of a central food-grain trading organization (Food Corporation of India), and not until 1968 that the organization became fully operative, with complete control over interstate movement of food grains and sole responsibility for management of imported stocks.

The Food Corporation was but one part of a package of institutional innovations and policy departures undertaken in the period 1960-65. The poor accomplishments of "community"-oriented development programs in the fifties and the growing fear of the economic and political consequences of rising prices persuaded the government to attempt a new strategy aimed at the individual commercial farmer. In this context, the corporation was expected to accomplish its ends through market operations and, if need be, to *support* farm prices in order to provide incentives. From a long-term perspective, it was the surpluses of the good years and not the shortfalls of the bad years that were the problem for the commercial farmer.[18] The latter problem could continue to be managed through imports.

There was already a huge but chaotic public operation in food grains, characterized by a complex set of arrangements between New Delhi and the respective state governments. Most deficit states were badly in debt in their food-grain operations, it was impossible to keep track of stocks, and such internal procurement of grain as did take place was entirely at the whim of the respective governments. Many in Delhi, therefore, perceived that the establishment of an autonomous, compact, and professional state trading organization would improve the situation. With its own capital, its own procurement organization, and its own interstate distribution system, the corporation could reduce costs and confusion. So long as most stocks were in fact imported, this was not a difficult decision to implement.[19]

However, the food crisis of 1967 eliminated any semblance of autonomy for this corporation. Prices, distribution arrangements, and interstate allocations became matters of intense political concern, subject to day-to-day control by the Ministry of Food. Finally, the crisis ended any hope that the corporation might actually establish itself as an independent force in the markets of the surplus states. As in the past, state governments became reluctant to permit external control of their food stocks and preferred to operate as the "agents" of the corporation, maintaining their physical control over procurement.

Moreover, many national-level politicians and administrators were not eager to bear the responsibility of controls. As market prices are disrupted, the functions they perform must be absorbed by administrative agencies. As John Mellor reminds us, these price functions include: adjustment of supply and demand, income distribution, resource allocation, and capital formation.[20] The regulation of the supply of food to one region or section of the population will affect supplies available to other regions and sections. This almost inevitably leads to demand for the extension of government protection to a larger and larger portion of the population. Most importantly, as Myron Weiner reminds us in *The Politics of Scarcity*, once a government enters into controls, like it or not, it does become *responsible* for vagaries of weather and market.[21] The administrative and financial cost of the operation aside, the political cost of failure to meet these responsibilities, once accepted, is enormous. Driven to avoid such failure, governments will be temped to expand their control over the nation's food supplies, both at the production and distribution end of the chain. This, in turn, disrupts existing distribution of functions between public and private sector, threatens existing distributions of political and administrative authority, and adds massively to the bureaucratic weight of government on the citizenry. The sources of political crisis are far broader than the cries of the hunger.

The moment one accepts the inevitability of securing a substantial portion of emergency reserves domestically, the problem of price levels presents itself. Those affected by hunger have little income-earning capacity and cannot pay market prices for food. A subsidy is the obvious answer. But the cost of a subsidy is not to be measured only in budget terms. On the contrary, as Morris D. Morris argues, the real cost is the missed opportunity for alternative investment.[22] Given the difficulty of raising taxes in Third World countries, the transfer payments that relief expenditure represents are not usually transfers from the rich to the poor but from the poor to the poor. Every rupee of relief could have been used toward productive investment elsewhere.

The alternative strategy is to restrict the price the government must pay for the grain in the first place. One method is a statutory levy on all farmers. This has the advantage of increasing the "market surplus," because it operates even on subsistence farmers. Few state governments are willing to accept the administrative cost of such a measure, however, and no one has forgotten the Congress Party defeats in the 1952 elections in areas where this method was employed.[23] If the government decides to buy in the market, however, the presence of such a large buyer will tend to force prices up, to the advantage of the larger farmer who will wait and take advantage of the unusually high prices prevailing after the government has drained the market.[24] In short, one must continually balance political, administrative, and economic costs in selecting a strategy for securing adequate stocks.

In summary, India now has the capacity to secure and store large reserve stocks; it has the capacity to manage a national food-grain budget and interstate allocation system (averaging 7.4 million tons between 1969 and 1972); and above all, it is committed to these tasks as a continuing public function. The cost is high and the system is not free from many difficult problems, but there has been a substantial increase in the institutional capacity of the government. The test of the system in the Bangladesh war proved its utility. Ten million refugees were fed with grain stocks approaching 9 million tons with an efficiency that probably few developed nations could guarantee.[25]

No tropical African government has a comparable capability. Where they exist, state food-marketing agencies appear to lack the purchasing networks, pricing policies, and other means with which to secure large quantities of foodstuffs relative to consumption needs.[26] For example, Kenya's Maize and Produce Marketing Board was charged by statute to ensure adequate supplies of maize through stocking in good years, selling from reserves in lean years at stable prices, and arranging for imports to cover domestic deficits. However, according to Leys, in both the 1965 and 1970-71 droughts, the board proved unequal to these responsibilites. It was unable either to stock sufficiently before the droughts or to prevent illegal exports and a flourishing internal black market during the scarcities.[27]

Kenya has been unusual in tropical Africa for its large grain-storage capacity; its maize-stocking facilities are equal to about a half year's demand.[28] In the other drought-prone states of the region, storage capacity has been very low relative to total consumption needs. Mali, for example, could store about 34,500 metric tons or roughly 4 percent of the expected consumption of the staples sorghum and millet for the 1974-75 crop year.[29] Chad's storage capacity in the same year was estimated at only 11,000 metric tons.[30]

The first and last steps in a food distribution system are the same— identifying the needy. The first step is to correctly identify the start of a crisis and to set in motion the public response mechanisms. The last step in the chain of events is to assure that the food reaches the needy and that the crisis does not destroy their earning capacity. This last point is often missed in discussions of famine. If the diversion of funds is not to continue ad infinitum, it is essential that those affected by crop failure not be forced to sell their land, tools, and animals. Once this happens, the region may take years to recover. The argument is essentially the same if the target group is not those hit by famine, but the historically destitute. The only way out of continued dependence on government is to increase their earning capacity.

Both the identification of crisis and the management of crisis depend, to a large extent, on the degree to which governments have *already* invested in development in the affected regions. Without communication facilities and official penetration of every village, hunger may well become widespread before anyone knows about it. This was the case in Bengal in 1943, where over a million starved, and in the Sahel and Ethiopia in 1973. Deaths in both areas may have numbered in the tens of thousands before their governments became aware of the mass scale of suffering.

One of the first clear indications of a drought crisis received by Ethiopia's central government was the appearance of about 1,500 destitute peasants on the outskirts of the capital city itself.[31] They had left their farms about 200 miles to the north in quest of food. Similarly, Sahelian governments began to suspect a crisis when nomads, their livestock lost, were reported flocking to administrative centers to obtain food and water.[32] In other words, the central governments began to appreciate the situation only *after* crops and animals had been destroyed and food reserves from previous years had been totally consumed. There was apparently little anticipation of the crisis, which could have been done by readying relief stocks so livestock could be saved and farmers permitted to remain in their villages. The lack of anticipation seems condemnable, since rains had been poor in the immediately preceding two or more years. The 1972 rainy season should have been watched with care.

The capacity to monitor was limited, however, by physical and political obstacles to communication between countryside and capital. Jack Shepherd reports that in 1973 eight out of ten Ethiopians "lived a full day's walk from any road."[33] Their needs were represented to the center, if at all, through a feudal-type of governance. In the Sahel, the 1970-73 drought tended to be most severe in northern areas, closer to the desert. Here, communications were poor and the inhabitants were mostly nomads, who, by tradition, avoid contact with governments. In addition, the Sahel's governments, like most in Africa, accorded a low priority to agriculture in their spending programs (see Table 10.8). Hence, they had few cadres in food-producing areas who could develop informed reports on the drought's impact on production.

Yet another factor in the Sahel was the absence of a recent-memory precedent of drought with sufficiently high political costs to make governments wary. Among such costs (which developed during 1973) were thousands of refugees crowding in and around cities and towns, severe losses of export revenues (because of reduced harvests of cash crops and livestock), and numerous starvation deaths blamed on the incumbent elites by their political rivals. The last major drought in the Sahel occurred in 1912-14.[34] In effect, there was no "Bengal famine" (India, 1943) to sensitize central governments to the imperative of preparing for another mass-impact drought. Adequate preparations would have been costly and would have included the development of data-gathering capacities sufficient to assess the food crop and livestock losses, the amounts of food reserves not yet consumed, and the deficits needed to be covered by imports. In the absence of such reasonably valid assessments, external relief sources could not determine how much help was needed. For example, on April 18, 1973, the French Foreign Ministry estimated that the drought-afflicted Sahelian states would require 530,000 tons of emergency food before the end of the crop year. The FAO thought otherwise, announcing on April 20 that the need would be 713,000 tons.[35]

Whatever the correct level, relief arrived too late in 1973 to prevent tens of thousands from dying.[36] It arrived late largely because the process of persuading donors to make commitments and to start shipping began too late. And the tragic delay in this process was due mostly to the Sahelian government's own failure to appreciate the seriousness of the

TABLE 10.8 Percentage of Government Expenditures Allocated to Agriculture[a]

	1963	1964	1965	1966	1967	1968	1969	1970	1971	1972	1973	Average All Years
Kenya	--	17.9[b]	18.1[b]	14.3[b]	12.4[b]	12.5[b]	12.8[b]	11.0	9.0	10.0	12.1	13.0
Malawi	--	8.8	--	10.4	--	12.5	--	--	11.9	15.4	15.4	12.4
Tanzania	13.6[b]	11.8[b]	8.6[b]	8.3	--	--	--	10.2	11.3	9.5	9.9[c]	10.4
Uganda	--	8.1[b]	6.7[b]	8.5[b]	8.0[b]	8.2	6.6	9.5	8.7	--	--	9.1
Ivory Coast	--	--	--	--	--	--	--	8.8[c]	6.3[c]	6.8	8.4[c]	7.6
Ghana	6.4	5.4	8.8	7.5	7.4	6.5	5.3	5.1	4.9	5.6	6.5	6.3
Rwanda	--	--	--	4.6	5.9	5.1	4.9	5.1	4.6	--	--	5.0
Ethiopia	--	--	3.0	2.7	2.8	4.2	--	3.6	5.0[b]	8.7[c]	8.4[c]	4.8
Sierra Leone	--	--	--	--	--	3.6[b]	3.1[b]	4.8[b]	4.9[b]	3.5[b]	7.8[b]	4.6
Liberia	--	--	--	--	--	1.8	1.8	1.5	2.7	3.8	3.8	2.6

Sources: Irving Kaplan, et.al., Area Handbook for Kenya (Washington, D.C., 1976); Kenya, Economic Survey, 1970 (Nairobi, 1970); United Nations, Survey of Economic Conditions in Africa, 1973 (New York, 1974); Harold D. Nelson, et.al., Area Handbook for Malawi (Washington, D.C., 1975); Allison B. Herrick, et.al., Area Handbook for Uganda (Washington, D.C., 1969); Allison B. Herrick, et. al., Area Handbook for Tanzania (Washington, D.C., 1968); Uganda, Statistical Abstract 5 , 1967 (Entebbe, 1967), 1970 (Entebbe, 1970), 1971 (Entebbe, 1971); Ghana, Statistical Yearbook 5 , 1965-66 (Accra, 1969), 1969-70 (Accra, 1973); Bank of Ghana, Annual Report 5 , 1971-72 (Accra, 1973), 1972-73 (Accra, 1974), 1973-74 (Accra, 1975); International Monetary Fund, Survey of African Economies vol. 5 (Washington, D.C., 1973); International Monetary Fund, op. cit. vol. 6 (Washington, D.C., 1975); Irving Kaplan, et.al., Area Handbook for Ethiopia (Washington, D.C., 1971).

[a]Actual recurrent and capital expenditures, unless otherwise indicated.
[b]Fiscal year.
[c]Estimated.

drought. They did not declare a "state of emergency" and make urgent appeals for external aid until March 1973, about four to five months after it should have been clear that the 1972 harvests were extraordinarily poor and the pasture cover woefully inadequate.[37] A similarly tragic time-gap occurred in Ethiopia: severe crop failures occurred in the fall of 1972, but no request was made by the Haile Selassie government for foreign relief assistance until April 1973.[38]

The case was different in India. Having experienced recurring crop failures, and knowing their potentially high human and political costs, the government had invested in elaborate administrative mechanisms to alert it to famine threats and to implement distributive programs. However, even when adequate staff is in place, the task of spotting the crisis is far from easy; the task of identifying the needy in individual terms is almost impossible.

In Sahel and Ethiopia during 1972-74, the governments were late in identifying the crisis and fumbled in distributing relief supplies. They had no "system" that could be activated once the famine threat was identified. With very little "upcountry" food reserves, they had to rely mostly on supplies shipped from abroad and on transportation means that were unsuitable for carrying large quantities of basic foodstuffs inland from ports. Severe bottlenecks developed at ports, along typically single-track railroads leading from ports, and at bridgeless rivers and other natural obstacles. Food spoiled. Other relief supplies were diverted to commercial markets for the profit of local officials.[39]

By late 1974, the high political stakes of mismanaging famine relief became clear. Three civilian governments of drought-stricken countries fell to military coups: those of Upper Volta (in February), Niger (April), and Ethiopia (September). Urban workers protested soaring food prices, student groups blamed government for the suffering of drought victims, and rumors circulated that officials were profiting from sale of relief supplies.[40] Such signs of popular disaffection doubtless encouraged the military in their ambitions and gave them grievances with which to justify their takeovers before national and foreign audiences.

The Politics of Production

Besides developing the institutional capability to distribute large quantities of relief supplies with reasonable efficiency and equity, vulnerable LDCs should follow India's example in trying to engineer increased domestic food production.

In sub-Saharan Africa, food farming has tended to be a seriously neglected sector. According to Table 10.8, the region's governments have spent relatively little on agriculture (even though from 60 to 90 percent of their people have obtained their livelihoods from that sector). Among the ten African countries surveyed, the highest average allocation was only about 13 percent (Kenya), the lowest, 2.6 percent (Liberia), and the median, 7.6 percent. In comparison, the state government of Punjab (India) devoted 11 percent to agriculture in 1974-75, without taking into account federal government expenditure in the state.[41] The expenditure neglect by African governments has meant little research on food crops, weakly staffed extension services for food farming, and inadequate investments in farm-to-market transportation. This last has meant that many areas of potentially significant surpluses are cut off from town consumers and consequently have no incentive to produce in surplus of family and local needs.[42]

What will induce African governments to invest more heavily in food farming, as Indian governments have? Among the persuasive factors may be the 1973-75 famine experiences, the increasing foreign exchange drain from food imports, and the soaring domestic food prices. Between 1970 and 1974, food prices rose by a reported total of 74 percent in Tanzania, 85 percent in Ghana, 102 percent in Zaire, and 145 percent in Uganda.[43]

In the early sixties, India embarked on what was a truly remarkable rural development strategy for an underdeveloped nation. Faced with rampant inflation and rapidly increasing demand for food (both of which threatened to disrupt the entire planning exercise), India opted for a "quick fix." On the advice of the Ford Foundation, the government decided to concentrate its investment in the most favored rural areas in order to maximize incentives to farmers and maximize the marketed surplus.[44] Technical assistance, credit, roads, electricity, and irrigation development were poured into districts (particularly in Punjab and Haryana) with good water supplies and soil fertility, among other advantages. When the new Green Revolution technology appeared, this same investment, particularly credit and irrigation, proved crucial to its adoption by farmers.

In the mid-sixties, a major breakthrough in plant breeding, termed the Green Revolution, permitted the hybridization of wheat and rice. The basis of these new hybrids was the ability to produce a dwarf plant that was very responsive to high applications of fertilizer. Traditional varieties of grains would typically convert the nutrients provided by heavy fertilizer applications into the overall growth of the plant rather than the growth of the grain. Not uncommonly, the resulting increased growth of the traditional varieties would cause the stalks to break, lodging the grain on the ground, and resulting in heavy crop losses. In these circumstances, the biological capacity for intensifying grain production simply did not exist, and a technological barrier existed to increased food production. The new hybrids, being genetically dwarf, absorbed increased nutrients in the grain, removing the constraint and permitting efficacious use of heavy dosages of fertilizer.

The new varieties were "revolutionary" in two senses. Of course, the genetic breakthrough was a discovery of major importance. In terms of farming techniques, however, the new varieties were not dramatically different from traditional varieties; only the results were. It was certainly not uncommon to double or treble yields by shifting from the old to the new varieties. This dramatic increase in farm yields and, therefore, in farm income was what made the new varieties truly revolutionary. Several consequences followed from this production breakthrough. First, a revolution occurred in thinking about the problem of agriculture. Farmers who were presumed to be hopelessly backward and conservative by government planners suddenly switched to these highly profitable seeds, thus demonstrating the potential dynamism of peasants when offered a workable technology. This, in turn, provided an opportunity for new investment in the rural sector to provide public support for the "revolution." Second, the new technology worked effectively only with plenty of fertilizer and plenty of water. In consequence, the capital outlay of farmers (for wells) and the production expenditures (for seed and fertilizer) increased rapidly, as did their risks. This in turn put pressure on governments to assist the revolution through the provision of credit, stabilization of market prices, and investment in rural infrastructure. Third, the new varieties proved very prone to disease compared with traditional varieties, and the rice, in particular, was very sensitive to variations in climate and growing conditions. These developments necessitated a heavy public investment in agricultural research (and extension) to protect the "revolution" from genetic failures.

Even at the time, however, some were cautious about the potential of this revolution. The success of the technology depended on heavy fertilizer imports. Many developing nations lacked governmental systems capable of maintaining the administrative and research support to sustain the highly vulnerable technology. Nevertheless, most observers assumed that the world's food problems had been solved. Today we are less optimistic.

In India, the application of Green Revolution technology to favored rural areas proved to be an unqualified success. However, it has meant that eight districts with 0.31 percent of India's cultivated area used 11.4 percent of the nation's fertilizer.[45] On the more extensive and effective use of fertilizer rests the key to increasing rural incomes in the Third World.

It was generally recognized that this strategy was one beset with enormous risk since it placed the future in such a restricted geographical region and in two crops.[46] Many argued that smaller investment spread over wider areas would produce greater aggregate yield. These arguments did not prevail, largely because of the uncertainty of farmers' responses in the more backward areas. In many ways, the gamble paid off, and Punjab and Haryana can now stock 65 percent of the buffer stock. Yet, although this eased some of the government's problems, it increased others. Nothing was done to reduce interregional income disparity; in fact, disparity grew. Nor was anything done to reduce the probability of crop disasters in less favored regions, which were neglected. It is not enough that governments give more attention to agriculture; they must be concerned with the pattern of that investment.

Greater investment in agriculture is hardly a difficult principle to sell if a nation is close enough to the margin of survival. Unfortunately, the distribution of the costs of such investment still remain to be decided. In most countries of the Third World, and especially in India, agricultural taxes are very low and very regressive. Yet, rural incomes have been rising, and at least some have derived enormous benefits from public investment. Faced with rising prices and high income taxes, urban interests are not likely to take kindly to rural public investment without correcting these inequities.[47]

In India, the emergence of the commercial farmer—encouraged by the policies of the sixties—has coincided with precipitous increase in government demands in the form of taxes, fees, price controls, etc.[48] This has led to the development, in the early seventies, of the embryos of farm lobbies in several states.[49] Such farm interests were strikingly absent in the decision-making process of the sixties. It is not that caste and language have disappeared as rural issues. Rather, these appeals are no longer sufficient to win support without sensitivity to the interests and demands of the commercial farming population. In various areas, these farm interests receive further strength from local government systems, cooperatives, and even the new agricultural universities.

Large landed interests had always been a political force in the subcontinent, but post-independence land reforms virtually eliminated the landlord class as a political force in many areas of India. Democratic elections then brought the middle farmers into increasing political prominence: first in the state legislatures, then in the state executives, and finally, by the late sixties, in New Delhi. Although it was never very effective at the national level, the "farm block" formed one of the components of resistance to the "leftist" policies of Indira Gandhi in the early seventies. Farm power in the states proved an effective buffer to those policies, as programs of further land reform, rural tax reform, and small farmer development were ground to a halt. It was evident that the progressive farm community felt that these new impositions were threats to their newly acquired prosperity and opportunities for social mobility. In Punjab, farm organizations attempted (unsuccessfully as it turned out) to disrupt government procurement operations. In Gujerat, farm disaffection contributed to the embarrassing defeat of the Congress Party in the 1975 elections—just before the declaration of emergency. In most states, the major institutions serving the rural sector—land development banks, marketing federations, primary credit cooperatives—have all come to be controlled by the farming castes and represent an important base for rural political organization. The *organized* farmer is now a force to be reckoned with in India. The reader should not assume that this "organization" is as yet as formalized and national in scope as, let us say, the American Farm Bureau Federation. Nevertheless, a revolution has occurred in that at least some sections of India's farm community can and do demand changes in policy and improvements in public services to serve their interests.

It might be expected that the food crisis will encourage rural investment but shatter the old alliance of urban and rural elites. A heavily regulated urban sector will no longer accept a virtually unregulated rural sector once growth spreads to the farms. In the rhetoric leading up to the Indian political crisis of 1975, it was evident that the "capitalist" farmer had replaced the "feudal" landlord as the target of the urban left. Similar rhetoric appeared in Kenya, when African "big farmers" replaced European landholders after the country's independence in 1963.

As Table 10.8 indicates, Kenya's government has ranked among the highest in Africa in terms of the spending priority accorded to agriculture. However, the flow of services (extension, production, and land-purchase credit) tended to favor large-scale farmers.[50] As of 1966, there were reportedly about 750 farms, averaging 800 acres, owned by African civil servants, politicians, and others.[51] Although much of the favored position of larger farms relative to government services may have been due to political connections, another factor (equally or more weighty) was those farms' capacity to utilize credit and other inputs. A study in Kenya's Nyeri district found a correlation between farmers' progressiveness on this dimension and their receipt of government services.[52] Moreover, whatever greater rural inequality government policies did promote may have had only minor political impact. Bienen notes that Kenya's former opposition party made little headway with this issue.[53] One reason appears to be that many large holdings are in fact owned jointly by groups of persons. Another is that owners tended to settle numerous relatives on their land.[54]

No response by the Third World nations that ignores these equity questions will be meaningful, for it is the destitute who represent the reality of the world food crisis. Dandekar and Rath presented the dilemma clearly.[55] In 1960-61, they report that 40 percent of India's rural population and 50 percent of her urban population lived *below* a consumption level of one-half a rupee a day. In the eight-year period (1960-61 to 1967-68) they examined, net national product more than doubled. Yet consumer expenditure increased by only 4.8 percent. Were this to continue, they argue, "The gulf between the rich and the poor will widen intolerably and inevitably undermine the democratic foundations of the economy." This aspect of the global food crisis will test the will and ingenuity of planners, administrators, and, above all, politicians. We must be able to design a development plan that will direct a greater proportion of the growth in national income to the poor and a choice of technology that will provide them with productive employment. John Lewis has called for a "relevant radicalism"— radical in its departure from existing growth strategies.[56] Too few planners have taken the advice.[57]

A model is emerging of how to handle this sort of crisis. It takes the form of increased agricultural productivity, sparked by public investment in technology and overhead. The consequent increase in farm income stimulates demand, which is then met by expanding small-scale consumer goods industries in smaller towns, close to their market. This in turn, it is hoped, will absorb the excess labor supply— productively. Rising income will hopefully slow population growth, but will also increase demand for food grains. These, in turn, must be supplied by an increasingly productive *domestic* agriculture. There are variations on the structure of this theme, but the basic bones are recognizable.[58] The Punjab is an area that fits the new development model. Double cropping has increased demand for labor, and rising demand has expanded employment opportunities in the small towns.

In many areas, however, the model faces serious institutional obstacles. Where "feudal" landlords are still the rule, land reform and other redistributive measures may be needed. Most of the existing rural institutions may have to be reformed or bypassed, because they have been largely captured by local elites, who are not inclined to use them productively.

The widespread "failure" of local participatory institutions in India requires some explanation. The scene is by no means a total disaster. In Gujerat state, for example, cotton-marketing cooperatives have proven highly effective and progressive. The credit cooperatives in Punjab appear to have been viable and to have made credit available even to small farmers if they were able to grow the new high-yielding dwarf varieties. Nevertheless, it is true that the rural institutions in the subcontinent have been a disappointment. There are essentially three explanations for this phenomenon. First, in areas where the new technology is unsuited, agriculture is still stagnant. There has not been enough economic pressure to divert local institutions from their traditional preoccupation with distributing patronage to the task of undertaking effective developmental roles. Second, in areas with highly unequal landholding sizes, politics is dominated by patron-client relations. The small farmer is dependent on the larger farmer and cannot bring effective pressure to bear for more widespread dispersion of needed inputs, such as credit, water, and fertilizer. The benefits, if any, tend to be highly concentrated among the few politically powerful "bosses." Third, even in technically dynamic areas with fairly equitable landholding patterns, the local institutions can be rendered ineffective if badly designed. This was certainly the case with local governments in both India and Pakistan, where indirect elections favored elite control in local bodies, and confusion and overloading of functions inhibited accountability. The combined effect of these technological, social, and institutional problems has tended to hamstring government efforts.

Finally, state administrators are often as reluctant to accept innovations as rural elites. This need not be because they are part of the "establishment," but may be because new departures threaten established bureaucratic power structures. Certainly, the Ford Foundation encountered this kind of resistance in trying to implement a program that would have directly benefited rural elites.[59] This suggests that national governments may have to risk classic "redistributive" radicalism in certain regions if the way is to be opened for new investment and new technology. This being the case, class issues are likely to dominate politics at the margin. The effects of this conflict and a way out of the crisis can be found with a combination of political skill and an adequate development model, but success is far from guaranteed. Let us look at three sets of basic decisions that must be made and at the factors that inhibit adequate responses.

(1) The greatest problem of an economic crisis is that it tends to encourage a concentration on the short-term responses, to the detriment of *long-term structural changes*. This is especially true where the crisis is

viewed as a temporary aberration. A recognition of the permanence of the food crisis and the corollary need for major structural changes is a first requisite of adjustment to the crisis. It is probably true that nothing short of pressure from urban consumers will produce the incentives for policy changes. On the other hand, extractive policies may well substitute for investment and rural structural change if the urban elite is too powerful.[60] Conversely, if rural elites prevail, solutions will be sought in higher agricultural prices, mechanization, and expanding farm size. These changes will increase the marketed surplus and farm incomes, but worsen the conditions of a growing portion of the rural community. Neither of these solutions resembles the labor-intensive, consumer-goods strategy outlined in the previous section. The difficulty is that in most developing countries, it is difficult to imagine the appearance of a coalition of political forces that might produce such a policy.

A labor-intensive strategy of development requires several policy innovations. First, it requires that the small farm, which tends to be more productive per acre, use labor more intensively than the large farm. Mere food shortage is not likely to persuade a government to risk a radical land reform especially when faced with the present economic and political power of landed interests. This means that the single structural change that could absorb the most rural labor is precluded. There are undoubtedly alternative ways of influencing farm size—tax and inheritance policy, for example. But lack of administrative capacity and lack of any clear predictions as to side effects of alternatives tend to eliminate the small farm option, even if the political will exists.

The other major source of employment opportunities would appear to be small consumer-goods industries. This solution is inhibited by a lack of appropriate technology, ideological mistrust of "capitalist solutions" in some areas, urban elites' preoccupation with imported luxury goods, and lack of a dynamic rural sector to provide a market for these goods. In addition to these problems, the small manufacturers' sector faces strong, if not overwhelming, competition when seeking government assistance—from heavy industry (supported by international investment), primary commodities development (sustaining food and luxury goods investment), and the growing vested interest of a farmer-dominated cooperative sector (as in India) which benefits from a monopoly of many of the services that would give the small-scale private sector a boost. Clearly, there are many more effective claims on public resources than the needs of small industry and market towns. Only a program of public works, with support from landed interests and contractors, promises to be a politically popular labor-absorbing one.

The farm community will be able to resist urban exploitation, on the one hand, and increasing concentrations of rural economic power on the other, only if reasonably broad-based rural political participation is encouraged. This may be accomplished by substantial decentralization to local governments, a mass-based party structure, or through lobby activities by broadly-based farm organization.[61] One way or another, it must be done. Unfortunately, such structures are often a threat to national or regional leaders, local elites, and to bureaucratic power—a formidable list of adversaries. In India, the power of the local government (*panchayats*) and autonomy of the cooperatives have been steadily eroded in most states. In 1974, for example, in Gujerat state, no elected governments at any level remained functioning. In the same year in Punjab state, both the apex cooperative bank and the apex cooperative marketing society faced delays of over two years in elections to their governing boards due to a combination of fiscal and political difficulties. Pakistan is still without functioning rural local governments, although the Bhutto regime has been considering the matter for four years. Yet, broad-based rural political participation would appear to be essential to a proper balance of rural development policies and socially optimal results.

However necessary for effective development over the long run, such participation may appear in the short-term to be too risky politically. The rhetoric of Tanzania's program for socialist rural development—*ujamaa*—calls for broad popular involvement in government.[62] A 1972 reform significantly increased the powers of local government at the expense of central ministries. However, one field study suggests that the farmers themselves have had very little influence on policy choices.[63] Another source concurs: "[The] practical effect of the decentralization policies pursued since 1967 has been to concentrate decision-making power in the hands of administrators, technicians, and political commissioners at Regional and District levels."[64] The problem may derive from the radical nature of the ruling party's rural development strategy, the opposition it has encountered, and the government's unwillingness to give its many farmer opponents formal means to influence policy. The strategy has been to communalize agriculture, and it has been strongly opposed by commercial farmers, who feel threatened with loss of income, and by poorer peasants, who object to being resettled away from traditional land in new communal villages.[65] As long as much of the clientele is hostile to its policy purposes, the governments of Tanzania and other countries pursuing transformationist strategies may repress grassroots participation. The hostility need not be long-lasting, particularly if, after trial and error, the strategy proves economically successful.[66]

The other factor that appears to be essential to restructuring the rural sector is public investment in agricultural research. It is widely recognized now that a steady program of agricultural technology is essential to rural modernization and to reducing production costs while increasing yields.[67] For many small nations, the cost of building educational institutions and research centers will be high, and there may be advantages to internationalization. But one way or another, relevant research must be encouraged. Politically, this is probably easier than institutional reform, since much of the current development will be funded by international sources in any case. Furthermore, technical education and research are usually matters within the control of the national elite. One can be reasonably optimistic about the future in this area.

(2) The second set of strategic decisions to be made by developing nations as they begin to consider restructuring the rural sector to handle the emerging food crises arises in defining the *proper relationship between the public and the private sector.* This involves decisions about the control of land, the manufacture and distribution of inputs, and the control of the grain trade. A related set of decisions involves the development of regulatory policies—on crops, prices, input packaging, and marketing. The former set of decisions, regarding nationalization, are typically made on ideological grounds and not on the basis of any particular theory of rural development. The latter decisions, regarding regulatory activity, are usually dictated by the extent to which policy is dominated by governmental purposes. In neither case does the preference, convenience, or efficiency of the farm community appear to be the primary consideration in the decision making.

In Indian Punjab, for example, a "crop loan system" specifies the "package" of inputs to be used on the specified crop. Both the loan and the inputs are supplied through the state cooperative system.[68] Yet, analysis of the production functions of farmers finds no appreciable difference in the efficiency with which fertilizer is used among farmers relying on the co-ops and those relying on the private sector. Some studies suggest that those following the official advice operate less efficiently.[69] In Pakistan Punjab, farmers preferred the larger and more expensive diesel pumps for their tubewells in the mid-sixties, because government regulation of electricity made the more efficient electric pumps too difficult to install.[70] For years in India—until 1965 in fact—food-grain procurement prices were set without the slightest attempt to calculate the actual cost of production.[71] Extension services act more often as the conduits of official policy than as service agents for the farmer; this has been true in India, Pakistan, Tanzania, and presumably many other LDCs. These examples are not given to suggest that these decisions have been either entirely pointless or wholly detrimental to farm interests—merely to show that farm preferences typically took a back seat to government needs.

The basic problem here is twofold. First, policymakers have often failed to treat the farmer seriously—as a rational, profit-oriented producer for whom considerations of efficiency are of some significance. This is reflected in the lack of concern for adequate profit incentives. When a government must control and regulate, it is usually bureaucratic convenience and efficiency rather than farmers that dictate the choice of institutional arrangements and the form of the regulations. Finally, when restrictions have been imposed, too little attention has been paid to finding a mode of enforcement that might contribute mutually to the interests of both government and farmer. There are examples of useful arrangements, but they are all too rare. Punjab's management agency (MARKFED) exchanges support for harvest season prices for an effective governmental monopoly of wholesale marketing. The Gujerat government trades strict crop and movement controls over the cotton crop for equally strict, publicly regulated quality control that improves farm prices.[72]

Far more common are the institutional failures. To assure maximum production rather than maximum profits, extension services have frequently been used to encourage farmers to employ more chemical fertilizer than the farmers found profitable. There are even reports of extension officers being ordered to require farmers to take complex fertilizers they neither wanted nor needed in order to remove stocks that had been overproduced by the factories. This type of professional advice to the farmer clearly weakens the effectiveness of the extension service. Cooperative societies have often been treated as administrative agencies of the government. They are asked to procure food grains for government stocks at very low profit margins. They are employed to enforce the use of certain technology packages favored by the government. In fact, governments have often preferred heavily bureaucratized systems of market management rather than reliance on the efficacy of free market mechanisms, because direct physical control over the crop was more amenable to traditional bureaucratic procedures than free market manipulations. The inability of developing nations to implement policies in the field and the high administrative costs that are frequently incurred are all too often due to a failure to reconcile the valid interests of the farmer with the public interests of the government in new and more efficient and reciprocal institutional arrangements.

Finally, politicians desiring control and administrators desiring effective "integration" of policy are far too likely to encourage the concentration of governmental power in the rural areas. Where a substantial portion of key inputs do end up in the public sector, this, in turn, means a concentration of control of inputs also. It is only slowly that India has learned the cost of this policy.[73] It has slowly become evident that services must be institutionally differentiated if specific rural groups are to be targeted. It has also become evident that, in general, differentiation of functions and multiple channels of access to key inputs and services may reduce access costs to the farmer and provide greater flexibility to him in adjusting his combination of inputs.[74] For example, given the additional administrative and political complications of using cooperative credit, it may not be attractive to all farmers. On the other hand, the existence of extensive cooperative credit undoubtedly has an impact on the private money lenders' rates of interest, level of services, and so on. Farmers can be expected to take advantage of these differences in decisions about borrowing.

As nations are compelled by food shortages to take agriculture more seriously, they will be forced, many for the first time, to think much more seriously about the impact of their administrative procedures, institutional patterns, and regulatory policies on the rural sector. Most will lack information, experience, and training in evaluating these impacts.

(3) *International relations* will continue to play a vital role in the strategy employed by Third World nations in their attempts to handle the food crisis. They constitute the third area of strategic decisions for these countries. Small nations and those in recurrent drought situations will continue to be dependent on international reserve stocks. The major grain-exporting nations can help to provide security to enable these states to risk radical departures in policy and high investment rates in order to transform their agricultural sectors.

Imported chemical fertilizer will also continue to be a vital component of any development strategies. Luckily, it now appears that the fertilizer shortages of the past few years have been rectified. New production capacity will ensure ample supplies, at least for the next decade.[75] Nevertheless, fertilizer imports will continue to absorb vital foreign exchange. For a few countries (those with adequate export markets), food imports may remain a viable alternative, but, even for these states, some stabilization of international commodity prices would appear essential to planned development.

The continuation of an import strategy despite rising international grain prices is, of course, a very restricted solution, not generally available. Furthermore, whether the grain is supplied on commercial terms or as relief supplies under bilateral or international agreements, grave political risks are involved in such dependence. Pakistan and India both felt the pressure from the United States when aid was manipulated to bring a stop to the 1965 war. With the United States supplying most of its fertilizer, Pakistan must be well aware of the intimate connection between the success of its agricultural programs and American views on its nuclear program. American agro-power may seem puny when applied to the Soviet Union, but in the Third World, dependence is very costly. This last statement should be treated with caution. We have stressed throughout that food strategies are the result of a complex set of demands and that there are alternatives available to developing nations. The costs of dependence are not necessarily determining—they are weighted against alternative costs. Similarly, in encouraging or discouraging import dependence, the United States should keep in mind its complex goals as well. When used carefully and targeted accurately, food imports can still be used to encourage job creation and to control inflation in the Third World. We have moved from a situation in which our food aid policies were dictated largely by our desire to unload our own large surpluses to one in which we must consider food stocks (like fertilizer, capital, technology, or military aid) as a scarce resource.

We can do much to encourage greater production in the Third World, the most important contribution being the use of our vast technical capacity to help solve the complex technological problems of tropical agriculture.[76] We should recognize, however, that, whereas development may help to keep population growth under control, it will also alter diets in the direction of more nourishing but less efficient uses of grain— meat, processed foods, milk, etc.[77] This reality suggests that poverty and inequality both will continue to be at the forefront of international politics in the Third World for some time, regardless of any likely level of "success" in rural development.

Domestic Political Constraints

It would be useful now to summarize briefly some of the domestic political factors that may inhibit or influence solutions to the food crises in Third World countries. Characteristically, seven dimensions of political conflict surround the food crisis.

First, and perhaps most severe in the initial stages, are interregional conflicts. Except in small countries, the crisis is seldom uniformly distributed geographically. Typically, rural growth increases inter-regional differences.[78] Planned investment tends to take place in those areas that promise the most return. Hard-pressed governments typically find the problems of the better endowed regions technically and administratively easier to resolve. In consequence, both efficiency and the national interest seem to conspire to increase inequality. There is certainly some evidence of this in India, where the Ford Foundation encouraged intensive investment in the best areas for a "quick fix" of the food shortage.

Where geographical cleavages also correspond with ethnic and cultural differences, the redistribution of the gains of growth is even more difficult. The Sahel offers a good example where governmental neglect was largely responsible for the severity of the food crisis there. Clearly the ethnic divisions between the pastoralists and the farming-town populations on which the region's governments were based contributed to the inadequacy of governmental responses. Even otherwise effective development programs, as in India, may shut ethnic minorities out of the benefits. In India, as elsewhere, tribal groups have not fared well at the hands of the majority population.

Investments based on the comparative advantage or superior resource base of a given region are therefore reasonable policy decisions where ethnic homogeneity or a responsive political structure can provide alternatives or transfer payments to the marginal areas. Where such political mechanisms fail, however, growing tension, conflict, and even separatism may result. In this case, the current attention of the international aid agencies to the poorest of the poor in the developing world may be good political economy. Additional resources, new technologies, and foreign pressure are provided to assist the needed transfer payments.

The second issue involves the character of rural politics. In most Third World countries, rural politics have become the politics of faction and patronage since independence. Rural politics depend, then, on the distribution of favors to clients. Political struggles are for a piece of a very small pie, and, short of the negative power of rural elites to prevent reform, rural influence is frequently dissipated in this factional struggle.[79] This may provide the explanation of why nations with such a large rural population can spend so little on the development of that sector. These rural coalitions of factions may break down as poverty increases, and we may well see the emergence of class politics in the villages. For the present, however, the inability of farmers, save in the most progressive areas, to articulate their economic interests in competition with the rural elites and the urban sector is a fact of life in most Third World nations.

Emerging class conflict is a third component of the emerging poverty in the Third World. In the past, rural social units—villages, tribes, and estates—stood against the hostile outside world. Throughout the Third World, a growing market orientation, combined with increasing population pressure, have destroyed the solidarity. One need not assume that this traditional solidarity was necessarily benign, but it was real. In areas experiencing growth, however, customary ties collapse and rural tension is common. For the first time in many countries, opportunities have appeared for political leaders to win support from the rural poor, who can no longer be controlled by their patrons.[80]

A growing class consciousness among the farm population will, of course, have a mixed effect. On the one hand, it may encourage governments to pay more attention to the agricultural sector, which, in the long run, is probably beneficial. On the other hand, the growing threat of a restive rural poor does not generally incline landowners toward "socially progressive" policies. Curiously enough, redistributive solutions to rising rural poverty make the most sense in those countries that face the least serious resource constraints. In India and Bangladesh, there are undoubtedly areas that might benefit from land redistribution, but in areas like Punjab, one could not redistribute further without endangering production. In the final analysis, there is simply not enough land to go around. The growing class conflict in rural areas will undoubtedly mean increased political participation, but its significance will depend on the overall resource situation and how that participation is structured.

The fourth element of the emerging political crisis is the role of technology. In the early part of this century in India, manufactured consumer goods destroyed a whole class of village artisans.[81] Today in some areas, resumption of cultivation and mechanization may be destroying a class of tenant farmers. Pakistan is a good example,[82] as is Ethiopia. Cohen observed in Ethiopia that a rural development program targeted at small farmers had the unintended consequence of dispossessing many of them. Through a demonstration effect, large landowners outside the project area adopted the improved seeds and use of fertilizers that proved successful in the project. Finding that these inputs made mechanization financially feasible and that, with machinery, they could dispense with tenant farmers, owners drove "thousands of tenants" off the land.[83] The tenants who remained found their rent rising and the prices of land climbing out of reach, despite their own higher incomes from Green Revolution inputs. Another unfortunate side effect may be a dramatic increase in the numbers of very small farms, as an expanding population, a land constraint, and a more productive technology combine to constrict the assets available to the poorest.[84]

To the contrary, there is now good evidence that technological innovation tends to economize on limiting factors in the production process. Sometimes the limiting factor is labor, as in the United States, or land, as in Japan. But, as Polanyi reminded us in *The Great Transformation*, these technical changes almost always help to speed up changes in social relationships, with associated changes in power relationships.[85]

Some questions have been raised about the negative impacts of technology. First, there appear to be no particular economies of scale in the new technology. Whether, in fact, operational holdings increase in size and tenancy disappears depends on a number of factors. Among them are the initial degree of inequality of holding sizes, the extent of supporting services to small operators available from the government, the availability of a stable water supply, and the flexibility of existing tenancy arrangements. In most areas, the new technology has been labor-deepening and has forced agricultural wages up. Whether this is an advantage to the poor or not depends on other factors. A tradition of payment of wages in kind rather than cash will permit workers to share in the increased productivity and rising prices. If off-farm employment is available, workers may, in fact, combine their high peak-season wages (which the new prosperity permits farmers to pay) with additional earnings in the slack season. Rising prosperity in the farm sector may, in fact, encourage the development of localized business investment to provide those jobs. Ultimately, the logic of the argument was based on the increasing gap between the (large) landowners and the rest of the rural population (tenants and laborers), a gap widened by the increased productivity of land. One's reaction to this argument depends on how one evaluates the political impact of the increasing gap compared with the significance of a rapidly growing real income. There have undoubtedly been tensions and conflicts in the regions affected by the Green Revolution. But the experience of ten years suggests that progress has been sufficient to contain them.

Intragovernmental and intergovernmental problems constitute the fifth aspect of political change. The integration of agriculture in the national economy has a profound influence on government administration. Technical bureaucracies expand and create tension with old-guard, law-and-order ministries and traditional, generalist civil servants.[86] The scale of social organization adjusts to the broadened interdependence of rural communities. Local leaders often become unresponsive to the needs of villagers unless they play a new brokerage role, and this dramatically alters authority relationships in rural areas.[87] New levels of government and administration emerge to correspond to the changing scale and functions of government. This, in turn, exacerbates problems of center-periphery conflict. These questions may be so serious as to virtually stalemate rural institutional development, as they have done in Pakistan recently.[88]

It could be argued that the success of the rural transformation, and, hence, the response to the food crisis, depend on the transformation of rural governance structures. In most cases, efficient allocation of public goods such as roads, irrigation facilities, and educational facilities can only be made by effective local authorities. Certainly, the maintenance of these goods and services depends on such decentralization. Of course, centralized control is necessary for sector-wide policies such as pricing, import/export decisions, and credit. Effective mobilization of the collective self-help capacities of the rural population demands considerable initiative in devising and encouraging new economic structures, such as water users' associations and cooperative societies. In short, collective decision making capacities are being expanded at the local level. For administrators and nationalist leaders who may view power as a zero-sum game, the self-help decisions on the local level are particularly difficult. Furthermore, the discretionary power invested in local institutions is not provided without some risk of wastage, corruption, and misallocation. A local base for opposition may also be inadvertently created. Drawing the lines of authority is not easy, and new institutions have frequently failed because it was inadequately done. But the organization of public authority at the local level is a major variable in the development process.

The sixth political dimension of the food crisis involves international dependency. Few Third World nations have the political capacity or resources to transform the rural sector without assistance. Yet as the Russian-American conflict spreads now to Africa and Latin America, as well as Asia, the costs of dependency become clearer. We have seen the frustration of the Third World leaders in the Cocayoc Declaration and in other international gatherings.[89] In the past, aid bought time and provided external resources for elites so they did not have to mobilize domestically. But as the crisis deepens, time runs out and poverty (in all but a few politically favored states) grows faster than external assistance. It seems unlikely that dependence will be an alternative to domestic reform for many nations much longer. More important, however, is the fact that, unless the nation in question has the technical, administrative, and political strength and skill to manage the relationship, dependence may well distort policy and institutional development as badly as colonialism did.

Seventh, and finally, ideological questions must play an important role in the solution to each nation's part of the global food crisis. Insofar as "ideology" means a model of the future (in this sense we should use Mannheim's "utopia," although our use is consistent with Geertz's)[90] and a broad strategy for the role of government in bringing that future into existence, one should perhaps encourage it. Many nations, including those of the West, have been content to deal with problems in ad hoc fashion and to let the future take care of itself. This seems unwise if the emerging global crisis is anywhere near as serious as the doomsayers suggest. The key problem identified by the Club of Rome, in political terms, is the inability of the future to place demands on the present.[91] All decision makers discount heavily distant events in time. The result is that events often catch us by surprise. Another key problem is identified by Garnett Hardin as the "commons" problem.[92] Expendable resources, or those that may be overtaxed, are poorly managed if responsibility and benefits are separated. This classic problem of political economy—the failure to secure collective goals—is becoming more frequently evident. Practical management and philo-sophical wisdom have never been more needed in directing the power of government.

Notes

1. Romesh Dutt, *The Economic History of India in the Victorian Age, 1837-1900*, vols. 1 and 2 (New Delhi: Government of India, 1963). These books give lucid descriptions of the economic history of India during the British regime.

2. Tetteh A. Kofi, "Peasants and Economic Development: Populist Lessons for Africa," *The African Studies Review* 20, no. 3 (December 1977):91-119.

3. John P. Lewis, *Quiet Crisis in India: Economic Development and American Policy* (Washington, D.C.: Brookings Institution, 1961). See also Wilfred Malenbaum, *Prospects for Indian Development*, (Glencoe: Free Press, 1962).

4. These rough percentages are derived from data on food aid shipments of two major kinds: those under Title I of Public Law 480, which provides for sales on concessional terms (twenty to forty years for repayment, low interest rates) and those under Title II of the act, which provides for grants. The data for Title I shipments were given for calendar years as follows: 1972, about 6 million metric tons; 1973, 3 million; and 1974, 1.2 million. Title II figures were given for fiscal years as follows: 1972, 2.5 million metric tons; 1973, 2.1 million; and 1974, 1.4 million. Sources: U.S., Congress, *1973 Annual Report on Public Law 480* (House Document no. 93-362, Washington, D.C., 1973), pp. 8, 50; and "The Annual Report on Activities Carried Out under Public Law 480, 83rd Congress, as Amended, during the Period January 1 through December 31, 1974" (preliminary draft, Agency for International Development, 1975), pp. 1, 95.

5. Theodore W. Schultz, "Value of U.S. Farm Surplus to Underdeveloped

Countries," *Journal of Farm Economics* 42 (December 1960):1028-29 and "Don't Feed the Starving Millions: Food Aid is Damaging to the Countries Which Receive it," *Economist*, September 28, 1968, pp. 60-1; Melvin Burke, "Does 'Food for Peace' Assistance Damage the Bolivian Economy?" *Inter-American Economic Affairs* 25 (Summer 1971):9. For a balanced review of the anti-food aid arguments, see Clifford R. Kern, "Looking a Gift Horse in the Mouth: The Economics of Food Aid Programs," *Political Science Quarterly* 83 (March 1968):59-75.

   6. U.S., Department of Agriculture, Economic Research Service, *The World Food Situation and Prospects to 1985* (Washington, D.C., 1974), pp. 81-83.

   7. The twenty-eight countries in question were ones for which both FAO and USDA per-capita food production estimates were available. See Table 10.1 for specific bibliographic references.

   8. Cited by Donald Heisel, "Food and Population in Africa," *Current History*, June 1975, p. 261.

   9. Ethiopia, Ghana, Guinea, Kenya, Mali, Niger, Nigeria, Senegal, and Upper Volta. Agency for International Development, *Special Report to the Congress on the Drought Situation in Sub-Saharan Africa* (Washington, D.C., 1975), pp. 17-44.

   10. Ethiopia, Ghana, Mali, Nigeria, and Senegal. See the sources listed in Table 10.1.

   11. See the entries for those eight countries in the following sources: U.S., Department of Agricultural Service, *Foreign Agriculture Circular: Reference Tables on Wheat, Corn, and Total Coarse Grains Supply-Distribution for Individual Countries* (Washington, D.C., 1976), and *Foreign Agriculture Circular: Reference Tables on Rice Supply-Distribution for Individual Countries* (Washington, D.C., 1976).

   12. Wilfred Malenbaum, "Scarcity: Prerequisite to Abundance," *Annals of the American Academy of Political Science* 420 (July 1975):76.

   13. During the decade of the sixties, imports of grain averaged 7.7 percent of India's domestic production, for example. More to the point, these imports represented 20.4 percent of the *marketed* supply of grain. See V. S. Vyas and S. C. Bandyopadhyay, "National Food Policy in the Framework of a National Food Budget," *Economic and Political Weekly*, March 1975, pp. A2-A13.

   14. John Moore et. al., *Indian Foodgrain Marketing* (New Delhi: Institute of Economic Growth, 1973), pp. 18-26.

   15. The data following on operating costs come from *Report of the Committee on Cost of Handling of Foodgrains by Food Corporation of India* (New Delhi: Government of India, 1974), pp. 23, 40-41.

   16. These dollar figures were converted from rupees at the official exchange rate then prevailing—one rupee equals thirteen cents.

   17. N. K. Nicholson, "The Politics of Food Policy in India," *Pacific Affairs* no. 1 (Spring 1968):34-39.

   18. The basic document in this change was the Ford Foundation report *India's Food Crisis and Steps to Meet It* (New Delhi: Ministry of Food and Agriculture and Ministry of Community Development and Cooperation, 1959). Regarding price policy, two subsequent reports indicate clearly the direction of

thinking in the Government of India: *Agricultural Price Policy in India* (New Delhi: Directorate of Economics and Statistics, Ministry of Food and Agriculture, 1966), and *Report of the Foodgrains Policy Committee* (New Delhi: Department of Food, 1966). In agricultural policy the innovations are presented in *Modernizing Indian Agriculture* (New Delhi: Ministry of Food, Agriculture, Community Development, and Cooperation, 1969). See also N. K. Nicholson, *Rural Development Policy in India: Elite Differentiation and the Decision Making Process* (DeKalb, Ill.: Center for Governmental Studies, Northern Illinois University, 1974); D. Brown, *Agricultural Development in India's Districts* (Cambridge: Harvard University Press, 1971).

19. This interpretation was derived from extensive interviews by Nicholson in India in 1974 with officers and politicians involved in making the decision or in its early implementation.

20. John Mellor, "The Functions of Agricultural Prices in Economic Development," in *Comparative Experience of Agricultural Development in Developing Countries of Asia and the South-East Since World War II* (Bombay: Indian Society of Agricultural Economics, 1971), pp. 122-40.

21. M. Weiner, *The Politics of Scarcity* (Chicago: University of Chicago Press, 1962), chap. 9.

22. Morris D. Morris, "What is a Famine," *Economic and Political Weekly,* Nov. 2, 1974, p. 885; Morris D. Morris, "Needed: A New Famine Policy," *Economic and Political Weekly,* February 1975, p. 283. See also N. S. Jodha, "Famine and Famine Policies: Some Empirical Evidence," *Economic and Political Weekly,* October 11, 1975, p. 1609.

23. For a discussion of the politics of decontrol, see Norman K. Nicholson, "Politics and Food Policy in India," thesis presented to the Graduate School, Cornell University for the Degree of Doctor of Philosophy, June 1966, chap. 2.

24. This possibility was demonstrated in the report by the Directorate of Economics and Statistics, Ministry of Food and Agriculture, *Report on Market Arrivals of Foodgrains—1958-59* (New Delhi, 1959).

The question of the effect of this control system on incentives has frequently been raised in public debate and in academic circles. Several answers are possible. First, the disincentive effect will depend on the extent to which higher prices would, in fact, be reflected in higher investments by the farmer. It could reasonably be argued that, in the absence of new technology, extensive farm investment was not to be expected. Second, controlled prices may be offset, from the perspective of the farmer, by higher average prices if the government does actually support the price at harvest and in bumper years. Third, some disincentive may be justified by the responsibility of the government to prevent starvation if this is what the grain is actually used for and there appears no other way to do the job.

25. A review of the relief problems can be found in the following documents: U.S. Senate, Committee on the Judiciary, Subcommittee to Investigate Problems Connected with Refugees and Escapees, *Relief Problems in East Pakistan and India* (Washington, D.C., June 28, 1971 and October 4, 1971. Senator Edward Kennedy, U.S. Senate, Committee on the Judiciary, Subcommittee to Investigate Problems Connected with Refugees and Escapees,

Crisis in South Asia, Washington, D.C., November 1, 1971.

26. See the discussions of state agencies in Kenya and Sierra Leone in William O. Jones, Marketing Staple Food Crops in Tropical Africa (Ithaca, New York: Cornell University Press, 1972), chaps. 7, 8.

27. Colin Leys, Underdevelopment in Kenya (London: Heinemann, 1975), pp. 106-7.

28. Ibid., p. 108.

29. Cf. War on Hunger (A Report from the Agency for International Development), vol. 8, August 1974, p. 27; and Food and Agriculture Organization, "Mission Multi-Donateurs dans la Zone Zahelienne: Republique du Niger" (Rome), 1974, p. 2

30. U.S., Agency for International Development, "Development Assistance Program: FY 1975, Section Three: Chad, Cameroon, Central African Republic, and Gabon" (Washington, 1975), p. 1-19.

31. Jack Shepherd, The Politics of Starvation (New York: Carnegie Endowment for International Peace, 1975), p. 1.

32. Victor D. DuBois, "The Drought in West Africa: Part I," American University Field Staff Reports: West African Series 15, no. 1 (1974):3.

33. Shepherd, Politics of Starvation, p. 4.

34. Derek Winstanley, "Climatic Changes and the Future of the Sahel," in The Politics of Natural Disaster: The Case of the Sahel Drought, ed. Michael H. Glantz (New York: Praeger Publishers, 1976), pp. 198, 164.

35. Victor D. DuBois, "The Drought in West Africa: Part II," American University Field Staff Reports: West African Series (November 2, 1974), p. 6

36. A field survey by the U.S. Public Health Service estimated for Mauritania, Mali, Niger, and Senegal that "the maximum number of deaths due to famine this year (1973) is calculated at 101,000." Public Health Service, "Nutritional Surveillance in West Africa" (July-August 1973) reprinted in Hal Sheets and Roger Morris, Disaster in the Desert, (New York: The Carnegie Endowment for International Peace, 1974), pp. 131-36. Shepherd reports, "In Ethiopia alone, at least 100,000 people starved to death in 1973 alone" Politics of Starvation, p. xiii.

37. "Drought in Africa: Part II," pp. 2-4.

38. Shepherd, Politics of Starvation, p. 17.

39. John D. Esseks "The Food Outlook for the Sahel: Regaining Self-Sufficiency or Continuing Dependence on International Aid?" Africa Today 22 (April-June 1975):46-47; and Politics of Starvation, pp. 60-64.

40. Jean Copans, ed., Secheresses et Famines du Sahel (Paris: Francois Maspero, 1975), pp. 133, 137-38, 140-42; Victor DuBois, "The Drought in Niger, Part II: The Overthrow of President Hamani Diori," American Universities Field Staff Reports: West African Series 15, no. 5 (1974):6-7; and Shepherd, Politics of Starvation, pp. 49-50.

41. Punjab Budget at a Glance: 1974-75 (Chandigarsh: Government of Punjab, 1974).

42. See Uma Lele, The Design of Rural Development (Baltimore: The Johns Hopkins University Press, 1975), chaps. 3, 4, and 6.

43. International Labour Organization, Bulletin of Labour Statistics, 2nd

Quarter, 1976, Table 9.

44. See Nicholson, *Rural Development Policy in India.*

45. See Gunvant Desai, *Growth of Fertilizer Use in Districts of India* (Ahmedabad: Indian Institute of Management, Center for Management in Agriculture, 1973), chap. 2. See also Gunvant Desai et al., *Dynamics of Growth in Fertilizer Use at Micro Level* (Ahmedabad: Center for Management in Agriculture, Indian Institute of Management, 1973); Brian Lockwood et al., *The High Yielding Varieties Program in India, Part I* (New Delhi: Programme Evaluation Organization, Planning Commission, 1971); National Council of Applied Economic Research, *Fertilizer Use on Selected Crops in India* (New Delhi, 1974).

46. Even at the time, according to the recollections of those involved in the decision, this was widely viewed as a considerable risk. In fact, most of the field trials of the new seeds were not encouraging, and the best economic opinion was against building up a dependence on imported fertilizers.

47. See *Report of the Committee on Taxation of Agricultural Wealth and Income* (New Delhi: Ministry of Finance, 1972); E. T. Mathew, *Agricultural Taxation and Economic Development in India* (New Delhi: Asia, 1968); A. C. Angrish, *Direct Taxation of Agriculture in India* (Bombay: Somarija, 1972); V. P. Gandhi, *Tax Burden on Indian Agriculture* (Cambridge, Mass.: Harvard Law School, 1966); S. L. Shetty, "An Inter-Sectoral Analysis of Taxable Capacity and Tax Burden," *Indian Journal of Agricultural Economics* 26 (July-September 1971).

48. In 1974, for example, attempts were made by the Finance Ministry to pressure the state governments into adopting agricultural income taxes. In addition, although the central government may not constitutionally tax rural income, the income tax laws were amended to take rural income into account in calculating the *rate* of income tax. Electricity rates were revised upwards by many states during the year and the price of fertilizer was doubled.

49. The two most obvious were the Kheti Bari Union in Punjab and the Kehdut Samaj in Gujerat. But interviews with Congress Party MPs in New Delhi indicated that by 1974, rural MPs from the northwest were becoming aware of their common economic interest, and some identified the "farm lobby" in the Congress as one of the major components of the attempt to oust Indira Ghandi in June 1975.

50. Lele, *Design of Rural Development,* pp. 75, 81; and Leys, *Underdevelopment in Kenya,* p. 101.

51. Henry Bienen, *Kenya: The Politics of Participation and Control* (Princeton, New Jersey: Princeton University Press, 1974), pp. 169-70.

52. Cited by Charles Elliott, *Patterns of Poverty in the Third World* (New York: Praeger Publishers, 1975). p. 27.

53. Bienen, *Kenya: Politics of Participation,* pp. 181-82.

54. Leys, *Underdevelopment in Kenya,* pp. 90-91.

55. V. M. Dandekar and N. Rath, "Poverty in India," *Economic and Political Weekly,* Jan. 2, 1971, p. 25; Jan. 9, 1971, p. 106. See also P. K. Bardhan, "On the Incidence of Poverty in Rural India of the Sixties," *Economic and Political*

Weekly, February 1973.

56. John Lewis, "Wanted in India: A Relevant Radicalism," *Economic and Political Weekly*, Special Number, July 1970, p. 1211.

57. In 1974, these issues led to the resignation of B. S. Minhas, at that time the leading economist on the Indian Planning Commission. This signaled the impending economic collapse that led to the declaration of emergency in June 1975. His book *Planning and the Poor* (New Delhi: S. Chand, 1974) takes on particular significance in the light of subsequent events.

58. The clearest recent presentation of this model can be found in John Mellor, *The New Economics of Growth* (Ithaca: Cornell University Press, 1976). A two-volume work by Sudhir Sen, *Reaping the Green Revolution* (New Delhi: Tata McGraw Hill, 1975) and *A Richer Harvest* (New Delhi: Tata McGraw Hill, 1974), is a comprehensive statement of the problems and solutions. An excellent statistical statement on the Indian case can be found in "A Report to the Nation on the Downtrodden," *Monthly Commentary on Indian Economic Conditions*, Indian Institute of Public Opinion, Annual Number, vol. 15, no. 5, 1973.

59. Nicholson, *Rural Development Policy in India*, pp. 39-43.

60. A good discussion of the "urban" focus of early agricultural planning in India can be found in C. H. Hanumantha Rao, "Agricultural Policy under Three Plans," in N. Srinirasan, ed., *Agricultural Administration in India* (New Delhi: Indian Institute of Public Administration, 1969), pp. 116-19. See also M. Lipton, "India's Agricultural Performance: Achievements, Distortions, and Ideologies," in *Agricultural Development in Developing Countries—Comparative Experience* (Bombay: Indian Society of Agricultural Economics, 1972), chap. 4.

61. See N. Luyks, "Rural Governing Institutions," in M. Blase, ed., *Institutions in Agricultural Development* (Ames, Iowa: Iowa State University, 1971), chap. 10; N. T. Uphoff and M. J. Esman, *Local Organization for Rural Development: Analysis of Asian Experience* (Ithaca, N.Y.: Rural Development Committee, Center for International Studies, Cornell University, 1974); D. E. Ashford, *National Development and Local Reform* (Princeton, N. J.: Princeton University Press, 1967).

62. See, for example, statements by Julius Nyerere, President of Tanzania, reprinted in *Freedom and Socialism: A Selection from Writings and Speeches 1965-67* (London: Oxford University Press, 1968), pp. 324-25, 353-55.

63. "As the review of *ujamaa* carried out under ARDS [African Rural Development Study] noted, there are only limited formal procedures for local people to influence TANU [Tanganyikan African National Union, the ruling party] officials, leaving little more than good will to assure these officials will, in fact, protect peasant interests," in Lele, *Design of Rural Development*, p. 153.

64. Paul Collins, "Decentralization and Local Administration for Development in Tanzania," *Africa Today* 21 (Summer 1974):25. In the same article (pp. 23, 25), Collins suggests that an exception to the concentration trend may be the interaction between local farmers and regional officials by means of *Ujamaa* planning teams which take officials to villages to assist in drawing up

feasible and realistic development plans for the villages.

65. See the discussion of farmer opposition to Tanzania's communalization of farming in Lele, *Design of Rural Development*, pp. 155-57.

66. Chinese experience in this regard is instructive. See B. Stavis, "People's Communes and Rural Development in China," (Ithaca, N.Y.: Rural Development Committee, Center for International Studies, Cornell University, 1974); J. C. Pelzel, "The Economic Management of Production Brigade in Post-Leap China, in W. E. Willmott, ed., *Economic Organization in Chinese Society* (Stanford: Stanford University Press, 1972), pp. 387-416.

67. See R. E. Evenson and Y. Kislev, *Agricultural Research and Productivity* (New Haven, Conn.: Yale University Press, 1975); Y. Hayami and V. W. Ruttan, *Agricultural Development: An International Perspective* (Baltimore: The Johns Hopkins University Press, 1971).

68. *Report of the Fertilizer Credit Committee of the Fertilizer Association of India* (New Delhi: Fertilizer Association of India, 1968), pp. 92-96.

69. P. L. Sankhayan, D. S. Sidhu, and P. S. Rangi, "Efficiency and Impact of Various Fertilizer Supply Systems on Production in Punjab," *Indian Journal of Agricultural Economics* (Oct./Dec. 1972):77-84; R. I. Singh, Ram Kumar, and Sri Ram, "Impact of Input Supply Systems on Crop Production in District Moradabad," *Indian Journal of Agricultural Economics* 28 (October/December 1972):130-36, J. G. Ryan and K. V. Subramanyam, "Package of Practices Approach in Adoption of HYV," *Economic and Political Weekly*, December 1975, pp. A-101 to A-110.

70. L. Nulty, *The Green Revolution in West Pakistan* (New York: Praeger, 1972).

71. This neglect was corrected in the mid-sixties with the establishment of the Agricultural Prices Commission in the Ministry of Agriculture, which prepares cost of production and price recommendations seasonally for the Ministry. The Commission's cost of production calculations are generally disputed by farm organizations, which feel they are too low. The Commission also appears to be of the opinion that, within broad ranges, prices do not influence the allocation of acreage, input use, etc. For discussions of various aspects of this problem, see Raj Krishna, "Agricultural Price Policy and Economic Development," in H. M. Southworth and B. F. Johnston, *Agricultural Development and Economic Growth* (Ithaca, N.Y.: Cornell University Press, 1970), chap. 13. Uma Lele is highly critical of government pricing policies in *Foodgrain Marketing in India* (Ithaca, N.Y.: Cornell University Press, 1971), pp. 220-23. That this is a widespread problem is argued by T. W. Schultz in "U. S. Malinvestments in Food for the World," reprinted in *Agricultural Development in Developing Countries* (Bombay: Indian Society of Agricultural Economics, 1972), chap. 21.

72. See N. K. Nicholson, "Local Institutions and Fertilizer Policy: The Lessons From India's Punjab and Gujerat States" (Paper presented to Food Institute Conference, INPUTS, June 7-17, 1976, at East-West Center, Honolulu, Hawaii). Also, "Differential Responses to Technical Change in Gujerat and Punjab: An Analysis of Economic Political Differentiation in India" (Paper presented to American Political Science Association, Annual Convention, San

Francisco, Sept. 16, 1975).

73. A good example is the Small Farmer Program evolved in the late sixties. It was designed to direct federal resources directly into programs to help the smaller farmer. Discussions of the problems and programs can be found in V. R. Gaikwad, *Small Farmers: State Policy and Program Implementation* (Hyderabad: National Institute of Community Development, 1971); *Rural Development for Weaker Sections*, Report of a Seminar sponsored by the Indian Society of Agricultural Economics and the Indian Institute of Management (Bombay: I.S.A.E., 1974).

74. N. T. Uphoff and M. J. Esman, *Local Organization for Rural Development: Analysis of Asian Experience* (Ithaca N.Y.: Rural Development Committee, Center for International Studies, Cornell University, 1974), pp. 63-75.

75. P. J. Stangel and J. H. Allgood, "World Fertilizer Situation 1976-1980" (Paper presented to Food Institute Conference, East-West Center, Honolulu, Hawaii, June 7-17, 1976).

76. See U. K. Srivastava et al., *Food Aid and International Economic Growth* (Ames, Iowa: Iowa State University, 1975).

77. See, for example, W. D. Hopper, "The Development of Agriculture in Developing Countries," *Scientific American* 235 (September 1976):196-205.

78. See N. Krishnaji, "Inter-Regional Disparities in Per Capita Production and Productivity of Foodgrains," *Economic and Political Weekly*, Aug. 1975, p. 1377; P. K. Bardhan, "Incidence of Poverty in Rural India," pp. 245-68.

79. There have been only a few attempts to relate the character of local politics to policy, but they are as yet somewhat primitive. See S. Hadden, *Decentralization and Rural Electrification in Rajasthan, India* (Ithaca, N.Y.: Rural Development Committee, Center for International Studies, Cornell University, 1974); R. N. Blue and Y. Junghare, "Political and Social Factors Associated with the Public Allocation of Agricultural Inputs in a Green Revolution Area," mimeographed (Minneapolis: University of Minnesota, Department of Political Science, 1973); B. W. Coyer, "The Distribution of Rural Public Policy Goods in Rajasthan" (Paper presented to Fourth Annual University of Wisconsin Conference on South Asia, November 7-8, 1975); N. K. Nicholson, "Factionalism and Public Policy in India," forthcoming in F. Belloni, ed., *Party and Faction* (CLIO Press).

80. Francine Frankel, "The Politics of the Green Revolution: Shifting Patterns of Peasant Participation in India and Pakistan," in T. J. Poleman and D. K. Freebain, eds., *Food, Population and Employment* (Ithaca, N.Y.: Cornell University Program on Science, Technology, and Society, Praeger Publishers, 1973), pp. 120-51; Jan Breman, *Patronage and Exploitation* (Berkeley: University of California Press, 1974).

81. M. L. Dantwala, *Poverty in India—Then and Now: 1870-1970* (New Delhi: MacMillan, 1973).

82. For India, see W. Ladejinsky, *A Study of Tenurial Conditions in Package Districts* (New Delhi: Planning Commission, 1965); Frankel, "Politics of the Green Revolution," W. Ladejinsky, "Agrarian Reform in Asia: The Green Revolution and its Reform Effects," in R. T. Shand, ed., *Technical Change in Asian*

Agriculture (Canberra: Australian National University, 1973), chap. 12; Mellor, *New Economics of Growth*, chap. 4; Nulty, *Green Revolution in Pakistan*, pp. 25-40; Hiromitsu Kanepa, "Mechanization, Industrialization and Technological Change in Rural Pakistan," in R. T. Shand, ed., *Technical Change in Asian Agriculture*, chap. 9.

83. John M. Cohen, "Effects of Green Revolution Strategies on Tenants and Small-Scale Landowners in the Chilalo Region of Ethiopia," *Journal of Developing Areas* 9 (April 1975):340-41, 350-51.

84. In Punjab, for example, farms of under two hectares constituted 17 percent of all holdings. In 1971, they increased in number until they constituted 57 percent of all holdings. N. K. Nicholson, "Local Institution and Fertilizer Policy," p. 23.

85. Hayami and Ruttan, *Agricultural Development*, chap. 3. See also K. Polanyi, *The Great Transformation* (Boston: Beacon Press, 1960).

86. A severe criticism of the recent role of government administration can be found in M. L. Dantwala, "From Stagnation to Growth: Relative Roles of Technology, Economic Policy and Agrarian Institutions," in R. T. Shand, ed., *Technical Change*, chap. 13. See also N. K. Nicholson and Silawar Ali Shan, *Basic Democracies and Rural Development in Pakistan* (Ithaca, N.Y.: Rural Development Committee, Center for International Studies, Cornell University, 1974).

87. Good discussions of the emergence of brokerage politics can be found in Richard Sisson, *The Congress Party in Rajasthan* (Berkeley: University of California Press, 1972); and S. Javed Burki, *Agricultural Growth and Local Government in Pubjab, Pakistan* (Ithaca, N.Y.: Rural Development Committee, Center for International Studies, Cornell University, 1974).

88. See *Integrated Rural Development Programme* (Islamabad: Ministry of Food, Agriculture and Rural Development, Government of Pakistan, 1973).

89. "Cocoyoc Declaration," *Ceres* (November/December 1974).

90. K. Mannheim, *Ideology and Utopia* (New York: Harcourt, Brace and Company, 1936, Harvest Books ed.), p. 55; Clifford Geertz, "Ideology as a Cultural System" in David Apter, ed., *Ideology and Discontent* (Glencoe, N.Y.: Free Press, 1964), chap. 1.

91. See D. H. Meadows and D. L. Meadows, *The Limits to Growth* (New York: New American Library, 1972); H. S. D. Cole et al., *Models of Doom* (New York: Universe Books, 1973); M. Mesarovic and E. Peskel, *Mankind at the Turning Point* (New York: E. P. Dutton, 1974); E. F. Schumacher, *Small is Beautiful* (New York: Harper & Row, 1973).

92. Garrett Hardin, "Living on a Lifeboat," *Bioscience*, October 1974, pp. 561-68, and "Tragedy of the Commons," *Science*, December 13, 1968, pp. 1243-48; W. M. Murdoch and A. Oaten, "Population and Food: Metaphors and the Reality," *Bioscience*, September 1975, pp. 561-67.

Index